More Praise for *FOUR HOURS OF FURY*

"Fenelon's epic account of the Allied invasion of Nazi Germany re-creates in stirring detail both the generals' strategies and the privates' emotions as their colossal effort climaxed in momentous achievement. *Four Hours of Fury* is a fine tribute to the gallantry of the men and women who, against overwhelming odds, vanquished a great evil."

—Craig Nelson, author of *Pearl Harbor, Rocket Men,*
and *The First Heroes*

"Diving into *Four Hours of Fury* is like opening the jump door on a C-46 transport high over Germany in March of 1945. You're an Allied paratrooper and the Rhine is fast approaching. Waiting are 55,000 *Wehrmacht* soldiers anxious to make sure you don't finish the day alive. Your orders are stark: *Keep taking ground!* A former US Army paratrooper, James Fenelon brings this story of the war's largest airborne assault to life as only he can, using the voices of the men who were there to deliver heart-pounding realism. The book is a gripping reminder that the crash of war is at its most deafening just before the end."

—Adam Makos, author of *Spearhead: An American
Tank Gunner, His Enemy, and a Collision of Lives
in World War II*

"Masterfully researched and written with a novelist's eye for detail, *Four Hours of Fury* hurls readers into the heart of one of World War II's most ferocious fights. . . . Readers will feel the buzz of bullets overhead, smell the vomit in the back of cramped plywood gliders, and duck as the enemy's artillery thunders. [This] is one helluva combat story."

—James M. Scott, author of *Target Tokyo* and *Rampage*

"Fenelon puts you in a transport plane, straps a parachute to your back, and sends you into an adventure commencing 1,000 feet over Nazi German skies. *Four Hours of Fury* is a brilliant tribute to the last great parachute assault, and the men who invaded Hitler's empire from the air."

—Jonathan W. Jordan, author of *Brothers, Rivals, Victors*

"Fenelon's experience as a paratrooper and his ability to describe in thorough detail what it takes to conduct an airborne operation, as either a private or a general officer, captures the lethal effectiveness of vertical envelopments, whether on the World War II battlefield with Operation VARSITY or today. Critics may question operations such as VARSITY as they assess the time involved, the distance traveled, what might have been achieved with alternative forces, and the total number of casualties, but there's no doubt that the psychological effect of an audacious paratrooper drop creates a force multiplier on the enemy that cannot be matched."

—Brigadier General David L. Grange, US Army (Ret.), former commander of the 75th Ranger Regiment and 1st Infantry Division

"A riveting chronicle of personal courage, overwhelming logistics, and inevitable mayhem that is as authentic as it gets. 'The ambition, scope, and execution of Operation VARSITY remains unparalleled in the annals of warfare,' Fenelon writes. The same can be said of his telling of the largest single-day airborne assault of World War II."

—Walter R. Borneman, author of *Brothers Down: Pearl Harbor and the Fate of the Many Brothers Aboard the USS* Arizona

"Told with a master's attention to detail and historical accuracy . . . James M. Fenelon emerges as a talented storyteller, anchoring this narrative of a grand military offensive with rich portraits of those whose sacrifices made it successful."

—Gregory A. Freeman, author of *The Forgotten 500* and *The Last Mission of the Wham Bam Boys*

"Deeply researched and richly detailed, *Four Hours of Fury* constitutes a major addition to the military history of World War II. A particular virtue of the book, among many, is the close attention paid to the GIs who carried out the mission."

—John W. Jeffries, author of *Wartime America: The World War II Home Front*

FOUR HOURS OF FURY

THE UNTOLD STORY OF WORLD WAR II'S
LARGEST AIRBORNE INVASION AND
THE FINAL PUSH INTO NAZI GERMANY

JAMES M. FENELON

SCRIBNER

New York London Toronto Sydney New Delhi

Scribner
An Imprint of Simon & Schuster, Inc.
1230 Avenue of the Americas
New York, NY 10020

First Scribner hardcover edition May 2019

SCRIBNER and design are registered trademarks of The Gale Group, Inc.,
used under license by Simon & Schuster, Inc., the publisher of this work.

For information about special discounts for bulk purchases,
please contact Simon & Schuster Special Sales at 1-866-506-1949
or business@simonandschuster.com.

The Simon & Schuster Speakers Bureau can bring authors to your live event.
For more information or to book an event, contact the Simon & Schuster Speakers Bureau
at 1-866-248-3049 or visit our website at www.simonspeakers.com.

Manufactured in the United States of America

1   3   5   7   9   10   8   6   4   2

Library of Congress Cataloging-in-Publication Data

Names: Fenelon, James (James M.), author.
Title: Four hours of fury : the untold story of World War II's largest
airborne invasion and the final push into Nazi Germany / James M. Fenelon.
Description: First edition. | New York : Scribner, [2019]
Identifiers: LCCN 2019002135 (print) | LCCN 2019010864 (ebook) |
ISBN 9781501179396 (eBook) | ISBN 9781501179372 (hardcover) |
ISBN 9781501179389 (pbk.) | ISBN 9781501179396 (ebk.) |
ISBN 9781508285533 (eaudio)
Subjects: LCSH: Operation Varsity, 1945. | World War,
1939–1945—Campaigns—Germany.
Classification: LCC D757 (ebook) | LCC D757 .F46 2019 (print) |
DDC 940.54/213553—dc23
LC record available at https://lccn.loc.gov/2019002135

ISBN 978-1-5011-7937-2
ISBN 978-1-5011-7939-6 (ebook)

For Frank Dillon. Thank you.

"He conceived the two armies to be at each other panther fashion. He listened for a time. Then he began to run in the direction of the battle . . . he said, in substance, to himself that if the earth and the moon were about to clash, many persons would doubtless plan to get upon the roofs to witness the collision."

—Stephen Crane, *The Red Badge of Courage*

CONTENTS

LIST OF DIAGRAMS AND MAPS

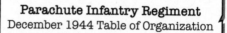

Parachute Infantry Regiment
December 1944 Table of Organization

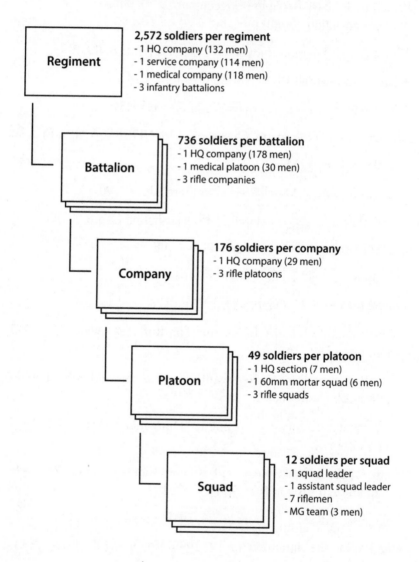

Regiment

2,572 soldiers per regiment
- 1 HQ company (132 men)
- 1 service company (114 men)
- 1 medical company (118 men)
- 3 infantry battalions

Battalion

736 soldiers per battalion
- 1 HQ company (178 men)
- 1 medical platoon (30 men)
- 3 rifle companies

Company

176 soldiers per company
- 1 HQ company (29 men)
- 3 rifle platoons

Platoon

49 soldiers per platoon
- 1 HQ section (7 men)
- 1 60mm mortar squad (6 men)
- 3 rifle squads

Squad

12 soldiers per squad
- 1 squad leader
- 1 assistant squad leader
- 7 riflemen
- MG team (3 men)

PROLOGUE

On Saturday, March 24, 1945, an armada of over 2,000 Allied aircraft droned through the bright morning sky over Belgium. Seventeen thousand airborne troops sat crammed in the cargo holds waiting to be dropped via parachute and glider into Germany. Consisting of transport planes and more than 1,300 towed gliders, the line of aircraft stretched back to the horizon for hundreds of miles. Flying at an altitude of just a thousand feet, the swarm generated a buzz that seemed to announce the fleet's arrival from every direction. Fighter escorts, biding their time and scanning for enemy aircraft, flew in lazy patterns above the staggered formations of lumbering transports.

Spearheading what Allied commanders hoped would be the final offensive in Europe, the transports carried troops from two elite divisions: the British 6th and the American 17th Airborne. Both were to be dropped over the same patch of German farmland five miles deep by six miles wide on the far banks of the Rhine River. As part of the largest operation since the Normandy invasion, the airborne units were to seize a bridgehead on the enemy side of the river and hold it until ground forces surged across the 400-yard width of the Rhine.

While the Allies had conducted several airdrops during the war, this was the first into the enemy's homeland. They were invading, not liberating, and the stakes were high. Nazi propaganda broadcasts made it clear that the element of surprise had been lost. The enemy was waiting for them. In addition to the expected 55,000 dug-in *Wehrmacht* troops, would fanatical German civilians attack with hunting rifles and pitchforks? Or would they cower in their basements? No one knew.

Sergeant John Chester and 384 other GIs of his battalion flew steadily on toward their drop zone in forty-two C-47 transports. Chester, a confident twenty-four-year-old section chief, occupied his time by writing a few postcards. Wanting to capture the novelty of his first combat jump, he scribbled the same note to both his mother and Kay, his gal back home in Missouri: "I am writing from a plane. We will drop into Germany soon. Hope to be seeing you soon. I love you."

Tucking away the postcards, Chester rested one hand on the buckle of his safety belt, remembering how he'd fought to stand up during his third training jump. Mortified by his body's unwillingness to rise to the occasion, panic had flooded through him before he realized he hadn't unfastened the buckle. That wouldn't happen today.

Chester knew most of the men in the plane, having trained and fought with them since 1943. Some pretended to sleep while others smoked or just stared into space. No one spoke. The roar of the engines and the rattling of the airframe made conversation impossible, which was just fine. Most were dwelling on their own thoughts anyway.

Chester briefly dwelled on the fact that this would be his thirteenth jump but chased the creeping feelings of doubt and hesitation from his mind with his simple, standard mantra: *You volunteered for this. You asked for it. Now go get the job done.*

The two-hour flight from France had been uneventful, but that couldn't last; as the planes approached the Rhine, it was time to go to work. From the cockpit, the pilot flipped on the red caution light, informing the men in back that they were nearing Germany.

As the aircraft began its descent, Chester unbuckled, stood, and yelled, "Get ready!" to the sitting jumpers. Those pretending to sleep snapped their eyes open and turned their attention aft where Chester stood by the open cargo door, wind whipping at his uniform.

The Rhine was the line of no return—once they crossed it, they'd be over enemy territory. More than ten minutes of flight time remained until they reached their drop zone, but given the possibility of getting shot down, they had to be ready to jump at any moment. This allowed the troopers to do what their pilots couldn't—bail out in the case of disaster.

As artillerymen, Chester's planeload of paratroopers also had to drop their 75mm howitzer. The disassembled artillery piece was divided into a door bundle, to be shoved out when the pilot flipped the jump light to green, and six bundles strapped to the underside of the aircraft, which would be released from inside the cabin.

"Stand up! . . . Hook up!" Chester bellowed over the sound of the deafening engines.

He reinforced his verbal commands with hand and arm signals that the men knew. They in turn echoed the orders, yelling them back in a ritual that ensured everyone understood what was happening and was engaged in the process. It gave them something to focus on other than their fears.

Overburdened with equipment, the troopers seated on each side of the plane struggled to get on their feet and form one line. Once standing, they attached their parachutes' static lines to the steel cable running the length of the cabin. Jumping at less than 500 feet, there wasn't time to deploy the chutes manually—the 13-foot static line took care of that, yanking the canopies open as the troopers fell away from the plane.

The jumpers jerked down on their static lines making sure the hooks locked shut. Satisfied everything was in order, they faced the rear of the plane and watched Chester and Manuel Pena shove the supply bundle to the edge of the open door. The bundle actually included multiple containers—made up of the howitzer's breech assembly, its wheels, and ten artillery shells—lashed together into a single awkward mass that required three parachutes. The two men wrestled the bundle onto a number of dowel rods, which facilitated the bundle's quick exit and eased the hassle of forcing the 720-pound bulk over the metal surface of the plane's decking.

At the Rhine, smoke and haze from the battle below obscured landmarks as the armada split up to head to their assigned drop zones. The ground forces had unleashed their attack before dawn and were still forcing their way across the Rhine under heavy fire. The pilots of Chester's unit, adhering to strict radio silence, watched helplessly as the seventy-two aircraft in front of them inadvertently veered off course. The C-47s carrying the artillerymen continued on the correct heading, but Chester, along with the rest of his battalion, was unaware that they would now be dropping first.

Having been alerted to the oncoming planes, German anti-aircraft batteries filled the sky with 88mm and 20mm flak rounds, the shells arcing up at the descending transports and bursting into dark clouds of exploding shrapnel. Streams of tracer fire from heavy machine guns stabbed at the planes and added to the mayhem.

The pilots felt like sitting ducks. To shake the aim of enemy gunners they needed to alter their flight path and airspeed, but that wasn't an option. Being in formation and approaching the drop zone required a steady speed and course. They shifted in their seats and flew straight into the growing maelstrom, following orders while ignoring their instincts.

Over the roar of the engines, the muffled detonations of flak could be heard from inside the plane. Behind the pilots, the troopers were buffeted about the shuddering cabin. Almost to a man they'd erred in favor of carrying as much equipment as possible: machine guns, rifles, pistols, hand grenades, extra ammunition, explosives, knives, bayonets, and brass knuckles. In many cases the parachute and equipment doubled a trooper's own weight; they supported themselves by holding on to one another, the airframe, or their static lines.

Chester caught glimpses of the action outside and was alarmed by what he saw: multiple aircraft in flames and a sky bursting with flak.

Looks like we are going to be real shorthanded, he thought. *Hope there are enough of us left to get the job done.*

As the men waited for the final command to jump, each struggled to stay on his feet as he pushed against the man in front, craning to get a glimpse of the jump light—still red. They wanted out and crowded toward the open door. Whatever awaited them on the ground had to be better than waiting to get shot down. One trooper, with his eyes on Chester, placed his hand on the command switch to salvo the howitzer bundles secured snugly to the belly of their C-47.

KABOOM! An explosion rocked the plane as a 20mm shell burst through the floor, shredding Melvin Boatner's leg. He crumpled to the deck, clenching his teeth and grabbing at the wound. Al Perry and Nick Montanino rapidly unhooked his static line and slid him to the other side of the plane—out of the way. There was no time to administer first aid to the increasingly pale Boatner, and he couldn't be allowed to hamper the jumpers' rush for the door.

Realizing shrapnel had severed the circuit to the now dead jump light, Chester yelled for the crew chief to stand in the cockpit door and relay the pilot's signal. Almost immediately the chief shouted, "GO, GO, GO!" while frantically waving both hands over his head.

Chester, Pena, and Perry shoved the bundle out and the troopers surged forward to exit right behind them. The salvo switches were flipped, releasing the bundles under the plane. Daisy-chained together to prevent them from drifting apart, all six were successfully deployed under their twenty-four-foot canopies.

The speed of the aircraft threw Chester forward over 500 feet as he exited. The first thing he saw was the ground below him, then the blue sky, then a jumbled kaleidoscope of both, as his deploying chute twisted him this way and that. The shock of the canopy snapping open took his breath away and sent the two grenades he had slipped into his jacket pocket ripping out the bottom. But he didn't have time to worry about them. He also didn't have time to enjoy the usual moment of elation following the successful deployment of a parachute. There'd be no blissful descent today. He briefly glanced at the departing aircraft and the chutes of those who'd jumped after him, before turning in his harness to keep an eye on the floating bundles of the howitzer.

The surrounding aircraft spewed paratroopers, filling the sky with hundreds of camouflage canopies. Supply bundles were mixed into the fray, descending under their distinct blue, yellow, or red chutes. The pilots, having delivered their cargo, gunned the engines and banked their aircraft for the return flight, finally free to dodge the flak and tracer rounds. Some trailed fire and oily smoke as they limped back to base. Others, more heavily damaged, arced into the ground.

With their adrenaline pumping, Chester and his fellow artillerymen were relieved to be out of the planes. But as the thrumming engines faded away, the crackle of gunfire and the *crump* of mortar rounds diverted their attention to the tilled fields of Nazi Germany rushing up at them. It was 10:20 a.m.

PART I

DECEMBER 1944–MARCH 1945

CHAPTER 1

"WHERE IN THE HELL
IS EVERYBODY AT?"

Northern France. Sunday, Christmas Eve, 1944.

Three months before they dropped into Germany, the troopers of the 17th Airborne entered combat for the first time in a manner entirely different from how they'd been trained. Without much warning, they'd been rushed to the front to set up blocking positions along the Meuse River on Christmas Eve 1944. Platoons of paratroopers, not fully aware of what was going on, found themselves digging foxholes in the Meuse-Argonne Cemetery, the final resting place for thousands of Americans killed in the previous world war. The men dug in and waited for orders, each contemplating the odds of becoming a permanent European resident himself. They were as ready as they could be, but like all unseasoned troops, most had no idea what they were about to endure.

Lynn Aas' platoon stopped to dig their defensive positions in a field littered with frozen American and German corpses. The cold, dead faces of the enemy reminded the twenty-three-year-old rifleman of his German and Ukrainian neighbors back in North Dakota. As he stood there in the snow, a nagging unease took hold of him . . . he had no desire to kill these people.

But knowing the task ahead required resolve, he walked over to one of the bodies and forced himself to stare. In life, the young German had been tall and handsome. Feeling the need to build up his hate, Aas kicked the corpse. *This is war,* he thought. *He is my enemy; I need to prove to myself that I can destroy him.* In the coming days almost all of his fellow troopers would get an opportunity to ignite their hate too.

On December 16, Hitler had launched a massive surprise assault to recapture Antwerp, Belgium, and divide British and American forces.

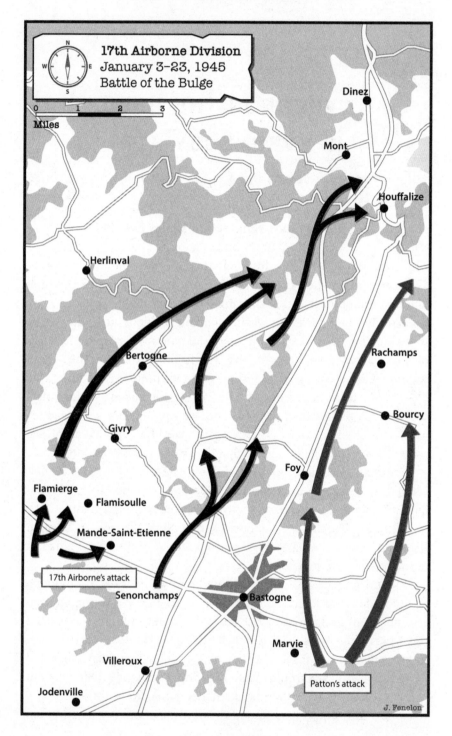

N
W   E
S

17th Airborne Division
January 3-23, 1945
Battle of the Bulge

0   1   2   3
Miles

Dinez

Mont

Houffalize

Herlinval

Rachamps

Bertogne

Bourcy

Givry

Foy

Flamierge

Flamisoulle

Mande-Saint-Etienne

17th Airborne's attack

Senonchamps

Bastogne

Marvie

Villeroux

Patton's attack

Jodenville

J. Fenelon

The desperate gamble, what would later be referred to as the Battle of the Bulge, caught senior Allied commanders flat-footed, and they scrambled to repulse the enemy's advance as *Wehrmacht* troops streamed out of the dense Ardennes Forest, decimating green American troops all along the front. Chased by panzer tanks, entire battalions fled from their positions while Allied commanders desperately tried to stem the retreat. Chaos reigned for several days, and accurate information was in high demand but short supply; defenses appeared to be crumbling all along the front.

It was into this maelstrom that the 17th Airborne was sent to bolster the lines. The initial plan of dropping them into Belgium had to be scrapped due to high winds and thick cloud cover. Thus the men of the 17th, who had trained for two years to descend into battle by parachutes and gliders, entered combat for the first time by jumping from the tail-gates of cargo trucks.

Joining the war in Europe after the venerable 82nd and 101st Airborne Divisions had each been involved in significant fighting and earned distinguished records, the troopers of the 17th knew they had a reputation to live up to and were keen to prove themselves.

They got their chance when they were assigned to protect the flank of General George Patton's counterattack out of Bastogne. They moved into the line for their first attack on the morning of January 3, 1945. Patton's Third Army intelligence officers assured General William Miley, the 17th's commander, that the enemy was fleeing before them; they would encounter only the delaying actions of small rearguard elements. Even so, Miley was concerned. His units were still assembling at their line of departure, his supporting artillery and anti-tank guns had yet to arrive, and timing prohibited even a cursory terrain study. Making matters worse, fog and snow significantly reduced visibility all along the front.

Miley's troopers, naïvely trusting Third Army's intelligence reports, left the line of departure in piecemeal fashion. It was their first mistake. Just as the forward elements began their advance, *Oberst* Otto-Ernst Remer's *Führer Begleit Brigade* launched an unexpected counterattack. The brunt of the German force, led by Panther tanks and half-tracks filled with two battalions of crack panzer grenadier infantry, hit the unprepared Americans like a brick in the face, stunning them to a halt.

Confronted by the heavily armed and battle-hardened enemy formations, Miley struggled to keep his units moving in concert with Patton's. In a fit of temper, Patton threatened to relieve Miley if he failed to keep his division on the move. Patton didn't realize until later that Miley's men had decisively engaged the enemy's main attack. Despite the retreat of an attached tank-destroyer unit, for which its commander was later court-martialed, the men of the 17th fought the German vanguard to a standstill, preventing a breakthrough into Patton's unprotected echelons from the rear.

On their second morning of combat, at 08:15, a battalion of Miley's paratroopers left the shelter of the Bois de Fragette woods near Flamierge. They were well into an open field when the Germans unleashed waves of artillery, mortar, and small arms fire. Casualties mounted quickly as the men loped forward through blankets of snow, seeking shelter in a depression on the south side of a small highway.

At the attack's height, two German tanks emerged through the dense fog like armored apparitions, clanking down the highway and firing into the exposed paratroopers. Corporal Isadore Jachman, known as Izzy to his friends, recognized the peril of the situation and sprinted from cover to salvage a dead comrade's bazooka.

Recovering the weapon and a canvas satchel of rockets, Izzy loaded the crew-served weapon himself and headed toward the German armor. He hoisted the bazooka to his shoulder, squinted against the blowing snow, and aimed. The high-explosive warhead slammed into the lead panzer, but with little effect. The tank's thick armor prevented serious damage, but the jarring detonation gave the crew pause and stalled their advance.

To get a better angle on the second tank, Izzy weaved forward through enemy fire, reloading on the move as he changed positions. The German commander of the trailing tank, witnessing the hesitation of the panzer in front of him, threw his machine into reverse and the two tanks crawled back to the protection of their lines. As Jachman pursued them, a burst of machine gun fire cut him down. The twenty-two-year-old corporal died moments after his comrades reached him.

Izzy's actions disrupted the enemy attack and provided his unit with a vital respite to consolidate their scattered positions and reorganize their defense. Izzy's parents, both German-born Jewish immigrants, would later receive their son's posthumous Medal of Honor.

In the next twenty-four hours, bitter skirmishes erupted over every yard of contested ground, with the adversaries trading possession of the same villages or hilltops multiple times.

German grenadiers attacked and pushed the paratroopers out of Flamisoulle at noon only to cede it back to them a few hours later. The frozen ground made digging protective foxholes almost impossible. The next morning, a German counterattack led by fifteen Mark IV and Mark V panzers overran the American positions, forcing them to withdraw with heavy casualties. All along their lines the evicted troopers regrouped and launched their own counterattacks. Bayonet-wielding paratroopers retook the village of Monty near Mande-Saint-Étienne at the sharp end of cold steel—screaming and whooping as they charged into the German defenders, who retreated in terror.

While the main line of resistance fluctuated, the troopers absorbed the German advance and stubbornly defended their assigned sectors. Patton, learning of the attack's ferocity, later acknowledged his best decision of the war might have been ordering the 17th to protect his flank. He was convinced that if they'd failed to hold their line, the German panzers would have wreaked havoc on his forces from the rear.

The division's vigorous defense earned praise from one of Patton's generals, Troy Middleton, who agreed, "The 17th saved the day." However, he also criticized their aggressive spirit, which he believed bordered on "recklessness." Another staff officer noted, "The 17th has suffered a bloody nose and in its first action lacks the élan of its airborne companions."

The troopers disagreed—when confronted with enemy armor, the choice was simple: bold violence or retreat. "God, how green we are, but we are learning fast," observed Colonel James R. Pierce, one of the division's regimental commanders.

Green they were. The lessons of launching poorly coordinated and piecemeal attacks came at a staggering cost—519 men killed in action and almost 3,500 wounded. At least one battalion commander was replaced, and several others probably should have been.

In the middle of February, after forty-six days of combat, the 17th rotated out of the front in Luxembourg, ending what Miley later referred to as their "long nightmare." The warming weather melted the snow, revealing a landscape dotted with rotting corpses, and an unbearable stench of decay followed the troops as they marched out of the splintered Ardennes Forest. Quartermaster troops piled the dead into the backs of trucks for transport and burial. The bodies, made stiff by freezing temperatures and rigor mortis, were difficult to stack and formed

a macabre heap of twisted limbs with arms and legs jutting out at gro-
tesque angles.

The weary men boarded a troop train for their journey out of Luxembourg and were soon rattling steadily toward France, watching as fields
of patchy snow gave way to those of wildflowers. Heading west, their
route took them through the Argonne Forest and Verdun, where long-
abandoned trenches from World War I could still be seen.

They rode in wooden, four-wheeled French boxcars known as "forty-
and-eights," named for the stenciled emblem on the exterior indicating
capacity for forty men or eight horses. Originally used as freight cars, the
French pressed them into service during the First World War to transport
men, horses, and equipment back and forth to the front. The men sat on
the wooden floor or on their packs. Some chose to sit in the open door;
others opted to scrounge enough straw from the floor for a makeshift pillow. They were used to fending for their own comfort, and the inevitable
cattle jokes or *mooing* sounds had long since lost an amused audience.

The cadence of the train rocked some men to sleep, but many others fidgeted in discomfort. Having agonized through one of the coldest
winters in Belgian history, enduring privation, snow, ice, frostbite, and
the flu—not to mention German artillery and tanks—almost all of the
troopers suffered from chronic diarrhea. As the forty-and-eights chugged
away from the sights and sounds of the front lines, the men now struggled against attacks from within.

It didn't take long for the GIs to note the lack of sanitary facilities on
what they christened the *Diarrhea Express*. In some boxcars men used
their bayonets to pry up floorboards to fashion a privy hole. But the shifting of the train frustrated accuracy and they abandoned that option. A
riskier, but more effective, technique was put to the test: the men took
turns standing backwards in the open door of the swaying boxcar, dropping their trousers and leaning back into a squatting position. To prevent their buddy from toppling overboard, two comrades held firmly
onto his arms and shoulders.

Those who managed to scrounge a scrap of paper or handful of hay
found wiping while dangling out the door required the dexterity of an
acrobat. However, solid teamwork prevailed over the active motion of
the train and the poor condition of the tracks. The troopers of the 17th
didn't lose a single man during the journey.

Laughing at the sight of bare bottoms continually appearing and disappearing along the line of boxcars, a company commander joked that the French farmers should thank his men for the free fertilizer.

Châlons-sur-Marne, France. Tuesday, February 13, 1945.

Disembarking at a small train station in the middle of the night, the men stretched their legs, grabbed their gear, and milled about until trucks arrived to complete the final leg of their journey. They'd arrived at Châlons-sur-Marne, a quiet town sixty-three miles northeast of Paris and home to the Cathédrale Saint-Étienne de Châlons, an imposing Roman Catholic monument consecrated in the twelfth century.

The division established its headquarters in the former barracks of a French cavalry unit, an impressive example of Second Empire architecture with mansard roofs and a high-walled parade ground. The Germans, during their recent occupation, had also used it as a temporary holding compound for American POWs. Now some of the 17th troopers were lucky to be billeted in the town itself, but most would reside in camps set up three or four miles out in the surrounding countryside.

One such tent city resident was Sergeant John Chester, whose camp was ten miles southwest of Châlons in the village of Soudron. After a long journey, he hopped from the back of the truck and plopped into a field of thick mud at a camp clearly still under construction. He squinted at the scene for a few seconds, deciding the quagmire and the camp's condition didn't matter—it was unquestionably superior to a foxhole in the snow.

Chester had first attempted to join the Army in 1938, on his eighteenth birthday, but his father refused to sign the enlistment papers. He had been raised on a Missouri farm during the Depression, and his parents had encouraged him to embrace a strong work ethic. Through this blending of circumstance and influence, Chester learned to accept the unavoidable in order to accomplish the necessary. As a teenager, he routinely rose at three o'clock in the morning to feed the animals and help his father bale hay, before starting his homework. With more chores in a day than there were hours, he often tackled tasks in a single-minded, pragmatic way.

For example, when picking up coal during the winter months, he found it more efficient to spend the night in the family truck parked outside the quarry gate so that he'd be first in line, rather than waste time waiting behind other customers in the morning. The bottle of milk he brought with him for breakfast often froze, so he treated it like a snow cone and ate his breakfast without complaint. By making his personal comfort a low priority he was often able to be in "the right place, at the right time." He just thought it common sense—a quality that would serve him well in combat.

The ranks of Chester's artillery battalion, originally filled by over 500 men of such varied civilian occupations as professional boxer, rumrunner, fisherman, feed store operator, and university instructor, had been whittled down to fewer than 300. He watched as his fellow survivors, whose uniforms were slick with two months of dirt and grime, took their issued cots and shuffled off to assigned tents.

Despite the camp's Spartan conditions, the men had reason to be happy; they were out of combat and among friends. Many dropped their gear and crawled onto their cots for some shut-eye. Some wandered from tent to tent, seeking buddies not seen since leaving England. Others spent time comparing or trading their spoils of war: German helmets, daggers, flags, badges, firearms, watches, and belt buckles emblazoned with swastikas. To navigate through the muck created by the spring thaw and rain, they wore their rubber overshoes, designed for coping with snow but equally effective when clomping through mud.

Private George Holdren and his squad, members of the division's anti-tank battalion, experienced a few hiccups while settling into life off the line. While adding wood to the tent's M1941 stove, one of the men accidently dropped the heavy steel lid, creating a sudden clanging noise that, because it sounded like incoming artillery, sent all of those nearby diving into the muck.

Recovering, the muddy troopers stripped off their uniforms in anticipation of a shower. But one of Holdren's buddies tossed his filthy boxer shorts into the stove and the resulting stench chased the men out of the tent, coughing and gagging for fresh air. They threw the rest of their soiled uniforms into a trench for burial.

The task of cleaning and clothing troops who had just come off the line fell to the Army's Quartermaster Corps. Its units could bathe, examine, and clothe 2,500 men in ten hours. Of chief concern was delousing: expelling lice and other infectious parasites helped maintain basic hygiene and prevented an epidemic.

Shower installations, established outside of the camps, pumped water out of ponds, through a large heater, and into an olive-drab semi-trailer, the interior of which was fitted with a row of showerheads.

In assembly-line fashion the men entered the shower six at a time; they were allowed ten minutes to bathe. The file of naked men extending down the trailer's wooden steps urged them on with shouts of "Hurry up!" and "Keep it moving!" After his first shower in two months, each man underwent a quick medical examination and then moved to the dressing station, where he donned a clean uniform. Rather than wait in line, in some cases up to two hours, many took advantage of nearby ponds or creeks to soap up and bathe themselves.

It was at one of the improvised bathing points that the troops announced their presence to the locals. Napping on a small dock after a swim in the Marne River, John Chester jolted awake as three loud detonations shook his resting place and rained water down on him like a monsoon. Some of the men had wagered that C-2 composition explosives would make excellent fish bait. Their hunch proved correct.

Within seconds, dozens of dead fish dotted the water's surface. Troops splashed into the river or rowed out in borrowed boats to claim their prizes. Seized by a vision of fresh fish for dinner, Chester joined in the melee, diving in and scooping up as many of the creatures as he could. He enjoyed seeing the men having fun and laughing again.

The blasts attracted the attention of the town's population, and soon parents, chasing their excited children, came running to discover the source of the commotion. The soldiers shared their haul with the locals, whose nervous smiles seemed to indicate all was forgiven, but it wouldn't be the last time the GIs startled their new neighbors.

The men of the division had four days to get their camps "squared away." They pitched additional tents and improved paths and roads, including hardstanding motor parks, latrines, and mess facilities.

"So this is a rest camp?" grumbled more than one trooper. "We got more rest at the front."

Laid out according to Army regulations, which recommended 8.3 acres for a thousand men, the camps were bracketed by latrines and vehicle parks on one side, and mess facilities on the other. In between were ranks of evenly spaced squad-sized, twelve-man tents. The open rows separating them were wide enough to facilitate company reveille formations and the movement of marching troops. The tents—made of non-breathing, fire-resistant, olive-drab canvas—had no floors. Each occupant had just enough room for his cot and duffel bag, and the savviest had scrounged wooden pallets for makeshift flooring to keep their equipment out of the mud.

After two months of poor diets and bad hygiene, many men had loose teeth or cavities. The division's dentists set up in a large tent to offer their services as needed. Waiting in line, patients watched uneasily as an Army private pedaled furiously on a bicycle contraption to power the dental drill.

The dentist looking into George Holdren's mouth surprised him by saying, "I see you are from Iowa." Apparently the quality of Midwestern dental work was well known in the profession.

Subsisting for weeks on cold rations stirs an obsession with hot food, preferably *good* hot food, and the local Frenchmen hired to assist the cooks rose to the occasion. Taking it as a matter of national pride, they worked hard to surpass the quality of anything the troops had eaten in England. The GIs appreciated English hospitality but had grown tired of meat boiled to the point that even spirited debate could never, with certainty, settle the identity of its origin.

Many took advantage of the downtime to write home, informing their loved ones they were still alive and safe, but official restrictions limited the details they could share. Every correspondence bore a "Passed by US Army Examiner" stamp and the signature of the officer who read, and, if necessary, censored the contents before it left camp. The smallest possibility of the mail falling into enemy hands forbade troopers from mentioning upcoming missions or revealing their location; instead they had to use generalities such as "somewhere in Europe" or "somewhere in France." Censors blotted out sensitive details with India ink or excised them with a razor blade before sealing and sending the letters on.

To get around the censorship, Private Joseph Clyde Haney, known as Clyde to his friends, had developed a secret code to conceal information in his letters home. Whenever he addressed a sentence directly to his wife, Vera, or mentioned "Tell Dad," his family knew to assemble a hidden message from the first letter of every following word.

Haney, an older-than-average private at thirty-two, was handsome, with thick, dark hair and a natural smile that belied the gravity of leaving his wife and four-year-old son back in Wisconsin. Before getting drafted in early 1944 he was a district manager for Fox Entertainment

Corporation, responsible for multiple theaters in the Madison area. It had been his duty on December 7, 1941, to interrupt a screening of *Shadow of the Thin Man* to inform the audience the United States had been attacked at Pearl Harbor, Hawaii.

Haney took the war seriously and was active on the home front, managing several successful War Bond drives and Red Cross fund-raisers, and he even set up a program to accept old tires in exchange for movie tickets at his theaters. The rubber would be recycled to make all manner of things from oxygen masks to galoshes.

Haney did lament his bad luck: two weeks after he was drafted, the War Department again exempted pre–Pearl Harbor fathers from service. But there was a war on and he accepted his lot. Arriving in England as a replacement in September 1944, he was assigned to the glider infantry as a rifleman four months before they were hustled into the Bulge.

From his rest camp Haney wrote to his in-laws: "Charles Holmen and Larry Owens need sales. 6 or 7 more in longs easy sold—so see what you can do—eh?" the hidden clue reading, "Chalons, 6 or 7 miles." Combined with "somewhere in France," it gave Vera a pretty good idea of her husband's location.

To get the division back to battle readiness, the First Allied Airborne Army, which had administrative and logistical responsibility for the airborne divisions in Europe, designated the 17th a priority recipient of men and materiel.

Officers, noting discrepancies and shortages, conducted a division-wide showdown inspection wherein each soldier presented his cleaned government-issued equipment. Five hundred planeloads of supplies were flown in from England to refit the men. Specialists rotated through the camps repairing damaged vehicles, radios, artillery pieces, and small arms.

Men, of course, are the most important assets of any fighting unit. Due to casualties, the division needed 4,000 to return to full strength. Upon arrival in Châlons, some rifle companies barely had enough men left to fill one platoon of 49 men; other units had lost all of their officers. One of the division's parachute infantry regiments had been reduced to less than 50 percent of its total manpower, with most of the losses suffered by its front line rifle companies. Invariably some of the wounded trickled back from hospitals as they recovered, but fully replenishing the ranks of the division required a significant number of fresh replacements.

The airborne divisions drew from a pool of trained parachute and glider replacements, but reconstituting the losses of the three American airborne divisions—all of which fought in the Bulge—drained the reserve entirely. To address the shortage, Supreme Headquarters Allied Expeditionary Forces sent a request to the Zone of the Interior (or the ZI, as the pencil pushers referred to the continental US), calling for 5,000 replacements in February and another 3,200 in March.

The replacements started arriving at the camps surrounding Châlons a day or two before the tired and depleted units themselves.

"Where in the hell is everybody at?" asked one of the replacements.

"There's seven guys here," said a sergeant, nodding to the few who were left of the company's original 120 men.

"The others," the sergeant added, "they're killed or in the hospital."

The veterans' haggard appearance startled the new men. In need of showers, haircuts, razors, and clean uniforms, they looked more like well-armed desperados than elite airborne infantrymen.

The veterans eyed the new arrivals warily if they eyed them at all. The old-timers, who'd trained together for over two years before their first combat, considered the replacements inexperienced outsiders. The replacements, witnessing the emotional reunions of returning comrades, felt ignored or slighted at their indifferent reception.

Private Tom Funk, a replacement paratrooper, noticed that many veterans seemed "to be in shock after the violent combat they had seen." He overlooked the cold reception and focused on fitting in.

The Army made an administrative attempt to improve replacements' morale by officially changing their designation to "reinforcements." But to veterans they were still just unproven unknowns to be regarded with doubt until proven otherwise. Rumors suggesting jailed inmates back in the States now had the choice to enlist in lieu of finishing their sentences didn't help the standoff.

After a short grace period, the officers reasserted the military discipline commonplace in a garrison environment. HQ issued directives preventing the use of tent guylines for hanging laundry and calling for the neat and orderly storage of equipment. Uniforms should be clean, worn correctly, buttoned correctly, headgear donned correctly, and boots polished. The camps soon took on the appearance and routine of well-organized military posts.

Officers and sergeants introduced physical training back into the division's daily routine. In the predawn darkness, the camps echoed with the cadence counts of calisthenics and the call-and-response running songs of units moving at double time:

> *We pull upon the risers and we fall upon the grass*
> *We never land upon our feet; we always hit our ass*
>
> *Aye, aye. Christ Almighty, who the hell are we?*
> *Zim zam God damn, we're parachute infantry!*

It soon became apparent that the replacements were out of shape. The veterans hounded the newcomers to meet the expected levels of physical fitness, adding to their misery. However, the growing intensity of training did provide an opportunity for camaraderie. Private Funk and others struggled through morning runs and forced marches to prove they could be relied on to carry their share of the load in combat.

A replacement later noted with pride that it took "two weeks of torturous physical training" before he started to feel welcomed by his squad.

Private Robert Fox, another newly arrived paratrooper, vividly recalled his reception: "The first person that we met as we disembarked was First Sergeant [John] Miletich. From his looks, I certainly was happy that he was on our side. The word was that he was from Chicago. To a kid from Iowa, with knowledge of the likes of Dillinger and Capone . . . that was about as tough as it gets. Somehow, I do not believe he was as happy with us as we were with him."

Miletich had the men fall into formation and called them to attention. The company commander, Captain Harry Kenyon, inspected the ranks of replacements and quickly found fault with Fox's posture. Getting in the newcomer's face, the captain yelled for him to "Stand at attention!"

"He was shouting so loud that I could have heard him from fifty feet," Fox remembered. "He kept finding fault so I was relieved when out of the corner of his eye he noticed that the guy next to me had one pants leg bloused in his boot while the other was out. . . . From the beginning, it was obvious to us new replacements that Captain Kenyon was held in high regard and respected by the Bulge veterans. All troops under his command were battle ready at all times. You did not go to the latrine otherwise—no exceptions. There would be no sneak attacks by the Germans when we were not ready."

The next morning, rising for early-morning calisthenics before he "had a chance to pee," Fox, in the back rank of the exercise formation, attempted to ease up on his exercises, thinking himself safely concealed in the darkness. As the men in front of him executed jumping jacks, he just threw his arms in the air.

A lieutenant roared into his ear, "Soldier, get your head out of your ass!" Immediately hopping into the rhythm of the exercise, Fox made note to use this new expression should he ever reach a position of authority.

As icy as they might have considered their welcome, the replacements integrating into the 17th had it pretty good. They at least enjoyed the luxury of joining a unit refitting in the rear. Infantry replacements commonly arrived at the front in the middle of the night, ushered straight to a foxhole on the line. In many cases replacements died before anyone even knew their name. If a replacement made it through his first forty-eight hours, his chances of survival slowly increased.

The survival rate of replacements was so low that a running joke among veterans was that the Army could save everyone time if the new men were just shot before bringing them to the front.

Although John Chester's artillery crew survived the Bulge without losing a man to enemy action or frostbite, they wouldn't be exempt from integrating replacements. To spread experience throughout Chester's unit, the 466th Parachute Field Artillery Battalion, several of the sergeant's men were reassigned to other gun teams that hadn't fared as well. Disassembling, inspecting, cleaning, and lubricating the section's 75mm howitzer became the first order of business for Chester's new crew.

Adopted by the Army in 1927, the M1A1 75mm howitzer was referred to as a pack howitzer; the design allowed the gun to be dismantled into seven components for transportation by mules through mountainous or jungle terrain. Its easy disassembly made it ideal for parachute delivery, the only disadvantage being the need for reassembly on the drop zone— after the crew had found all of the components. With a maximum range of a mere five miles, this peashooter drew sneers from conventional artillerymen, but airborne troops valued it for its simple operation and reliable firepower.

The howitzers of the 466th were divided into three batteries with four guns each. Chester, as section chief of the first gun in A Battery, prided himself on being an artillery guru. Before joining a gunnery crew, he'd spent time in the fire direction center and the unit's instrument and survey team. He pored over training manuals and questioned experts with the diligence of a religious scholar unlocking heavenly mysteries. Not one to accept doctrine blindly, he reverse engineered the Army's artillery practices, not only for deeper understanding but also to improve them. He devised an unorthodox method of resetting aiming stakes, which shaved vital minutes off the standard procedure for repositioning his howitzer.

Yet Chester did reverently adhere to the Army's maxim of retention through repetition. He ran his men through endless iterations of the Cannoneer's Hop—a drill in which each man rotated through all of the crew positions, practicing the steps necessary to assemble, prepare, and fire their howitzer. Each position had specific, well-defined responsibilities, and the drill provided a way to evaluate the replacements' competency, reinforce teamwork, and ensure they could perform all of the tasks necessary to accomplish a fire mission.

Once satisfied with his crew's expertise in each position's prescribed procedure, Chester worked them through drills to increase their speed. The Army manual asserted an ace crew's rate of fire should be one round every ten seconds; Chester thought that was too slow. The value of his rigorous training had been validated during the Battle of the Bulge when a forward observer (FO) radioed a fire mission to A Battery. Each of the four howitzers fired its first round, which Chester's gun crew immediately followed with another four shots.

The FO radioed back, "Cease fire, mission accomplished."

Chester's crew destroyed the German target before the other guns managed to fire a second round.

Upon the division's arrival, Châlons-sur-Marne had been placed off-limits. Authorized passes would be required to enter the town, and before the men got time off to *parlez* with the local ladies or hoist a few drinks, they needed to get their respective camps in order. Once the essential tasks were completed, HQ posted requirements for issuing passes, and forays into Châlons and neighboring villages became frequent.

But soldiers heading into town needed cash. Since there was no use for money at the front, they hadn't been paid since leaving England. Dutifully, the troopers lined up by last name and waited their turn to step up to the small field desk and sign for their pay. Many elected to send an allotment home to their families. Chester earned a base pay of $78.00 a month, plus another $50.00 for parachute duty, an additional $10.00 for combat pay, and $15.60 for foreign service. Because his father had died in 1940, Chester requested only $10.00 per pay period for himself, and sent the balance of his $143.60 home to his mother and sister. Given his aversion to drinking, gambling, and smoking, and the fact that the Army provided his meals, $10.00 covered minor incidentals until the next payday.

The influx of troops significantly increased the town's population, literally overnight, and strained the local economy accordingly. Soon GIs crowded into town, flipping through their little blue Army-supplied phrase books, attempting to order champagne or a glass of watery French beer. To mutual delight, children soon learned they could trade bottles of wine for a few cigarettes.

Five days after issuing the first passes, division headquarters started publishing a slew of directives to reduce tensions between the local inhabitants and their new, albeit temporary, neighbors. But trying to police troopers who viewed bucking the system as a right became an unwinnable match of wits.

So many of the GIs enjoyed swaggering through the streets munching on long French baguettes that it produced a civilian *famine pour le pain*, resulting in a directive prohibiting the purchase of local foodstuffs. The habit of swigging from open bottles of wine and champagne so offended the locals that another posted edict required concealing spirits in paper bags or satchels. Soldiers tearing down narrow streets in jeeps, mindless of civilians, necessitated the division to crack down on traffic and limit access to vehicles. Like circus clowns, the enterprising troopers got around the prohibition by stuffing as many men into a jeep or on a motorcycle as humanly possible. In short order, the clown-car routine was banned by a decree formalizing the explicit number of passengers allowed per vehicle type.

The camp's Red Cross coffee and doughnut bars provided little distraction, and the troops preferred going out for their entertainment. On weeknights, the division's Special Services unit utilized the town theater to show movies, and on the weekends the venue presented live entertainment. The vaudeville-type show *Oui, Oui, Oui* featuring a juggling act and a female tumbler—who also played the vibraphone—was so popular that the two nightly performances played to full houses with standing room only.

The more burlesque revue *Straight from Paree* soon replaced *Oui, Oui, Oui*, and due to the number of women in the production—and the corresponding amount of exposed flesh—it became a local sensation. Soldiers eagerly paid their forty francs to ogle bare midriffs, long legs, and much to their delight, the occasional breast.

The lure of Châlons so tempted troopers that many risked trips into town without passes rather than spend a dull night in camp. After a week or two of turning a blind eye, division headquarters decided to apprehend offenders with a cordon of surprise checkpoints. For troops trained to operate behind enemy lines, evading the checkpoints became a sport.

To reduce brawls and rowdy drinking, airborne divisions relied when possible on their own MPs rather than those of rear-echelon units. The hope was that using MPs from the same division would, because they were at least paratroopers, curtail the inevitable scuffles at checkpoints or during curfew enforcement. To soldiers returning from the front, where battle had forged an easy camaraderie, pedantic requirements for pressed uniforms, orderly paperwork, and salutes rankled—as did the petty indifference of rear-area personnel.

Those looking for cultivated options beyond the rustic environs of Châlons had the opportunity for a forty-eight-hour pass to either Reims, Nancy, or Paris, with the capital city being the most popular destination.

The Army's official *Guide for Leave Troops*, recognizing that Paris could accommodate the whims of any visitor, encouraged GIs to "take advantage of the things that interest you." While the guide promoted such sights as Notre-Dame, Sacré-Cœur, the Louvre, and the Eiffel Tower, it attempted to dampen the desire for other indulgences by warning those seeking negotiable affections that 42 percent of all venereal disease cases suffered by American troops originated in Paris. An enclosed map plotted available activities, including athletics, free theaters, movies, music, architecture, the English library on the Champs-Élysées, and for gamblers, the location of twenty-five prophylaxis stations scattered throughout the city.

Readily identifiable by a green light over the door, the prophylaxis treatment centers—known to the GIs as "pro stations"—provided a remedy for sexually transmitted diseases. Soldiers were urged to seek treatment within three hours of sexual intercourse. However, waiting in line, embarrassment, and the procedure itself often discouraged would-be patients. The preventative entailed a silver protein solution injected into the penis, which had to be held in the urethra by clamping the thumb and forefinger over the end for an agonizing five minutes. After expelling the fluid, soldiers were directed to avoid urination for at least four hours. The stations' medical staff often had more free time than patients.

George Holdren, with his recently cleaned teeth, won a pass to Paris and the city made quite an impression on the twenty-year-old Midwesterner. Fortunate to be billeted in the luxurious Le Grand Hotel, Holdren found himself staying in the city's center, not far from the Louvre. But on his first evening in the City of Light, unable to speak French and afraid of getting lost, he retreated to a nearby theater where he spent several hours relaxing and tapping his foot to the beat of American big band music.

The next night, after touring the Eiffel Tower, Napoleon's Tomb, and the Arc de Triomphe, he ventured out to a show billed as the *Olympian Follies*. Having heard of the *Folies Bergère*, he decided to check out what might be a cheaper version of the world-famous revue. Weaving through the dim basement, the mâitre d' led him to a small table with a good view of the stage.

When Holden was asked what he wanted to drink, he glanced at nearby tables for clues. The other patrons appeared to be drinking either champagne or orange soda, so he opted for a soda. The waiter asked him for 110 francs—or $2.20—a steep price given that a Coke at the Post Exchange cost 5 cents.

The cost of the soda was just the first surprise. The Iowa farm boy did a double take when the dancers took to the stage. Each woman's costume consisted of an almost nonexistent rhinestone ensemble that circled the neck, ran down between her breasts, and tied into a wide belt resting high on her waist. The women completed their outfits with large white feather headbands and high heels.

Holdren's eyes grew even bigger when he spotted the lead starlet, who was wearing just a headband and sparkly shoes. Feeling obligated to stay for the whole show—given his soda investment—he ordered a glass of champagne and settled in. Holdren returned to camp the next day penniless but feeling considerably more worldly.

As in Châlons, economic sanctions in Paris limited a soldier's purchases to wine, beer, liquor, soft drinks, and costume jewelry. To ease inflation's effect on the population, the rules required GIs to eat at designated service clubs and prohibited them from dining in restaurants. Allowing the well-paid troops to buy food on the local economy would have soon driven prices beyond the means of most Parisians.

During his seventy-two-hour pass, John Chester learned the hard way that he shouldn't question all Army regulations. Strolling down a boulevard, a sign for "American Style Hamburgers" caught his eye and proved too tempting. Having gone without a burger since leaving the States, he eagerly approached the sidewalk concession stand to place his order. The proprietor slid a plate of cold vegetables and bread through the small window, after Chester had handed over his money.

Confused, Chester complained to the vendor, "I ordered a hamburger!"

The man shrugged, pointed at the plate, and said, "American style hamburger."

Chester dumped the plate and its contents into the trash bin and stormed off.

Another paratrooper, John Baines, had his brief sabbatical ruined by Axis Sally while sipping a beer in a small bistro. Her German propaganda program readily found an Allied audience willing to endure her often clumsy attempts to lower GIs' morale in exchange for hearing popular American music.

Sally got Baines' full attention when he heard her say, "Welcome to the 17th Airborne Division! We know you're going to jump over the Rhine River soon, and we want you to know we'll be waiting to greet you!"

He noticed everyone in the bar staring at his highly polished paratrooper boots and the 17th Airborne's golden talon patch on his shoulder.

Baines raised his glass toward the radio in the gesture of a toast, uttered a curse, and hoped the Berlin Bitch was wrong.

CHAPTER 2

THE SPARTAN

On the road to Brussels, Belgium. Friday, February 9, 1945.

General Matthew Ridgway, the Americans' most experienced airborne commander, rattled down a narrow dirt road in the passenger seat of a mud-splattered, olive-drab jeep. Flanked on either side by the towering fir trees of the Ardennes Forest, he and several members of his staff were on their way to Brussels to plan what would be the war's largest airdrop. It was a week before the troopers of the 17th Airborne would withdraw from the Battle of the Bulge's blood-soaked front lines and head to Châlons, but events that would determine their future were already unfolding.

Described as a Roman senator who lived like a Spartan hoplite, Matthew Bunker Ridgway was comfortable with every facet of battle: from carrying grenades and a bolt-action rifle to spearheading invasions as a division commander. His uncanny ability to recall names and his preference for getting information firsthand from as close to the front as possible made him popular with his troops, who, inspired by the two grenades he wore on his combat suspenders, nicknamed him "Old Iron Tits."

Commissioned as an officer in 1917, he had missed service in the First World War but spent the interwar years serving in China, Nicaragua, and the Philippines. In 1942 he took command of the 82nd Infantry Division, leading its transition into the Army's first division-sized unit of parachute and glider troops.

Ridgway literally jumped into his command of the 82nd. Wanting to be the first man in his new division to parachute out of a plane, he went to Fort Benning, Georgia, for a short familiarization course and one jump. He enjoyed the "beautiful feeling of serenity" during his descent but admitted his landing felt "like jumping off the top of a freight car, traveling at thirty-five miles an hour, onto a hard clay roadbed." He then traveled to Ohio for a glider flight at Wright Field. It went well, but again the landing didn't; he had to leap from the glider as it careened down the runway, escaping just before it crashed into a row of parked aircraft.

At forty-seven, Ridgway, who suffered periodically from bouts of malaria and a debilitating back injury, had known he was putting himself at risk in his new career as a paratrooper. But in spite of his precarious introduction to airborne life and the real threat of permanent injury, he stuck with the 82nd and led the division through the invasions of Sicily, Italy, and France. Now at the age of fifty he commanded the XVIII Airborne Corps, which controlled the deployment of the US airborne divisions, including General Miley's 17th.

On his way to Brussels, Ridgway contemplated what senior Allied commanders had already determined, and the Nazis in the German High Command took for granted: an assault crossing of the Rhine River would be necessary to defeat Germany and end the war. Despite the Third Reich being up against the ropes, it was becoming increasingly clear that Hitler had no intention of throwing in the towel; his minions continued to give the Allies a bloody nose at every opportunity.

While the Germans deliberated over the *when* and the *where* of the Rhine crossing, General Dwight Eisenhower, the Supreme Commander of all Allied expeditionary forces in Europe, decided the *who* would be British Field Marshal Bernard Law Montgomery. Montgomery in turn would determine the *how*, and few American generals were happy about that, least of all Ridgway. If his superiors thought he would welcome the opportunity to work with the British and help Montgomery attempt to cross the Rhine a second time, they were mistaken.

In August of 1944, after three months of fighting to gain a foothold in Normandy, the Allies had pushed forward into France. Advancing on a wide front, with British forces in the north and the Americans to their southeast, Allied armored units led a sweeping hook through the country, liberated Paris, and by September the British were in Belgium, poised to attack into Germany through the Netherlands.

But there had been more than just the enemy to contend with. The more ground the Allies gained, the further they taxed their extended supply lines, constraining the potential of their advance and heightening inter-Allied competition for precious resources. Allied divisions were carnivorous in their consumption of "bullets, beans and batteries,"

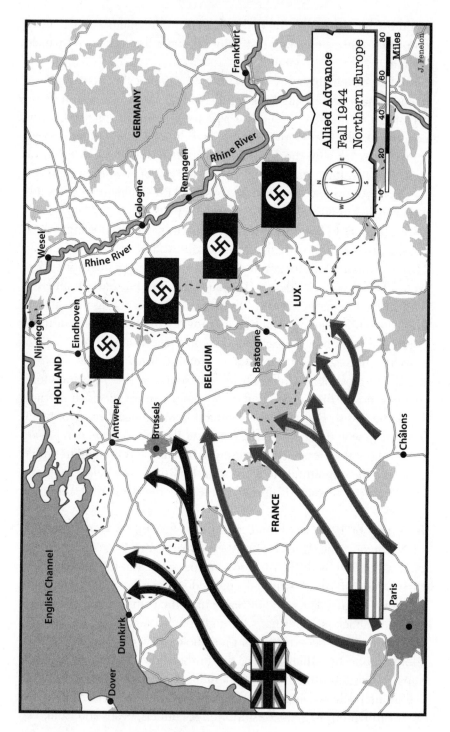

requiring almost 750 tons of daily supplies for a total of 20,000 tons a day across the entire front. The systematic destruction of the French rail system prior to the invasion forced supply convoys to rely on a network of dirt roads snaking out of Cherbourg to deliver the food, gas, ammunition, and medical supplies necessary to sustain the rolling offensive.

Montgomery had a solution. Favoring his British forces with the lion's share of supplies would allow them to punch a hole in the German defenses all the way to the Rhine River and simultaneously complete the liberation of Antwerp's harbor. Eisenhower considered access to a second port an "indispensable prerequisite for the final drive into Germany." Supplies flowing from Antwerp would allow the Allies to move materiel to the front more quickly, which in turn meant a faster end to the war.

Montgomery's plan, code-named MARKET GARDEN, was considered ambitious by many and a calculated risk by all, but it provided appealing opportunities. The proponents reasoned that if the plan to storm into Germany through Holland went well, the Allies would bag a second harbor and the war might be over by Christmas. It did *not* go well.

MARKET GARDEN kicked off on the morning of September 17, 1944, with the American 101st and 82nd Airborne dropping to seize bridges in the Dutch towns of Eindhoven and Nijmegen respectively. The British 1st Airborne Division had the most daring mission: landing on the far side of the Rhine to secure the Rhine bridge at Arnhem, seventy miles behind the German lines.

The ground forces rumbled forward, led by the British Guards Armoured Division, intending to use the captured bridges to their advantage for the dash into Germany. The advance maintained its fragile timeline for forty-eight hours before German counterattacks and logistical problems unraveled the plan.

Departing from airfields in England, the three airborne divisions needed more aircraft than could be mustered. Thus, delivery of the complete complement of airborne troops had to be divided across multiple serials, flying in over a multiday period. Unfortunately, an unforeseen weather front descended on England, bringing with it an impenetrable fog and low clouds that further delayed the schedule, forcing men and materiel to dribble in whenever a break in the weather permitted. Additionally, having to defend the landing zones for the arrival of their overdue reinforcements stalled the airborne troops from seizing their primary objectives in force.

The interrupted timetable forced the British 1st Airborne to alter their plan. Immediately after landing, instead of a full regiment, a mere 500 paratroopers rushed to the bridge over five miles away. Only able to occupy the north side, they were soon surrounded by gray-clad Germans.

By this point the *Wehrmacht's* ranks included pressed-into-service clerks, trainees, and cadets—still, the Germans were successful in severing the Tommies into two groups. The cordon prevented all British attempts to break through to their men at the bridge. With the bulk of the British division still defending the drop zones—lingering there for the anticipated follow-on serials—the men holding the bridge were on their own. It became apparent to the dwindling group that reinforcement now depended on the Guards Armoured Division rather than their own division. But the British tanks were still miles away, encountering heavy resistance as they moved up a single Dutch highway. Hit-and-run ambushes slowed their advance, and waiting for burning vehicles to be towed off the narrow road further hampered momentum.

After an epic feat of arms lasting five days longer than expected, all of the paratroopers at the Arnhem bridge had been killed or captured. The rest of the division, surrounded with its back to the Rhine, stealthily withdrew across the river on the night of September 25.

This first attempt to cross the Rhine had cost the British 1st Airborne Division a staggering 1,485 men killed in action and an additional 6,525 missing or captured. Of the 11,920 men who landed on the east bank, fewer than 4,000 made their way back to Allied lines. During the same nine days of fighting—September 17 through 25—the 101st Airborne Division suffered 2,110 casualties and the 82nd lost 1,432 men. Both American divisions continued to fight in Holland, nearly doubling their losses in the following weeks.

While the Allies seized Antwerp and had punched a narrow corridor to the Rhine, their brief hold on the far side of the river evaporated with the withdrawal of the 1st Airborne Division. Montgomery's attempt to claim a "ninety percent success" fooled no one. At best, MARKET GARDEN provided an indecisive result. Ridgway, citing a lack of "vigorous command supervision," viewed it as a British "failure to strike hard and boldly."

✳   ✳   ✳

The complexity of Montgomery's newest plan to cross the Rhine River rivaled both the invasion of Normandy and of Holland. Similar to MARKET GARDEN, the goals were ambitious. This time the prime objective was to seize the Ruhr, Germany's industrial region, which continued to belch out at a surprising rate the materiel necessary to wage the Nazis' war. Cutting off the production of their factories and foundries would be another nail in the Third Reich's coffin.

But crossing the Rhine could not be taken for granted. Winding over 760 miles, the river is one of the longest in Europe. With an average width of 430 yards, it forms a natural and traditional obstacle to armies intending to force their way into Germany's western frontier. The ancient fortifications built by the Romans as part of their occupation in AD 6, as well as the dozens of medieval castles dotted along both banks, provide mute testament to the historical importance of this imposing geographical barrier.

Adopting Montgomery's proposal would once again require that the British receive the majority of supplies, which incensed the American generals. They felt that the United States' contribution to the war — almost two-thirds of men and materiel — warranted the lead role in Germany's defeat. They advocated continuing to push forward on a wide front with both the British and the Americans attacking forward and cited the MARKET GARDEN debacle as evidence against another single-thrust campaign.

Both plans had merits: a single-thrust focused Allied might, while a broad attack prevented the Germans from massing an effective defense and kept their reserve forces scattered.

Montgomery argued that ignoring his strategy limited the combat potential in any one sector and kept the Allies competing for resources. Crossing the Rhine in the British sector favored a rapid breakout — once on the other side — and cutting off the Ruhr would be a devastating blow to the enemy. Farther south, where the American forces were advancing, there were fewer options. The mountainous terrain favored the German defenders and retarded a rapid breakout.

Montgomery maintained that his plan stood the best chance of success. But to execute it he first had to get to the Rhine. To clear the Germans still holding out on the west side of the river he divided his plan of attack into three stages.

The first two stages would get his divisions to the banks of the Rhine:

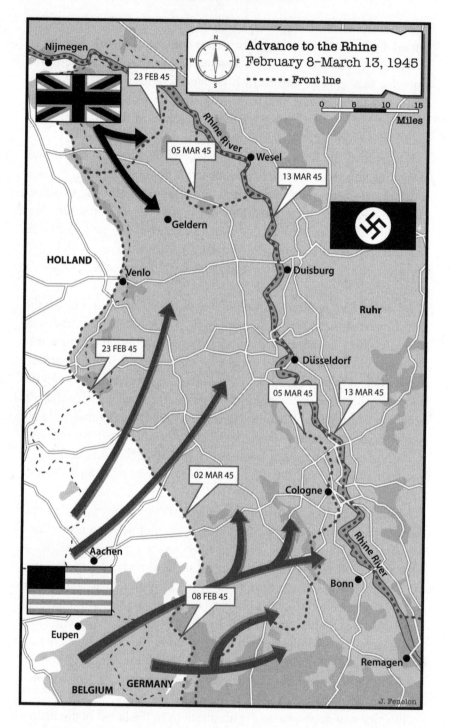

Advance to the Rhine
February 8–March 13, 1945
•••••• Front line

Operation VERITABLE, with more than twelve divisions attacking southeast, and Operation GRENADE, led by US General Bill Simpson's Ninth Army advancing northeast. The two attacks would end in a converging assault, known as a pincer movement or double envelopment, crushing the Germans between them. Simpson's army, consisting of ten divisions of over 300,000 soldiers and 1,394 tanks, would be the only American ground forces participating in the offensive.

After securing the west bank, which Montgomery estimated would take six to eight weeks, the third stage, code-named PLUNDER, would be a mammoth crossing of the Rhine in early April. During the subsequent sprint to the Ruhr, Montgomery's forces would bypass the dense urban areas to avoid heavy casualties and instead swarm through the open terrain to surround and isolate the industrial sites.

Attacking on a twenty-two-mile front, PLUNDER, which necessitated a naval admiral to oversee the flotillas of landing craft, would be the largest river crossing in military history. In support of his final stage of the plan, Montgomery wanted three airborne divisions of nearly 39,000 men to land on the German-held banks of the Rhine to seize vital terrain and secure a bridgehead for his advancing forces. Montgomery and his subordinate commander, Lieutenant General Miles Dempsey, whose British Second Army would spearhead PLUNDER, both stressed that the airborne landings were critical to their plan.

Eisenhower, after spirited debate within Supreme Headquarters, approved PLUNDER and the supporting airborne mission, code-named VARSITY. Predictably, designating Montgomery to lead the primary push into Germany angered American officers who viewed the British field marshal as an overrated, plodding, political peacock keen for more than his fair share of the glory. The decision inspired one incredulous American general to conclude that Eisenhower was probably the best general the British had.

VARSITY, like all other Allied operations, obtained its name from a list of available code words consisting of nouns and adjectives culled from an unabridged dictionary. Organizing the logistics for Montgomery's airdrop would fall to specialists in the First Allied Airborne Army, a unique joint American-British command that reported directly to Eisenhower's Supreme Headquarters. Airborne Army consolidated the expertise and logistical assets necessary for the increasingly complex choreography of

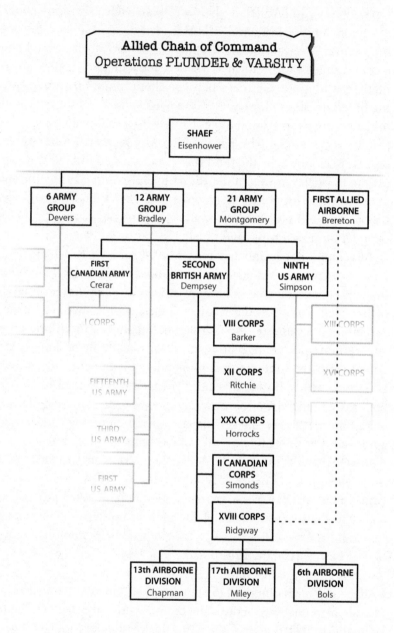

Allied Chain of Command
Operations PLUNDER & VARSITY

dropping men into battle, which had grown from small battalion-sized operations in 1942 to the multi-division missions of Normandy and Holland. They managed the administration, rather than the direct operational control, of airborne divisions.

Airborne Army was composed of two subordinate corps, divided along national lines: Ridgway's American XVIII Airborne and the British I Airborne. After landing and seizing their objectives, the HQ ceded control of the airborne troops to the ground units whose advance they were supporting.

The Airborne Army's American commander was General Lewis H. Brereton, by all accounts a fastidious little man who often referred to himself in the third person. He carried a swagger stick and shamelessly courted the press corps. With a wide forehead and nose, he could, on demand, flash an equally wide smile for photographers. Almost as if embracing his reputation as a fop, he had his personal aircraft decorated with the moniker *Debonair Duke*.

Brereton, one of the Army's first military aviators, had earned his wings in 1913 and since then believed airpower alone could win wars. In 1942 he relished being assigned to command the Ninth Air Force, but allowed himself to be distracted by the glamour of its fighters and bombers, ignoring the mundane troop carrier squadrons under his command. Even with deficiencies noted after the July 1943 airdrops in Sicily, Brereton failed to procure the proper radar equipment for his troop carrier aircraft. He also failed to push night navigation training for pilots who needed air time to master that witches' brew of inexact science and luck.

Brereton was again soundly criticized a year later for the poor performance of his troop carrier units, which had mis-dropped paratroopers all over Normandy. Many senior officers called for his reassignment to a narrower, sideline role. Omar Bradley led the effort, considering Brereton "marginally competent" and too enchanted with his sleek fighters and powerful bombers to coordinate effective support for the ground war. According to Bradley, Brereton "resisted any effort to work together."

Marginalizing Brereton by placing him in command of the Airborne Army was a questionable decision. Brereton himself took a dim view of his airborne assignment, believing it to be a demotion. In fact, his charge *was* important: effectively, it was up to him to mind and manage logistics, where it could be argued many battles are won (or lost) before they even start. But therein lay the problem: Brereton would again be responsible for coordinating troop carrier operations, an area in which he'd already demonstrated gross negligence.

How to explain Brereton's remit? War planners hoped that, by surrounding Brereton with competent professionals, the fallout from his mercurial temperament would be minimized. But hope is never a plan.

Indeed, Brereton had already run afoul of Montgomery's staff by openly complaining that the field marshal's demand for three airborne divisions ignored wider strategic realities. Simultaneous to VARSITY, Airborne Army's staff was planning three additional airdrops to support other Allied units crossing the Rhine, as well as an emergency operation to drop a division into Berlin in the event of a Nazi collapse. With an arsenal of five divisions under his command, Brereton had more missions to support than he had divisions.

Brereton initially assigned the commander of the British I Airborne Corps, Major General Richard Gale, to plan and command VARSITY. Because PLUNDER was primarily a British undertaking, they both felt it appropriate Gale's corps should command VARSITY. Supporting Gale were the twelve men of the Airborne Army's Plans Section, who devised and revised options for deploying the Allied airborne divisions by anticipating the needs of field commanders and maintaining up-to-date information on enemy dispositions. Their advance planning reduced the time necessary to prepare a full-scale airborne operation, thereby mitigating one of the hindrances of leveraging airborne forces: ground units having to pause their operational tempo while the airborne units readied themselves.

Gale and Brereton selected the American 13th and 17th Airborne as well as the British 6th Airborne Divisions to support Montgomery's crossing. But in Brereton's mind, he had only temporarily assigned the divisions to VARSITY.

Gale met with Montgomery's commanders on Thursday, February 1, 1945, to review his initial plan. They gathered at the Airborne Army's Parisian headquarters in the Hôtel Royal, located near the Seine, across from the well-manicured grounds of the seventeenth-century baroque Château de Maisons-Laffitte.

Gale, known as "Windy" to his friends, had begun his military career commanding a machine gun company during the First World War. He'd endured gas attacks and suffered in the quagmire of the Somme and Ypres—an experience that gave him a sober appreciation for leadership's responsibilities. Perhaps his experience with trench warfare is what drew him to the parachute forces in 1941; a soldier with a background in static tactics would find the dynamic nature of airborne operations more appealing. Subsequently, Gale became one of the most experienced airborne officers in the British Army. After leading the 6th Airborne Division into Normandy, he spent a year in the War Office Directorate of Air, where he ensured proper coordination between the Army and the Royal Air Force. Gale preferred blunt, direct communication with subordinates and superiors alike, a trait that when combined with his uncompromising approach to soldiering reinforced his reputation as a boisterous buccaneer. In dealing with Montgomery's staff, he would enjoy no such direct communication.

A few days after the meeting in the Hôtel Royal, Montgomery's staff informed Brereton that Montgomery wanted Gale replaced by Matt Ridgway and his XVIII Airborne Corps. Their rationale: there'd be two American divisions taking part in the operation, and Ridgway's corps had more combat experience and possessed superior signal capabilities. The concern over communications went back to British I Airborne Corps' failure to establish radio contact with its own troops during the first three days of MARKET GARDEN. Their poor performance had contributed to the operation's breakdown, and no one wanted that to happen again.

But Brereton refused. He planned to use Ridgway's corps for the other pending operations; nevertheless Montgomery remained adamant.

With the situation at an impasse, appeals were made directly to Eisenhower, who resolved the argument in Montgomery's favor. Brereton went so far as to personally present his case to Eisenhower, who continued to back Montgomery, reminding Brereton that the primary effort to breach the Rhine would be made by the British. Supreme Headquarters would afford them all the support necessary for success, and the same was expected of Brereton. Ridgway's XVIII Airborne Corps would command VARSITY.

Having lost his first request, Brereton pressed Eisenhower to release one of the three airborne divisions. He argued that two airborne divisions were sufficient to establish Montgomery's bridgehead and that conventional infantry, crossing the Rhine in the wake of the main assault, would be a more effective way to reinforce the east bank. He concluded by pointing out that committing three divisions left just one each for the other planned airdrops to cross the Rhine, not to mention the potential drop into Berlin. Unmoved by the objections, Eisenhower reiterated that Montgomery's plan would stand.

A deflated Brereton left Eisenhower's Versailles headquarters and reluctantly started the process of transitioning command of the operation from Gale to Ridgway.

Ridgway reacted to news of the transfer by immediately lodging a protest with his current superior, General Omar Bradley. Ridgway had been leading several divisions actively engaged in the American sector of the front, and the decision to subordinate his corps to a British operation annoyed him. Both he and Bradley were certain that with a few more weeks their attack would splinter the German defenses and they would be well on their way into Germany. Bradley wanted to keep Ridgway in the fight, but his appeal to Eisenhower had been cut short as well—the assignment was final.

Ridgway, driving his divisions forward with the confidence of a centurion, wanted to stay at the front, and he was livid about being ordered to relinquish command in the middle of a battle. He preferred a fighting command and going toe to toe with the Germans to what would largely be an administrative role of coordinating and planning the airborne landings for Montgomery. A corps commander for an airdrop wouldn't have much to do once the troops landed in enemy territory, and he relished his place in the vanguard of Bradley's ground advance, later describing the challenge as "one that no professional soldier could turn down."

After his journey on Friday, February 9, Ridgway and William "Bud" Miley—the 17th Airborne Division commander—arrived late to VARSITY's initial planning conference. When they walked into Room 445 on the fourth floor of the British headquarters in Brussels, they found that Montgomery's chief of operations, Brigadier General David Belchem, had started the meeting without them.

The two airborne generals had both come directly from the front, still wearing their battle gear and muddy combat boots. Miley hadn't bathed in weeks, and Ridgway remained in a sour mood. Belchem waited for them to take their seats and, using a large map for orientation, continued his overview of PLUNDER, pointing to the German town of Wesel, on the Rhine's far bank, as a primary objective.

Belchem briefed the group on the four principles behind Montgomery's airborne plan: drop them in a single lift; time it to coincide with PLUNDER's river assault; drop onto landing zones within range of Allied artillery; and ensure a linkup with ground forces as soon as possible.

Everyone in the room realized that the last point—a quick linkup—depended on ground forces punching through German defenses, the speed of which could not be predicted. Preparing for a worst-case scenario, they planned for two aerial resupply drops of ammunition, food, water, and medical supplies.

Airborne troops, because they were limited to the equipment they could airlift with them, favored packing firepower and medical supplies over food and water. Arranging for airdrops of additional supplies ensured the airborne troops could sustain themselves in the event ground forces were delayed. But heavy weapons still posed the biggest challenge. The largest artillery piece that could be dropped via parachute was a disassembled 75mm pack howitzer. Theoretically, cargo gliders provided a more reliable method of delivering heavy equipment by air. But whereas the British had two types of gliders, one of which could carry a light tank, the Americans fielded a single, smaller glider, the Waco CG-4A. In addition to the two pilots, it could either carry thirteen troops, a jeep (with three men), a 75mm pack howitzer, or, if squeezed in just right, a modified version of the larger 105mm howitzer.

The briefing transitioned to Montgomery's chief of plans, who disclosed VARSITY's proposed objective: to seize the high ground—a forested rise of 500 feet called the Diersfordter Wald on the far bank of the Rhine—to prevent German artillery fire from hampering the crossing. He assigned two divisions, the 17th and 6th, to accomplish the task. At a later phase the 13th Airborne would drop ninety miles farther inland to exploit the advance and facilitate the crossing of a second, smaller river, the Lippe.

After a brief pause, Ridgway said he understood the mission of the first two divisions but thought the request for the 13th Airborne premature. Any reduced momentum—a reasonable concern given Montgomery's record—would allow the Germans to fall back and occupy the proposed drop zones in strength. Characteristically, Ridgway sat ram-rod straight in his chair—a posture he adopted to both reinforce the intensity of his focus and to respect his back injury. His deportment also reflected his inflexibility on the topic. While Eisenhower may have agreed to the use of three divisions, he hadn't.

Belchem decided to defer the argument for another time, and the group agreed to at least put the 13th Airborne on alert while the justifi-cation for their participation was further explored.

Moving on, Belchem then polled the room for a proposed launch date of March 15.

"Absolutely out of the question," responded Ridgway.

Having already studied the governing factors, he rapidly fired off the facts: still on the front lines at that point, the 17th had sustained almost 4,000 casualties; the 13th, having just arrived in Europe, would not even be operational until the first of March—at the earliest.

Gale piled on, stressing that if the 6th—also still at the front—got pri-ority movement back to England they could be ready within four weeks. He pointed out that the current schedule had them withdrawing at the end of February, making them available for an airborne mission some-time at the end of March or, more likely, early April.

Ridgway stated the airborne point of view: the earliest possible date for the operation would have to be April 1. He warned that if the Rhine jump were conducted any earlier they should expect higher casualties due to less-than-thorough planning and training. Begrudgingly, Mont-gomery's staff accepted Ridgway's launch date.

Later that afternoon, over lunch, Ridgway listened to Gale summa-rize the VARSITY plan he and his staff had developed before having to relinquish command to the Americans. Ridgway recognized that he and Gale shared similar concerns and perspectives, and so ordered the British general, now his deputy commander, to continue planning on his behalf.

Ridgway wanted detailed planning for the ground phase of the oper-ation to be conducted directly with General Miles Dempsey's Second Army staff. Since the divisions under Dempsey's command would lead the river assault, Ridgway dispatched Gale and a small team of British airborne officers to coordinate with them until XVIII Airborne Corps could be relieved from the front. At that time, the men agreed, Gale's corps would transition to managing the preparation of 6th Airborne in England while Ridgway's staff took over VARSITY planning and attended to the logistical needs of the two American divisions on the continent.

Before departing, Ridgway sought out Montgomery to make another attempt at getting Gale's corps assigned to command VARSITY so he could return to the front. Finding the field marshal away for the day, Ridgway discussed the matter with Belchem, who frankly shared his doubts over any change of plans but agreed to present Ridgway's case to Montgomery.

Ridgway left to complete his transfer and relocate his headquarters to Épernay. The small French town, best known for its champagne vineyards, was seventy-five miles east of Paris and just a forty-five-minute drive to Miley's 17th Airborne HQ in Châlons.

The next day a British operations officer at Supreme Headquarters, apparently confused as to why Gale hadn't ceded command to Ridgway, telephoned Brereton's HQ and irately demanded that Gale terminate his planning efforts at once. It was up to Brereton's chief of staff, Floyd Parks, to smooth over the misunderstanding. He explained that Gale had Ridgway's full confidence and emphasized that his participation as deputy commander allowed planning to start straightaway, rather than be delayed until Ridgway himself became available.

Somewhat mollified, the caller then tried to change the operation's launch date, stressing Montgomery's desire to conduct the crossing no later than March 15. To accommodate the acceleration, Montgomery would withdraw the 6th Airborne to their bases in England no later than February 15, and the 17th Airborne would soon be relieved from the front as well.

Parks agreed the divisions' combat readiness was a major factor, but not the only one. The conditions of the twelve French airfields from which the American divisions were departing also hampered the timeline. The abandoned *Luftwaffe* airstrips had been bombed mercilessly by the Allies and were in appalling condition. Engineers estimated it wouldn't be until the third or fourth week of March that the fields would be repaired. The effort required to get them operational could hardly be exaggerated. To hit their deadline 3,200 American and British engineers, with 750 French civilians, would labor 700,000 hours around the clock over the next thirty-four days. They needed to mend and upgrade runways, taxiways, service roads, and hangars. They had to erect crew barracks and storage facilities, build hardstands for parking aircraft, and construct marshaling areas for the airborne troops.

Reluctantly, the British officer acquiesced. D-Day would remain April 1—for the time being.

CHAPTER 3

THUNDER FROM HEAVEN

Châlons-sur-Marne, France. Mid-February 1945.

While senior commanders debated logistics, olive-drab cargo trucks rumbled into the camps around Châlons-sur-Marne with daily deliveries of replacement troops. Wounded veterans, having recovered from their injuries, also trickled out of hospitals and back to their units. General William "Bud" Miley, with the thoroughness of a nervous accountant, monitored the growing troop numbers as his division climbed back to full strength.

Despite an available pool of trained parachute and glider replacements, there was still a shortage of qualified airborne troops. Reconstituting the losses of the three American airborne divisions—all of which had fought in the Bulge—had drained the reserve entirely. To address the shortfalls, Supreme Headquarters sent repeated requests to the US for more replacements.

Miley had learned the details of the forthcoming mission when he attended the British planning conference in Brussels with Ridgway. With a few exceptions on Miley's staff, the rest of the division would remain ignorant of the mission for now. But they were in good hands; Bud Miley had plenty of experience to get them squared away for their first combat jump.

On the outside Miley had the quiet demeanor of a benevolent schoolmaster and the dimpled chin of a Hollywood leading man, but at his core he was steeped in the discipline and dedication of his family's military pedigree. As a fourth-generation graduate of the Army's prestigious West Point academy, he approached his chosen profession as a point of honor and with a warrior's ethos.

During the interwar period, Miley's protracted climb up the Army's career ladder had reflected the scant opportunities for advancement in America's small peacetime military. After graduating in 1918, he'd spent the first fifteen years of his service at the entry-level rank of lieutenant. His early assignments varied from managing the acrobats of the 1st Infantry Division's circus in post–World War I occupied Germany to attending the Air Corps Tactical School in 1930. He later spent several years in Panama and the Philippines assigned to an infantry regiment. He returned to West Point as the director of athletics and advanced to the rank of captain in September 1933.

Seven years later, after another promotion and with war looming, Major Miley organized a group of over 400 volunteers into the Army's first formal parachute unit, the 501st Parachute Infantry Battalion. In preparation for his new assignment he made his first parachute jump in October of 1940. After landing, he casually observed, "Hell, there's nothing to it."

It became obvious to Miley that the Army's standard-issue personal equipment was insufficient to meet the needs of his paratroopers' unique mission. Much of what they required simply didn't exist. As pioneers of parachute tactics and techniques, his battalion would need to develop their own equipment. Miley organized a prototyping regimen for each platoon to experiment with various models of helmets, boots, and field uniforms.

First up were the standard service shoe and canvas leggings, which provided little ankle support during landings. They had to go. A boot of some kind was needed, so they tested several designs. The selected model was made of dark reddish leather, mid-calf height, featuring a reinforced toe cap and stiff canvas supports sewn inside the ankle. Rubber soles prevented slipping, and the front of the heel angled to the rear to avoid catching on the edge of the aircraft door or entangling the parachute's suspension lines. These specialized boots became a status symbol for the elite troops who spent hours polishing them.

Miley, who was forty-two years old at the time, earned his troops' respect by personally testing the unfamiliar and unproven equipment, and he made sure that the battalion's officers did likewise. He had the unit's parachute rigger shop develop experimental weapon cases and quick-release harnesses so that the troops could jump with their equipment. His principles landed him in the hospital after he became the first in the unit to jump with an oversized load and suffered a broken collarbone.

Made up entirely of volunteers, the Army's first parachute battalion demanded more of its men—mentally and physically—than an average infantry unit. Captain William Yarborough, one of the company commanders, said of Miley, "He was always in superb physical condition and it was one of his major goals in life to make sure that we were too. . . . If Bud Miley had the power of decision, paratroops would be hard to join and easy to get out of."

A visiting British parachute instructor commented, "The percentage of failures, which were colorfully described as 'washed-outs,' was extremely high, but the net result was the production of a force of supermen imbued with very high morale and fighting qualities."

Successfully completing the Army's toughest training course earned the graduates a certificate of completion as a token of their accomplishment. Miley believed the men's elite status deserved something more than a document barely suitable for framing, so he instituted a number of uniform modifications to distinguish his parachute troops from the rest of the non-jumping Army.

In early 1941 the Army approved the battalion's request for a parachute qualification badge. Miley, after rejecting several disappointing designs submitted by the Quartermaster General's office, dispatched Captain Yarborough to take charge of the matter. The final insignia incorporated a fully inflated parachute with feathered wings curling out from each side. Known as "jump wings," the men proudly wore the sterling silver badge over the left breast pocket of their uniform.

Miley's paratroopers ditched the standard service hat—a despised round design with a leather visor that evoked the image of a milkman—in favor of a more practical garrison cap adorned with a round parachute patch on the front left side.

Miley also encouraged his paratroopers to leave their standard-issue low-cut leather shoes in their footlocker and instead wear their spit-shined jump boots with their dress uniform. To make the entire boot visible, troopers tucked their trousers and bloused them over the top. The Army Uniform Board approved the modification, which led to the troopers referring to non-parachutists as "straight-legs" or simply as "legs," and not infrequently as "dirty" or "nasty" legs. The more loquacious favored "dirty, nasty, stinking legs."

The combination of the sleek garrison cap, shiny jump wings, bloused trousers, and polished jump boots made paratroopers instantly recognizable and bolstered an already cocky pride. And as a Signal Corps recruiting film advised prospective volunteers, "The dolls don't exactly put on a chill when they get a load of the wings or these boots."

The unique uniform made a different impression on Fort Benning's other elite troops: the nasty leg tankers of General Patton's 2nd Armored Division, who declared an open season on forcibly collecting jump boots. A battle royal ensued off base, and whenever the two groups crossed paths, the tankers found the paratroopers more than willing to engage in "knuckle maneuvers." At such times, Miley's emphasis on hand-to-hand combat training proved useful. On more than one occasion a barefooted and bruised paratrooper returned to barracks with his boots around his neck and an even more arrogant spring in his step.

Officers in both units turned a blind eye to the brawling despite constant protests from local law enforcement and military police. After all, they wanted aggressive men spoiling for a fight. Miley actively encouraged the hostilities. Calling the troops together for a "fight talk," he told them, "It isn't a disgrace to get a black eye but it is a disgrace to run away from a fight and let your buddies get beat up." The "battle of the boots" was never brought to a successful cease-fire, and the men of the 501st Parachute Infantry Battalion bragged that they could whip a whole division of tankers.

As a new unit with no lineage or traditions, Miley and his officers invented their own. One of the first was a rite-of-passage drinking game named after the gust of wind that smacks a jumper as he exits the aircraft, the "Prop Blast."

One of Miley's lieutenants created a ceremonial mug from a cut-down 75mm artillery shell with two reserve parachute ripcord handles welded on each side. The elixir consisted of vodka, for strength, and champagne, to represent the youth and energy of the parachute troops. Lemon and sugar could be added for taste.

The ritual followed a defined protocol: the parachutist stood on a chair and on the command "GO!" jumped into the air, performed a parachute landing fall, rolled into a standing position, and grabbed the mug as his comrades yelled out a count, "One thousand! Two thousand! . . ." He had to down the entire drink before "Four thousand!" He then announced to the room the first thought that popped into his head.

Miley was unable to attend the inaugural Prop Blast due to recovering from a parachute injury, but some of his officers smuggled the chalice and the concoction of alcohol into his hospital room so that he could have the honor of the first official sip.

In March 1942, three months after the attack on Pearl Harbor, the Army promoted Miley for his innovative leadership and assigned him to organize the first full regiment of parachutists. As the Army began its rapid expansion to meet the demands of fighting wars in both the Pacific and in Europe, Miley, like other career professionals, was quickly promoted to even higher leadership positions.

By September he had attained the rank of brigadier general, becoming Ridgway's assistant division commander at the 82nd Airborne. Then in early 1943 he managed the formation of the Army's fourth airborne division, the 17th, whose motto "Thunder from Heaven" was inspired by a biblical quote from the Book of Samuel: "The Lord thundered with a great thunder on that day upon the Philistines and terrified them."

Distinguished by their shoulder patch, featuring a gold eagle's talon on a circular black background with a black-and-gold "AIRBORNE" tab crowning the top, the men of the 17th embraced the aggressive attitudes expected of elite infantry. Their insignia symbolized striking from the darkness to seize opportunity; anyone foolishly mistaking the talon for a chicken's foot was readily corrected with a sharp comment or a punch in the face.

Now, in the spring of 1945, Miley managed the recovery of his division from its losses in the Bulge and its preparation for VARSITY while at the same time managing a divisional reorganization.

When the 17th was formed, like the other airborne divisions, it had consisted of approximately 8,500 soldiers divided into two glider infantry regiments and one parachute infantry regiment, plus smaller specialty units. This structure, known as the triangular division, mirrored conventional infantry divisions and allowed commanders to engage the enemy with two regiments, with a third in reserve to exploit tactical opportunities. But combat had proven that the airborne divisions needed an overhaul. Originally scaled down due to lack of sufficient air transportation, they were 3,500 men short of a regular infantry division but still expected to hold the same frontage once in the line.

Ridgway had been a strong proponent of increasing manpower since before the invasion of Sicily in 1943. He likened the unreasonable expectations for the understrength divisions to "calling in a very large man and saying, 'Here are two yards of cloth. Go make yourself a suit of clothes.'"

He admitted, "The only thing to do was to ignore these limitations." To sidestep bureaucratic constraints, independent parachute units were attached to the divisions rather than officially assigned. Upon disembarking in England, the 17th had a second parachute infantry regiment attached, giving Miley four regiments and manpower above his authorized count.

Ridgway's multiple attempts to have the War Department increase the manpower and equipment allocations for airborne divisions had been habitually rejected. The chronic shortage of infantrymen required the airborne to wait their turn, but America's production of C-47s and trained aircrews made the expansion feasible from a transportation aspect.

In December 1944 Ridgway made yet another request, this time directly to the Army's Chief of Staff in Washington, DC. In late February the War Department gave its approval. The airborne divisions expanded to just over 13,000 men, making them roughly equivalent to a regular infantry division.

The reorganization shifted Miley's triangular formation from two glider regiments—the 193rd and 194th—and a parachute regiment— the 513th—to a single glider regiment and two parachute regiments. The new Tables of Organization consolidated the two glider regiments into a larger, single unit and formally assigned the 507th Parachute Infantry Regiment to the 17th. The division's artillery firepower increased from forty to sixty 75mm howitzers.

While the headquarters staff transferred men and materiel across the division via typewriters and paper, the officers and sergeants managed the reorg at the unit level.

✱   ✱   ✱

Enjoying a bright but chilly spring morning outside of Châlons, Lieutenant Frank Dillon, a platoon leader in the 194th Glider Infantry Regiment, sat in his four-man tent contemplating his platoon's training schedule.

Dillon, a twenty-four-year-old forestry major from northern Massachusetts, had been pursuing a career in the timber industry before the war started, but like thousands of other young men, he put his plans on hold to volunteer for service. After completing jump school in the

States, he joined the 17th shortly after their arrival in England and was assigned to replace a platoon leader who, along with all thirty of his troops, had died in the crash of a British Horsa glider during training.

In the course of fighting in the Bulge, Dillon's company was in reserve when the men of Baker Company trudged out into the swirling snow to storm the heights of "Dead Man's Ridge." During three days of brutal effort to clear the summit and overrun the enemy positions, the German defenders shredded the men of Baker. All of the officers were killed or wounded, and of the original 150 men who went into the attack fewer than 40 still stood after the melee. Given command of the decimated company, Dillon knew he had his work cut out for him. It was a textbook leadership challenge: a broken group of survivors who'd known one another for years, and a newly arrived, unknown lieutenant. By all accounts Dillon rose to the task, organizing the glider infantrymen into a platoon and leading them through the next month of combat.

Unlike the parachute outfits, glider units were manned by non-volunteers, many of whom were often bitter about being pressed into such a dangerous assignment with few perks. Denied the extra hazard pay enjoyed by paratroopers, glider riders were also neglected by the Army when it came to any unique insignia or badges. But the most egregious offense was that they were forced to fly without parachutes, contrary to standard practice for military aircrews.

In the barracks, men hung handmade posters featuring photos of twisted and burned gliders; the caption read: "Join the glider troops! No flight pay. No jump pay. But never a dull moment!" A few stanzas from a popular drinking ditty, "The Gliderman's Lament," summed up their position:

> *Oh! Once I was happy, but now I'm Airborne,*
> *Riding the gliders all tattered and torn,*
> *The pilots are daring, all caution they scorn,*
> *And the pay is exactly the same.*

> *We glide through the air in our flying caboose,*
> *Its actions are graceful, just like a goose,*
> *We hike on the pavement till joints come loose,*
> *And the pay is exactly the same.*

Once I was in the infantry, now I'm a dope,
Riding in gliders attached to a rope,
Safety in landing is only a hope,
And the pay is exactly the same.

We glide through the air in a tactical state,
Jumping is useless, it's always too late,
No chute for the soldiers who ride in a crate,
And the pay is exactly the same.

The lack of elite status and inequality of pay created a class system within the division. In the mind of the jumpers, the glider riders weren't exactly legs but close enough.

A grassroots campaign, which included mailing copies of "The Gliderman's Lament" to congressmen, resulted in House Resolution 4466, the Glider Pay Bill. The bill gave the glider troops the same hazardous duty pay as paratroopers: $50 a month for enlisted men, $100 a month for officers. The rationale for paying an officer $50 more than an enlisted man to jump out of the same aircraft or buckle into the same glider went unaddressed. The glider troops also received authorization to wear jump boots and a glider badge, similar to jump wings in appearance but with the distinct nose of the CG-4A glider replacing the parachute. But rowdy paratroopers, looking to remind non-parachute-qualified glider troopers of their station, were known to attack those foolish enough to blouse their pants over their jump boots, cutting their trousers off at the knees as a symbol of who'd earned this exclusive right.

Private Gene Herrmann, like all glider riders, relished the extra pay and recognition. Before the war the twenty-one-year-old Cleveland native held numerous odd jobs trying to put food on the table: grocery stocker, shipping clerk, and factory worker. He possessed a pleasant disposition, a mop of thick, dark hair, and a full smile that made his eyes squint. But the morale of his unit, the 193rd Glider Infantry Regiment, was at a low point after their mauling in the Ardennes. It sank further when the men were called to formation on a rainy morning in Châlons. From his position in the back, Herrmann had a hard time hearing the announcement until the bad news rippled through the ranks: they were being disbanded. As they shuffled back through the mud to their tents, Herrmann learned that they'd be reassigned to their sister regiment, the

194th. Not only had they lost friends in combat, now it seemed that they'd be split up from the few they had left.

The troops from the disbanded 193rd would be used to expand the 194th by augmenting each platoon with an additional squad of twelve men and building out a third battalion. Collapsed into a single regiment, the transfers boosted the regimental strength from 1,678 men to 3,114.

The paratroopers might still look down on them, but the glider regiment now became the most lethal unit in the division. Their allocation of 81mm mortars soared from six to eighteen, 60mm mortars increased to twenty-seven, over a hundred bazookas were added, and the number of .30-caliber belt-fed machine guns quadrupled to thirty-six.

With the regiment's reorganization, Frank Dillon became the lieutenant in charge of 1st Platoon in the reconstituted Baker Company. Having arrived in the rest area with 35 men, the company now swelled back to 200, building out a headquarters section, three rifle platoons, and a weapons platoon.

Dillon's training regime for his men followed the division plan, which began with marksmanship. They built a rifle range in an open wooded area near their camp, scrounging cans and bottles from the mess tents for targets. For two days the area rang with the loud *pop, pop, pop* of the platoon zeroing their M1 Garands and carbines.

Dillon's veterans found that the replacements could load and fire their weapons but do little else. They knew nothing about how to clear stoppages or place crew-served machine guns into action quickly. It was clear that they needed more practice.

Training progressed from squad- and platoon-level exercises to the full company acting in concert. Squads loaded into the backs of large cargo trucks to practice assembling. Having bumped their way randomly out into a large field, the men charged off the tailgates of their "gliders" as soon as they came to a halt and made their way to the platoon's designated rally point.

In combat, waiting for squads to arrive was a tactical trade-off: the longer the delay, the stronger the unit became, but it also gave the enemy time to react. When enough troops had arrived at the assembly area, procedure called for the highest-ranking man to lead them out. Gliders guaranteed that squads arrived on the battlefield as a group, but seizing and holding an objective required the company's full firepower. Those failing to assemble on time had to find their own way or catch up to the troops already on the move.

Jeeps, trucks, and trailers that had been arranged to simulate the lay-out of farm buildings or small villages served as objectives for practic-ing assault tactics. Platoons and companies bounded forward, yelling, "Pow! Pow! Pow!" as they assaulted through the "villages."

They ran the drills over and over. Their harrowing ride in a motorless glider, through anti-aircraft fire and an uncertain crash landing, was just the commute. The real action, the payoff for all their training, would be what happened after they landed. Despite the rudimentary conditions, Dillon made sure they took advantage of every opportunity to get ready for the trial ahead. Plus, the replacements needed more work.

Rehearsing patrol formations and small unit tactics, the veterans bad-gered the new men to avoid bunching up, especially during attacks. The idea was to fire one or two shots, roll behind cover, and select the next position before rushing forward. The safest place during a German mortar or artillery barrage, the rookies learned, if not in a foxhole, was in a recent shell hole, given the unlikely chance of a round hitting the same spot twice.

Damaged glider fuselages recovered from the Dutch landing zones of MARKET GARDEN were brought in for troopers to refresh on loading and lashing down equipment. An improperly balanced jeep or shifting cargo in flight could result in disaster. Knot-tying classes emphasized slipknots to secure equipment that could be undone rapidly once on the ground.

Over at the 466th Parachute Field Artillery Battalion's camp, John Chester took notice of the reorganization. His battalion, having oper-ated with twelve howitzers since the previous June, added three more. But something about the new arrivals' attitude bothered him. Perhaps he picked up on their hesitation. None had fired a howitzer in over a year due to serving as scouts in the division's reconnaissance platoon. They needed practice, but there were no artillery ranges near Châlons. Seeing that their training lacked the appropriate sense of urgency, Ches-ter suspected the new men would be more of a liability than an asset.

As his crew had learned, living up to Chester's standards required maximum effort. The results, however, were hard to argue with: five of the battery's gunners and three of the section chiefs had been promoted up from his section. But they did get a small break from their rigorous routine when Chester attended a short combat leadership course.

In spite of his recognized leadership abilities and being "the best gunner in the battalion" (in his own opinion), Chester didn't consider himself "the military type" nor did he plan to turn his service into a career.

After returning from the leadership course, he approached his commanding officer, Captain Charles Duree, to share the results of his soul-searching and resign his position as section chief.

"You're doing a fine job and that's why you're wearing stripes now," the captain told him, hesitant to accept Chester's self-demotion.

Chester replied that he appreciated the compliment but felt that "a career type soldier should be giving the commands that might get some of the troops killed."

Duree reluctantly agreed, telling Chester, "You're my choice but if you want out, we'll respect your wishes. Who is qualified to take your place?"

Chester nominated Ralph Foulk, a former section chief whom the previous commanding officer had busted in rank.

"Who will be the gunner?" asked Duree.

Chester replied, "That's me, as long as there is no command authority involved."

It did not take long before Chester regretted his decision. Having led his crew through the Battle of the Bulge, he now had a more refined appreciation for leadership and noticed that "Sergeant Foulk was rather hesitant when it came to the making of even minor decisions. He nearly always felt the need of checking with higher authority first."

That kind of indecisiveness could sure get people killed, thought Chester. And not just "people," they were "his boys," with whom he'd trained and fought for the last two years.

After watching Sergeant Foulk in action, or inaction, it dawned on Chester that "being a career military man does not mean you will be good at command decisions. On the other hand, being a civilian type doesn't mean you can't make proper military decisions if need be." But it was too late now.

In neighboring camps, shouts of "GO, GO, GO!" could be heard as parachutists used mock aircraft doors to practice their exit drills. Made of wood and constructed to the same dimensions as a C-47's rear door, the mock-ups helped retrain the muscle memory originally honed at jump school. The men spent hours lining up, left arms raised to guide imaginary static lines, and, following the orders of their jumpmaster, shuffling to the mock door and launching themselves out in the prescribed body position. Snapping into a tight posture and bent slightly at the waist with chin tucked into the chest reduced the possibility of tumbling during the chute's deployment. Combat equipment made exiting in the correct position more difficult, but a poor exit could result in suspension lines fatally entangling the jumper.

As the men jumped, they yelled out their count, "One thousand! Two thousand! Three thousand!" and hit the ground a few feet below the door before the final "Four thousand!"

Instructors reminded them that on an actual jump, if they didn't feel the opening shock of their chute by 4,000, they had the rest of their lives to deploy their reserve.

When bored with mock-door drills, they stacked crates into "three-foot towers" from which they leapt to practice their PLFs—parachute landing falls. Executing a proper PLF prevented snapped ankles or broken legs by dispersing the impact with the ground across the jumper's body. With feet and knees together, jumpers were taught to roll in the direction of the parachute's drift. Upon the soles of his feet hitting the ground, the jumper curved his body into the roll using the balls of his feet, his calf, buttocks, and push-up muscles to absorb the impact. Those out of practice usually found a textbook execution impossible, and with the grace of a falling sack of potatoes, most only narrowly avoided a "feet, knees, face" landing.

The refresher training culminated with the troops trucking out to airfields twenty-five miles outside Châlons where the Air Force provided aircraft for both glider flights and parachute drops. The training also benefited the aircrews that had spent the last several months focused on supply runs rather than airborne operations.

★   ★   ★

On Thursday, February 14, Ridgway met with Montgomery's Second Army commander Miles Dempsey, the orchestrator of PLUNDER's execution. Widely regarded by his peers as a humble man, Dempsey preferred to wage his war quietly and readily surrendered the spotlight to his boss, Montgomery, who took more naturally to basking in its glow. But those in high places recognized Dempsey's talents and unpretentious contributions. During a visit to the front in 1944, King George VI knighted him for his many wartime accomplishments—a rare battlefield honor that was last recorded to have taken place at Agincourt in 1415.

Ridgway was surprised to find that Dempsey, who was not present at the original planning conference, had developed his own VARSITY plan. Dempsey, either ignorant of or disregarding the previously agreed-upon objectives, wanted one of Ridgway's divisions to seize the town of Wesel—an industrial community of almost 25,000 inhabitants and an important *Wehrmacht* communications hub. The second division would link up with Dempsey's troops crossing the Rhine, while the third airborne division occupied the high ground east of Wesel.

It was uncharacteristically naïve of Dempsey to task an airborne division with attacking Wesel; they lacked the tanks and heavy artillery required for such an urban assault, which meant the defenders had all the advantages. Knowing senior commanders often wanted to appear "imaginative and bold in their thinking," Ridgway was used to them reaching for the "magic key" of an airdrop. He'd been fending off misguided proposals that ignored the tactical realities and limitations of airborne troops since the invasion of Sicily in 1943.

After patiently listening to Dempsey defend his decisions by elaborating on his previous assault experience in Sicily, Italy, and Normandy, Ridgway said he'd be "completely frank" in his assessment.

He told Dempsey that he seemed to be approaching the landings "purely as a map problem" and "that no consideration appeared to have been given to two fundamental factors, namely, the practicability of the drop area between the city and the hill mass, and the nature of hostile defenses."

Ridgway, looking over the map, acknowledged that the plan for the second and third divisions was conceptually sound. However, recollecting a previous study of the area, he reminded Dempsey that his proposed landing zones east of Wesel were "adequate for a maximum of one division," not three.

Ridgway concluded by suggesting that Dempsey develop an alternate plan, "because it seemed very likely that the one he proposed would not be practical."

Dempsey preferred to wait for Ridgway's formal assessment before making any modifications. Ridgway agreed to have conclusions ready in four days.

The next morning Ridgway informed Brereton that Dempsey's current plans for VARSITY were unsuitable. Ridgway considered sending airborne troops, without armor support, to attack a fortified town, an exercise of "useless slaughter." In his experience, "the hard decisions are not the ones you make in the heat of battle. Far harder to make are those involved in speaking your mind about some hare-brained scheme, which proposes to commit troops to action under conditions where failure is almost certain, and the only results will be the needless sacrifice of priceless lives."

The Americans, and Brereton in particular, considered Dempsey to have a better understanding of airborne forces than other British ground commanders. Yet Dempsey's plan baffled the Americans and they closed ranks against it.

The impasse escalated. Four days later, with the planning process floundering, Eisenhower's deputy, General Bedell Smith, attempted to arbitrate the matter between Brereton's chief of staff, Floyd Parks, and Montgomery's diplomatic and well-respected chief of staff, Brigadier General Sir Francis de Guingand.

Smith opened by scolding Parks for "putting the cart before the horse." Before he would agree to involve Eisenhower, Smith recommended Dempsey be given the opportunity to modify his plan—a victory for the planners at Airborne Army. Smith made it clear he knew Ridgway wasn't a "British man," but he'd be expected to find common ground on a mutually acceptable plan, just as he had in the past and despite initially resisting their proposals.

Parks, spreading out prepared map sketches, turned the conversation to the disagreement over the location of drop zones. De Guingand advocated Dempsey's preference to drop east of Wesel, as opposed to the northwest as originally agreed. Responding to Parks' protests over the concentration of German anti-aircraft batteries, de Guingand assured him that air support could sufficiently neutralize the defenses to a point where they "would not cause undue damage."

Parks reminded de Guingand of his own comments made just fifteen minutes earlier when he had shared recent findings that the number of enemy anti-aircraft positions destroyed by Allied aircraft were "insignificant and but a fraction of the percentage claimed by pilots."

Feasibility of suppressing enemy air defenses aside, Parks pointed out that the undulating terrain east of Wesel hindered glider landings and the distance forced a longer march to the objectives. The British tacticians should have recalled the poor decision from MARKET GARDEN, where the distance between the drop zones and 1st Airborne's objective had factored greatly into their failure.

"The ideal airborne landing is to land directly on the objective," an American commander later elaborated. "It is in general far better to take landing losses and land on the objective than to have to fight after landing in order to reach the objective."

The need for glider-friendly terrain weighed equally with the need for proximity, and the Airborne Army's Ground Information Team had armed Parks well. Staffed with experts in photo reconnaissance and interpretation, they specialized in identifying areas suitable for landings and noting hazards of unique concern to parachutists and glider pilots: ditches, fences, power lines, and trees. Poorly chosen landing zones in Burma the previous year had resulted in an Allied glider mission suffering 11 percent casualties and significant equipment losses before the enemy even fired a single shot.

Parks, supporting Ridgway's position, refused to yield; de Guingand reiterated Montgomery's conviction that crossing the Rhine absolutely required airborne support. The committee adjourned after Smith concluded that Dempsey and de Guingand would have to reformulate their plan. Brereton's staff had done their job, ensuring that their specialized units were deployed in a manner suitable to their capabilities and limitations.

Simultaneous with the ground planning, debates about the logistical challenges of transporting two divisions over the Rhine were occurring at Airborne Army's Maisons-Laffitte HQ in Paris. The initial planning focused on lifting the 17th and 6th Airborne, with planners recognizing that if a third division was used, it would drop later.

MARKET GARDEN had shown that making up for aircraft shortages by flying multiple, round-trip serials could be unreliable. VARSITY needed over 3,000 aircraft to drop the full complement of British and American parachutists and gliders in a single lift. The planners realized that they were over 700 planes short. The deficiency raised the question: Should they just transport one full division or parts of both? They decided to defer the decision until it could be determined how many serviceable aircraft could be scraped together.

★   ★   ★

The troops were largely oblivious to the arguing and logistical gymnastics taking place echelons above them. Even so, they began picking up clues that an operation would shortly be under way.

One evening as Frank Dillon and his men ate chow and took a break from training, he noticed fresh paint concealing the unit identification marking on one of the company jeeps. No one was supposed to know it yet, but now Dillon did: the division was preparing to move without being identified.

CHAPTER 4

DELIBERATE AND DISCIPLINED

West of the Rhine River. Early March 1945.

As the 17th Airborne Division refitted in France, Montgomery's plan to clear the west banks of the Rhine unfolded in what Eisenhower later described as "a bitter slugging match in which the enemy had to be forced back yard by yard." The double envelopment of operations VERITABLE and GRENADE slowly pushed the Germans back toward the Rhine. VERITABLE had commenced on February 8, with the British and Canadians attacking from their northern sector with five infantry divisions of over 50,000 men. Fifteen days later the US Ninth Army launched GRENADE, swinging out from the American sector to form the southern pincer of Montgomery's attack. When the operations were successfully concluded, the Allies would be well positioned to cross the Rhine. But they had to get there first.

*   *   *

Marshaling the opposing forces in Western Europe was *Generalfeldmarschall* Gerd von Rundstedt, the German Commander in Chief West, who held this post for the second time. His small gray Hitler-esque mustache and deep jowls pulled the corners of his mouth into an omnipresent scowl, complementing his Prussian bearing. The sixty-nine-year-old field marshal, whose family traced their military service back to Frederick the Great, had retired in 1938, been reappointed in '39, dismissed by Hitler for perceived failures in Russia in '41, and recalled in '42 only to be dismissed again by the Führer after failing to stop the Normandy invasion. In September 1944 Hitler called upon him once more to resume his post just prior to the Allies launching MARKET GARDEN.

Driven backwards since the Ardennes campaign, Rundstedt's ground strength of eighty divisions appeared to be a force greater than what the Allies had arrayed against him. But by the spring of 1945 the German

Army was a tiger on paper only. Declawed by fighting simultaneously on multiple fronts for nearly four years, Rundstedt could muster a capable defense, but little else.

He knew the undermanned and poorly equipped divisions at his disposal had suffered irreplaceable losses. However, while the Allies enjoyed an advantage of roughly ten to one in tanks, more than three to one in aircraft, and over two to one in troops, Rundstedt planned to exact heavy casualties on the attackers. His commanders would lead a dogged defense for every yard of ground, blunting and delaying the approaching Allies by any means at their disposal. Germany had started two world wars but had yet to experience any ground fighting on its soil; Rundstedt knew firsthand what carnage would be unleashed if the enemy's grinding momentum crossed into the Fatherland.

As Montgomery's divisions closed on the Rhine, they encountered the fixed defensive line of Germany's *West-Stellung*. This in-depth defensive perimeter consisted of anti-tank ditches, layers of mutually supportive concrete gun emplacements, and a myriad of engineering obstacles. Constructed by more than 40,000 forced laborers, the miles of fortifications were integrated into the original defensive line known as the *Westwall*, which had been built between 1936 and 1940.

Hitler, with an unshakable faith in his own unique genius to fathom the front line situation from Berlin, wanted all of Germany's might concentrated on stalling the Allied advance. This was critical. He was convinced that with enough time he could either reverse the course of the war or cause such a crippling number of Allied casualties that they would agree to a negotiated conclusion. His certainty of victory deluded the naïve and inspired the zealots into believing that prolonging the war could salvage the Third Reich.

To gain that time, Hitler demanded a *hold at all costs* strategy—a maxim he'd been hammering into the *Wehrmacht* since 1941. There would be no abandoning defensive positions for more favorable ground—ever.

Hitler's willingness to disregard the fundamentals of defense for what he viewed as the bigger political picture didn't permeate down to his tactical commanders, many of whom were well-trained and experienced combat leaders capable of managing their dwindling assets with deadly competence. Contrary to Hitler's belief that fortified positions discouraged aggression, his underlings knew falling back to more advantageous terrain was often tactically sound. Nevertheless, facing enemy guns was one thing, disobeying the Führer was another matter. Thus field commanders fought desperate battles of attrition, splintering any hope of keeping their units intact as effective fighting forces.

As they were pressed farther into Germany, commanders requested permission to partially withdraw some of their forces over the Rhine. They wanted to take advantage of the river as a natural obstacle and establish an in-depth defensive line along the far bank, from which they believed they could stop the Allies. Their requests were met with consistent and unequivocal rejection. "My generals only look behind them," Hitler often lamented.

In the first week of March, Montgomery's pincer attack converged at

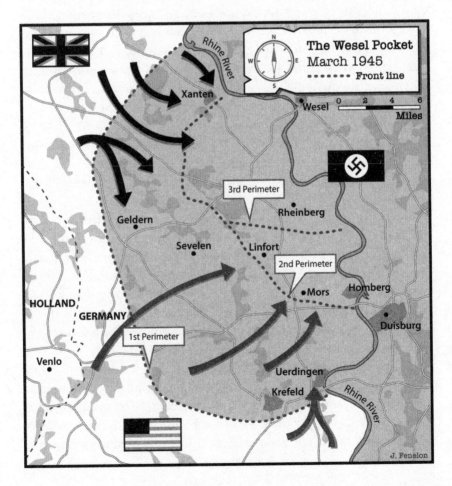

the German town of Geldern, located just sixteen miles from the Rhine. The *Wehrmacht* had put up a stubborn defense, inflicting over 20,000 Allied casualties, but at a staggering cost: an estimated 20,000 killed and more than 50,000 of their own captured.

The Allies continued rolling the Germans up along the banks of the Rhine. To the south the Americans were advancing through Luxembourg on their way to Remagen. At Geldern, Rundstedt's forces still on the western side of the river, with their backs to the Rhine, were encircled on three sides by the uniting of Montgomery's armies. The holdouts formed a half-moon defensive perimeter. A wide arc—roughly thirty miles long—ran from Xanten in the north, southwest to Geldern, and then southeast back to the Rhine at Duisburg. Centered on the town of Wesel, located on the east bank, the "Wesel Pocket" stretched sixteen miles deep from its apex near Geldern to the Rhine.

General der Fallschirmtruppen Alfred Schlemm commanded the 50,000 troops in the Pocket. Schlemm's short stature, dark complexion, and wide Slavic features made him a physical anomaly in the upper echelons of the Aryan Third Reich. One observer offered "anthropoidal" as the best adjective to describe the fifty-one-year-old general.

Whether he looked vaguely simian or not, Schlemm's abilities and agile mind were respected by his peers as well as his adversaries. Awarded the Iron Cross twice as an artillery officer in World War I, he'd spent the interwar years in Germany's hibernating military, studying and refining his craft.

In 1938 he transferred to the *Luftwaffe*, where he qualified as a pilot and planned anti-aircraft defenses along the western borders. In early 1941 he became chief of staff for the newly formed *Flieger Corps*, which consolidated the elite parachute and air landing troops into a unified command. That same year he played a key role in planning the invasion of Crete, Germany's largest airborne assault of the war. Shortly thereafter, with a promotion to major general, he commanded a division on the eastern front and later led field corps in Russia and Italy.

His career had matured in an age of technological advances: from temperamental biplanes to thundering jet fighters, from static muddy trenches to blitzkrieging panzers and dive-bombers. Now as commander of the I *Fallschirmjäger-Armee* (1st Parachute Army), he leveraged his three decades of military experience to stubbornly hold his position in the Pocket.

In addition to organizing his four parachute divisions, two panzer divisions, and a panzer grenadier division into a cohesive defense, Schlemm obsessed over the nine Rhine bridges in this sector. To facilitate the flow of materiel to the front lines, the *Oberkommando der Wehrmacht*—the German Army's High Command—desperately needed to keep the remaining bridges intact as long as possible. Schlemm knew Allied doctrine would normally dictate destroying the bridges to prevent reinforcement of the Pocket, but apparently they were letting them stand in the hopes of seizing one to aid their own crossing over the formidable water obstacle.

The implications of the Allies capturing one of the bridges became an anxious preoccupation. Schlemm later recalled the potential consequences: "[I was] personally responsible for the prompt and thorough destruction of all Rhine bridges in my sector. Special courts were ready to judge immediately the responsible person in case he let a bridge fall undamaged into enemy hands. Every dereliction of duty was to be punished by death. . . . I designated an officer to be responsible for each bridge. He had engineers and troops who had to insure that the demolition of the bridge was carried out successfully." Each officer reported via radio directly to Schlemm, who reserved exclusive authority to demolish the bridges.

Hitler's plan to utilize the Pocket and its bridges as a launching point for a counterattack added to Schlemm's complications. Given the demand for more troops, armored vehicles, and aircraft in Russia, Italy, and along the length of the Rhine, Schlemm was privately dubious Hitler could assemble the forces required for such a strike. However unlikely that was, Hitler continued to overrule reality with bombastic demands that the *Wehrmacht* prepare to burst across the Rhine just as they had out of the Ardennes Forest. From the *Führerbunker* he officially declared the Wesel Pocket a "fortress," a designation that brought even greater dictatorial scrutiny. Schlemm's requests to remove useless equipment or personnel across the bridges for refitting were denied as a matter of course, since assent violated Hitler's order to hold the fortress for the imminent offensive.

As the oversight governing his tactical options became more draconian, Schlemm took disobedient, life-threatening risks to fulfill his primary task: keeping the enemy at bay. Without seeking permission from his chain of command, Berlin, or the Führer, Schlemm quietly ordered fifty howitzers, sitting idle at the *Westwall*, moved to the Pocket to buoy his defenses.

He needed every gun he could find as Montgomery's 21 Army Group probed for a weakness in his perimeter that could be exploited for a route to the Rhine. To Schlemm's surprise, he found most of the British attacks to be uncoordinated and piecemeal feints rather than committed thrusts en masse.

On Thursday, the first of March, from a spot of high ground, he observed an attack on his southern flank near Krefeld. Scrutinizing the maneuver through his binoculars, Schlemm watched as the attackers began a very cautious advance led by Sherman tanks.

It seemed the primary mission of the tanks was to draw the fire of his concealed anti-tank guns. Those tanks fortunate enough to survive the ploy then pulled back as artillery hammered the revealed positions. Once the shelling ceased, the attackers again moved forward with flame-throwing tanks now in the vanguard; occupants of any remaining bunkers had to choose between fleeing or getting burned alive. The Allied units repeated the process every hundred yards or so. Schlemm found the tactic a fascinating study of using overwhelming firepower at the expense of speed. But despite the impressive display, the plodding tactics allowed him time to reposition his defenses and repulse the attack.

"The disadvantage for the enemy was that he never surprised us," Schlemm later said. "We could determine from the kind and location of artillery fire and from the assembly positions of the tanks where and when the attack would take place."

He later confessed that had all the tanks simply stormed forward at once, they could have overrun his defenses and been in Wesel within twenty-four hours.

Schlemm often directly influenced such events from the front lines himself. As the attacks rolled in, he shifted his forces to meet them, sometimes beating the Allies to vital road junctions or key terrain by mere minutes. He used his *Fallschirmjäger*—parachute infantry—to great effect, relying on their aggressive fighting spirit to zealously blunt Allied advances, which provided the time he needed to reorganize.

In one hilltop battle, just north of Xanten, a group of *Fallschirmjäger* beat back attacks for five days before withdrawing after getting flanked. The weeklong struggle had been a bloody ordeal of man versus machine, and in their wake the Axis paratroopers left behind the corpses of 276 comrades and a scrapyard of 320 smoldering Allied tanks. Montgomery later wrote, "Not in the course of the entire war had enemy units offered more bitter resistance, as did the German Fallschirmjägers during the fighting for the Rhineland."

Schlemm also used the terrain to his advantage. Cratering and mining the raised roads forced the Allies into either exposed, creeping advances or bold rushes across open, muddy meadows, which risked bogging down the heavy tanks and favored German artillery. But in spite of the slow progress, the Allies continued to advance steadily, threatening to seize several of the bridges. Their never-ending supply of artillery shells and their ability to rapidly replace losses allowed them to nip at Schlemm's forces around the clock.

As his perimeter shrunk, Schlemm ordered the demolition of the bridges his army could no longer protect. Having first razed the bridge at Uerdingen just as the Allies attempted to cross it, Schlemm next ordered the destruction of the Homberg Bridge on Saturday, March 3. After ten minutes of waiting for the affirming sound of explosions, he radioed to inquire about the delay. The radio operator told him a *Wehrmacht* colonel, claiming higher authority, had countermanded his orders, preventing the engineers from completing their task.

Furious, Schlemm evoked the specter feared by every German: Adolf Hitler. Emphasizing that *his* authority came directly from the Führer, Schlemm promised he would personally shoot the colonel, the radio operator, and anyone else he found at the bridge if they failed to blow it immediately. Seconds later he heard the explosions.

To avoid such precarious incidents at the other bridges, Schlemm dispatched military police units with orders to arrest anyone attempting to usurp his authority.

Schlemm had carefully considered his decision to blow up the Homberg Bridge. Days before, engineers had spent hours systematically rigging the span for explosives, but to prevent accidental detonation, they installed only the infrastructure and detonation cord, not the actual charges. This cautionary measure was a gamble, as the engineers would potentially have little time to install the charges, or to troubleshoot their handiwork should the explosives fail in the face of the enemy barreling forward.

Schlemm also had to keep the resulting retardation of river traffic in mind. Given the need to prevent rapid repair by the Allies, the bridge had to be totally destroyed, and the ensuing wreckage would likely impede river traffic, preventing delivery of essential fuel and ammunition to the Pocket.

Inevitably there would be questioning from the Berlin cabal of micromanagers demanding he justify his decisions from over 300 miles away. After the event, Schlemm had to be able to prove the demolition a military necessity, not the act of a panicked defeatist.

A few days later, wondering how he could be expected to lead an army under such ridiculous conditions, Schlemm raced to intercede on behalf of a court-martialed subordinate. The officer, after twenty-one days of heavy combat and losing all the soldiers under his command, crossed the Rhine seeking a new assignment. Arrested for desertion and sentenced to be hanged as a warning to others, his life was saved by Schlemm's intervention.

By Monday, March 5, the Allies' continued advance had driven Schlemm's forces into a smaller perimeter centered on the only two remaining bridges at Wesel. The Pocket now contained a growing collection of damaged tanks, vehicles without fuel, artillery without ammunition, and idle personnel without training for the task at hand. To avoid the unwanted attention of Allied aircraft, the abandoned equipment was pushed off roads and concealed. But the growing detritus of war accumulated to the point of impeding Schlemm's ability to shift his forces within the Pocket.

It was time to appeal to his superior, *Generaloberst* Johannes Blaskowitz, the commander of *Heeresgruppe H* (Army Group H). Schlemm hoped the more senior officer, who understood the local situation, might prevail in arguing his point with Berlin. The High Command reluctantly authorized the removal of the useless materiel, but with its consent came a list of specific types of equipment and personnel permitted for withdrawal. In turn, each unit commander had to testify by signature that the evacuated men were unable to contribute to the fighting; the documents were then forwarded to Berlin for review and filing.

All around the perimeter, the British, Canadians, and Americans repeatedly used isolated tank attacks in attempts to break through what they believed to be thinly held lines. In one effort, Schlemm's competently manned and well-camouflaged anti-tank guns destroyed twelve of fourteen Sherman tanks. In another, near Rheinberg, where the Allies endeavored to cut the Pocket in half, a determined defense took out thirty-nine of fifty-four Allied tanks before the attackers retreated.

Schlemm maneuvered his treasured anti-tank guns and artillery adroitly, shifting them to specific hot spots, which the removal of obstructing debris had made easier. The Pocket's shrinking footprint also helped, providing the paradoxical benefit of allowing him to concentrate his firepower and reinforce the perimeter in depth; his artillery could now swivel and fire across the width of the Pocket to defend any section of the perimeter. He also leveraged the withering fire of his anti-aircraft guns by pressing them into a direct fire role against Allied tanks and troops.

On the night of March 6, streams of RAF bombers pummeled Wesel for the fifth time in three weeks. Schlemm recognized it as yet another attempt to cut his supply lines. From altitudes of over 16,000 feet the British dropped combinations of 4,000-pound blockbusters and 500-pound general-purpose munitions, targeting the rail network, depots, and suspected troop concentrations.

Across the river, from the relative safety of the Pocket, Schlemm's troops watched in awe for hours as wave after wave of explosions and concussions ripped the town apart. Occasionally they could hear the whine of German jet aircraft cutting across the steady droning of bomber engines, but Hitler's wonder weapons seemed to make little impression on the never-ending flow of British aircraft. The glow of fires reflected off the Rhine's black current, and dark clouds of smoke billowed up to blanket the stars.

Sunrise revealed the extent of the devastation. Covered in ash, the craters and rubble looked more like a monochromatic lunar landscape than a city. Schlemm's assessment of the damage and its impact on his logistics was interrupted by more bad news. Ninety miles upstream, outside of his sector, an intact, dual-track railway bridge had fallen into Allied hands. After confused authority caused a delay, and explosives failed to topple it—due to only half of the charges detonating—the Ludendorff Bridge at Remagen was seized by forward elements of an American armored division. By order of Berlin four German officers were executed for their incompetence.

The capture of the bridge was a dramatic loss as GIs dashed across the span under German machine gun fire while frantically searching for and cutting any remaining demolition cord.

"The bullets didn't worry us half as much as the bridge," recalled Gaccarino Mercandante, a mortarman from Brooklyn. "We expected the Heinies to blow the bridge right out from under us at any minute so we didn't waste any time getting to the other side."

Desperate to destroy the bridge, Rundstedt sent bombers, floating mines, and even frogmen to finish the job. Finally after ten days, the thousand-foot span, structurally weakened from the original detonations, heavy Allied traffic, and multiple attacks, collapsed into the Rhine. Almost 200 US Army engineers went with it.

In the intervening days before the bridge gave way to stress and gravity, the Allies built several pontoon bridges adjacent to it; these temporary floating trestles allowed for the steady flow of tanks and men into Germany. Rundstedt, in an attempt to stem the growing American bridgehead at Remagen, shifted several divisions south. With virtually no reserves to call on, he moved units from around Wesel, their departure draining vital manpower from Schlemm's perimeter.

In the Pocket, the Allies targeted Schlemm's artillery with increasingly effective counter-battery fire, which he estimated to be 20 to 25 percent heavier than any return fire he could muster. To protect his howitzers, he wanted to shift them to concealed positions on the far bank, from where they could still engage Montgomery's oncoming forces.

Once again he had to seek permission from the High Command. This time, with Berlin focused on the Remagen crisis, oversight had loosened and Schlemm received authorization to relocate a portion of his artillery. Taking advantage of the opportunity, he shuttled every howitzer he had across the Rhine.

Schlemm's prospects for holding out were getting dire. Now down to 8,000 men, and seeking to prevent annihilation, he demanded Berlin send an officer to verify his tenuous position firsthand.

On the morning of March 9, an *Oberstleutnant* (lieutenant colonel) from the High Command arrived. Schlemm and his men eyed the junior officer as he entered the makeshift headquarters, noting with amusement that he'd elected to wear a new, freshly pressed dress uniform. The pink stripes on his trousers were hard to ignore—officially a pale shade of carmine to designate a staff officer of the *Oberkommando der Wehrmacht*, as well as veterinarians, meteorologists, librarians, and other specialists who failed to impress combat troops. If the dapper officer intended to instill confidence by radiating Berlin-blessed officialdom, he was wasting his efforts. The exhausted men had been under fire for the last thirty-one days, and thus could muster little curiosity about unworthy outsiders.

Schlemm ensured the errand boy fully appreciated the situation by making the *Oberstleutnant* crawl with him to a forward position in the midst of an Allied artillery barrage. After a few near misses and now covered in mud from head to toe, the *Oberstleutnant* concurred that holding the bridgehead was hopeless. He radioed Berlin stating the Wesel bridges were in critical danger of an Allied breakthrough, advising evacuation to save the remaining troops.

Anticipating this small triumph, Schlemm had previously organized his men for a methodical withdrawal, and that night his I *Fallschirmjäger-Armee* initiated the retreat plan.

The two remaining bridges, although damaged from overshot Allied artillery fire, were still solid enough to support the crossing of heavy armored vehicles. While the infantry held the perimeter, the remaining tanks and self-propelled guns made their way across.

Schlemm stationed himself at the foot of one of the bridge's east spans, shaking the hand of each man as he came over, thanking him for his courageous stand. He saw that his men were filthy and dead tired, but a passing *Fallschirmjäger* demonstrated the unit's élan when he encouraged Schlemm not to worry and assured him that once established on the other side they wouldn't sell so cheaply. Safe for the moment, Schlemm knew that it was just a matter of time before he and his men would be expected to defend this new piece of real estate down to the last bullet and the last man.

To create the illusion of a fully manned front line, two of Schlemm's infantry regiments remained in defensive positions along the perimeter. These rearguard units covered the withdrawal by launching localized counterattacks and laying down barrages of mortar fire to occupy the Allies' attention. They were to make their crossing by small assault boats and commandeered rafts after the destruction of the bridges.

Schlemm wanted to blow the bridges at 04:00, but men were still streaming across at the designated time. He delayed the destruction by two hours, but again, troops carrying, pushing, and towing as much equipment as possible filled the bridge. Civilian refugees escaping the Allied invaders crowded over the bridge as well. Mixed into the flow were the walking wounded, ambulances, supply trucks, carts loaded with ammunition, and even cattle—anything that might be of use once on the other side.

Finally at 07:10 on Saturday morning, with reports of approaching Allied tanks, Schlemm could wait no longer. After a stressful delay caused by failed ignition fuses, he watched as four massive explosions launched the bridges skyward before they buckled into the Rhine. The remains of the two bridges jutted out of the flowing river like a petulant child's abandoned erector set.

Several of the straggling German troops, abandoned on the west side when their escape route literally went up in flames, shot at their own engineers in the fury of having their fate decided for them.

The next day, on March 11, the High Command's Daily Report stated that "in order to use the better defensive lines on the east bank of the Rhine, our forces evacuated the left side of the Rhine in the Wesel Bridgehead in a deliberate and disciplined manner."

*   *   *

The skillful withdrawal caught the Allies by surprise. Upon reaching the banks of the Rhine, General Simpson, commander of the US Ninth Army, the only American troops assigned to Montgomery's army group, anticipated a quick assault crossing. In his and his staff's opinion, the Germans were falling back in disarray and would be unable to react effectively to a hasty, violent river assault. But Montgomery vetoed Simpson's plans. The crossing of the Rhine in the British sector would be executed according to Montgomery's strategy, and there would be no impromptu expeditions.

There is little doubt that an immediate crossing, forced before the Germans properly reorganized on the far bank, would have succeeded and kept Schlemm on the run. Instead, the Allied advance in the British sector sputtered to a standstill at the river's edge, just as many American generals had predicted.

Allied intelligence officers scrambled to develop an accurate understanding of the German situation across the Rhine. How effective had the withdrawal been? What was the enemy's morale? What was Schlemm's strength? The enemy's disposition and intentions would be more difficult to determine now that the Rhine separated the two belligerents. The 3,000 German soldiers left on the west bank became prisoners of war and the Allies' initial sources of information.

Interrogations led to the estimate that Schlemm's 116 *Panzer-Division* and the 15 *Panzer-Grenadier-Division* had escaped with only thirty-five tanks between the two of them. However, as the dust settled, it became clear that while Schlemm had retreated, he'd done so in a well-organized manner. An Allied intelligence officer noted, "From the enemy's POV, the evacuation from the Wesel bridgehead can be considered successful. At no time was this withdrawal disorderly."

Schlemm, despite fanatical meddling from Berlin and overwhelming Allied firepower, managed to save almost all of I *Fallschirmjäger-Armee*'s remaining artillery and evacuate enough troops and armor to establish a formidable defense on the far bank. Consequently, the Allies' immediate intelligence goal was to determine the rate at which Schlemm's army would be reinforced and how effectively the German commander could array his defenses to repel Montgomery's river crossing.

CHAPTER 5

"FIFTY PERCENT
OF TWO IS ONE"

Châlons-sur-Marne, France. Mid-March 1945.

As Schlemm and his *Fallschirmjäger-Armee* retreated across the Rhine, Thad Blanchard, a twenty-three-year-old sergeant in Able Company, 1st Battalion, of the 507th Parachute Infantry Regiment, returned from a week in the hospital to find half his squad manned by replacements. Wounded during a patrol in Luxembourg by either a land mine or a mortar round—he never knew which—Blanchard had spent two more weeks on the line with his lacerated face covered in bandages and sulfa ointment. Only after the division was withdrawn from the front did he consent to proper medical attention.

Blanchard empathized with the replacements; having been one himself, he knew how tough it was to join a veteran outfit, and he appreciated that while the new men were certainly green, they'd all volunteered to be there.

His own journey into the parachute troops had been a long one. Blanchard's hometown of Fallon, Nevada, was so small—population 2,400—and remote, that he had to report over 300 miles away, at Fort Douglas, near Salt Lake City, on December 23, 1942. Because his family had been in the construction business and he was familiar with operating heavy equipment, he figured he'd be tapped to be an engineer or a tank driver, but instead the Army designated him a rifleman.

After spending his first eighteen months of service as a stateside infantry instructor, he finally shipped to Europe as a volunteer for the parachute troops. Upon completion of jump school in England, he joined the regiment in July 1944 when they returned from France after the Normandy jump.

*   *   *

The 507th, originally an independent regiment attached to the 82nd Airborne for the invasion of France, transferred to the 17th Airborne in August 1944 to bolster Miley's division with a fourth infantry regiment. The move irked the veteran paratroopers, who were proud to be part of the legendary 82nd. At the time, the 17th had yet to be tested, and the 507th's arrival made it the only unit in the division with any combat experience—the reality of which the regimental commander, Colonel Edson Raff, made sure everyone was aware.

Raff's nickname, "Little Caesar," reflected both his aggressive attitude and his diminutive height of five-foot six-inches. Raff had taken over the regiment after the founding commander was captured in Normandy. Viewed as an outsider by the men of the 507th, Raff made it clear that his command style would be in direct juxtaposition to the more relaxed manner of his predecessor. Raff's brash attitude and his reshaping of the regiment polarized opinions of subordinates and superiors alike.

Chester McCoid, a captain in the division's intelligence section, considered Raff a "miserable monster" when it came to dealing with staff matters and noted that Little Caesar "seemed to relish savaging his own tall subordinates, or anyone else's." But McCoid conceded, "Despite his queer quirks of character, Raff was a terrific combat leader." Other officers held a less charitable opinion, regarding Raff as a loudmouth publicity seeker.

A 1933 graduate of West Point, Raff's credentials could inspire professional jealousy. In 1942 he had led the Army's first parachute assault of the war into North Africa, and shortly thereafter Eisenhower personally promoted him to full colonel. The fighting in Algeria and Tunisia, against first the Vichy French and then the Germans, reinforced Raff's belief in the value of grueling training. He developed several adages on unit readiness from his combat experiences in North Africa. One of his favorites, "The squad and platoon must be perfectly trained. They win battles," was perhaps his men's least favorite.

His focus on the smallest element in the Army's inventory capable of inflicting violence was often mistaken for micromanagement. Many of the Normandy veterans took offense at Raff's back-to-basics approach of relearning fundamental field tactics, viewing it as a vote of no confidence. His physical training regime was unpopular as well. Raff liked to exercise—a lot. However, after the cauldron of the Ardennes, many of his critics begrudgingly admitted his approach saved lives.

While other regimental commanders might limit their interactions to senior leaders—battalion or company commanders—Raff took a direct interest in the welfare of each man behind a rifle. As one reporter noted, Raff let his authority and rank remind his men that he was in command, not his distance or aloofness from them.

His men didn't always appreciate the attention. The occasion of Private Donald Greene getting "clapped up" instigated Sergeant Blanchard's first meeting with his regimental commander. Raff, who abstained from drinking, gambling, and smoking, waged a one-man war against vice and venereal disease. If during one of the many "short-arm inspections" a medic discovered a case of "Cupid's itch," Raff required the guilty party, his squad leader, his platoon leader, his company commander, his battalion commander, and the regimental medical officer to report to him and explain their combined ineptitude at maintaining unit hygiene. Disease affected the regiment's combat strength, and therefore Raff deemed a man's poor decision between the sheets to be official business. Raff viewed Blanchard's defense—that he wasn't present at the time to enforce the use of prophylactics—as a weak excuse and a leadership failure. Concluding his tirade, Raff reminded them all that the boxes of condoms available at the main gate were there for a reason.

Having led the final drive of the division's assault in Luxembourg, Raff's Ruffians licked their wounds in Châlons. Indeed, Blanchard's squad reflected the state of the regiment, which had suffered 700 casualties: 100 killed, 600 severely wounded or injured. The losses from the Ardennes fighting had been top down, including two of Raff's three battalion commanders.

With his wounds mended and his position as squad leader reclaimed, Blanchard now set his mind to getting his new men up to Raff's standards. The regiment's training cycle once again focused on the basics, with plenty of monotonous road marches and textbook field tactics.

The men also needed to conduct training jumps, not only to maintain proficiency but also to familiarize themselves with new equipment. The latest parachutes incorporated a modified version of the standard T5 harness. The original harness' three connection points used D-rings and snap links to secure the chest and leg straps, but combat conditions had proven the original design to be a liability. Unable to undo or even reach all three links in a crisis, parachutists had been dragged to death in high winds, drowned in marshes, or machine-gunned while helplessly entangled in trees. As an initial solution, the Army issued each para-trooper a switchblade to cut himself out of the harness in an emergency.

The new design replaced the three connection points with a sin-gle-point release mechanism. The quick-release box, centrally mounted on the chest above the reserve parachute, allowed a jumper to escape with just a twist and a punch. While the more efficient design had been developed in 1943, it took over a year and inquiries by the House Appro-priations Committee to ensure that the new releases were produced in bulk and dispatched to front line units.

During one training jump, Blanchard and his squad, having com-pleted their descent, watched from the ground as the next serial of nine aircraft passed overhead. Their interest turned to horror as two of their fellow troopers plunged to their deaths. One jumper, close enough for Blanchard to witness, clawed at the ripcord of his reserve parachute until the moment he slammed into the dirt field with a sickeningly soft thud. Both of the men's main chutes had failed to open, triggering sev-eral troopers to profanely wonder aloud who packed them.

Another new gadget introduced to Blanchard's squad was the M18 57mm recoilless rifle. The M18, more of a rocket launcher than a rifle, was intended to replace the M9A1 bazooka, which, due to the evolv-ing thickness of German tank armor, had become virtually obsolete as a tank-stopping weapon even before it reached the front lines in 1942.

"Them bazookas were like swatting against those tanks—you had to hit 'em just right," lamented one paratrooper.

Certainly taking out an enemy tank with a bazooka took a combina-tion of skill, patience, and bravery. Firing from a relatively safe distance from the tank increased the likelihood that the round would simply explode harmlessly on impact or ricochet wildly off the sloped armor. To overcome the bazooka's inadequacies, intrepid gunners stalked their prey, working around a tank's flank to either disable it with a shot in the tracks or damage the engine from the rear.

The revolutionary M18 had more in common with a Buck Rogers weapon than with its predecessor. Its rifled barrel, with twenty-four right-handed lands and grooves, significantly improved its accuracy and range over the smoothbore bazooka. When combined with its twenty-eight-power scope, the barrel gave the M18 an effective range of over 4,000 yards, more than a dozen times the bazooka's meager 300 yards. For the first time in the war, paratroopers had a legitimate and lethal anti-tank weapon.

Recoil-reducing technology was not new, but it was new to the US Army. German engineers at Krupp—a Ruhr-based arms manufacturer—had perfected the technique of channeling gases from a projectile's ignition rearward through a series of orifices to eliminate the weapon's recoil while also reducing the weapon's size. Krupp's advances had armed *Fallschirmjäger* with small, hand-towed recoilless rifles in 1941. The American design took the German innovation a step forward by further reducing size and weight. At just over sixty-one inches long and forty-four pounds, the M18 was man portable and could be fired from either the shoulder or a tripod. The shaped-charge projectiles fired by the weapon proved to have greater penetrating power against German armor than bazooka rounds.

But there were a few issues. First, no one really knew how to use this new piece of hardware. Airborne Army scrounged up a captain who had trained with the weapon back in the States and tasked him with developing a training regimen. Over seven days, 138 officers and enlisted men of the 17th Airborne rotated through his improvised school.

Divided into three-man crews consisting of a gunner, a loader, and an ammo bearer, the troops drilled getting the rifle into action and practiced their marksmanship. After firing a few rounds, Blanchard and the others learned to respect the recoilless rifle's significant back blast—almost fifty feet deep and forty feet wide. The choking cloud of dirt and debris thrown up behind the gunner, caused by the redirected gases, could not only kill someone but also telegraph the crew's position. The troops realized that firing the M18 in combat would require frequent displacement in order to avoid drawing retaliatory fire.

The other issue was supply. To fully equip the airborne divisions, Supreme Headquarters had requested 200 M18s but had received only two. General Miley, after witnessing a demonstration, became "extremely anxious" to get them for his men and pressed Brereton to procure more M18s in time for VARSITY. Brereton agreed, designating the 17th as the priority recipient of the new weapon—if they could get more in time.

All of the training culminated in a series of regimental exercises, including a full-scale dress rehearsal of the upcoming operation. On Thursday, March 15, Blanchard's squad, along with the rest of Raff's Ruffians, moved to nearby airfields for briefings that lasted until midnight.

The next morning, the sky was clear and the air cool as the men marched down the flight line to the idling aircraft. They would be taking off at 07:30 for a twenty-four-hour field exercise.

In addition to testing the regiment's readiness, the exercise also tested the men's nerves. Several troopers refused to jump. Whether due to shaky premonitions related to the training drop or the upcoming combat operation itself, they were immediately booted out of the regiment and transferred to a leg unit. Two men were Normandy veterans who claimed they wanted to jump but were unable to exit the plane before it passed over the drop zone. Since it wasn't feasible to organize another drop, they had to go.

*   *   *

Ridgway, having studied and rejected Dempsey's VARSITY plan, drafted his own proposal and presented it to Dempsey and others at his XVIII Airborne Corps HQ in Épernay. He'd developed three options for VARSITY and reviewed each in order of preference.

Dempsey dismissed Ridgway's first two plans, which called for the airborne troops to land within three miles of the Rhine's far banks. In Dempsey's opinion those options were too conservative and more hindrance than help; they lacked the depth he was looking for, and dropping so close to the Rhine hampered his artillery support. Instead Dempsey selected Ridgway's third option, the one he considered least desirable: dropping farthest inland from the riverbank to create the deepest bridgehead.

A deeper bridgehead appealed to Dempsey because it offered the best chance to throw the enemy into disarray by landing troops among Schlemm's rear echelons and thus probably on top of his artillery positions. The deeper targets also included two road networks that could facilitate Schlemm's movement of reinforcements into the area of the crossing.

Ridgway listed this option last for several reasons: The surrounding high ground, from which the enemy could pour fire into the assembling troops, would require attacking uphill "with practically no heavy weapon support." The distance from the drop zones to the friendly side of the Rhine also meant a loss of artillery support, and it put his lightly armed troops in the most likely path of advancing enemy armor, which is of course exactly where Dempsey wanted them.

Ridgway was also concerned that dropping farther behind enemy lines would increase the time it took to link up with British ground forces. Unwilling to gamble on Montgomery sticking to a reliable time-line of advance, Ridgway wanted his troops resupplied immediately. Because the troop carrier aircraft couldn't drop the two divisions, return to base, and be reloaded and refueled for a resupply drop in the same day, there'd be no return flights until the second day. Further, if unfavorable weather closed in overnight, it would leave the troops low on ammunition and stranded without vital supplies.

Dempsey thought he could alleviate Ridgway's apprehensions by bringing up heavier guns on his side of the Rhine, extending the zone of direct artillery support. Pressing medium bombers into service would solve the supply issue. They could fly in on the tail of the airborne armada to drop twenty-four hours' worth of supplies. With the pledge of long-range artillery support and immediate resupply, Ridgway agreed his divisions could tackle the mission.

Once the scheme of maneuver was settled, the discussion turned to the timing of the drop. Initial plans called for the amphibious assault and airdrop to occur simultaneously several hours before dawn. Miley, preferring a night drop, liked that plan; Ridgway, however, wanted a daylight operation. Both options had merits.

The cover of darkness aided the element of surprise and robbed German anti-aircraft gunners of clear targets. But night operations were fraught with risk, and the Allied track record of dropping troops accurately in the dark ranged from a near disaster in Sicily to mediocrity in Normandy and Southern France. Ridgway had another concern: the poor condition and short runways of the French airfields made glider operations at night a hazardous proposition.

Daylight provided maximum visibility for accurate navigation and thus tighter drop patterns, which allowed the troops to assemble faster. It also allowed the Allies to take advantage of their vast air superiority to protect the armada and suppress anti-aircraft positions. Conversely, *Luftwaffe* night fighters posed a legitimate threat; just a few could wreak absolute havoc on the formations of lumbering, unarmed transports.

Dempsey had his own unique idea and proposed that the drop occur hours *after* PLUNDER kicked off. He wanted to launch his assault during the protective hours of darkness before dawn, which would hinder the accuracy of German artillery. By delaying VARSITY until after sunrise, his men would have several hours of supporting artillery as they established a foothold on the far banks. Once the inbound transport planes and gliders were on final approach, Allied artillery batteries would have to cease fire to avoid hitting the descending aircraft, leaving Dempsey's men on their own. After the airborne landed, his artillery support would still be somewhat restricted by having to closely coordinate fire missions to prevent fratricide.

Dempsey reasoned a later landing would also be perfectly timed to disrupt German forward observers just as they were attempting to call in accurate artillery on the bridging operations and assault craft chugging across the Rhine.

Ridgway liked Dempsey's plan. The sequence, while unorthodox when compared to previous operations, wherein the airborne exploited the element of surprise by dropping prior to the main assault, offered a number of advantages. It allowed more time for artillery and fighter-bombers to pound anti-aircraft positions, and flipping the traditional tactics might even catch the Germans off guard. Miley too conceded that the advantages outweighed the complexities of a night drop.

It was thus settled that the main crossing, near Xanten, spearheaded by the 15th Scottish Division, would launch at three in morning. The Scots were to crack the Germans' river defenses and push inland as soon as possible to link up with the airborne troops, who in turn would drop seven hours later, at 10:00.

The agreed-upon mission statement called for Ridgway's XVIII Airborne Corps to "disrupt the hostile defense of the Rhine in the Wesel Sector by the seizure of key terrain by airborne attack, in order to rapidly deepen the bridgehead to be seized in an assault crossing of the Rhine by British ground forces, in order to facilitate the further offensive operations of the Second Army."

Meanwhile, Ridgway sought resolution to the unsettled matter of the 13th Airborne Division's commitment to VARSITY. Montgomery and Dempsey still maintained that the best way to reinforce PLUNDER's bridgehead was dropping in a third division. But Ridgway remained unconvinced.

By Dempsey's calculations, it would take forty-eight hours for his initial ground divisions to cross the Rhine via pontoon bridges. Dropping the 13th provided an attractive way to get thousands of additional troops onto the east bank quickly. His idea did have precedent. Ridgway himself had employed a similar tactic over a year ago in Italy when the 82nd Airborne dropped two regiments onto the Salerno beachhead. However, at Salerno, the Allies were on the verge of being thrown back into the sea by the *Wehrmacht* and the situation called for expediency over pedantic adherence to doctrine. Emergency action helped save the day in that case, but Ridgway viewed Dempsey's river crossing quite differently. The Allied inventory contained dozens of readily available infantry units to support PLUNDER but only a handful of specialized airborne divisions.

Responding to a communiqué requesting further explanation of "how it is intended to employ this additional division," Montgomery's chief of plans dispatched a snippy reply, "This question was discussed by Commander-in-Chief [Montgomery] with Supreme Commander [Eisenhower] and understand decision was firm."

Since Eisenhower had, in Montgomery's eyes, designated PLUN-DER to be "the main effort," the British commander felt that all his requests should be approved without question.

Ridgway wound up placating the British by agreeing to place the 13th Airborne officially in reserve for VARSITY. Meanwhile, Brereton, who was embroiled in yet another impasse with Montgomery, wired Eisenhower requesting permission to reassign the 13th to CHOKER II, a planned American crossing of the Rhine at Worms, currently scheduled for March.

With the 13th Airborne awaiting the call to arms in their billets south of Paris, Ridgway issued orders to the commanders of the two confirmed divisions.

Outlining PLUNDER's overall scheme, he focused on their specific roles in VARSITY. As Dempsey's troops assaulted across the Rhine on a twenty-two-mile front, the airborne divisions would drop farther inland to seize key terrain and block enemy counterattacks.

The 17th Airborne would drop on the right flank, while the British 6th Airborne, commanded by General Eric Bols, would drop west of Miley's division to defend the northwest flank of the bridgehead. The forty-year-old Bols was relatively new to airborne warfare, but his experienced staff were veterans of the Normandy jump.

The two divisions would tie their perimeters together to repel the expected German counterattacks. Underscoring the obvious, the orders concluded by reminding both commanders that their objectives were to be "held at all costs." With their orders in hand, the division staffs commenced their detailed planning.

Looming over Miley and his staff's planning was a shortage of transport aircraft. An assessment of MARKET GARDEN's failure had resulted in new doctrine requiring the entire complement of airborne troops be delivered in a single lift. While the mandate prevented troops from being dropped piecemeal, with their follow-on serials subject to unexpected weather cancellations, it limited the number of troops Miley could bring in. The Air Force and RAF planners estimated they could muster enough aircraft to drop about 17,000 troops in a single lift. Together the two divisions totaled about 21,000 men.

Miley streamlined his load, planning to prioritize combat units for aerial delivery while the division's supporting units would cross the Rhine later in vehicle convoys.

At a coordination meeting in late February, the Air Force told Miley they could give him 400 parachute aircraft and 588 glider tugs. Miley countered that he wanted fewer aircraft for his two parachute regiments and more to serve as tugs to bring in the glider troops.

Two innovations radically shifted lift capacity in Miley's favor. The first was the arrival of the new twin-engine C-46 Commando transport aircraft. The hulking Commandos flew faster and farther and doubled the cargo capacity of the C-47 Skytrain, the ubiquitous workhorse of the troop carrier squadrons.

The Skytrain, built by Douglas and held together by over 500,000 rivets, was based on the prewar DC-3 airliner. With a reinforced floor and a widened cargo door, the C-47 had proven itself to be a rugged airframe that delivered cargo, shuttled personnel, dropped troops, and towed gliders in every theater of the war. But it was not ideal for parachute operations. It could only carry twenty combat-equipped paratroopers and had a single jump door in the rear. In comparison, the C-46 could carry up to forty jumpers and had doors on both sides of the fuselage. The double doors provided a faster exit, and a faster exit meant a tighter drop pattern.

But the Commandos had just started arriving in the European theater, and only a handful of pilots were rated to fly them. Getting the Commandos operational for VARSITY required that Troop Carrier Command accelerate the pilots' transition training. Additionally, Miley and Ridgway wanted some familiarization jumps for the men who would be delivered via the C-46s. The double doors posed a challenge to troopers whose muscle memory had been honed to make a right turn when exiting the C-47. That adrenalized moment when a soldier rushed for the exit wasn't the time to learn how to turn left. The Air Force agreed that the C-46 units would be made available for joint training as soon as practical.

Rushing the pilots' training was worth the effort. Including 72 of the larger C-46s in the lift provided the equivalent of 144 C-47s. The reduction in parachute aircraft gave the Air Force the flexibility to shift more C-47s to serve as tugs for Miley's glider lift, providing a total of 610 tugs.

The second, more controversial innovation was the decision to double tow the gliders. Simple enough in concept, double towing used a single C-47 to serve as the tug for two gliders. The C-47's twin 1,200-horsepower Pratt & Whitney engines were capable of such a feat, but safety made it an uncommon practice.

Many tug or "power" pilots were wary of flying double tow. They joked that in addition to severely increasing their aircraft's fuel consumption, pulling two gliders stretched the fuselage by several inches—the exact amount varied by pilot and the number of drinks he'd consumed at the officer's club.

The technique required that the left-side glider use a 350-foot towrope and the glider on the right side, a 425-foot rope. The 75-foot difference provided a safety margin to avoid midair collisions, but glider pilots had to exercise extreme diligence to prevent drift and avert entanglement. The longer rope was actually made up of two ropes, which when under the strain of a fully combat-laden glider, increased the risk of breaking. The nylon towropes were designed to expand by 40 percent before snapping, but the more likely point of failure was the connecting shackles.

The advanced technique would almost double Miley's combat

strength, but the Troop Carrier Commander, General Paul Williams, rebuffed the idea. Brereton stopped short of making a direct order, but he and Ridgway strongly urged Williams to reconsider. Ridgway favored double tow for obvious reasons, and Brereton was confident a daylight operation would reduce accidents.

Within a few days, after a series of successful tests had been conducted, Brereton directed Troop Carrier Command to "utilize double tow to the fullest possible extent." The 610 C-47s would now be pulling 906 gliders.

The British also had their airlift challenges. Unable to leverage double tow, as the Horsa gliders were too heavy, the RAF drafted every spare bomber they could find to serve as a glider tug. The press-ganged aircraft needed modifications to fulfill their new role, and ground crews went to work on over a hundred Stirling and Halifax bombers to install the correct towing equipment.

Lift capacity so taxed the RAF that they requested an additional 275 C-47s and crews from the Americans to make up for shortages. But Williams could only spare 243.

This put Bols in a tough spot. The shortage reduced his lift capacity by 576 men—a full battalion. While the loan of the American aircraft allowed his division to go in with more manpower than any previous British operation, it was little consolation in a fight where every rifle would matter.

The combined effort amassed the largest air armada in history, and for the first time in the war, two divisions would be simultaneously dropped into battle in a single sortie.

*   *   *

Senior Allied officers harbored growing concerns about the Germans' espionage network on the continent. Hiding in plain sight, as well as lurking in the shadows, the enemy was closer than many realized. Even the somewhat aloof Brereton was alarmed, writing in his diary, "Intelligence reports that it has captured a document which indicates that the enemy had possession of correct information about the proposed Operation NAPLES II, a landing across the Rhine at Cologne—had the correct area and date."

Not long after that, another disturbing report reached Brereton. An Allied counterintelligence agent, dressed in civilian clothes, had spent an hour at a bar eavesdropping on American aircrews discussing troop carrier movements and, more revealing, complaining about the ongoing hassles of installing parachute rigging equipment in the aircraft. Brereton sent a strongly worded letter to Williams at Troop Carrier Command admonishing him to take immediate steps to "stop this violation of security."

Indeed, Brereton's staff struggled to keep their own safeguards in check. Eisenhower's intelligence team chastised them over their own "serious breach of security" following the delivery of a VARSITY planning report through unsecure channels—including a cover elaborately illustrated with gliders and parachutes. The terse communiqué from Supreme Headquarters reminded Brereton that plans were to be "enclosed in a folder which gave no indication of the nature of its contents." The artist had further compounded his gaffe when in his zeal to decorate the cover he forgot to add the "Top Secret" designation. At least thirty-two copies of the report were distributed without the proper classification label. Obviously, the rigid security precautions that characterized the invasion of France had largely fallen into disuse and given way to complacency.

But the main threats to security were the French airfields, the feverish construction of which was impossible to hide from informers. As the airfields became operational, the US troop carrier units transferred aircraft to France from their bases in England. In addition to their thriving espionage network in France, Belgium, and Holland, the Germans' jet aircraft routinely flew reconnaissance missions with near impunity over the growing airfields.

✯   ✯   ✯

Troopers took advantage of the downtime between training events by playing football or baseball, or improvising their own entertainment.

The division's anti-tank unit assembled a formidable band led by Private Bill Keller, who organized several impromptu jam sessions. Keller, whose trigger finger had been severed when a German bullet crushed the trigger guard of his rifle, now played his accordion—or squeezebox—upside down. The unit's musical prodigy, Robert Beyers, who'd played piano in Cincinnati speakeasies before the war, was Keller's sax man. Rounding out the band were troopers on guitar, clarinet, harmonica, fiddle, and an improvised set of drums fabricated from purloined fuel barrels. The band's front man, red-haired Robert Wagner, sang and tap-danced atop a wooden crate. The noise attracted passersby, who ducked into the tent to enjoy the music.

Elsewhere, recently promoted Clyde Haney, now a private first class, and his tentmates pooled various ingredients from belated Christmas packages to make chocolate fudge. The men combined canned milk, sugar, chocolate bars from field rations, and nuts and boiled the concoction over a cut-down five-gallon jerry can to create a GI version of the homemade treat.

After the disbanding of the 193rd, Haney had been reassigned to King Company in the 194th Glider Infantry. As a combat veteran, he now received an extra $10 monthly bonus. To make it official, the Army awarded Haney, along with his comrades, the Combat Infantryman Badge. Known as the C.I.B., the badge, worn above the left breast pocket of the dress uniform, indicated that the bearer had engaged in ground combat as an infantryman. The badge featured a silver musket on a rectangular field of infantry blue, with a silver wreath forming the background. It remains one of the most prestigious awards in the US Army, and Haney regarded it as the "nicest looking medal the Army has." He kept it polished as a proud symbol of his service during the Battle of the Bulge.

Along with the intensive training, rumors too increased in both quantity and velocity. The men were convinced that their rigorous preparations were for a combat jump across the Rhine, but when and where was still unknown. Spreading or swapping rumors was a favorite pastime, and any new speculations filtered through the ranks like gossip in a small-town barbershop.

After Haney heard about the captured bridge at Remagen, he was convinced they were off the hook. He figured the Allied crossing of the Rhine had alleviated the need for an airborne mission. Contrarians soberly pointed out that their training regimen hadn't even slightly abated since Bradley's crossing of the upper Rhine.

After a few glider troopers in Haney's regiment witnessed a British tank officer being escorted into their headquarters tent, a flurry of rumors circulated that they were dropping into the "Limey's sector."

John Chester's opinion was that he and his fellow troops would be jumping in front of Patton's advancing legions to secure vital objectives and speed up the sacking of Berlin.

Most of the troops knew better than to pay much attention to rumors, but some took them to heart, wrapping their anxieties or hopes around whichever one appealed to their own sense of mortality. Some relished the confusion as a form of sport, actively starting their own rumors to both wind up their friends and see if the scuttlebutt came back full circle. A cruel game to be sure, but one well within the rights of those whose futures were starved of detail.

Master Sergeant Frank Macchiaverna, an old hand in the 513th Parachute Infantry Regiment, didn't believe any of the gossip. But he did confide to his diary, "We are preparing for something big. . . . I can see it in the air."

✷   ✷   ✷

Several blocks east of Châlons' Canal Saint-Martin, on the Avenue de Valmy, Miley's three regimental commanders arrived at the old French Calvary barracks serving as division HQ. They were among the lucky few learning the truth behind the rumors as they received their first VARSITY briefing.

Miley's 17th Airborne Division had two tasks: capture the high ground of the Diersfordt Forest and seize ten bridges over the Issel River and its offshoot canal. The river, four miles inland from the Rhine, provided a natural defensive line, and capturing its crossing points early would prevent German reserves from attacking into the ground forces. Seizing the bridges intact was also vital to ensuring that Montgomery's columns could attack out of the bridgehead when ready. At the same time, the British would drop farther west to seize the village of Hamminkeln and another three bridges over the Issel in their sector.

The commanders each returned to their camps to commence regimental-level planning. Large tents, known as "War Rooms," were set up inside the camps and surrounded by barbed wire and armed guards. The tents would serve as secure briefing areas, and intelligence officers carted in trunks stuffed with maps and aerial photographs of Germany.

Regimental briefings were conducted down to the level of company commanders, but it would be several weeks before the rank and file had their suspicions confirmed. They would receive full briefings once they were sequestered at the secure marshaling airfields. There they'd have a few days to conduct final preparations and memorize what would be expected of them once on the ground.

The War Rooms attracted attention and generated more rumors. The bustle of officers making multiple trips to and from the briefing tents heightened the feeling that a major action was imminent, especially when visiting senior Air Force pilots were noticed.

The need for repeated briefings and map study was best explained by an experienced airborne officer who remarked, "Never yet has [there] been an airborne operation in which every unit has landed in its proper area. . . . Every battalion commander must know the plan of every other battalion commander. . . . He must be prepared to undertake the execution of any of those other plans immediately upon landing as well as his own."

Private Paul Reed, a 513th paratrooper, was assigned a guard duty shift on the perimeter of his regiment's War Room. He later recalled how he and another trooper "each marched half way around the tent, turned around and did it again."

"It wasn't long though before we actually had something to guard. The regimental commander and his staff entered the tent and shortly after jeeps carrying the battalion commanders and their staffs arrived."

As he patrolled his monotonous route again and again, Reed strained to eavesdrop. He overheard two distinct comments: the regiment would get corps-level artillery support and they should expect 50 percent casualties.

Turning the corner of the tent, the odds became easy to compute. Face to face with his fellow sentry, Reed realized, *Fifty percent of two is one.*

Executing an about-face for his return route, he wondered to himself, *Does that mean one of us is going to be part of that 50 percent?*

The three regimental commanders and their respective battalion commanders had a week to prepare their plans before returning to division headquarters on March 8 for a coordination conference. In addition to his senior officers, Miley also hosted their British counterparts from the 6th Airborne Division.

That same morning Eric Bols, the British general in command of the 6th, along with his retinue of regimental and battalion officers, boarded aircraft in England for the short flight to France.

Among the entourage of British officers was Lieutenant Colonel Napier Crookenden, commander of the 9th Parachute Battalion, who'd donned his best service uniform to impress his American counterparts. But a sergeant with strict orders dashed Crookenden's plans. Intercepted before boarding the aircraft in England, Crookenden had his red beret confiscated and the airborne patches roughly cut off his uniform by the sergeant wielding a pair of dull scissors. Embarrassed by a lack of headgear—a required part of the uniform in any army—and picking at the shabby red threads sticking out on both shoulders, Crookenden climbed aboard to find his peers' uniforms had suffered similar wounds at the hands of the amateur haberdasher. The crude alterations were intended to conceal the fact that British airborne officers were meeting with an American airborne division.

Arriving in Châlons, the British were driven through the main gate of Miley's HQ, which was manned by a sharply saluting paratrooper standing guard in front of his red-and-white-striped sentry shack.

Once inside, they were escorted past a cordon of MPs and down a wide hallway bustling with "clerks, orderlies and staff officers, going about their business very briskly." Crookenden was impressed by their military bearing, which contrasted with his stereotypical impression of the Yanks' more casual approach to authority. After a warm welcome from their American counterparts, the British filed into the briefing room and split up according to rank. The senior officers sat up front while Crookenden stood with the American battalion commanders in the back of the room.

Miley started the conference by stepping up in front of several large maps flanked by enlarged reconnaissance photographs. Injecting bits of wry humor, he gave an outline of his plan before transitioning the brief to his chief of staff, who provided more detail.

It was all very familiar to the British, who'd conducted similar briefings themselves. That changed when thirty-seven-year-old Colonel Edson Raff stood up in front of the map to brief his regiment's plan.

Despite his gruff manner, Raff's "unruffled professionalism" during the Ardennes campaign had stuck out above "the less imaginative performances" of Miley's other regimental commanders. The 507th would be spearheading VARSITY, and Raff intended to be the first man to land in Germany.

Raff took in the assembled group and radiated back his own cocky confidence. Pointing to an area of open terrain to the east of the Diersfordt Forest he said, "The 507th are flying in west to east and jumping here. . . . And I jump Number One from the lead ship. . . . We get together here," he added, his hand indicating the eastern edge of the forest. "In these woods are a bunch of Heinies and we sort 'em out." He sat down.

When everyone realized he was actually done, they burst into laughter. The British officers eyed one another in amusement; this sangfroid was certainly more in line with what they'd expected from the Yanks. For his part, Miley couldn't have been surprised. He'd known Raff since early 1942, when he served as a battalion commander in Miley's 503rd PIR. The other two regimental commanders briefed the assembly in more traditional detail, including how their battalion's scheme of maneuver would unfold.

British and American battalion commanders met after the group briefing to discuss specifics. Crookenden coordinated with Colonel Allen "Ace" Miller, the 513th's 2nd Battalion commander, whose objective would border that of Crookenden's 9th Battalion. The two officers confirmed where their units would establish contact on the battlefield to avoid fratricide.

As the British contingent departed, Miley shook the hand of each man and presented him a bottle of liberated *Luftwaffe* brandy. If the fortunes of war were with them, they'd next meet in Germany.

CHAPTER 6

EVERY HOUR A GIFT

Wiesental, Germany. Sunday, March 11, 1945.

Two nights after Schlemm's troops evacuated the Wesel Pocket, a chauf-feured dark blue Mercedes-Benz limousine turned onto a narrow, for-ested road hidden under a web of camouflage netting and leading to Schloss Ziegenberg, the headquarters for the western front located sixty-two miles east of Remagen, atop a small spur at the foot of the Taunus mountain range. In the Mercedes' backseat sat *Generalfeldmar-schall* Albert von Kesselring on his way to assume the post of *Oberbe-fehlshaber West*—Commander in Chief West.

As he ascended the stone steps to the main building, Kesselring would have noticed the towering keep silhouetted against the night sky. The five-story, circular stone edifice was the only surviving element of the original medieval castle. The headquarters offices were in an unre-markable adjacent three-story rectangular structure.

The Führer himself had dismissed Kesselring's predecessor, *Gener-alfeldmarschall* Gerd von Rundstedt, for the third and final time. With the Allies over the Rhine at Remagen, Hitler needed a scapegoat, and consequently Rundstedt's fifty-two-year military career ended with a phone call from Berlin.

Hitler now placed his confidence in Kesselring to reverse the current misfortunes on the western front. And the field marshal felt up to the challenge. Known as "Smiling Albert" for his omnipresent toothy grin, he greeted his staff with the quip "I am the new V3!" The comment was a reference to Hitler's series of wonder-weapon rockets, an arsenal of vengeance to which Kesselring now added himself. But it would soon become clear that more than optimism and punchy analogies would be needed to halt the Allies' grinding advance through western Germany.

The fifty-nine-year-old field marshal sat down for a briefing by his old

comrade and new chief of staff, *General der Kavallerie* Siegfried Westphal. The highly capable Westphal had retained his post, providing con-
tinuity for the incoming commander and a valuable perspective on the
current state of the western front. The two men had worked together in
Italy, and Westphal provided a trusted, candid overview.

Kesselring found the situation to be far grimmer than the Führer had
led him to believe. He'd inherited a crisis: Berlin had just ordered ten
panzer divisions, ten artillery corps, eight rocket launcher brigades, and
six infantry divisions transferred from the west to the eastern front. With
the Soviet Red Army just forty miles outside of Berlin, Hitler believed
the more immediate threat lay to the east. Kesselring realized that his
remaining beleaguered legions now consisted of fifty-five divisions. His
celebrated smile continued to fade as Westphal revealed that even that
number was misleading. Most of those divisions, still not recovered from
their losses in the Ardennes, were down to 7,000 men each—about half
strength. The good news? They had a formidable barrier between them
and the enemy: the Rhine.

To orchestrate his defense of the Rhine, Kesselring opted to relocate his staff to several outbuildings in a secluded wooded area a short
five-minute drive from Schloss Ziegenberg. The complex, constructed
by the *Wehrmacht* in 1940, was code-named *Adlerhorst*—the Eagle's
Eyrie. From the exterior, the cluster of buildings appeared to be tra-
ditionally built two-story timber-framed cottages with flower-boxed
dormer windows. In reality, each was a fortified bunker protected by
three-foot-thick walls of reinforced concrete. The interiors were simply
appointed but far from austere. The floors were oak and the walls pan-
eled in pine. Hunting trophies and ornately framed Teutonic paintings
added visual interest. The compound, ringed by several anti-aircraft
positions along the surrounding ridgelines, hosted a full-time garrison
of over a hundred troops.

Kesselring's decision to vacate the main building would prove to be
almost clairvoyant.

Kesselring's two immediate tasks were obvious: halt—or ideally repel—
the spreading American foothold at Remagen and protect the *Ruhrge-
biet*—the Ruhr industrial area. The best way to defend the Ruhr was
to prevent Montgomery from crossing the Rhine. But containing the
Americans upriver required transferring units from somewhere else,

thereby reducing the strength available to repulse Montgomery's 21 Army Group.

At Remagen, elements of four American divisions had managed to push across the Rhine before the Ludendorff Bridge collapsed. And still more tanks and infantry were crossing on hastily constructed pontoon bridges. While the rugged terrain and narrow mountain passes on the east bank hampered their immediate breakout, Kesselring knew it was only a matter of time before they amassed enough firepower for serious concern.

Arguably, the Ruhr was Kesselring's most pressing issue. While Berlin may have been the ideological heart of the Third Reich, it was the Ruhr's 3,000 square miles of coal mines, factories, and industrialized cities that belched out the tanks, guns, and other materiel necessary to wage war. Prior to Germany's expansion, the region produced 65 percent of its crude steel and 56 percent of its coal. After the Soviets seized Silesia, a resource-rich area on the border of Poland and Germany, and the Americans had overrun the Saar, the Ruhr became vital to continuing the war.

In the spring of 1945, in spite of their industrial losses, the Third Reich continued to crank out war materiel at an alarming rate. While Allied bombing had cut expected production in half and wreaked havoc on transportation networks, rapid reconstruction of damaged facilities and the shift to underground factories had allowed the Germans to maintain a steady stream of manufacturing output that peaked in late 1944. In November of that year, the *Luftwaffe* fielded over 5,000 operational aircraft, and factories were still producing them at a rate of over 4,000 a month. Every thirty days, the *Kriegsmarine* received 25 new U-Boats. Almost 1,600 tanks and self-propelled guns rolled off assembly lines monthly as well. If the Allies cut Germany's industrial umbilical cord, the Third Reich's forces in the field would wither and collapse. Hitler was relying on Kesselring to prevent that.

For the last nineteen months Kesselring and his retinue had deftly kept the Allies at bay in Italy, a campaign marked by bitter battles of attrition for every hill and valley. With seas on both sides and soaring mountain peaks to their front, the Allies had been forced to claw their way north through Italy. But Kesselring knew Germany's western frontier provided more open invasion routes than the constricting width of the Italian peninsula.

To defend the Ruhr Kesselring would continue to rely on Blaskowitz's *Heeresgruppe H*, already in position along the Rhine. And in turn it would once again fall to Blaskowitz's most experienced commander, *General der Fallschirmtruppen* Alfred Schlemm, to bear the direct brunt of the fight when Montgomery attacked.

Schlemm could take little satisfaction in having successfully withdrawn back across the Rhine. To repel the British he needed more time, more tanks, more munitions, and most of all, more troops—ideally, well-trained and well-equipped troops. What he had were the exhausted remnants of his combat-hardened I *Fallschirmjäger-Armee*. While establishing his defensive line, Schlemm knew he had to simultaneously be on guard in the event Montgomery attempted to force an immediate crossing. If the British pressed a speedy assault before he was ready, Schlemm would be hard-pressed to stop them.

But Montgomery seemed willing to give him time; inexplicably, the British appeared to have paused at the Rhine. A relative calm had descended on the front with the collapse of the Wesel Pocket. Not knowing how long the lull would last, Schlemm focused on reinforcing his defensive positions and marshaling replacement troops to fill his depleted ranks.

All things considered, Schlemm was faring better than expected. Through his decisive—if not subversive—maneuvering he'd escaped with almost all of his artillery batteries intact, much more than either Berlin or his adversaries had anticipated. Additionally, his casualties were lighter than he could have hoped and well below enemy intelligence estimates.

Schlemm had ordered the construction of defensive positions along the east bank of the Rhine back in February. As he gradually moved troops out of the Pocket, combat engineers took charge of them on the far bank, organizing work parties to erect field fortifications, machine gun positions, tank barriers, barbwire obstacles, and minefields. But being short of concrete and construction equipment, Schlemm still needed more men and materiel to build a defense in depth worthy of halting the Allies at the Rhine.

Schlemm's I *Fallschirmjäger-Armee* consisted of seven divisions and several anti-aircraft battalions, divided among three corps. He assigned each of his corps commanders a sector of the front; they in turn arrayed their divisions. Always mindful of their shortages, Schlemm and his staff shifted troops and heavy weapons, including precious batteries of artillery, to strengthen the units along their forty-five-mile front.

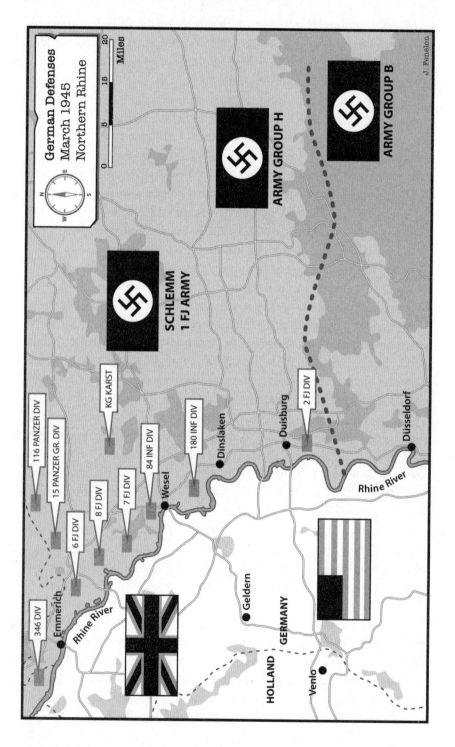

German Defenses
March 1945
Northern Rhine

Typical of the *Korps* taking up positions on the right flank was the *7-Fallschirmjäger-Division*, one of the last units withdrawn across the Rhine. The paratroopers had doggedly defended the Pocket, exacting a heavy toll on the Allies, but in the process they'd also suffered severe losses. In spite of the casualties, the commander considered his men's morale to be high, and they knew more fighting was expected of them.

The center *Korps* anchored their sector with the *84 Infanterie-Division*, commanded by *Generalmajor* Heinz Fiebig. He positioned his three regiments along the Rhine to the north of Wesel. A provisional division of assorted infantry troops occupied Wesel itself.

On his left flank, Schlemm's remaining *Korps* established positions down to Duisburg, arranging two divisions along the riverbank.

Studying the map, Schlemm knew he had the front covered as best he could, but the lack of manpower nagged at him. Like Kesselring, he realized his divisions were that in name only. Most had made it back over the Rhine with barely 3,000 soldiers each. The three parachute infantry divisions on his right flank totaled just 11,000 men, essentially the number in a single, full-strength division.

But the Third Reich still had resources to draw on. Just two months earlier, in January, Hitler had increased the military service age limit to forty-five years. In February, eight new full-strength divisions had been drafted. But a significant portion of the new recruits were conscripted from previously reserved categories: workers whose factories had been destroyed, men previously designated as medically unfit, youths just entering their adolescence, or older men who'd hoped to enjoy their twilight years in front of a fireplace rather than in the front lines. Among the replacements were thousands of *Kriegsmarine* and *Luftwaffe* personnel who were transferred into the *Wehrmacht* as Berlin stripped the idle from their branches of service for combat duty.

And time was not on their side. The replacements received only rudimentary infantry training at best before being sent to the front. Schlemm integrated them into his existing divisions, hoping they would benefit from combat-experienced supervision and on-the-job training. Manning static defenses didn't require as much training as assault tactics, but it did necessitate staying power. Rumors reflecting the gravity of their situation spread among the new rank and file: SS troops were setting up blocking positions to hinder any retreat and force deserters back into the fight if necessary.

• • •

Schlemm's logistical problems were eased somewhat by the shortening of his supply line, which no longer had to traverse the Rhine, but Allied air attacks, intermittent since late February, were increasing in both intensity and tempo. Allied bombers targeted railroad lines, bridges, road junctions, and maintenance facilities. The ten bridges and viaducts supporting rail traffic in and out of the Ruhr were hit by dozens of attacks. Meanwhile, low-flying Allied fighters were on the prowl for targets of opportunity, pouncing out of the sky to strafe vehicles and trains. The marauders littered the countryside with the spoils of their victories, destroying over 100 locomotives and 3,000 railcars. The zealous attacks went after anything that moved, restricting most movement to the hours of darkness.

In response to the growing air raids, Kesselring ordered his commanders to shift their anti-aircraft batteries to better protect the threatened transportation network. Over a hundred of the devastatingly lethal 88mm guns and several hundred lighter-model, multi-barreled 20mm and 40mm guns were set up in positions along the Issel River and the two railroad lines running out of Wesel. These gunners knew their business, having had years of experience combating enemy aircraft in the Ruhr Valley, and favored orchards to conceal their guns from prowling enemy fighters.

Despite the relentless air raids, crippled rail network, and widespread fuel shortages, reinforcements trickled into I *Fallschirmjäger-Armee* at the rate of over 3,000 men a week. But instead of experienced front line troops, Schlemm received training units, either in their entirety or cannibalized for the purpose of supplying replacements. While inexperienced, however, the fresh troops had the advantage of not being exhausted from months of combat. And in many cases they were buoyed by naïve notions of National Socialism and held fast to Hitler's proclamations of *Deutschland*'s ultimate victory. Schlemm knew their convictions would be put to the test soon enough.

Schlemm realized that he didn't need to meet the enemy on equal terms. Experience had taught him that a well-positioned and determined machine gun squad in the defense could hold up an entire platoon. The key, though, was "well-positioned."

Given the deficiencies in almost every column of his field commander's ledger, he needed to maximize the terrain to his advantage. Since before the time of the Chinese warrior Sun Tzu's writings in 500 BC, soldiers have studied terrain and the art of effectively using topography. Schlemm was no different. Unfortunately for him, the German side of the Rhine was relatively open farmland, not ideal terrain on which to anchor a defense—which was also why Montgomery wanted to ford the river there. However, the farms were crisscrossed with man-made features suited well enough for a stubborn defense: dikes that were thirteen feet high and sixty feet wide as well as a railroad embankment stretching across Schlemm's entire eastern boundary. Both would serve as effective tank obstacles. Schlemm's soldiers constructed fighting positions every twenty to thirty yards on the reverse slopes of the dike, supported by forward machine gun pits. To the front of the dike they strung double lines of barbed wire to entangle and impede the attackers.

Schlemm directed his men to turn suitably placed farmhouses into strongpoints. Further inconveniencing an already inconvenienced populace, they evicted residents, dug trenches in gardens, knocked out windows, barricaded exterior doors with furniture and sandbags, and punched crawl holes through interior walls for greater freedom of movement. When completed, some homes concealed as many as four or five machine gun emplacements. Off-duty crews slept in the cellars.

Artillery batteries set up positions on local farms too, digging in their howitzers in orchards, front yards, or wherever they saw fit. They commandeered the cellars for communication posts or command centers. Many of the farms boarded soldiers in their spare bedrooms, living rooms, basements, and barns, whether the owners liked it or not.

The disruptive activity made it clear to the civilians that the *Wehrmacht* was expecting a fight and planned to make a stand. Anticipating the carnage, many families evacuated, departing in military convoys or piling what they could into farm carts or onto bicycles. Some families, however, opted to stay, lingering to work and watch over their farms—their sole source of income.

Helga Kleinherber's parents evacuated their family to nearby Hamminkeln after five anti-aircraft guns were positioned in neighboring fields. They made several expeditions back to the house to rescue valuables, navigating sheltered routes through the woods to avoid unwanted notice. The *Wehrmacht* had posted hand-painted signs along the roads to remind civilians and soldiers, "*Achtung! Feind in Sicht!*"—"Attention! Enemy in sight!" Careless movement in the open often drew British artillery fire from the far bank. During one visit, the Kleinherbers interrupted a group of German officers conducting a staff meeting at their dining table, which was covered in maps.

"It was extremely dangerous to be in the open fields during the day," recalled then thirteen-year-old Friedrich Sons. "My father was once shot at by fighter planes when driving his horse cart to the dairy farm in Hamminkeln. The wagon was hit several times; luckily he and the horse got away unharmed." The family had another close call when a stray bomb missed their house but destroyed the fruit garden.

Vicar Heinrich Müller, who scolded his departing wife and daughter for evacuating with the "faint of heart," nonetheless took heed of warnings passed along by German refugees migrating from the opposite side of the Rhine.

"The conquerors steal like ravens," they told him.

Before leaving, Müller's wife had buried her favorite linen and porcelain under the family's chicken coop. Now Müller snuck out at night to conceal a few of his own valuables, including several bottles of his favorite brandy.

But civilians had to worry about more than just Allied thieves. The Tinnefeld farm had half of their dairy cows confiscated by the *Wehrmacht*, and other farms had horses and wagons pressed into service for hauling military equipment. Bored soldiers ransacked vacant homes or liberally helped themselves to poultry, eggs, and the fruits of family gardens.

The looting became so problematic, and the number of complaints grew to such volume, that the Führer himself was said to have issued execution orders for those found guilty of pilfering from their own countrymen.

The effectiveness of Schlemm's defense depended on his ability to anticipate Allied intentions. Across his front line, efforts were under way to develop an accurate understanding of the enemy's plan of attack. He and his division commanders knew that if they could mass their limited resources at the most likely avenues of assault they stood a better chance of stopping Montgomery's crossing.

By day observers scoped the far shore, and by night patrols in small rubber dinghies paddled quietly across the Rhine to reconnoiter the far banks. While patrols often disappeared into the gloom never to be heard from again, several returned having identified likely crossing points; some even located engineering depots stockpiling equipment in advance of the attack. *Generalmajor* Rudolf Langhaeuser, one of Schlemm's division commanders, recalled, "Reports from our systematic reconnaissance and careful observation—organized down to the smallest infantry post—left no doubt as to the fact that the enemy was preparing a large-scale offensive across the Rhine river." Langhaeuser continued, "The results from recon and observation led to the conclusion that the enemy would launch his main attack either near Emmerich or near Wesel."

Scouts from units adjacent to Langhaeuser's division collected evidence indicating that the potential zone of attack extended farther south to include Dinslaken. This focused Schlemm's attention to a thirty-mile stretch of the riverbank centered on Wesel.

Schlemm and his staff were increasingly confident they'd established the *where*; they still needed to uncover the *when*. The Third Reich's intelligence services, still very active in France, pressed their web of over 2,000 stay-behind collaborators to find out. Spies had also parachuted into France via captured American bombers or had been smuggled across the borders of Spain, Switzerland, and northern Italy. The missions of these agents ranged from espionage and sabotage to supplying existing networks with wireless transmitters. To deliver their reports when radios failed or were unavailable, some agents resorted to carrier pigeons.

Most of the agents were French, either sympathetic Fascists or those willing to ink a deal with the devil to get back home. Several refugees were given safe passage into France in exchange for reporting observed Allied troop movements. In some cases agents were aided and sheltered by former members of the *Parti Populaire Français* (French Popular Party), a Fascist and anti-Semitic political organization active in France during the German occupation.

In spite of the inevitable double-crossers and deserters, there were notable successes. One intelligence coup purloined an Allied after-action report on MARKET GARDEN. A copy of the document made its way to Schlemm, who found the up-to-date Allied doctrine for deploying airborne troops of particular interest.

Miles above the skullduggery the *Luftwaffe*'s aerial photoreconnaissance missions also contributed to the developing intelligence picture. While their numbers were limited, Germany's advanced jets— Messerschmitt Me-262s and Arado Ar-234s—provided formerly lacking aerial imagery, and they could range across Allied lines with near impunity. Streaking over France, the jets' equally high-speed cameras photographed Allied airfields bulging to capacity with aircraft and gliders. The airfields were not hard to find; the *Luftwaffe* had built them.

Allied attempts to preserve the element of surprise were partly undone by the scale of their pending invasion, which made it impossible for them to conceal their preparations. But they tried, using deception and camouflage wherever possible. German intelligence officers diligently pored over photographs to identify supply dumps and bivouac areas while trying to determine which were dummy installations built to draw their attention away from the real sites.

Like they were assembling a jigsaw puzzle, the Germans started with the edges and worked inward, sifting through the shapes, looking for patterns. The collection of reports, photographs, and sightings provided a hazy but discernible image of Montgomery's intentions. The missing pieces not obtained from rubber dinghies or jets were filled in by years of combat experience and expert terrain analysis.

Oberst Rolf Geyer, one of Blaskowitz's staff officers, summarized what their analysis had revealed of the enemy's most likely courses of action: the first was a British assault below Arnhem; the second was a crossing farther south along the thirty-mile stretch of river between Emmerich and Dinslaken. In either case, Geyer noted, a supporting airborne operation should be expected.

Kesselring and Blaskowitz both considered the second scenario the more probable. The advantage was obvious: it would allow the British and Americans to protect each other's advance and reunite after flanking the Ruhr. It was a given that the Allies wouldn't directly assault the Ruhr but instead use the open terrain to encircle and isolate it.

"Nevertheless," wrote Geyer, "in absence of clear indications to the contrary, the first possibility still had to be taken into account. . . . Furthermore it was assumed that the Americans would cross the river simultaneously south of Wesel [near Dinslaken]." Enough uncertainty remained that Kesselring continued to hold several divisions near Arnhem just in case.

Blaskowitz and Schlemm, in turn, kept their plans flexible. Schlemm placed an infantry division in reserve near Wesel so they could, depending on the scenario, attack toward either the Americans crossing upstream or the British downstream.

Blaskowitz had a *Panzer-Korps* available to Schlemm as a mobile reserve of tanks and infantry if he needed them. Tucked inland behind the Issel River, the *Panzer-Korps* formed the fulcrum of their defensive plan. Commanded by *General der Panzertruppe* Heinrich Freiherr von Lüttwitz, an aggressive and experienced Prussian, their task would be to swing in like a sledgehammer, smashing the Allies against the banks of the Rhine. But only after Blaskowitz had identified the British main point of attack would he commit the reserves to the battle. Both Blaskowitz and Schlemm expected their adversary to launch feints to draw out the *Panzer-Korps* units prematurely.

The sledgehammer consisted of two veteran divisions equipped with approximately ninety tanks and twenty self-propelled guns. It was a far cry from the impressive force that cut its way across Europe in 1940, but if wielded correctly it could do considerable damage. German tank crews still had the advantage in target acquisition, firepower, and armored protection. Their most feared adversaries weren't Allied tanks, but rather *Jababombern*—or *Jabos*, the Allied fighter-bombers that would invariably hound their movement to the front.

The two divisions contained over 4,000 men each; however, their refitting was progressing more slowly than Blaskowitz needed. They were each only receiving 500 replacements a week. And while these units had priority for receiving mechanized vehicles—they had to be able to move fast—transportation for the infantry ranged from armored half-tracks to platoons equipped with bicycles.

During a conference at I *Fallschirmjäger-Armee*'s headquarters on Wednesday, March 14, Schlemm briefed Kesselring and Blaskowitz on the state of his preparations to date. He admitted that while most of his fortifications had been hastily constructed, his men had used the four days since crossing the Rhine to advantage and would continue to do so. Positions just inland from the riverbank, as well as those along the railroad line running parallel to the Rhine, had been occupied and reinforced. Of course he was still concerned about his lack of defensive depth, which would be an issue in the event of any enemy airdrop.

Were more troops available?

Kesselring was doing what he could to get more men, he had a meeting scheduled with Hitler the next day to discuss it, but the situation on Schlemm's flanks was grave. Those units also desperately needed more replacements. Reviewing the disposition of the defenses, Kesselring knew his forces would be unable to repel the invaders indefinitely. Even with the relative certainty of knowing Montgomery's crossing points, he realized his troops were spread too thin, and too much mass was being arrayed against them.

He later admitted he felt "like a concert pianist who is asked to play a Beethoven sonata . . . on an ancient, rickety and out-of-tune instrument."

Of course recognizing the inevitable end game doesn't release a soldier from fulfilling his duty. The three generals were committed to resisting the invasion as best they could. But none relished being on the defense. While they appreciated that a solid defensive line could compensate for smaller numbers, by training and disposition their forte was the offense—attacking. After years of chasing their prey, they were now in the position of absorbing Montgomery's assault without the firepower and agility they were used to. Motivated by a complicated combination of loyalty to the Führer, their professional pride, and a strong desire to avoid a repeat of 1918's humiliating armistice, they would continue to fight with the troops and equipment available. If any of them had doubts about their chances of holding out, they remained silent.

Schlemm continued his briefing; his plans for addressing the potential enemy airdrop to his rear were in progress. The first component, fortifying farms near the anticipated drop zones, was well under way. The second, converting the 4,000 men of a reserve division into a specialized anti-airborne battle group, would be completed soon.

Blaskowitz confirmed the availability of the two reserve divisions. They were poised to launch coordinated battalion-sized infantry and armor attacks at any point along Schlemm's front, or flank, within five to six hours' notice.

The three officers debated where Montgomery's main attack should be expected. Schlemm believed the main attack would occur near Wesel, while Kesselring and Blaskowitz thought it would be farther north, closer to Emmerich.

They all agreed Montgomery would certainly use airborne troops. But each general had his own opinion as to where the airdrop would occur. Schlemm, referencing the captured MARKET GARDEN report, cited the Allies' new unwillingness to drop troops too far away from advancing ground forces. His terrain analysis, coupled with his own airborne experience, led him to believe the Allies would drop close to the Rhine, just northwest of Wesel. Blaskowitz suspected they'd land farther north and more inland, as much as ten miles, to give the bridgehead added depth in the direction of the Ruhr. He'd witnessed firsthand the havoc of an Allied airdrop—during the invasion of Southern France the previous August, his staff had been surrounded and taken out of the fight by American paratroopers. Blaskowitz had barely managed to escape.

Time would prove that Schlemm had a more acute understanding of their adversaries.

✶   ✶   ✶

For their part, Allied intelligence officers were desperate to determine what the Germans were up to across the Rhine. The task of developing an accurate assessment of Schlemm's manpower and the disposition of his units was frustrated by the lack of direct engagement.

The intelligence staff used every available asset to gain a better understanding of the enemy's activity. Radio eavesdropping was complemented by aerial reconnaissance flown by camera-equipped Spitfires and P-38s. Occasionally, the intelligence officers were lucky enough to get a captured German reconnaissance scout or deserter for interrogation. But the German situation was so fluid—and ad hoc units were being created, renamed, or relocated with such frequency—that it was challenging to maintain a coherent understanding of what the Allies would be up against.

The intelligence estimates predicted that by March 10, Schlemm's I *Fallschirmjäger-Armee* had already received 18,500 troops, to be followed by another 27,000 before VARSITY's target date.

On March 18, the staff of 21 Army Group's intelligence section were alarmed when communication intercepts revealed the enemy had correctly anticipated not only the use of airborne troops but also where they'd be dropped: "[Allied] preparations of forces on the mainland for an airborne landing must be regarded as completed, so that the possibility of the beginning of one or a number of enemy airborne landings on the Western Front must be taken into consideration . . . in the following areas, in order of probability: Wesel—Bocholt—Doetinchem—North of Arnhem—Veenendaal."

The communiqué concluded with a reminder to German ground commanders that "the key to success [lies] exclusively in immediate bold attack with all available forces."

The element of surprise had been lost.

CHAPTER 7

SEQUITIS BASTATII

Châlons-sur-Marne, France. Friday, March 16, 1945.

The atmosphere had changed in the 17th Airborne camps, and rumors were crystallizing into facts. The troopers had no doubt *something* was about to happen. The frequency of visitors to the guarded War Room tents continued to climb. And as equipment and weapons inspections became annoyingly more frequent, passes out of camp became harder to get.

The reduction of passes was a ploy by the division's counterintelligence officers, who wanted to slowly decrease the presence of airborne troops in the nearby towns so as to avoid notice of their sudden departure. Nevertheless, troops disappearing from other locales were drawing attention.

In nearby hospitals airborne officers combed the wards seeking discharges for men who'd recovered enough from their wounds to return to duty. The implication was obvious: the officers wanted experienced veterans back at their units sooner rather than later. Clearly something big was afoot. The curious activity compelled other patients, whose officers were less proactive, to slip out of the hospital without a doctor's release or official authorization.

The Army tracked its soldiers like all its assets: on paper. No one moved from point A to point B without documented orders. Every GI had to be accounted for, but paperwork took time and who knew how long that would take. Going through proper channels could mean missing the operation. Few if any of those breaking out were motivated by patriotism or a love of war; their reasons were far less complicated. Simply put, they were unwilling to let their buddies down. Comrades were counting on them, and that was more important than personal safety. Some were no doubt driven by the nagging worry that they'd be considered a coward if they stayed behind. Miley had long known that his men, particularly the paratroopers, had built a culture wherein they "became more afraid of the unfavorable opinion of their fellows than of death itself." Anyone who'd worked hard to gain acceptance within a group of combat men wanted to avoid the shame of shirking the brotherhood.

By sneaking back to their units without orders the men risked the stockade—in the eyes of Army bureaucrats, they were Absent Without Leave. George Streukens, a captain in the glider regiment, welcomed his men back regardless of their means or motivations. With a wink he subjected each escapee to his own court-martial. Charging them with being AWOL, he sentenced the guilty to a week's confinement in camp—a verdict that generated the Army's required paperwork and prevented outside authority from taking further action. Once word got out that officers were either turning a blind eye or actively aiding those without proper authorization, even more veterans returned.

In spite of their suspicions, none of the troopers knew exactly when the operation would launch. Unknown to them, General Miley and his staff of logisticians had been working toward a D-Day of April 1. But as is customary in war, the enemy failed to cooperate. Schlemm's unexpected escape across the Rhine put VARSITY's timeline back in question.

Montgomery wanted to attack sooner. With the Americans already across the Rhine at Remagen and the Germans in his own sector organizing their defenses on the far bank, Montgomery knew the clock was ticking. If the Americans pressed their advantage, their breakout might drain the supplies earmarked for his operation, and he knew the enemy across the river would only get stronger with time.

Montgomery again angered the Americans by complaining bitterly to Eisenhower that the crossing at Remagen ran counter to the agreed plan. But as frustrated as Montgomery was that American field commanders were crossing the Rhine as fast as they could—and thus taking more gas and supplies—their attacks did stretch the Germans' defenses, causing the enemy to transfer troops out of Montgomery's sector to repulse the Americans.

While Ridgway understood Montgomery's newfound sense of urgency, he felt the airborne troops needed two weeks' notice before they could launch. Up at Airborne Army, however, Brereton overruled him, telling Montgomery they only needed one week. He caveated his commitment with the understatement of a man who would be sitting it out in the rear: such a hasty option, he added, "would lack the smoothness of deliberate planning and preparations." Both Ridgway's diary and history are silent on how the experienced combat commander reacted to being overridden by someone who'd never led troops.

Montgomery's desire to move up D-Day was more optimistic than practical. His unwillingness to scale down his plans still required stockpiling vast amounts of supplies. The essential landing craft and 30,000 tons of bridging equipment had yet to arrive at the front. Sixty thousand tons of artillery shells still had to be moved up to gunners manning 1,300 howitzers — and that was merely for the opening salvos of the pre-invasion artillery barrage.

The G-4 section at Supreme Headquarters, the supply guys, estimated that keeping Montgomery's bridgehead stocked with rations, fuel, batteries, and medical supplies would require over 500 tons of provisions per day, per division. Moving all of that materiel forward necessitated widening roads and building depots, which still needed to be completed.

After a sober assessment, Montgomery and Dempsey agreed they could, at most, advance D-Day by one week.

The day before St. Patrick's Day, Miley informed his regimental commanders that the drop had been moved from April 1 to March 24. They now had eight days to prepare.

Shortly thereafter, without explanation or fanfare, small convoys departed from the various 17th Airborne rest camps. In some cases the heavier equipment, such as the 105mm and 75mm howitzers, were towed away. In others, lines of jeeps with overloaded trailers rumbled out of camp. The departing convoys made it obvious that equipment was being relocated somewhere, perhaps to airfields for staging.

The next day officers conducted another series of weapon inspections. Platoon sergeants drafted personnel rosters and organized aircraft loading plans. The activity sparked rumors that restriction to camp was imminent.

Sergeant John Chester didn't wait around to confirm the scuttlebutt. He needed his clothes, which were in the possession of a local gendarme's wife. Chester, grabbing his entire stash of cigarettes and a large bag of candy, bolted into Soudron.

He had a pretty sweet deal. For a pack of American cigarettes, the woman washed, pressed, and folded his duffel bag of dirty clothing. The bargain saved him from competing for access to his camp's limited laundry facilities. As a nonsmoker, Chester stockpiled his weekly ration of smokes for such bartering.

He found the family at home and after a bit of small talk exchanged the requisite cigarettes for his duffel bag, gave the husband a smart salute, and turned toward the door.

Pausing, he handed the bag of candy to the couple's nine-year-old daughter and simultaneously tried to discreetly slide three cartons of cigarettes onto the table. But his sleight of hand needed work. The over-joyed wife descended on him in a flash, planting a big kiss on his cheek.

Chester, nervous that her husband would get the wrong idea, was relieved when the man laughed and pointed to a mirror. A perfect, bright red print of the woman's lips highlighted Chester's right cheek. As a fan of symmetry, Chester pointed at his left cheek, whereupon the woman planted another perfect kiss. Chester nodded his approval, set his garrison cap at a rakish angle, and with a spring in his step returned to camp.

Passing through the maze of tents, Chester was hounded by catcalls and questions from "a bunch of very jealous and curious troopers." Relishing the attention, he simply replied, "Boys, you've got to know your way around." He'd been back less than an hour when everyone was confined to camp.

Clyde Haney also had a close call. Just before all outgoing mail was bagged and held until after the operation, he managed to send a letter to his family. Continuing to encode sensitive information, Haney concluded his note of March 19 with "Dad [the indication a hidden message followed]: Am in really beautiful ozone training now easy. Meal in several seconds—I'm off now. Seldom overlook our noonmeals." Translated, the slightly jumbled message read: "Airborne Mission Soon."

Lieutenant Frank Dillon and his platoon were called to an unexpected company formation, where their commander explained why no one was allowed to leave: they'd soon be conducting a combat drop and preparations were to start immediately.

Dillon had just received a warning order—stripped of details and dates, it was just enough information to put the gears in motion. He and the rest of the men would get the details in the marshaling camp.

Dillon didn't need to know the particulars, nor did he require a lot of guidance; he knew what to do.

First, he told his troops to return to their tents and pack all of their nonessential articles and extra uniforms into their duffel bags. These were then to be left at the supply tent for storage. They'd now be living out of their combat packs. He reminded his men to keep their mess tins, with army-issued knife, fork, and spoon, with them.

Later that day, while Dillon's Baker Company scrambled in anticipation of their departure, another thirty-two replacements arrived. Yesterday these men had been drowning in the monotony of a replacement depot, and now they were caught in a whirlwind of soldiers preparing for combat. The new arrivals were assigned across the four platoons; at least they didn't have to unpack.

Dillon, along with every other platoon leader in the division, ordered the men to remove their golden talon shoulder patches and all other airborne insignia from their uniforms. They unbloused their trousers to conceal their distinctive jump boots. The men hid their weapons and combat equipment in duffel or kitbags to further aid the ruse. Since they'd be traveling through civilian areas en route to their departure airfields, the uniform modifications were intended to rob observers of any clues that they were witnessing airborne troops on the move.

The next evening, well after sunset, Dillon's platoon loaded into the backs of cargo trucks for a short ride to the rail station in Châlons-sur-Marne.

The men boarded the familiar forty-and-eight boxcars for their journey to their marshaling camp adjacent to the airfield near Melun, officially designated A-55. Most tossed their packs on the floor for a pillow and settled into the rhythm of the swaying boxcar for some sleep.

Before Gene Herrmann, who'd been reassigned to a mortar squad in the 194th's Dog Company, left camp, his platoon sergeant, Mardell Kreuzer, asked for a volunteer to stay behind. Headquarters needed a few men to guard equipment and bring it overland later in the campaign. Volunteering would mean missing the drop. No one stepped forward or raised his hand. Kreuzer approached each man individually but still got no takers. The last trooper he spoke with got the job.

Between March 19 and 20, the entire division snaked through the darkness of Northern France via jeeps, trucks, and trains as unobtrusively as

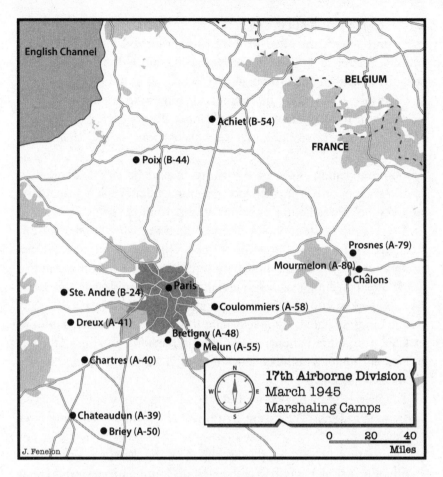

English Channel

Achiet (B-54)

BELGIUM

Poix (B-44)

FRANCE

Prosnes (A-79)

Mourmelon (A-80)

Châlons

Ste. Andre (B-24) Paris

Coulommiers (A-58)

Dreux (A-41)

Bretigny (A-48)

Melun (A-55)

Chartres (A-40)

17th Airborne Division
March 1945
Marshaling Camps

Chateaudun (A-39)

Briey (A-50)

0   20   40
Miles

J. Fenelon

9,000 men could. At the same time, across the English Channel and well over 200 miles away, the British 6th Airborne Division moved to their eleven departure airfields northwest of London.

Both divisions were on their way to camps where they'd be briefed on the mission's details. The troopers would have three days to memorize the plan and get themselves ready. The Americans were staging out of twelve camps constructed at the departing airfields, each with a capacity for 1,200 to 2,400 GIs.

Structurally and aesthetically, the camps were similar to those in Châlons: rows of generic olive-drab army tents. Inside the tents each trooper would find a standard-issue cot and three wool blankets awaiting him. There were some differences though, the most notable being the seven-foot-tall barbed wire fence and patrolling MPs surrounding the camps—both intended to thwart unauthorized entrance or exit. Outside the fence and extending around the airfield's perimeter were recently emplaced anti-aircraft guns.

On display throughout the compounds and inside briefing tents were posters bearing cautionary axioms: "Home Alive in '45, Don't Talk!" and "Enemy Ears Are Listening!" and "What You See and Hear Here, Leave Here."

Communication between the camps would be strictly limited to landline telephone or messengers traveling by liaison planes, jeeps, or motorcycles. No radio transmissions were permitted.

A segregation system had been established to ensure briefed personnel couldn't mingle with the uninformed. Guards would escort visitors in and out of the encampments, preventing contact with those in the know. Separate dining facilities and latrines for administrative personnel had also been set up. Any briefed personnel who fell ill were to be quarantined in designated hospitals where they'd remain under guard and isolated from other patients until after the mission launched. All such briefed personnel had the code word "UNDERDONE" written boldly on their medical tags.

The men *could* write letters, but all outgoing mail would be bagged and sent to the censors for extra scrutiny. It would all be held until after D-Day.

The routine at each camp would be the same. Briefings would start shortly after arrival, beginning with battalion commanders who attended the first of several scheduled planning sessions. The briefings were to be conducted on a rotating basis, working down to the platoons. Men waiting their turn would be made as comfortable as tents, cots, and barbwire would allow. Sporting equipment was made available, and each camp set aside a tent for showing movies. Red Cross volunteers were on hand to dispense cigarettes, gum, doughnuts, and coffee.

Issues of *Stars and Stripes*, the armed forces newspaper, would be made available at each camp. Men flipping through the pages read about plans back home to build a nationwide interstate highway system. There were satisfactory reports of the Air Force doing their job, both locally and abroad. Over 1,300 heavy bombers had again plastered Berlin, and in the Pacific, B-29s were bombing Japan. The Marines were in a bitter battle for the island of Iwo Jima. Also of interest were cautionary tales of treacherous German civilians: an elderly woman was caught riding her bicycle through American lines, waving at GIs in their foxholes for the benefit of enemy artillery observers. Those less engrossed by current events would find entertainment in the comic-strip adventures of Dick Tracy or the antics of Li'l Abner. The sports section provided updates on the Stanley Cup semifinals; baseball season wouldn't start until April.

Marshaling Camp A-80, Mourmelon-le-Grand, France.
Tuesday, March 20, 1945.

Sitting in his tent, Bud Miley once again mentally reviewed his division's plan. In accordance with doctrine, he'd bolstered his three regiments by assigning them supporting units of engineers, anti-tank gunners, and artillery to form three combat teams. The operation itself boiled down to two primary tasks: seizing high ground and establishing a perimeter to protect Montgomery's bridgehead from counterattack.

Miley's two parachute regiments would be used to attack a six-mile stretch of high ground in the Diersfordt Forest from which German artillery gunners could observe and fire on exposed Allied troops traversing the wide river below. The division's most lethal regiment, the glider riders of the 194th, would seize and hold positions along the Issel River to form the perimeter's defensive line. The Issel ran roughly parallel to the Rhine six miles inland and virtually boxed in the 17th Airborne's area of operations to the east and southeast. Originally a tributary, whose banks had been steadily built up since the Roman era, its high embankments and thirty-five-foot width created a natural obstacle and prevented tanks and vehicles from crossing anywhere other than bridges. Taking and holding these crossing points would be critical for Montgomery's forces to break out of the bridgehead. The British airborne would seize bridges farther up the Issel in their sector to complete the perimeter.

Hazy intelligence suggested one potential problem with the setup, which was that the Germans had arrayed their reserve formations behind the Issel. This placed them in a position to reinforce units already along the Rhine. If they got to the bridges first, they could strike the still-maturing and vulnerable bridgehead. The location of these reserves also made them a danger to Miley's troops mopping up enemy positions between the Rhine and the Issel.

Reading the March 22 intelligence report, Miley noted the blunt realities: "The reserve activity in this area against airborne operations cannot really be evaluated. There is a squeeze on petrol and motor transport, but, on the other hand, the Germans have been rehearsing to counteract airborne landings at the earliest possible moment with reserves in selected areas." The report went on to estimate that "by the time the airborne assault takes place, there is a possibility of 100,000 troops of all types and caliber being within a 30 mile radius and from 10,000 to 12,000 within a 10 mile radius of the area."

Miley knew that the *Wehrmacht*, even with its resources stretched, would be a formidable opponent. German infantry and tank crews continued to wield an expert level of lethality that made them infamous.

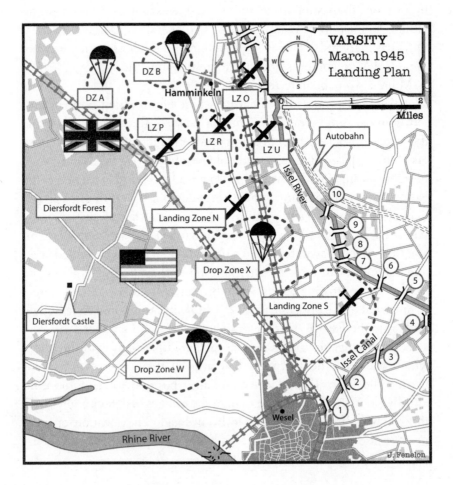

They'd come back from the brink of destruction multiple times and had shown, both at Arnhem and in the Ardennes, that they still had a vote in the outcome of any battle.

Miley realized that delaying the drop until after commencing the river assault created two possible scenarios. First, the Germans might hastily commit their armored reserves to repel the assault crossing, in which case his men would be landing virtually on top of the enemy units as they moved toward the river. Or, more likely, Montgomery's crossing would not draw out the reserves by the time of the drop. In that case, they'd be mustering behind the Issel awaiting developments along the riverbank. If Miley's troops could beat the Germans to the bridges — after overcoming the enemy occupying the landing zones — they stood a good chance of keeping them at bay.

Regardless of how the Germans reacted, Miley knew he had the advantage of mass. It would be a concentrated drop with the two airborne divisions landing in an area roughly five miles wide by six miles deep; there was little chance of units becoming isolated. In contrast with MARKET GARDEN, they'd be dropping virtually on top of their objectives, allowing them to pounce on their targets almost immediately and at full strength. The division would drop into a rough triangle shape, with the 507th, including Miley himself, jumping in first, followed by the 513th farther north and the 194th gliding into the east.

In the other marshaling camps, Miley's troops were learning the details of their specific roles.

Camp A-40, Chartres, France. Tuesday, March 20, 1945.

Thad Blanchard's squad, along with the rest of the 1st Battalion of the 507th Parachute Infantry Regiment — Raff's Ruffians — traveled over 140 miles by train to get to camp A-40, located west of Paris, at Chartres. The regiment's other two battalions staged out of airfield A-79 near Prosnes, just twelve miles due north of Châlons.

Like newly arrived convicts, the GIs strolled along the seven-foot fence line in small groups inspecting its thoroughness and heckling the MPs outside the wire. Counterintelligence agents roamed the camp, keeping their eyes and ears open for lapses in security and randomly spot-checking troopers, patting them down for diaries, letters, and other sensitive documents.

Overall, the troops were impressed with the camp. Here the mess tents had wood flooring and electric lighting. Some of the men made their stay even more luxurious by smuggling in bottles of champagne.

The heat of the bright, sunny day brought out the dusty smell of the canvas tents. While waiting for their briefings, many of the troopers took advantage of the sports equipment and the pleasant weather to organize games of horseshoes, softball, football, and volleyball. Some troopers used their downtime to gamble, read, write letters, or just lie on a blanket and loaf in the sun. Outdoor speakers blared songs by Glenn Miller, the Mills Brothers, Tommy Dorsey, and other popular musicians. The occasional news broadcast kept the soldiers informed of current events.

While some pined for distractions of the outside world, others got down to the task at hand. Clustered to the side of the sports fields, small groups of men whetted the blades of their fighting knives, shaving the hair off their arms to dramatically demonstrate their razor sharpness. Others, hoping to avoid getting that close to the enemy, meticulously cleaned tommy guns and loaded extra ammunition magazines. Some troops dragged their cots out into the sun to field strip and oil their rifles.

One of Blanchard's fellow paratroopers recalled, "Days before the operation we went to the marshaling area and were sealed in. . . . But we didn't mind it because the process was much more like a religious knight fasting before an important ceremony. As a matter of fact, like monks we couldn't afford to think of anything but what we had before us."

Contrary to the cavalier simplicity of his briefing to the British, Raff had a comprehensive plan for his combat team. He assigned each of his three infantry battalions a specific role in accomplishing the regiment's mission to "liquidate the enemy" occupying the Diersfordt Forest.

Raff's regiment, divided into three serials of over forty planes each, were jumping into Drop Zone W—or more simply DZ W—an open area of farmland hugging the boundary of the forest. At their first briefing Thad Blanchard's squad learned the Ruffians were slated to be in the vanguard of the invasion, jumping in first.

After assembling on the western edge of the DZ, Blanchard's 1st Battalion, commanded by Major Paul Smith, would form Raff's reserve element. There they would wait for orders to either seize the wooded area to the northwest or assist one of the other two battalions who would be simultaneously seizing sectors of high ground to the north and southwest. The Ruffians also had an archaic objective in their area: a castle. Raff had noticed the small group of buildings surrounded by a moat when studying the mosaics of aerial photography and recognized its potential as an enemy strongpoint. He decided they needed to storm Diersfordt Castle.

Blanchard's squad studied maps and aerial photos of the DZ. They noted it was roughly egg-shaped: 2,000 yards long on its east-west axis and 1,500 yards wide. At just over a mile inland from the Rhine's east bank, they'd be landing closest to the river, making them the first to greet the advancing British Tommies of Montgomery's 21 Army Group—if all went according to plan.

The DZ, essentially solid farmland, did however contain a number of obstacles: the forest's fifty-foot trees bordered the north and west, with shallow drainage ditches and wire fences crisscrossing the open fields; along the northern boundary ran a single-track, narrow-gauge railroad line parallel to a main road. An embanked road also bisected the DZ. The squad noticed that the roads each had twenty-five- to thirty-foot telephone or power line poles running along both sides. No one wanted to get entangled in those.

Huddled over aerial photographs, Blanchard and the other troopers could see enemy trenches dug along the road. They also recognized that the road could facilitate the rapid movement of German troops and tanks into their DZ.

Blanchard reminded his men to pay attention to their flight path. Knowing the aircraft would pass over the DZ from west to east gave them a handy navigation reference. After landing, all they had to do was face the same direction as the departing aircraft and turn left. They'd then be facing north, the direction they needed to move to find the assembly point on the edge of the woods.

Dropping with the Ruffians in a fourth serial of forty-five planes would be the 464th Parachute Field Artillery Battalion, or "Branigan's Bastards" as they'd dubbed themselves. Commanded by Lieutenant Colonel Edward Branigan, the Bastards were newcomers to both the division and the war itself. They'd joined the 17th in Châlons as part of the division's reorganization, arriving just nine days before moving into their marshaling camp, A-80, at Mourmelon-le-Grand.

During those nine days, Branigan thought Miley's staff kept "coolly distant, and never really made us feel accepted." He admitted it felt like being "the bastard son at the family reunion." Ironically, Raff warmly welcomed the Bastards, despite their lack of combat experience.

The two commanders viewed themselves as outsiders. Branigan, a thirty-six-year-old lieutenant colonel, had started his military service as a private in 1933 when he enlisted in the New York National Guard. A year later he earned his commission and then steadily rose through the ranks surrounded by West Pointers. Raff, in spite of his West Point pedigree, viewed most of his fellow officers as politicians rather than warriors, and he took pleasure in distancing himself from them. The two developed an immediate rapport.

Camp B-54, Achiet, France. Tuesday, March 20, 1945.

After departing Châlons on the evening of March 19 in staggered groups, the paratroopers of the 513th Parachute Infantry Regiment took seventeen hours to make their way to their marshaling camps.

When they disembarked from the train, they were amused by the heavy-handed security: the station's signs had been covered up. While it impressed the replacements, the old hands wondered if the Army realized it was more important the Germans remain oblivious to their location than that they themselves be kept in the dark.

The paratroopers milled about in the dark smoking and waiting to board the cargo trucks for the final stretch of their journey. They didn't know it at the time, but they were in the sleepy village of Bapaume, which had been leveled by German shells in the First World War. After an uneventful fifteen-minute ride, they arrived at the airfield designated B-54, near Achiet. Because they'd all be taking off from the same airfield in the larger-capacity C-46 Commandos, the regiment's two marshaling camps were located next to each other.

The rank and file of the 513th PIR embraced the superstition of the unlucky number thirteen in their unit's designation. While historians have never agreed on the origins of the cultural phobia, the paratroopers didn't spend much time dwelling on it. As Private Harold Green recollected, "We were called the 'Thirteeners' and wore our parachute insignia on the opposite side of our cap than the others did. The day we were activated . . . we had 13 paratroopers jump from a plane numbered 13, at 1,300 feet at 1300 hours."

Legend has it that the first man to jump, Captain John Spears, carried a black cat out the door with him. The daredevil feline was incorporated into the regiment's insignia, which featured a wide-eyed Disney-esque black cat with pants bloused into the tops of its jump boots. "Little Joi," as the mascot was known, was portrayed in an aggressive pose, descending through the clouds under a black parachute canopy and wielding a bayonet-tipped rifle. The bayonet was covered in blood to eliminate any doubt about the cat's ferocity. In another nod to superstition, a monstrous number 13 dominated the background. A favorite regimental pastime was a game called "Matching the thirteen in 513," which consisted of downing thirteen beers in a single sitting.

The thirty-six-year-old regimental commander, Colonel James Coutts, shared his men's sense of humor. He was a 1932 graduate of West Point who, when asked about his academic achievements, joked, "I ranked 20th in my class . . . 20th from the bottom." What he lacked in academic discipline, he made up for in physical pursuits. He ranked second in his class for horsemanship and excelled at boxing. Coutts volunteered for parachute duty in 1941 and enjoyed the demanding physical training. As a captain in Miley's first parachute battalion, his name was one of those engraved on the first Prop Blast mug.

In the planning tent at camp B-54, First Lieutenant Ed Tommasino, a company commander in Coutts' 2nd Battalion, shouted, "Issue the tissue, you're wasting the tax payers' money!" This was Tommasino's way of telling his men they were expected to take notes.

Tommasino became Dog Company's second commanding officer after his predecessor had been killed in the Ardennes. He wouldn't be their last.

Among those with pencils poised was Private Curtis Gadd. Wiry, with a cocksure smile that revealed his fondness for mischief, Gadd had held a high-paying, draft-deferred job with Thompson Aircraft Products, a defense contractor. But after being asked, "Why ain't you in the Army?" one too many times, he volunteered to enlist. After his induction he volunteered again to join the paratroops, motivated by the extra $50 a month, which would soften the blow of his pay cut.

Undoubtedly Gadd's commanding officers wished he'd stayed back in Ohio. In his first year of service the rise and fall of his rank reflected his boredom with garrison life: private, private first class, technical sergeant 5, technical sergeant 4, private, sergeant, private.

It's possible Gadd holds the Army's record for the fastest double demotion. The same morning he was busted in rank from technical sergeant 5 to technical sergeant 4, he thought he'd get a laugh by attaching the new rank to his fatigues with laundry pins. He made it until lunch, when an officer spotted him in the chow line and busted him down to private. Trying to get rid of the troublemaker, his commanding officer "volunteered" Gadd for pathfinder training, hoping he'd wash out and be reassigned elsewhere; but no such luck. He made it.

Gadd's true character was revealed in combat, where he shined, earning a Silver Star for bravery, a Bronze Star, and two Purple Hearts.

In the briefing tent Tommasino oriented the men to the map: the rough rectangle of the regiment's drop zone, DZ X, was located two and a half miles northwest of Wesel. It was approximately 2,500 yards long by 1,000 yards wide with two distinct features: a series of ninety-foot-tall, T-shaped steel pylons supporting high-tension power lines cutting diagonally across the western section, and a double-track railroad—the Wesel/Hamminkeln line—running along the western boundary. Like all farmland in the area, the zone was littered with small fences and dirt roads. Several wooded areas, with trees ranging from thirty to seventy feet tall, dotted the terrain as well. Reconnaissance photography revealed enemy positions peppering the DZ.

The lieutenant pointed to the railroad line and told the men that in the event they got lost, just head west until they ran into it.

The Thirteeners would be flying twelve minutes behind the Ruffians and into the farthest point of the bridgehead. Once assembled, they were expected to clear their zone of enemy positions and establish their section of the northern perimeter along the Issel River. Gadd's Dog Company and the rest of the 2nd Battalion would seize the high ground on their side of the Diersfordt Forest while the other two battalions occupied positions along the Issel and established roadblocks against potential enemy incursions from the north.

In his written operations order, Colonel Coutts hinted at a possible shortage of body bags, reminding each battalion commander to bring mattress covers and safety pins, but he hoped they wouldn't need them.

The twenty-three-year-old Gadd "had absolutely no apprehension about the jump, just looked forward to it as a great exciting adventure." He recalled that "morale among all of us appeared to be extremely upbeat."

Private Jerzy Spitzer, a twenty-two-year-old whose family had escaped the Nazi occupation of Poland, had more on his mind. Just before the operation he wrote to his father, "I am not afraid of anything, and I do not worry about myself. I am fighting and working for my ideals and believe that God will help me. My ideal is that all people are individuals and should be treated as such, regardless of their origin, understanding of God, and appearance. That is my faith, ideal, and religion. The goal of my life is to do whatever I can to spread that faith among people, so that finally everybody may recognize that truth and unite as citizens of the world and live together in friendship, so that the ideals of peace on earth, goodwill toward everyone, and brotherhood among men should be realism in life, thinking, and deeds of men."

The letter would arrive almost the same day as the notice informing the Spitzer family their son had died of wounds suffered in Germany.

Texan Lendy McDonald, a twenty-year-old staff sergeant, and his platoon spent hours each day studying maps to memorize the terrain, the location of their assembly area, and routes to their objectives. McDonald took his responsibilities as a platoon sergeant seriously, ensuring each of his squad leaders understood their assigned tasks. As members of Able Company in the 1st Battalion they were responsible for setting up roadblocks.

To aid the troopers the regiment's S-2 intelligence section constructed a twenty-foot terrain model. Terrain models—or more informally, sand tables—were large, shallow-framed wood boxes filled with dirt that could be shaped into hills and valleys to match the operational terrain. The scale was dictated by the string grid pattern over the table, held in place by evenly spaced nails along the frame. The pattern replicated the kilometer grid squares on the issued maps.

Creative flourishes brought the sand table to life: ration boxes for buildings, sprinkled weeds for wooded areas, various colors of string for roads, streams, and railroad tracks. Other markers indicated assembly areas, objectives, and enemy positions. The tables gave troopers a three-dimensional interpretation of the terrain. When they were coupled with maps and aerial photographs, the men developed a mind's eye view of the geographical features that would help orient them to the ground on which they'd be operating.

On the second day in camp, someone from the intelligence section added to the table a note card with "2,200" written in red—the expected number of enemy troops on, or surrounding, DZ X.

"There were only about 1,500 of us and this bit of news was alarming as hell," recalled Sergeant Mac McKirgan.

Perhaps the estimate was alarming, but McKirgan also noticed, "The increase in morale these days was truly amazing. These guys had really come to life. This type of operation was their forte. This was what they had been trained for and they were looking forward with gleeful anticipation."

With each visit to the planning tent McDonald and his platoon noted an increase in the number of dots indicating enemy anti-aircraft positions. Daily reconnaissance flights provided a mountain of material, and intelligence teams worked in twenty-four-hour rotating shifts to plot the new information. Estimates of enemy troop strength were continually revised. As the men studied their predicament via aerial photographs and the sand table, the regiment's motto came to mind: "*Sequitis bastatii.*" Roughly translated, the Latin meant "Follow the son of a bitch."

As one trooper clarified, "It doesn't mean to follow your leader. It means get after the bloody enemy. It means get the Krauts whether a sergeant is in front of you or not."

Based on the growing number of enemy emplacements, McDonald and his men agreed that, upon landing, they wouldn't have any trouble finding plenty of sons of bitches to go after.

VARSITY would be the first airborne mission of the war to be conducted in "enemy" versus "occupied" territory, and the implications weren't lost on the troops. Each briefing generated new rumors. Wherever the men gathered to clean their weapons, pack supplies, or wait for chow, they shared the latest scuttlebutt.

"The Germans are committed to hold or die."

"The Rhine River has never been crossed by an invading army since Napoleon."

"Old men, women and children have been trained to maim or poison us."

"Sharpened sticks have been set up to run us through as we land."

"Wide areas have been wired to detonate when the landings are made."

Some thought Hitler might finally resort to poison gas. Indeed,

Supreme Headquarters sent down an official memo drawing attention to "the possibility that the Germans will employ gas as an extreme measure."

Often coupled with swapping rumors was the inevitable debate about taking prisoners. Specifically, what to do with them: take or kill them?

"We had direct orders," said Private John Cobb, a replacement from New Jersey. "We weren't allowed to shoot anybody that surrendered. . . . They just preached and preached to us. Don't shoot nobody. Don't shoot nobody." However, several officers followed the official position with unofficial wisdom: "If you do, make sure you don't do it out in the open."

Army regulations contained no such ambiguity. Prisoners were to be treated humanely and escorted to the rear for interrogation — never executed. Many troopers rationalized that there was a difference between rules and reality. Weren't the regulations written before airborne operations existed? When you're surrounded, where is the rear? *Aren't we here to kill Germans? Wouldn't they do the same to us?* When every rifle was needed against a numerically superior enemy, relegating men to guard duty seemed foolish. One trooper summed up the feelings of many, "A prisoner is a liability."

Several of the veterans were already familiar with the ugly realities. The Thirteeners had killed enough prisoners during the Ardennes fighting that a rear-echelon MP had taunted them with a nickname that reflected their growing reputation, "The Baggy Pocket Butchers."

Regarding the Rhine operation, most expected to be executed themselves if captured by the Germans. The murder of eighty-four American POWs at Malmedy had made it clear what the enemy was capable of, and Allied propaganda ensured that every GI and Tommy knew of the massacre.

Take prisoners, or kill them? Until faced with the realities of the situation, it was an academic argument. One thing was certain on the battlefield: there'd be both unbelievable examples of humanity and tragic outbursts of rage.

Flying in eight minutes behind the Thirteeners would be their artillery support, the 75mm howitzers of the 466th Parachute Field Artillery Battalion. In their marshaling camp, A-80 at Mourmelon-le-Grand, John Chester and his comrades studied their sand tables. Their battalion would take off in a serial of forty-five C-47s and form up with the 513th's seventy-two C-46s already in flight.

Chester noticed the chaplains had made themselves conspicuous between briefings, milling about for anyone wanting to make his peace with God before facing the enemy. In total, nine chaplains and their enlisted assistants would drop with the division. They were respected for their willingness to run the risks of combat unarmed in order to bring comfort and last rites to GIs in the field. And certainly the job was risky. Since June 1944, five airborne chaplains had been killed in action, ten wounded, three taken prisoner, and two were still missing.

All of the crews in Chester's battalion had to disassemble and pack their howitzers for the airdrop. They stripped the gun down to its component parts: the rear trails, the two wheels, the gun sleigh, cradle, tube, and breech. After adding ten rounds of ammunition to the pile, they packed it all into seven bundles, six of which would be strapped underneath their aircraft, with the seventh being pushed out the door before they jumped.

Chester recalled, "We had practiced for this event, we could have almost gone through the procedure in our sleep. I recall no inspection. Our officers seemed quite busy with many other things to look after." Chester's howitzer would be one of fifty-one being brought in by the division on D-Day.

Chester's crew also meticulously cleaned and oiled their .30-caliber folding-stock carbines. As artillerymen, their primary weapon was their 75mm howitzer, but they'd be jumping with a carbine in an oversized canvas holster attached to their equipment belt and tied down on their leg, just above the knee. Chester also carried a .45-caliber automatic pistol.

Sequestered alongside the paratroopers were several reporters accompanying them into Germany. One of the more notorious was Robert Capa, a thirty-two-year-old Hungarian combat photographer. Known for pursuing his passions with a bravado that ignored potential consequences, Capa was famous for landing in one of the early assault waves on Omaha Beach armed with only a camera, and infamous for not letting a woman's marital status interfere with his affections. On or off the battlefield, Capa marched to his own drum.

"Capa was notorious for his daring," wrote fellow war correspondent Ernie Pyle. This was high praise from Pyle, who himself often got as close to the action as possible. Capa's approach to this assignment for *Life* magazine cemented his reputation: he planned to jump into Germany right behind the 513th's commander.

Capa was one of those enviable few who seemed either to know exactly where he stood in the context of the events happening around him, or to have the wisdom to understand that none of it mattered. Just as important, perhaps even more so, he knew how to take advantage of a situation.

Born as Endre Friedmann to Jewish parents in Budapest, Capa changed his name to sound more American and obtain freelance work in Paris, where he fled after leaving Berlin University in 1933. Since then he'd photographed the Spanish Civil War, where he palled around with Ernest Hemingway and tragically lost his lover and photography partner, Gerda Taro, to a violent accident. He documented the Chinese struggle against the Japanese in 1938 and was living in New York City at the war's outbreak, having been chased out of Europe as the Nazis advanced west. As a citizen of the world, Capa reportedly spoke eight languages, but according to his friends, "none of them well."

Although technically designated an "enemy alien" due to Hungary's Axis alliance, Capa's talent and willingness to go where others hesitated kept him gainfully employed. Between assignments he oscillated from trying to stay out of trouble to actively seeking it.

Elmer Lower, the manager of *Life* magazine's Paris office, had tipped off Capa about the VARSITY assignment. Capa liked the idea and readily agreed. He joined the Thirteeners in Châlons, hitching a ride with them in the forty-and-eights to the airfield.

Capa's participation was part of the plan to overcome what Brereton viewed as lackluster press coverage of his Airborne Army. The supercilious Brereton went so far as to have one of his staff officers develop a comprehensive public relations plan to ensure VARSITY would be properly celebrated in the press. All told, there were close to thirty correspondents assigned to cover the operation. The total head count almost represented the strength of a full platoon—a questionable prioritization given that Miley was still asking for additional aircraft.

Brereton had also arranged for a B-17 bomber filled with cameramen to document the armada's entry into Germany. They would get closer to the spectacle than they could possibly imagine.

Settling into camp B-54, Capa recalled, "we had a short time left for the usual preinvasion cleaning of rifles and consciences."

Camp A-55, Melun, France. Wednesday, March 21, 1945.

After a few hours of sleep, Frank Dillon and his fellow officers shuffled into the War Room tent for their first formal briefing. They'd arrived at Melun's train station at 02:00 that morning. With only a few minutes to mingle about in the dark, they huddled in small groups passing around cigarettes before the short ride to the airfield.

To a man, they were unaware that their brief occupation of Melun was a mere footnote in this suburb's storied history. Twenty-five miles from the center of Paris, the area had been witness to numerous campaigns, including Roman occupation during the Gallic Wars and a Norman sacking in AD 845. The town surrendered to the English in 1420 during the Hundred Years' War—after a siege that became so desperate the inhabitants resorted to eating rats. More recently, the *Wehrmacht* had passed through Melun, on their way both in and out of France.

Bumping through the town on benches in the back of their trucks, the glider riders of the 194th were hardly noticed as they quietly made their way to the airfield.

The briefing started with an overview of the big picture. "We saw the situation from the standpoint of armies on large maps down to the action of individual regiments, companies and platoons," Dillon recalled.

Confidence was high in Dillon's unit. "I definitely recall there was a general feeling of enthusiasm and eagerness about the operation once we were in the marshaling area."

Dillon would spend the next three days applying the leadership lessons he learned in both Officer Candidate School and while under fire in the Ardennes. VARSITY's dedicated planning time allowed him to employ the fundamentals of Troop Leading Procedures.

After the briefing, he took time to review his orders, ensuring he understood the assigned tasks. He took stock of what they knew about the enemy's disposition, which was inadequate at best. Finally, he studied the maps and aerial photographs, taking note of prominent terrain features in the area.

Dillon knew that sharing as much information as possible with his men helped instill confidence. The more they understood their role in the context of the overall plan, the more in control they'd feel.

He started his platoon's briefing at the high level: the 17th would be in the vanguard of Montgomery's massive crossing of the Rhine, and as part of the 194th Combat Team they were tasked with destroying the enemy in the immediate area and seizing bridges over the Issel.

The plan: thirty-six minutes after Raff's Ruffians jumped, the 194th's gliders would be released over Landing Zone S and land to the east of the two parachute regiments, completing the right corner of Miley's triangle formation. Located in the southeastern sector of the division's area, their landing zone, or LZ as they called it, was a goose egg–shaped area, covering almost four square miles.

The 2nd Battalion would land first, closest to the bridges along the canal. Coming in next, the 1st Battalion, including Dillon's platoon, planned to rush to the bridges along the river. Meanwhile the 3rd Battalion would assemble on the eastern edge of the Diersfordt Forest, just north of the Ruffians. There they were to await orders as Miley's divisional reserve—his fire brigade—ready to attack where needed.

The last four serials into LZ S would be the artillerymen and howitzers of the 680th and 681st Glider Field Artillery Battalions, landing in the center to provide fire support. This contribution of heavy weapons would help the glider riders secure and defend the bridges.

Bringing up the rear of the division's air armada would be over 300 additional gliders delivering supporting units of engineers, signals, forward air controllers, medics, and the towed 57mm anti-tank guns. Their destination, LZ N, placed them adjacent to the British 6th Airborne sector just to the north, in the middle of the airborne perimeter. The heavier 57mm anti-tank guns were critical to Miley's plan. Until those heavier guns arrived, the two parachute regiments would be relying on their new M18 recoilless rifles for defense against German armored vehicles.

Dillon reminded his troops that the plan was just that—a plan. The enemy would largely dictate events and they'd have to stay flexible.

Putting enemy reaction aside, there were some misgivings about the bigger plan. Some of the men were perturbed at having to rely on Montgomery's ground troops for reinforcement. The failure of the British to reach their own airborne troops in Arnhem during MARKET GARDEN still burned.

Additionally, their LZ would be unsecured when they cut loose overhead. Traditional doctrine called for paratroopers to have cleared the area, pushing back enemy gunners to protect the vulnerable gliders during the landing. But Miley wanted all of his troopers to dash directly for their objectives rather than linger to provide security. The glider riders would be on their own.

Together, Dillon and his platoon studied the terrain mocked up on their sand table, pointing out and memorizing details. They took in the relatively flat and rural geography that consisted of cultivated fields and pastures dotted with stone farmhouses and barns. Upon study, the men saw that sections of the LZ were unsuitable for glider landings; pilots would have to watch out for scattered trees, streams, and ditches—all of which might cause a devastating crash.

In their sector the Issel split, the river marking the northern boundary, the canal cutting down into Wesel marking their southern limit of advance. Both the river and the canal were approximately thirty-five feet across with steep banks that made for a natural tank obstacle.

Dillon recalled, "We saw aerial maps and photos taken by reconnaissance planes—sometimes at an elevation of only 50 feet."

A fellow trooper was also impressed: "The briefing was thorough and included photos so detailed that we could pick out German foxholes."

Reviewing the aerial photography, Dillon's men realized the advantages belonged to the Germans, while the disadvantages were all theirs. The fields were scarred with zigzagging trench lines and fortified positions, and the open terrain favored the enemy too—there'd be no cover. They all agreed speed and aggression would have to carry the day.

Dillon's briefing detailed the platoon's specific actions down to each squad, including where they should assemble. They'd be divided between multiple gliders for the ride in and they had to plan for the likelihood of separation during their descent. They'd assemble at a pie-shaped patch of woods jutting out on the east side of their LZ.

Also preparing for the mission in camp A-55 was Clyde Haney. While he sat in a briefing tent, his wife in Janesville, Wisconsin, sat down to write him: "The radio news commentator, Kaltenborn, said on the radio tonight that there were several airborne divisions ready to go into action on the east side of the Rhine River. So I suppose that means you. . . . I'm anxious to know. All Our Love, Vera & Richard."

VARSITY may have been the worst-kept secret of the war.

CHAPTER 8

SECRET DESTINATIONS

Saint-Germain, France. March 11–20, 1945.

Once again Helmut Steltermann went through the ritual of erasing his past to become someone else. For his latest masquerade he'd become Erich Reddig, an *Unteroffizier*—sergeant—in the *Wehrmacht*. His forged German pay book informed anyone inspecting it that he'd enlisted in 1942 and was assigned to the *84 Infanterie-Division*. The picture stapled inside presented the clean-shaven, twenty-year-old émigré in his well-pressed *Wehrmacht* uniform with the silver embroidered Nazi eagle on his right chest. His hair was perfectly coiffed; parted on the side and swept back in the style of the day. What an observer would miss on examining the black-and-white photograph was the intensity behind Steltermann's deep blue eyes and any trace that he was actually an extremely capable intelligence agent.

The ruse was just the latest in his distinguished clandestine career. His first cover identity had been that of a British soldier. In many ways his new alias would be easier to master than that of a Tommy from Manchester; having been born in Mülheim, he spoke German fluently.

In reality Specialist X First Class Helmut Albert Lorenz Steltermann worked for neither the English nor the Germans but rather as an operative of the Office of Strategic Services, America's first clandestine intelligence organization and the predecessor of the Central Intelligence Agency. Established by a Wall Street lawyer in 1941, the OSS was responsible for coordinating the United States' wartime espionage activities in both the European and Pacific theaters. The organization was infamous for its subterfuge and bag of dirty tricks.

Steltermann's intelligence career started routinely enough. The Navy had drafted the nineteen-year-old after his unsuccessful attempt to enlist in the Marines. Sworn in on March 18, 1943, he completed six weeks of basic training before attending radio school in Indianapolis. After the OSS recruited him for his language skills and radio acumen, the organization sent Steltermann to Washington, DC, for a battery of aptitude and personality tests. Once he passed the rigorous selection process, he was shepherded through the training pipeline for the OSS Special Operation Branch, where he mastered land navigation, parachuting, hand-to-hand combat, urban field craft, reflex shooting, and demolitions.

He spent several weeks at a 6,000-acre OSS training camp thirty miles outside of Washington, referred to as Area C. Here he built on his conventional radio skills, learning clandestine communication techniques, Morse code, antenna theory, direction finding, coding, and ciphers.

In February 1944, he shipped out to England on the *Queen Mary*, leaving behind "Honey," his nineteen-year-old girlfriend Anneliese Jaeger. The two had met two years earlier at a church function and had been inseparable ever since. As he sailed across the Atlantic, he wondered when he'd see her again.

Upon arriving in England, Steltermann swapped his American uniform for that of a British Tommy. The OSS changed his first name to Harold and dropped the second "n" from his last name. In this guise he attended Oxford as a subject of the Crown. Having immigrated to America in 1929 when he was five years old, he'd grown up speaking both German and English. Oxford professors helped perfect his High German dialect.

Since his brief tutelage at one of the world's most prestigious universities, Steltermann had completed an operation serving as the wireless operator on a team working behind German lines for six weeks during the Battle of the Bulge. During that time his teammates nicknamed him "Easy" for his easygoing demeanor and the low-key nature with which he accepted his harrowing assignments.

Now Steltermann, recuperating in London, had his R & R interrupted by a summons for "a secret operational mission to a secret destination for the purpose of accomplishing a secret mission in connection with Office of Strategic Services activities." The overly dramatic prose of the order was soon made clear: he'd be leaving for France to join a team of agents currently preparing for something behind the lines.

His partner for the op would be Second Lieutenant Robert Staub, a former enlisted soldier who was half-French and half-German. Staub enjoyed a reputation for determination. Rumor had it that in 1940 he carried his ailing Jewish father over the Pyrenees Mountains into Spain to escape the advancing German Army while his mother remained behind in occupied France. Staub would adopt the guise of a *Wehrmacht* officer to accompany Steltermann.

The two agents received standard gray German uniforms, helmets, field equipment, and forged identification papers. Steltermann was also provided with a *Wehrmacht* driver's license to complement his pay book.

As expected, the exact details of the operation hadn't yet been revealed. They'd learn more in France. Regardless of the circumstances or the nature of the work, the two knew of Hitler's 1942 Commando Order directing that captured Allied saboteurs and agents be executed without a trial. If Steltermann had any concerns, he kept them to himself and took the assignment in stride.

On March 11, he and Staub reported to the OSS office in Paris, located on the once rollicking Avenue des Champs-Élysées. From there they were driven to a safe house in the suburb of Poissy on the edge of the Saint-Germain Forest. Private First Class David Doyle, assigned to the team in a support function, described the three-story timber-and-stucco château and its surrounding grounds as "palatial."

The other members of the group, divided into a headquarters element and the agent teams, were already there. In addition to Steltermann and Staub, the eight other agents were an international collection of Americans, Frenchmen, Belgians, and a former member of the Luxembourg resistance. Steltermann was happy to find fellow Specialist X First Class Leo Jungen assigned as a wireless operator for the headquarters element. The two had met during their naval training in Indianapolis. Jungen, a native German speaker from Iowa, had been recruited at the same time as Steltermann.

Captain Stephen Vinciguerra commanded the sixteen-man detachment, collectively code-named Algonquin. Vinciguerra, a former stockbroker and native New Yorker, was well suited to lead the team. He'd served as an instructor for teams parachuting into occupied France and had jumped into Holland during MARKET GARDEN. There he served as a liaison officer furnishing American airborne troops with reports from OSS agents in the field. While in Holland he observed that the initial confusion of an airborne drop might be an ideal way to infiltrate agents into enemy territory. VARSITY provided the opportunity to validate his hypothesis.

He'd spent the interim working with Ridgway's corps during the battle in the Ardennes, where he infiltrated agents and recruited local informers and guides, as well as secured safe houses for future missions.

At the well-appointed manor Steltermann, Staub, and the others were briefed on their mission: they were going to be inserted into the battlefield during the chaos of the airborne landings to gather tactical intelligence for Ridgway's XVIII Airborne Corps. Vinciguerra had divided Algonquin's agents into four teams of two, all of which were to be equipped with radios. Their reports would be made immediately available to Ridgway's intelligence team via Vinciguerra's co-located field detachment. This allowed for quicker processing of agent reports to supplement information gathered from conventional patrols and prisoner interrogations.

Steltermann and Staub, dubbed Team S&S, had the diciest mission: dressed as *Wehrmacht* soldiers, the pair were going across the Rhine in the back of a glider. For transportation they had a captured a *Kübelwagen*, the German equivalent of a jeep made by Volkswagen. It easily fit in the back of a glider, and OSS communication specialists had already rigged the four-door, open-top vehicle with modified long-range radios. They hoped to land on the edge of the LZ in order to quickly flee into the enemy lines.

Team Poissy, consisting of the two Frenchmen, would be dressed and documented as foreign civilian workers. They were arriving in a separate glider headed into LZ S alongside Team S&S. The agents of Team Alsace, both of whom spoke German, planned to conduct their mission as a composite team: one in German uniform, the other in civilian clothes. Outfitted with standard US Army radios normally mounted on backpacks, both teams were jumping in with Raff's Ruffians, with the thirty-pound SCR-300 radios concealed in civilian suitcases. These two teams planned to take advantage of the pandemonium, slip through German lines, and proceed to predetermined points to set up concealed observation posts and report back to Vinciguerra's command element still on the DZ. They'd then mingle with the inevitable flow of retreating civilians and soldiers, reporting as they went for as long as they felt safe.

Team Student, the two French-speaking Belgians, would also be disguised as foreign civilian workers. As the reserve team, their first priority would be to find a safe place on LZ N to hunker down, await orders, and stand by to pursue intelligence requests as the situation developed.

The missions were a variation of what the OSS called "tourist" drops: shorter-duration assignments wherein the agent made his or her way back to friendly lines on foot after parachuting in as either a German soldier or a civilian. The agents were to make note of enemy troop movements, identifying insignia, depots, and anything else of interest. The risky technique allowed for the collection of intelligence in a sector to the front of advancing Allied army groups. The OSS had given up on infiltrating agents overland through the front line due to the inherent dangers coupled with the risks of minefields and growing enemy counterintelligence measures.

But help from the OSS was frequently unwelcome. Conventional soldiers often viewed the OSS' cloak-and-dagger work as unnecessarily dramatic and of questionable value. Because the organization was known for recruiting Ivy League talent and female spies, its detractors referred sardonically to it as "Oh So Social" or the "Office of Sexual Satisfaction." Indeed, the OSS had already disappointed Brereton's Airborne Army planners by being unable to provide local guides or any intelligence for the immediate vicinity of VARSITY. But Vinciguerra had formed a good working relationship with his counterparts on Ridgway's staff. They'd initially viewed the attached OSS field detachment as a distraction, but in Holland and the Ardennes, Vinciguerra had worked diligently to add value and build relationships with the skeptics. His efforts paid off, and both the OSS and Ridgway's XVIII Airborne Corps staff later complimented his contributions.

The agents had twelve days to prepare. While they worked, Steltermann and Staub practiced their German and sang *Wehrmacht* marching songs, including the anthem of the Nazi Party, the "Horst Wessel Song"—also known by its opening line, *"Die Fahne hoch"*—"Raise High the Flag."

The two knew their cover required absolute attention to detail. During the week, the intelligence section at Airborne Army again vetted their identification, verifying that their "assigned" German units were still in the Wesel area. Issued what captured German rations were available, they supplemented them with civilian provisions. The OSS could only procure two *Wehrmacht* maps of the area, and Allied photoreconnaissance stills and maps complemented the agent's briefings. Like their airborne counterparts they spent a lot of time studying the terrain. They also memorized their ciphers and rehearsed radio procedures.

They planned to conceal their German uniforms under olive-drab American mechanic coveralls, which they would wear when in the marshaling camp and during the flight. They tied down a tarp emblazoned with a large white star over the hood of their *Kübelwagen*. They would remove it once they were off the LZ and driving into the German lines, pretending to be frantically escaping the Allied landings. Both men practiced driving the *Kübelwagen* and familiarized themselves with its working components, including changing tires.

Steltermann and Staub would carry captured German MP-40 submachine guns and pistols. Both operatives were already familiar with the enemy weapons.

★   ★   ★

On Tuesday, March 20, Ridgway sent a quick note to Bud Miley sequestered at camp A-80: "My present schedule may prevent seeing you before you leave. I know you and your 17th will do a splendid job, and give the German another lesson he will never forget. We will support you in every possible way. Good luck and God bless you. . . . Faithfully, M.B. Ridgway."

Undeniably, Ridgway's schedule had been full. Not only had he been attending to VARSITY's hundreds of operational details, but also to those of CHOKER II, the 13th Airborne's new mission. After much haggling, Eisenhower had released the 13th Airborne from VARSITY to support Omar Bradley's crossing of the Rhine at Worms.

Ridgway had also been heavily engaged with VARSITY's contingency planning. The expected "what if" scenarios had to be scrutinized and allowed for—the first "what if" being, what if foul weather grounded VARSITY's aircraft? That eventuality could lead to only one airborne division being able to take off or, alternatively, neither taking off. The planners considered that while conditions might allow troop carrier units in France to fly, the opposite could be true for the RAF in England, where inclement conditions and fog "so thick you could tack pin-up pictures to it" often curtailed flight operations.

Ridgway advocated that both divisions depart from France to mitigate poor weather, but the limited number of airfields on the continent negated this option. Thus the RAF and 6th Airborne would stage and depart from fields on England's east coast.

Should the weather hamper either division, the delivery of a lone division into the combat zone would leave Ridgway with just a single option: seize all of the airborne objectives with the one division. It would require a monstrous improvisation of the plan, spread the division too thin to effectively hold all of the objectives against the assured German counterattack, and create the potential for a slaughter. Ridgway opposed this option vehemently and recommended VARSITY be canceled in its entirety should weather prevent one of his divisions from taking to the air.

Brereton overruled him: in the event the weather "what if" became a reality, the operation would proceed as scheduled. To be disregarded by a senior officer with no experience leading men in ground combat must have been a bitter pill for Ridgway, who'd learned his lessons the hard way. He later wrote that a commander who "forgets that he is dealing with men's lives, and through callousness or stupidity sacrifices them needlessly, is more butcher than battle leader. He is a fool and not a guiltless one."

Ideal weather conditions for the drop would be at least three miles of visibility, a ceiling over 1,500 feet, and winds on the landing zones less than twenty miles an hour. Additionally, Ridgway and the Air Force planners wanted forty-eight hours of clear weather before D-Day to conduct anti-flak operations and interdiction bombing at German airfields.

As the Allied meteorologists noted, March in northwest Germany "is not a pleasant month." They estimated that only half of the days between March 15 and April 15 would meet operational conditions, and they projected that planners could expect, at best, just two periods of uninterrupted good weather for three consecutive days.

Montgomery believed VARSITY critical enough for his crossing that in February he'd agreed to postpone PLUNDER by up to five days should the Air Force be grounded.

But shortly before D-Day he appeared to have a change of heart. Representatives from his 21 Army Group requested Brereton's Airborne Army draft an alternate plan should the weather prevent VARSITY. PLUNDER would launch on schedule, and Montgomery now wanted the two divisions to drop twelve miles farther east, near Erle, within twenty-four hours of weather scrubbing VARSITY's current plan.

Brereton would rush an alternate plan, but only if the British complied with a forty-eight-hour window, not twenty-four, for anti-flak operations and re-briefing the airborne divisions. Montgomery agreed, while Ridgway begrudgingly accepted the two-day lead time, having requested three from Brereton.

The alternate plan had problems. The drop area near Erle was barely large enough to accommodate two divisions, and dropping farther inland would put them beyond the range of friendly artillery, a prerequisite Ridgway had demanded of the British for VARSITY in the first place.

Revising the flight plans was no simple matter either. The Air Force had just finalized the air routes to Wesel on March 20. The alternate drop near Erle, where the concentration of flak batteries was described as "a formidable issue," required reworking the routes from scratch. Any delay of VARSITY created aviation-resourcing challenges for CHOKER II, which was already stretching the number of available aircraft.

The planning materials for the Erle drop—maps and aerial photographs—were distributed to Miley's intelligence officers in the marshaling camps, who tucked them away. No one would distract the troops with "what if's" now; they had plenty of realities on which to focus.

General Ridgway visited the troops at one of the marshaling camps on the same day he'd written Miley the good luck note. Stepping into a baseball game as a pinch hitter, he immediately regretted his vigorous swing at a fastball as the sudden twist enflamed his old back injury. Ridgway waved off the next pitch and left the game as gracefully as possible.

He summoned the corps surgeon to tape up his torso. "The pain was excruciating," he later confessed. "I remember lying on a board in my room one evening, trying to sleep, for lying on a mattress on a saggy Army cot was agony. I was trying not to move a muscle, but even so, spasmodic and convulsive reflex actions of the muscles deep in my back sent such waves of pain shooting through me it was hard not to yell out loud."

He spent the next several nights trying to sleep on the board, his mind filled with apprehension that the injury, which had flared up multiple times during the war, would end his career. The injury may have influenced his decision to cross the Rhine via boat rather than parachute, a choice that would later generate criticism.

•   •   •

Gliders were an essential component of the Allied airborne capability, but also a continual pain point for the logisticians at Airborne Army. Comedian Bob Hope often joked about them in his USO show, telling the audience that "a glider pilot in Texas once asked me to fly with him. I told him I was not interested in his three-knot ship.

" 'What do you mean, three-knot?' he said. 'They're faster than three-knots.'

" 'They'll always be three-knot ships to me,' I told him. 'Not comfortable . . . not safe . . . and I'm not going.' "

For Brereton's planners there was a fourth knot, as in not having enough of them. The demands of supporting both VARSITY and CHOKER II, scheduled to launch within days of each other, taxed their ability to field the required 1,832 serviceable gliders.

There were multiple reasons for the shortages, but the primary one was lack of foresight. While gliders weren't considered expendable, operational landings often damaged them, and recovery required significant logistical effort. Additionally, the constant exposure of the gliders' wood and fabric to rain and heavy storms destroyed many of the aircraft. The Airborne Army needed a steady supply of gliders to maintain its inevitably shrinking inventory, and the shortage reflected both the realities of getting them to Europe and poor asset management.

Gliders were a simple and cheap solution to a complex tactical and technical problem: landing an organized unit of troops in an area inaccessible by traditional aircraft, with weapons and equipment impractical to drop by parachute.

The gliders' lack of engines provided several advantages, not the least of which was a lower production cost. But more significant was the relatively low wing load, which gave them a higher glide ratio and thus a far lower landing speed. A low landing speed required less distance and therefore allowed the gliders to land in smaller fields.

America's combat glider, designated Cargo Glider 4A—or CG-4A— lacked any pretense of aerodynamic aesthetics. Its appearance was so awkward one pilot, upon seeing it for the first time, exclaimed, "It's all right to fly a box car, but why fly it sideways?" Passengers didn't care for the glider's ungainly appearance either, often referring to it as a crate or a flying coffin.

The pilot and copilot sat side by side in the snubbed nose of the glider, which was hinged across the top, lifting upward to facilitate the loading and unloading of cargo. Large Plexiglas windows riveted into the metal frame of the cockpit provided a wide arc of visibility. Under the nose, three parallel wooden skids allowed the pilot to bring the full weight of the glider to rest upon the front end and thus reduce the stopping distance on uneven terrain.

To support heavy loads the cargo area had a heavy-duty, honeycombed plywood floor with a load-bearing capacity of 4,060 pounds. It was durable enough to sustain the wear and tear of loading and unloading jeeps, artillery, and small bulldozers. Removable wooden troop benches served as seating for thirteen combat-equipped men, and four small circular portholes on each side provided limited visibility for the curious. Personnel exits were located on each side of the fuselage.

However functional, the design contained critical flaws. The unique ability to load and unload cargo through the uplifted nose, originally hailed as a strongpoint, became the source of complaints after combat experience revealed that most gliders "ended up against fences, stone walls, or trees, thus making it almost impossible to remove the combat cargo." The cockpit design also required the pilots to scramble back over their seats and into the main compartment, often over the cargo, to egress the glider after landing. A repeated—and repeatedly ignored—request from combat-savvy pilots called for the installation of escape panels in both sides of the nose or a redesign of the large windows to double as emergency exits.

Operation MARKET GARDEN had required using 90 percent of the Americans' on-hand inventory of CG-4As. The Air Force Commander in Chief pressured Brereton to recover as many as possible. He wanted to avoid a repeat of the poor retrieval efforts in Normandy, where 97 percent of the gliders used in the invasion still sat rotting.

Repair and recovery teams scoured the LZs in Holland for salvageable gliders. What they found was appalling: mangled cockpits, broken landing gear, sheared wings, and pilfered instrument panels. In many cases, fabric had been ripped off the fuselage in great chunks for foxhole covers. Troopers also cut out huge sections around the Army Air Force insignia to secure to the hoods of their jeeps so Allied aircraft overhead could identify them.

Using small bulldozers, the mechanics towed the abandoned gliders into corners of the LZs and started field repairs. Using spare parts and components stripped from airframes too damaged to fly again, they cobbled together airworthy gliders. The recovery mission suffered a major setback when a storm swept through Holland, destroying over a hundred of the recovered gliders. Upon conclusion of the two-month effort, only 281 of the 2,000 gliders—barely 14 percent—had been retrieved.

In an embarrassingly belated effort, Brereton advised the War Department on Tuesday, March 6, that the "present production of gliders is insufficient to meet the operational requirement" and requested "all gliders be shipped immediately to this theater on highest priority as soon as they are manufactured." Given the lead time necessary to get a glider from the assembly line to the flight line, it was unclear in which operation Brereton hoped to use these gliders.

Gliders couldn't be flown over the Atlantic like powered aircraft. They had to be delivered via cargo ship, requiring each CG-4A to be disassembled and boxed into five large crates.

At this stage the gliders battled for priority over all of the other vital materiel necessary to wage war: soldiers, food, gasoline, artillery, tanks, jeeps, half-tracks, trucks, weapons, medical supplies, a cornucopia of ammunition, and pallets of bottled beer. Logisticians, with the greed of misers, loaded supplies into every available square foot of cargo space and were often reluctant to surrender the space to the massive wooden crates taking up over 6,000 cubic feet for a single glider.

Once the gliders were unloaded in Europe, the exacting process of attaching the wings and the tail section, securing the cockpit, running control cables, installing tie rod cables, and tightening horizontal tension bars took a well-trained team almost 250 man hours to reassemble a single CG-4A. Even presuming east coast harbors had stacks of crated gliders awaiting a berth, it would still take several weeks for any to arrive—far too late for either VARSITY or CHOKER II.

A few days after his plea for more gliders, Brereton ordered troop carrier units to curtail training flights to avoid damaging any of the remaining gliders.

Through the combined efforts of construction and recovery, Troop Carrier Command confirmed in mid-March that their inventory contained the 906 CG-4As for VARSITY as well as the 926 necessary for

CHOKER II, with the caveat that the two operations would again essentially drain their entire supply.

Watching all the activity from the sidelines were the glider pilots themselves. From their tents they could see the sequestered airborne troops preparing behind barbed wire fences and witness the CG-4As being maneuvered onto hardstands around the runway. While they too had been restricted to base and recognized the activity of an imminent mission, they'd been neither briefed nor given any official details.

As they debated what lay ahead, the demands of supporting both VARSITY and CHOKER II continued to strain Airborne Army's resources, this time in the form of personnel. They finally had enough gliders; now they just needed to find pilots to fly them. Operational flights required gliders to be manned by both a pilot and a copilot, the standard operating procedure stating that "only in emergencies will there be but one rated pilot in the glider."

With these parameters as a barometer, it can be said American glider missions had been operating in a state of emergency since their debut in the November 1943 invasion of Sicily, when the CG-4As were launched with a single pilot in the cockpit. The shortage occurred again in June 1944, during the invasion of France. About that mission, the 82nd Airborne's commander later noted, "Each co-pilot's seat was occupied by an airborne trooper. Incredible as it may seem, these men sitting in the co-pilot's seat had been given no training either in flying or landing the glider, and some of them found themselves with a wounded pilot and a fully loaded glider on their hands as they came hurtling in through flak-filled space." Preferential selection of a copilot in these cases went to one of those troopers in the cargo area who answered positively to the pilot's question of "Have any of you ever driven a bus or a tractor? . . . or a car?"

By MARKET GARDEN in September 1944 the situation had only improved because planners waived the copilot requirement altogether. The Air Force had enough pilots to put two in each cockpit, but doing so would have drained their reserve pool, and thus only a fraction of gliders had copilots. After the Holland operation, the Air Force addressed the perennial shortage by extending the training of stateside C-47 pilots by two weeks to get them dual-rated prior to overseas duty. The transport pilots complained bitterly about being "forced" to fly the CG-4As, but after a handful of flights they were officially rated as glider pilots.

A few weeks prior to VARSITY, Brereton and the Air Force commanders solved their shortage of glider pilots by seeking 300 volunteers from the ranks of troop carrier pilots.

Twenty-year-old Lieutenant Zane Winters, a C-47 pilot, recalled how he volunteered to copilot a glider in VARSITY. A few days before the mission, the squadron commander "called us out, and when we were all lined up, he said, 'will all power pilots who are qualified glider pilots take one step forward.' When we had taken one step forward, he thanked us for volunteering to go on the glider mission coming up."

Fundamental to the glider pilots' experience in World War II was that no one knew what to do with them. The Air Force treated them as second-class aviators, and once on the ground, where they served as poorly organized quasi-infantry, they were forced to rely on their wits and the charity of airborne troops to stay alive. Their commanders ignored them, and the airborne units only paid them attention *after* they became an operational burden.

Many pilots took advantage of the poor coordination. During MARKET GARDEN, hundreds of disorderly pilots struck out on their own, reportedly leaving the battlefield to seek the pleasures of Brussels. Glider pilot Don Pinzel recalled, "They got into Brussels, most of them, and that was it. They never reported out to the airfield to be flown back to England." Some of the pilots, wanting to experience combat, went so far as to attach themselves to airborne units for a few days of fighting.

General Jim Gavin, commander of the 82nd Airborne Division, sent Troop Carrier Command a scathing critique following MARKET GARDEN, describing the glider pilots as more of a "liability" to his division than an asset.

Gavin caveated his evaluation by stating that he did "not believe there is anyone in the combat area more eager and anxious to do the correct thing and yet so completely, individually and collectively, incapable of doing it, than glider pilots." But Gavin made it clear, they were mostly "in the way" and "aimlessly wandering about."

The troop carrier units contributed to the problem by neglecting to properly equip their glider pilots. Only half received maps and those were 1:100,000 scale, upon which one centimeter equaled one kilometer on the ground—virtually useless as a navigational aid once on the battlefield. None of the pilots were issued compasses. The pre-mission briefings, deemed as "unsuitable," failed to orient the pilots as to where and when to assemble.

Without proper equipment or a fundamental understanding of the evacuation plan, it's unsurprising that the pilots became an "amorphous mass, almost without organization."

While Army doctrine dictated that "all glider pilots should be given intensive combat training consisting of basic infantry drill, infantry tactics, and the use of infantry weapons," after-action reports described their training as "short and relatively sketchy." Squad-level drills, where team building and organizational discipline take place, had been largely ignored.

To function effectively, teams must have opportunities to build trust and familiarity; the lack of a consistent organizational structure in the troop carrier units—caused by constantly transferring glider pilots from squadrons not scheduled to fly glider missions to those that were—negatively impacted morale and training, which in turn handicapped the glider pilots' performance on the ground. As one postwar report noted, better organization would have allowed the pilots to follow "a coherent and continuous training program of their own working with . . . slack periods [spent] on realistic infantry practice instead of stagnations during the long periods when the squadrons they were assigned to were preoccupied with non-glider activities."

Flight Officer Bill Knickerbocker candidly recalled, "We were bitter about the up-rootings and were generally treated as the enemy by our new outfits, but we felt the same about them so it worked out evenly."

Changes had to be made for VARSITY. In the aftermath of the criticism, troop carrier units agreed to issue glider pilots the necessary infantry equipment that had been lacking in previous missions: compasses, maps, canteens, and entrenching tools to dig foxholes.

Airborne Army directed the 17th Airborne to provide additional infantry training for the pilots to improve their level of readiness for ground operations. The training taught the pilots vital battlefield skills and served to boost the airborne commanders' confidence that the pilots would be better prepared to carry out their ground assignments. In early March, before moving into their marshaling camps, the glider riders of the 194th jammed into two weeks 200 hours of training for their future chauffeurs.

The curriculum included 75 hours of weapons training with rifles, carbines, submachine guns, automatic rifles, light machine guns, bazookas, grenades, and mortars; 14 hours on the subject of "technique of rifle fire, landscape and field firing"; 18 hours on scouting and patrolling; and a vital 20 hours on "tactics, rifle platoon in defense," with the remainder of the training including map reading, demolitions, hasty field fortifications, employment of land mines, first aid, personal field sanitation, an assembly exercise, and overviews on military government, the organization of an airborne division, and the lawful rules of land warfare.

A vocal minority of the pilots complained about the intensified training—which required fourteen-hour working days—protesting that if they were withdrawn rapidly enough there'd be no need for the extra training. The majority, however, welcomed the renewed focus on their welfare and realized—some from previous experience—that evacuation out of the combat zone had the potential of varying wildly from a few hours to a few days.

★   ★   ★

While air and ground crews remained ignorant of VARSITY's details, squadron commanders and key personnel had already been briefed. Their knowledge, and the need to ready the aircraft for the complex choreography required to get them off the ground in an organized manner, sent activity at the airfields into a fevered crescendo.

Enterprising ground crews headed to an Army ordnance depot outside of Paris to scavenge armor plating from destroyed tanks. They installed the chunks of metal under the seats of their pilots and copilots; at a minimum it provided psychological comfort and reinforced the "flak resistant" seat pads.

To carry the paratroopers' external equipment—bundles of weapons, additional supplies, and howitzers—racks had to be bolted into place on the bellies of the C-47s and C-46s. The para-racks increased drag and fuel consumption but boosted the amount of equipment dropped in the first wave of the assault. The ground crews installed the racks, and the paratroopers would later rig them with the supply bundles.

The C-46s, however, arrived without the Air Force having settled on a safe means to drop external loads. The aircraft was so new that experiments on how to best secure and drop external bundles were still under way in the States. The planes did have the shackles necessary to attach bundles to the belly; missing was a way to protect the bundles from being torn off by the slipstream during flight. Stateside testing had yet to provide a solution.

Flight engineers and ground crews in Europe improvised an answer, cannibalizing the external fuel tanks of P-51 Mustangs. The nose cone of the tanks proved rugged enough to effectively shelter the bundles in flight. In the days before launch, crews procured enough tanks to construct 1,350 hoods, more than enough for VARSITY.

Several crates of self-sealing gas tanks arrived late, causing rushed installations in as many C-47s as possible. The tanks were designed with an internal rubber bladder, which prevented leaking fuel from escaping when punctured by flak. The special tanks significantly reduced fire hazards, but shortages meant many would fly without. None of the newer C-46s had self-sealing tanks, which later proved to be calamitous.

The CG-4A gliders also required last-minute upgrades. Specialized devices such as deceleration parachutes needed to be installed. Troop Carrier Command had requested 3,000 from the States on a high-priority basis, but only received a little over 300 before D-Day. Fortunately, when these were combined with the on-hand stock, there was enough to ensure the majority of gliders would be equipped with the chutes.

Another important attachment was a contraption known as a "Griswold nose," which bolted to the front of the cockpit. The reinforced steel cage resembled a five-point spiderweb and provided protection to the pilots from trees and fence posts. However, a shortage of them, and the thirty-two man-hours required for installation, meant only a handful of VARSITY gliders would go in with this life-saving amenity.

In far better supply were "Corey Skids." When anchored under the cockpit, these four-foot-long, one-foot-wide wooden skis served to deflect logs or other objects that could damage the glider's nose or the pilots' legs. They offered scant protection when compared to the Griswold nose, but were better than nothing.

After retrofitting the gliders, ground crews manhandled them into position on the airstrips. They needed to be maneuvered into their staggered formation for takeoff and made accessible to the infantrymen for loading equipment.

Personal survival equipment continued to flow in daily from supply depots for distribution to aircrews and glider pilots: 1,554 flak aprons, 1,865 flak vests, 1,732 flak helmets, 2,074 flak pads, 361 fighting knives,

650 Thompson submachine guns, 1,187 pistols, 524 carbines, and 1,658 fragmentation grenades.

At camp B-54 Thirteeners lined up in their baggy olive-drab combat uniforms to collect their parachutes. The division's parachute maintenance personnel issued the chutes early so paratroopers could work out the intricate strategy of how they wanted to rig their equipment. Successfully snaking out of a parachute harness while lying down and under fire depends on one's familiarity with the equipment and how it's arranged.

To their advantage, the chutes had the new single-point quick-release harness; but some troopers still viewed the device with suspicion, afraid it might snap open during descent. As the troopers shuffled through the distribution point, each grabbed a main and a reserve parachute. Invariably some glib soul cheerfully commented, "If it doesn't work, just bring it back and they'll issue you a new one."

Jumping with a reserve parachute stimulated debate. *Do we even need this thing?* Many troopers thought dropping at 600 feet made the second chute pointless. By the time you realized you needed it, it would be too late.

Paratrooper John Magill decided he would jump with his. "It was psychologically comforting to feel it on the midriff, and it could be an important buffer against flak or small arms fire on the way down."

Those who wanted them could grab padded canvas containers for their weapons. Miley himself had been the first to prove it possible to jump with a rifle in both hands, but doing so meant the jumper's hands were full in the vital seconds he might need to yank the handle of his reserve. The containers allowed troops to jump with their weapons attached rather than dropping them separately.

The original design required disassembling the M1 Garand rifle into two sections to fit inside. Not ideal. So the riggers of the parachute maintenance company added extensions to the bottom to accommodate an assembled and functional rifle. The elongated container snapped to the right side of the parachute harness. The placement required a jumper to focus his landing to his left to avoid injury by rolling onto the rifle.

Those jumping with tommy guns or M3 grease guns often opted to tuck them under the parachute harness on their right side or secure them horizontally across the top of their reserve parachute. It came down to personal preference. Several troopers taped two of their thirty-round submachine gun magazines together for a quicker reload in a tight spot.

Troopers spent a lot of time configuring their equipment, making adjustments and trade-offs to their loads; it was the one thing over which a soldier had control. And the better soldiers were known to obsess over the details: oiling a rifle to make sure it wouldn't jam; taping up extra webbing to keep it out of the way; cutting the handle off a toothbrush to carry a bit less; packing brass knuckles to make it that much more personal. Being prepared meant a better chance of survival. Magill noticed that the veterans preferred to pack extra ammunition or grenades rather than the additional rations favored by replacements. Magill, a veteran himself, focused first on surviving his landing: "Being equipped with the 45 caliber pistol did give me access to a weapon while descending, even though it was short range in effectiveness."

He was lucky to have a Colt 45. Pistols were much sought after as every paratrooper wanted a sidearm at the ready upon landing. Troopers carried them in hip or shoulder holsters; the more cavalier wore theirs in a cross-draw fashion, emulating their favorite western bandit. Some cut down the holster flaps to ease their quick-draw.

Magill pinned a grenade to the upper pocket of his combat jacket for "quick emergency use immediately upon landing." Weighing just over twenty-one ounces, the Mark 2 hand grenade was light and deadly. Its explosive charge sprayed iron shrapnel up to thirty yards. A fuse delay of four to five seconds gave troopers plenty of time to throw it after pulling the pin and releasing the spoon, which activated the fuse. Anyone familiar with a baseball could easily throw one. Most troopers opted to carry at least two.

Magill also strapped his fighting knife to his right calf for easy access. As a forward observer for the artillery, his primary weapon was his radio, but he'd later have cause to wish he'd armed himself with more than just a pistol and a knife.

Each trooper also picked up an individual first-aid pack. Containing a field dressing, a tourniquet, and a syrette of morphine, the hermetically sealed packet was covered in a lightweight olive canvas that could be easily ripped open. Two attached eleven-inch cotton ties allowed the kit to be secured to equipment.

Having the packet readily available was critical. In the event of injury during the landing it would be up to the individual and his buddies in the immediate vicinity to administer first aid to one another. Medics would be otherwise engaged or simply not around. Standard operating procedure called for using the casualty's aid packet, not your own. You might need it later yourself.

For VARSITY, officers ordered the troopers to tie the packets to the front of their helmets. Not only would this make them accessible, but it also gave the Americans a distinct silhouette. This detail would help friendly troops identify one another at a distance and also serve as a recognition aid to the advancing British. The British airborne troops dropping to the west would in turn don their maroon berets upon landing, giving them their own visual identity.

Each GI in the division also received a US invasion armband. Featuring a five-inch, forty-eight-star American flag printed on weather-resistant oilcloth, the armbands were safety pinned or stitched onto the right shoulder of the combat jacket.

These friendly identifiers were vital when dropping in the midst of enemy troops.

At airfield A-55, Frank Dillon and his platoon sergeant distributed bright yellow silk triangular signal panels to their men as an additional measure to aid friendly identification. Both British and American airborne troops would be wearing them. Each corner had a loop of cord to facilitate tying it down as necessary; the panels could be worn as a scarf, tied over a helmet, across the back, or tied down to the hood of a jeep. Their bright color facilitated both ground-to-ground and ground-to-air identification. The glider riders were instructed to wear theirs looped over one shoulder.

Dillon discovered that they were one short, so he cut the last one down the middle and shared it with his platoon sergeant. Each man laughed and shoved his half into a pocket. Most troopers scoffed at the highly visible bullet magnets, hiding theirs away or securing them around their neck, tucked under the collar of their combat jackets. But the panels would save more than one life on D-Day.

Officers ensured that their men knew the operation's password combination for the first twenty-four hours: "Hither-Thither." The tongue twister would be used as a challenge for anyone advancing on their position at night. Passwords were often selected in the belief that Germans had a hard time pronouncing "th," so even if they tried to use it, their noticeably hard Ds and Ts would give them away.

Troopers could be heard mumbling "Hither" and "Thither" to have the two words front of mind. No one wanted to be shot down by a GI with an impatient trigger finger.

✶   ✶   ✶

Since the airfields were jam-packed with troops and overcrowded with aircraft, station commanders were concerned that even a small German air strike could put dozens of planes out of action. The unfilled bomb craters and confined conditions of the former German airfields hindered ground crews from disbursing the transports and gliders, making them vulnerable to attack. The grounded aircraft were literally sitting ducks, all grouped together as if huddling for warmth.

Anti-aircraft guns ringed each airfield and several American night-fighter units stood on alert to intercept enemy raiders. While the Allies enjoyed air superiority by day, radar-equipped *Luftwaffe* fighters menaced the skies after dark. Earlier in the month, several had cozied up behind a flight of returning bombers and followed them back to their British airfield. Aircrews at a nearby base witnessed the resulting carnage: "A few spurts of gunfire were heard and almost immediately a bomber was seen to go down in a great ball of flame . . ." Peeling away from the attack, the marauders then strafed two other nearby airfields before vanishing as rapidly as they'd appeared.

Hitler's *Vergeltungswaffen*—vengeance weapons—were also proving to be a menace. On the night of March 21, and again at dawn the next morning, the impact of V-2 rockets' high-explosive detonations jolted aircrews and ground personnel from their slumber at airfields in England. The rockets caused alarm, but no one on the base was injured.

Upper-echelon commanders also worried about all the activity drawing the enemy's attention. Montgomery grew increasingly nervous about *Luftwaffe* reconnaissance flights, and his staff hounded the RAF to do something about them. The new jet-engined Messerschmitts and Arados gave the Germans a tactical reconnaissance asset that could range over the front with almost complete freedom. Thwarting them was easier said than done.

The single-seat Messerschmitt Me-262, with its two turbojet engines and sharklike appearance, was the most common nuisance. With nose-mounted oblique cameras, the 262 gave the Germans access to previously unavailable intelligence, and Montgomery wanted them stopped.

The 262's speed was its greatest asset—it flew at an astonishing 530 mph. So fast, in fact, that Allied radar stations couldn't fix its echo accurately—the 360-degree sweep moved too slowly. By the time it came back around, the jet had screamed past.

The RAF assigned the perplexing task of stopping the 262s to units flying the Allies' fastest single-engine fighter, the propeller-driven Tempest, with a max speed of 435 mph.

The disparity was obvious. By the time the Tempests scrambled and were vectored to where the 262 had been spotted, the *Luftwaffe* jets had vanished. Even if the Tempests got close, the 262 easily outran them.

Wing Commanders Peter Brooker and John Lapsley developed a workable solution that they dubbed the "rat code." Within a few days the Tempest pilots renamed it the "bastard code."

Flight Lieutenant Pierre Clostermann, an ace multiple times over with twenty-six kills, recalled how the system worked: "Two pairs of Tempests were permanently kept at a state of immediate alert—i.e., the planes were actually in scrambling position on the runway, with the pilots ready, strapped in their cockpits, their finger on the starter, engines warmed up, radio switched on."

When a 262 crossed the Rhine heading toward the front, the control tower radioed the bored pilots, "Hallo, Talbot Leader, scramble, rat, scramble, rat!"

Alert ground crew fired three red flares skyward to clear the flight pattern and give the rat-catchers priority for takeoff.

The Tempests headed in the opposite direction of the enemy jets, making no attempt to intercept them. Instead, they flew to the 262's airfield, where they took up patrol positions at 10,000 feet to await the returning jet. When the Messerschmitt pilot lowered his wheels and reduced his speed for landing, the RAF swooped in for the kill.

It took the *Luftwaffe* the loss of eight rats in a week before they devised an effective countermeasure.

To counter the RAF tactic, the 262s started returning to base at full speed and at treetop level, which made them tricky to spot. The Germans sent up their own fighter patrols to cover the returning jets and also built an impenetrable "flak lane" of several dozen four-barreled,

20mm anti-aircraft guns. The flak positions, arranged in a five-mile corridor extending from the runway, allowed the 262s to touch down under their protective fire.

"In one week we lost three Tempests which tried to attack an Me-262 in this flak lane," Clostermann recalled. "There was no point in persisting." The wing commanders ordered their pilots to avoid attacking 262s within six miles of their base as the losses were unsustainable.

But the aggressive pilots often ignored orders regarding personal safety. On March 15, Clostermann's rat patrol was circling a *Luftwaffe* airfield, hoping to get lucky, when "suddenly we saw at ground level a Messerschmitt 262 without any camouflage, its polished wings glittering in the sun. It was already in the flak corridor and about to put down. The barrage of tracers was already up to cover its approach. In accordance with the new orders I decided not to attack in these conditions, when, without warning, my No. 4 dived vertically towards the small bright dot which was nearing the long cement runway. Hurtling through the air like a bullet Bob Clark miraculously went through the wall of flak without being hit and fired a long burst at the silvery Me-262, which was in the final phase of its approach. The Messerschmitt crashed in flames just on the edge of the airfield."

Below the rat patrols, *Wehrmacht* troops on the far bank of the Rhine harassed and hampered British efforts to finalize their D-Day preparations. They fired machine guns set on fixed trajectories into areas of known activity, which was more of an annoyance than anything else. But they also lobbed artillery shells, and those were less predictable and far more deadly.

Trucks traveling too fast over dry dirt roads kicked up clouds of dust, drawing enemy artillery fire. Soon MPs posted signs along all of the roads leading to the Rhine, urging drivers to slow down: "DUST MEANS DEATH."

In mutual attempts to frustrate watchful eyes, artillery duels became a sport with no perceived vantage point safe from shelling. Artillery spotters found it more and more difficult to gain elevation for effective observation. German gunners turned Xanten's church tower on the Allied side of the Rhine into a sieve, and in retort, British artillery brought down the church towers at Wesel and Bislich.

Because Montgomery felt that the "dummy supply points, parks of inflated rubber vehicles, aggressive patrolling, construction of faked approaches, and even the use of sound effects" were insufficient to baffle his adversaries, he approved the use of smoke to screen the entire seventy miles of his front.

The airborne commanders and Air Force liaison officers had advised against it. Asked for input before igniting the screen, Brereton and his Airborne Army staff "definitely disapproved" of the tactic, fearing it would mask navigational features from pilots on D-Day. Montgomery took the risk and soon had dozens of smoke generators, built by the Standard Oil Company of New Jersey, intermittently belching out walls of smoke during peak activity. He planned to have them billow continuously from sunrise on March 21 until sunset on March 23, the eve of D-Day.

The smog was primarily intended to conceal the Royal Engineers who had to complete their work along the Rhine's banks. They were responsible for laying causeways down to the river's edge to ease the entry of amphibious vehicles and assault boats. Additionally they taped routes for mustering infantry and installed small, battery-operated signal lamps; these were faced away from the river so they could guide friendly troops but remain out of sight to the enemy.

The engineers found the smoke "a mixed blessing." It screened their activities and prevented accurate German shelling, but the stench was overpowering and several men complained of chest pains.

The swirling clouds of white smoke certainly frustrated German observation, but it would also have unintended consequences on Montgomery's master plan—just as the planners at Airborne Army predicted.

CHAPTER 9

"SATANIC PLAN
OF ANNIHILATION"

German side of the Rhine. Sunday, March 18, 1945.

On the east bank of the river, German lookouts sat in the swirling haze of Montgomery's massive smoke screen. Generated by boiling cauldrons of oil-based wax placed along the far bank, the smoggy veil stymied observation. The smoke drifted across the river and inland over two miles into the German-held side, blanketing the ground and making breathing a chore.

The troops closest to the riverbanks donned gas masks to mitigate the effects of the smog. The continuous wearing of the masks was uncomfortable and shook the morale of the younger troops, who found them claustrophobic. *Feldwebels*—sergeants—in charge of work details, removed theirs, encouraging the younger ranks to muscle through the discomfort. The lookouts continued to stare into the haze, hoping it would part long enough to reveal a hint of what might happen next.

Apart from causing discomfort and frustration, the smoke didn't particularly alarm Schlemm's troops. The veterans were familiar with the Allied tactic and had used smoke themselves the previous autumn to conceal the Rhine's bridges and ferry sites from Allied air raids.

But expecting it and doing something about it were different. Directed by irritated forward observers, Schlemm's artillery batteries lobbed shells into areas engulfed by the thickest smoke on the Allied side. The hope was that the harassing fire had hit something, but it was impossible to know.

Generalmajor Heinz Fiebig, whose troops were deployed around Wesel, contemplated generating his own smoke screen, just to mock his adversaries, but he lacked the means. Montgomery's smoke screen

146

did conceal activity, although for trained professionals it failed to mask where the battle would unfold.

It was "purely a case in which the territory most suitable for AFVs [armored fighting vehicles] would be bound to be used," Fiebig later observed. His reconnaissance patrols had already identified the most probable launch points, and of course, the corresponding landing sites capable of supporting armor on their side were well known to the Germans.

★   ★   ★

Hitler's *Reichsminister*, Joseph Goebbels, held the dual titles of Reich Plenipotentiary for Total War and Minister of Public Enlightenment and Propaganda. Through these two offices, he worked feverishly to drum up support for his "People's War"—a last-ditch effort to defend the Third Reich by any means available.

While publicly Goebbels held firm to the Reich's inevitable victory, privately he believed Germany's only salvation lay in its embrace of total war. If he could inspire every man, woman, and child to dedicate themselves to repelling the enemy, Germany could achieve a stalemate. In spite of overwhelming evidence to the contrary, Goebbels had convinced himself that staggering Allied casualties would divide their alliance and bring them to the negotiation table.

Toward this goal, Goebbels had used his position to drain industries not directly contributing to the war effort and had drafted over 500,000 new recruits for national service. As head of propaganda, he leveraged his ministry's control of film, radio, and print to infuse the German population with a sense of the pending catastrophe should the Allies win the war.

His machinations to stir up fear and national pride were aided by an unwitting ally: the United States Secretary of the Treasury, Henry Morgenthau. Morgenthau had authored *Suggested Post-Surrender Program for Germany*, a proposal arguing for stripping postwar Germany of all industrial production and limiting Germans to an agricultural economy.

The public release of the report, aptly referred to as the Morgenthau Plan, played to Goebbels' favor, and he ensured that radio and newspapers fanned the fires of fear. *Völkischer Beobachter*, the newspaper of the National Socialist German Workers' Party, proclaimed, "Roosevelt and Churchill Agree to Jewish Murder Plan!" The article warned, "The German people must realize that we are engaged in a life and death struggle which imposes on every German the duty to do his utmost for the victorious conclusion of the war and the frustration of the plans of destruction planned by these cannibals."

The *Berliner Morgenpost* referred to Morgenthau's document as a "satanic plan of annihilation," and the *12 Uhr Blatt* concluded that the "aim of these conditions, inspired by the Jews, is the annihilation of the German people in the quickest way."

Goebbels deftly tied these themes to the Allies' stated policy of unconditional surrender, first announced by American President Franklin D. Roosevelt in 1943. Goebbels assured Germans they could expect a reign of terror and enslavement if the Allies were allowed to turn Germany into a "giant potato patch."

The newspaper *Neue Zürcher Zeitung,* a Zürich-based German-language daily journal, recognized Goebbels' success: "The conviction that Germany had nothing to expect from defeat but oppression and exploitation still prevails, and that accounts for the fact that the Germans continue to fight. It is not a question of a regime, but of the homeland itself, and to save that, every German is bound to obey the call, whether he be Nazi or member of the opposition."

Goebbels' plan seemed to have the desired effect. In the battle for Aachen, the first German city conquered by the Allies, just over 18,000 defenders held up 100,000 Americans for five weeks of bitter fighting. President Roosevelt's son-in-law, Lieutenant Colonel John Boettiger, an Army Civil Affairs officer, believed Morgenthau's document was "worth thirty divisions to the Germans."

A declaration issued by the Führer on March 19 reinforced the desperate measures necessary to reclaim a German victory: "The struggle for the very existence of our people forces us to seize any means which can weaken the combat readiness of our enemy and prevent him from advancing. Every opportunity, direct or indirect, to inflict the most lasting possible damage on the enemy's striking power must be used to the utmost. It is a mistake to believe that when we win back the lost territories we will be able to retrieve and use these transportation, communications, production, and supply facilities that have not been destroyed or have been temporarily crippled; when the enemy withdraws he will leave us only scorched earth and will show no consideration for the welfare of the population."

Hitler's order, known as the "Nero Decree," went on to outline the targets of destruction: "all types of bridges, tracks, roundhouses, all technical installations in the freight depots, workshop equipment, and sluices and locks in our canals. Along with this all locomotives, passenger cars, freight cars, cargo vessels, and barges are to be completely destroyed and the canals and rivers blocked by sinking ships into them." Ironically, if carried out to the letter, the order ensured Germany would become nothing more than a potato patch.

One of the more celebrated efforts of Goebbels' call for total war was the Volkssturm—"People's Storm"—a paramilitary organization whose ranks were filled by conscripted civilians: those too old, too young, or too unfit for military service. Organized into company-sized units of sixty to seventy-five men, Volkssturm units were composed of men from the local region who were mustered for active service when their district became operationally relevant. Goebbels claimed his home district alone had marshaled 100,000 recruits.

The militia in the Wesel area had been called up the first week of March, before the collapse of the Pocket. Most of the Volkssturm companies descending on Wesel were from the neighboring towns or villages, but some groups marched as far as forty miles to reach Schlemm's front.

They arrived sporting a potpourri of uniforms and armed with a hodgepodge collection of weapons. Most carried thirty-year-old Danish or Italian Army rifles. The fortunate were armed with modern German K98 bolt-action rifles obtained from replacement depots. An unfortunate few still retained their personal single-shot hunting rifles.

Almost all had managed to scrape together at least part of a military uniform. Some wore their tunics from the last war; most had obtained long gray field coats. Trousers ranged from riding breeches to slacks. Very few had steel helmets. They were identified as combatants by the only consistent part of their uniform: black-and-red armbands. The cloth bands, worn around the left bicep, bore the words "Deutscher Volkssturm" above "Wehrmacht" in white letters and were flanked by Nazi eagles clutching swastikas. The number of silver pips worn on the left collar denoted rank. The more pips, the more authority.

Their motley appearance reflected their military prowess. With the exception of squad and platoon leaders, who'd attended four weeks of training the previous November, most hadn't received any formal military education. Their lack of training aside, the militia's numbers could

be a factor in defensive plans; almost 5,000 *Volkssturm* participated in
the Battle of Aachen. A well-aimed bullet fired by a sixty-year-old farmer
would inflict just as much damage as one fired by a twenty-two-year-old
Grenadier.

As the militia units reached the front, they reported to *Wehrmacht*
quartermasters who supplied them, as stocks allowed, with helmets,
heavy machine guns, *Panzerfaust* anti-tank weapons, and most important, ammunition. Some men had arrived with only forty rounds of
ammunition.

After inspecting eight battalions of *Volkssturm* reinforcements, *General
der Panzertruppe* Heinrich Freiherr von Lüttwitz reported to Schlemm,
"Defense of the Rhine line with these forces would be madness."

Schlemm agreed. He had no intention of anchoring his defense with
militia; their equipment and training were inadequate to operate independently, and they couldn't be relied on to hold their ground. But he
did intend to use them where it made sense. Originally integrated as
platoons in the front line *Wehrmacht* regiments in the event of a hasty
crossing by Montgomery, the *Volkssturm* were gradually relegated to
fulfill the role of rear-echelon troops, freeing more soldiers for the front.

In one of Schlemm's divisions, each regiment had a *Volkssturm* battalion assigned to it. The commanding officer, *Generalmajor* Rudolf
Langhaeuser, recalled how the system worked: "The *Volkssturm* battalion of the 18th Regiment consisted of five companies with high
standard personnel of middle age, most of them minors, whereas the
Volkssturm battalion of the 16th Regiment had rather old and exhausted
men who were no longer fit for line duty. . . . The battalion with the
old personnel was soon filled up with young soldiers fit for action from
the supply services of the Division, while the men from the *Volkssturm*
were transferred back to the rearward services." Behind the main line
of troops, they would construct field fortifications and man checkpoints
at crossroads.

Relations between the militia and the soldiers weren't always amia-
ble. The younger Army conscripts, as adolescents are apt to be, thought
of the militiamen as "useless old dodderers." The constant switching of
assignments and shuttling from unit to unit left the *Volkssturm* unsettled, and they often drew the dregs of rations and billets.

That *Wehrmacht* officers assigned the militiamen menial tasks did little to boost morale either. Wesel's district commander ordered a squad

of eight *Volkssturm* to guard his personal car and cache of wine. The men had a narrow escape when Allied artillery shells destroyed both. Far from their homes and families, the militiamen doubtlessly hadn't envisioned that their contribution to the People's War would be safe-guarding cases of alcohol.

Schlemm continued to bolster the depth of the defenses in his sector despite his bosses' estimate that the Allies would drop farther inland. He'd been suspicious of an Allied airborne attack since mid-February when he anticipated Montgomery might drop troops to cut off the Wesel Pocket. As Schlemm withdrew his anti-aircraft and artillery bat-teries back over the Rhine to take up better stations on the east bank, he cautioned them to the possibility of airborne troops landing among their positions. After it became obvious Montgomery wouldn't pursue a brazen, improvised crossing, Schlemm shifted plans accordingly, con-vinced that when the attack came Montgomery would use airborne troops closer to the Rhine for better support.

Generalmajor Heinz Fiebig, one of Schlemm's division command-ers, agreed. "According to the English system of security, which had been confirmed again and again, one had to expect an attack across the Rhine with very strong forces, exploiting all available means. . . . For our troops it was important, then, to prevent the enemy from crossing the Rhine by all means and to have alert units participate in the smashing of any enemy unit that landed in the depth zone."

But unlike in Normandy, where suspected Allied drop zones were laced with anti-personnel mines and wire obstacles, Schlemm didn't have the resources for such elaborate countermeasures. He did, how-ever, ensure that combat engineers constructed both actual and dummy minefields to channel advancing troops. He inspected machine gun emplacements to verify they adequately covered the suspected DZs. Artillery survey teams also preregistered the locations of potential assem-bly areas. Their data would later allow German gunners to swiftly adjust their howitzers onto these targets.

Observation posts, often manned by *Volkssturm* troops, were set up to provide an early warning network. From these points alarms would send the defenders into action. Because telephone lines or other forms of ground-based communications were susceptible to interdiction by para-troops, alternate signals such as the use of red and white flares or sirens were instituted. Lookouts were reminded, "The commanding general has ordered our highest degree of alertness against airborne landings."

Kanonier Peter Emmerich, a member of an anti-aircraft crew, witnessed all the activity. His battery had dug in three of their quad-barreled 20mm Flak 38 anti-aircraft guns in a cornfield.

"The gun position was worked on, ammunition storage was made," he recalled. "The ammunition cases were filled. As the Allied aircraft had armor plating on their belly, the ammunition cases were filled with first an armor-piercing bullet, next a high explosive followed by an incendiary. As I could see later on, this combination had a disastrous impact."

Emmerich's commander, *Leutnant* Amtmann, ran daily drills to decrease the time it took the crews to reload the guns and change barrels. His shrill commands underscored the anxiety of the imminent action.

"One always talked here about an airborne operation. From where these rumors came nobody knew for certain. However, they seemed to be believed by everybody. The message that was transmitted everywhere was: 'We defend till the last drop of blood.'"

Schlemm and Blaskowitz were improvising, playing a risky shell game, just as they'd done when trapped in the Wesel Pocket. To supplement the fixed anti-aircraft positions surrounding Wesel they transferred in almost all of the mobile batteries from the Netherlands. The move built up the anti-aircraft arsenal in Schlemm's sector to almost 400 guns of various calibers. Crews positioned their guns so that by lowering their barrels they could engage ground targets and serve as anti-tank guns if necessary.

General der Panzertruppe Heinrich Freiherr von Lüttwitz, *Volkssturm* critic and commander of Blaskowitz's XLVII *Panzer-Korps*, contributed as well: "I stripped the entire Ruhr District of its defensive weapons and rushed guns, men and materiel to Wesel."

Visible anti-aircraft positions drew unwanted attention, and the tempo of Allied air attacks increased daily. *Generalmajor* Heinz Fiebig studied the attacks with interest. He was not "particularly impressed" by what he saw. While the Allies consistently targeted his guns in the Diersfordter Wald, those positioned farther east, in the area he suspected would be used as a DZ, were "left relatively undisturbed." Fiebig felt the

Allied fighters didn't press their attacks "with sufficient vigor or determination, retaliatory fire being sufficient to keep attacking aircraft too high to do their job effectively." He thought their efforts "haphazard" at best.

He took solace from the realization the Allies probably believed their efforts to be more successful than they actually were, just as all commanders tended to do. Those positions not under attack often held their fire to remain unmolested until D-Day.

However inaccurate, the attacks against anti-aircraft guns were constant enough to be revealing to the waiting Germans.

"Through very active fighter bomber activity the enemy tried constantly to paralyze our anti-aircraft defense, whereby the impression was increased that in the beginning of the attack, the enemy intended to employ airborne troops," said Fiebig.

Oberst Rolf Geyer concurred: "The targeting of German anti-aircraft weapons made the use of airborne soldiers obvious."

From his position, *Kanonier* Peter Emmerich did not feel so detached about the situation. As his crew witnessed Allied aircraft blasting a neighboring gun position, Emmerich's sergeant muttered, "Many dogs are the rabbit's death. Hopefully it will not be our turn soon."

Schlemm had dogs too: an anti-airborne *Kampfgruppe*—battle group—positioned adjacent to the expected landing areas to serve as quick reaction forces. *Kampfgruppe Karst*, named after its commander, *Generalleutnant* Friedrich Karst, was a recently drafted replacement unit of 4,000 raw recruits. Karst divided his unit into five smaller combat teams, which were organized into companies of well-armed squads. Some squads were designated as special anti-tank units, wherein each man carried multiple *Panzerfausts* in addition to his rifle. The *Faust* was a single-shot, handheld weapon that fired a shaped charge capable of destroying any Allied tank. It required little training and was perfect for ambush-style warfare.

Each combat team contained its own artillery and an assorted collection of six to twelve tanks, ranging from the smaller Mark IIIs up to the behemoth Royal Tiger.

When the drop occurred, Schlemm expected the *Kampfgruppe* to engage the enemy as rapidly as possible—every man would participate in the maximum effort. He knew from his own experience that airborne troops were most vulnerable upon landing, and it was his intention to maul them at that crucial point. At a minimum, 80 percent of the *Kampfgruppe* was to be committed to hasty attacks. Platoon leaders were instructed to attack immediately and independently; speed and initiative would be paramount. They were to deploy straightaway, even with inferior numbers. Some platoons were issued bicycles to reduce their reaction time.

The initial attacks, supported by self-propelled guns, were to be followed quickly by additional waves of small armored forces of three to five tanks with infantry companies and artillery support. Their mission was to wreak havoc among the still-organizing paratroopers and pin them down until the mobile reserves could be brought in to crush them. Hitting the parachutists before they could consolidate and mass their firepower would be critical.

German intelligence efforts culminated on Sunday, March 18, when Blaskowitz and Schlemm received a communiqué from the High Command confirming their suspicions: "[Allied] preparations of forces on the mainland for an airborne landing must be regarded as completed."

Later that same day, Kesselring advised Blaskowitz to place his units in a state of alert as soon as possible. He also recommended setting up more roadblock positions, reinforcing the lookout points with additional sentries, and ensuring Schlemm's *Kampfgruppes* were in position and ready.

Forty-eight hours later Blaskowitz placed the entirety of *Heeresgruppe H* on high alert and ordered anti-aircraft crews to sleep at their guns.

Peter Emmerich recalled leaving the relative comfort of a nearby barn for his crew's gun pit: "I tried to sleep at our gun position. It was a sleep with 'eyes closed and ears open.'

"Everybody received a tent for camouflage. I got myself a spade, and was able to obtain two hand grenades," said Emmerich. "So I was 'equipped' for the final battle."

Emmerich's crew was told, when the enemy arrived overhead, to focus their fire on the lumbering transport planes. Just before the parachutists jumped, the planes would slow down—making them easy targets.

The alert stirred a renewed sense of urgency. *Generalmajor* Heinz Fiebig later recalled that his infantrymen sped up the reinforcement of their defenses "in feverish haste." His units between Hamminkeln and Wesel positioned their heavy artillery to cover both anticipated avenues of approach, from the river and the open fields that might become enemy landing zones. The flat terrain lacked natural cover, so the best countermeasure for an air landing was fortifying farmhouses. While not ideal, Fiebig admitted it was "the best that could be devised in the circumstances."

Schlemm knew preparation and propaganda would only get them so far. The battle itself would be the payoff; hyperbole would not stop the enemy from crossing the Rhine. It would come down to tenacity and relentless violence.

He later wrote, "Officers and men did not fight out of slavish obedience, to benefit individual persons, or from a false regard for honor to prolong the suffering of the German people. Rather, they hoped that the unbroken, stubborn German resistance would cause the enemy, in consideration of his own losses, to grant a mild peace, one which would not ruin the future of Germany."

Schlemm was only being partially honest. The reasons they fought were as personal or as numerous as the men waiting in foxholes. Some fought for Prussian tradition, some fought to defend their homeland, some fought for their comrades, some fought for personal survival, and some fought to defend the ideals of National Socialism.

Regardless, there was mounting evidence that each man would need to draw on the strengths of his individual cause at any minute. Increased Allied reconnaissance flights over the Wesel area had been noted, but the most compelling proof was the systematic attacks on the command structure itself.

The Allied decapitation campaign started subtly enough on March 16 with an air attack on the VI *Flakkorps'* command post. The *Flakkorps* controlled the various anti-aircraft units assigned to Schlemm's I *Fallschirmjäger-Armee*. The attack undoubtedly meant to disrupt coordination between the disbursed flak units.

Two days later another raid was directed at Blaskowitz's *Heeresgruppe H* headquarters near Deventer in Holland. British Typhoons and Spitfires screamed in at first light, dropping bombs and firing rockets at the country estate occupied by Blaskowitz and his staff. Daring the ring of anti-aircraft guns, the RAF fighters zoomed in from 200 feet, making two direct hits on the main house. Blaskowitz managed to escape without injury, but his dentures did not. They were lost in the fire.

Twenty-four hours later it was Kesselring's turn. Using similar tactics, a formation of American P-51 Mustangs swept through mountain valleys to attack the *Adlerhorst*. Their explosive and incendiary bombs were dropped on Schloss Ziegenberg itself, leaving the concealed bunkers a short distance away largely undamaged. While Kesselring and his staff suffered only mild inconvenience, ten civilians perished in the raid.

The pinpoint air raids, clearly intended to dismantle the chain of command prior to the river assault, resulted in Blaskowitz ordering all of his troops into an even higher state of alert. But the precision attacks continued.

In the early hours of March 21, Schlemm was distracted from his morning shave by the low, throbbing sound of approaching aircraft. Seconds later, explosions ripped through the darkened cottage that served as his headquarters. Allied fighter-bombers had dropped their payload directly into the stand of trees concealing the bungalow. The *General der Fallschirmtruppen* was pulled from the rubble, alive, but unconscious and severely wounded.

Exploration of the area revealed what appeared to be a large arrow, formed by piles of leaves, pointing to the smoking cottage. The searchers also discovered a group of displaced civilians sheltering in the nearby woods—in possession of a shortwave radio. Putting potential coincidences and explanations aside, a firing squad executed them on the spot.

✶   ✶   ✶

On the evening of Thursday, March 22, one of Goebbels' propaganda tactics landed a direct hit. In the airborne marshaling camps, GIs listening to Axis radio over the loudspeaker system heard the commentator announce, "Allied airborne landings on a large scale to establish bridgeheads east of the Rhine must be expected. We are prepared."

Apparently, it would take more than MPs and barbwire to keep their secrets safe.

That same night, after hearing the broadcast himself, Brereton admitted to his diary that "the pattern of our air attacks and various other factors [are] easily apparent to all military men, plus information picked up from their agents in France, undoubtedly has warned the enemy that we are preparing an airborne operation, but it's a hundred to one he does not know where and when."

Later Axis Sally chimed in as well: "Come on Seventeenth, we're waiting for you. You can leave your parachutes at home. The flak will be so thick you can walk down."

At camp A-40, Thad Blanchard recalled lying in his cot and hearing the propaganda broadcast and marveling how "they seemed to know exactly where we were all the time." The propaganda ploy had hit its target, setting off a chain reaction of rumors about the pending slaughter.

Blanchard later wrote sardonically, "But we enjoyed the music."

CHAPTER 10

"TWO IF BY SEA"

Allied Airfields, France. Friday, March 23, 1945.

After breakfast, Lieutenant Frank Dillon and his platoon marched out to the flight line. They passed down the long row of gliders, in some cases three deep, staged and ready to be matched with tug aircraft the following morning. Ground crews were still busy towing gliders across the runway with jeeps, installing arresting chutes, directing taxiing C-47s into position, and testing engines. Fuel trucks made their way up and down the line topping off the transport planes. Jeeps darted back and forth carrying officers, messages, or more supplies. Dillon's group proceeded along the seemingly endless string of CG-4As until they found theirs—easily identified by the large "155" scrawled in chalk on its nose. The large numbers individualized the identical gliders and allowed the troops to find their assigned aircraft. The practice gave rise to referring to the passengers as "chalks." As in "Chalk 155, over here!" Or, "Get your chalk loaded up." And so on.

The glider riders at Melun were on the flight line to finish loading their equipment. Two serials would be taking off from A-55, each consisting of thirty-six twin-engined C-47s towing a pair of gliders. Stuffed into the 144 gliders would be several companies of glider infantry, the regiment's anti-tank unit, and part of the headquarters element.

The replacements that had arrived just before the unit departed Châlons were now seeing a glider in person for the first time. Many were unsettled by its apparent flimsiness; one trooper lamented, "It looked like a reinforced egg crate and I admit I had my doubts."

Dillon's platoon split up to stow several cases of 60mm mortar rounds, crates of rifle ammunition, litters, water cans, rations, and entrenching equipment. When done with their gliders, they fanned out to help other squads with the heavier stuff. To ease loading, five or six troopers would heave the glider's tail up and prop it into position with two-by-four braces. This lowered the nose, and once the cockpit had been locked open, jeeps could be gingerly backed in. The width of the cargo area barely accommodated a jeep; it was a tight fit and the maneuver required patience.

Once loaded, everything had to be securely lashed into place, as cargo shifting in flight or during landing could be fatal. Heavier equipment, such as the jeeps and howitzers, was chained to tie-down rings embedded on the edges of the honeycombed-plywood floor, which had an impressive load-bearing capacity of over 4,000 pounds. The lighter equipment—machine gun ammo, land mines, picks, shovels, bazooka rounds, water cans, and boxes of rations—was tied down with hemp rope.

Farther down the same flight line, Captain Bill Barrett supervised as his company loaded multiple gliders with jeeps, trailers, and the regiment's nine towed 57mm anti-tank guns. Barrett's unit used British guns owing to their cargo hold–friendly narrow carriage. The crews worked together on the awkward process of getting the massive "six pounders" (as they were called because of the weight of their projectile) on board: one trooper would put all his weight on the long barrel to lift the tail; then, with several men bracing themselves to pull, others took a running start to get the 2,000-pound beast up the small ramps and into the glider. It was a tight fit, and the blanket-wrapped barrel protruded into the cockpit between the two pilots. During the flight, Barrett's six-man crews would be divided across multiple gliders since only three could ride with the gun due to its weight.

The troopers were responsible for loading and lashing the equipment, but the glider pilots were ultimately responsible for conducting the final inspection to ensure everything was shipshape for a safe flight. Except for a handful of the curious, though, there weren't any pilots around. They were still unaware of tomorrow's operation; to the glider riders waiting for them, it was a typical Army SNAFU.

On the flight line, correspondent Hamilton Whitman watched several troops killing time by partaking in what many thought to be the airborne's official pastime: putting a razor-edge on their M3 fighting knives. For a nineteen- or twenty-year-old airborne trooper, looking cool was part of the job. Sharpening a knife looked cool, and witnesses got the message: *I'll get as close as it takes!* In addition to their fighting knives, troopers often carried bayonets or machetes, sometimes even a backup switchblade, just in case. At least one always needed a finer edge. Of course, a sharp blade had a practical purpose: hacking at half-inch hemp with a dull knife could cost vital minutes, or even lives, when trying to extract equipment under fire.

Not far from the hubbub of the A-55's flight line, glider pilot Bob Casey waited to be told what was happening. Upon entering the mess tent that morning for his breakfast pancakes, he'd learned that all pilots were restricted to base. The twenty-two-year-old Casey had flown glider missions into Normandy and Holland and was considered an old hand. He liked to wear his flight hat at a rakish angle as if to confirm his status. Like everyone else on base, he knew something was going on and was keen to find out what. The briefing would start shortly, at 13:00.

When after lunch Casey finally took a seat in front of the operation's briefing tent, the atmosphere was casual and everyone had on what they'd worn to the chow line: leather flying jackets, short-waisted Ike coats, olive-drab sweaters, garrison caps, flight hats, knit beanies, and various scarves and mufflers.

At other bases the briefing procedure called for squadrons to be trucked to the closest town theater, with armed MPs guarding the doors. But at Melun, the briefings took place outside, in front of a large tent. Regardless of where they were conducted, the format was nearly identical. In many cases, like what occurred with the 439th Troop Carrier Group, the briefing opened with a chaplain's prayer, asking "God to give those going on the mission the strength, the skill and the courage [to] successfully and safely perform their dangerous mission on the morrow."

Briefing officers, with a microphone in hand, stood before large maps—mosaics of pieced-together aerial photographs and oversized drawings of the LZs. The lectures were divided by topic and delivered one after the other over a period of five hours.

After a review of the forecast—visibility was expected to be over four miles with no low cloud cover—the flight routes were discussed. Indicated by colored yarn stretching across the maps the routes were masterworks of intricate mathematics and precision timing. They accounted for the varying airspeeds of C-46s, C-47s, C-47s pulling a single glider, C-47s towing two gliders, and RAF bombers towing the larger British gliders, all of which consumed fuel at different rates, but were expected to deliver the two divisions simultaneously.

The armada of over 1,500 powered aircraft and 1,300 gliders, which was departing from twenty-three airfields in England and France, would converge over Belgium. The town of Wavre, code-named MARFAK, would serve as the Command Assembly Point, over which all serials should pass to change course for their run to the Rhine. At MARFAK the armada would form three lanes, spaced one and a half miles apart, with the glider serials flying at a higher altitude so that the faster parachute serials, which should arrive over the Rhine first, could overtake and pass under them. Casey and the rest of the pilots flying out of Melun would form two serials, which would cut loose over LZ S after the two lead serials—flying out of airfield A-58 with 160 gliders—arrived before them.

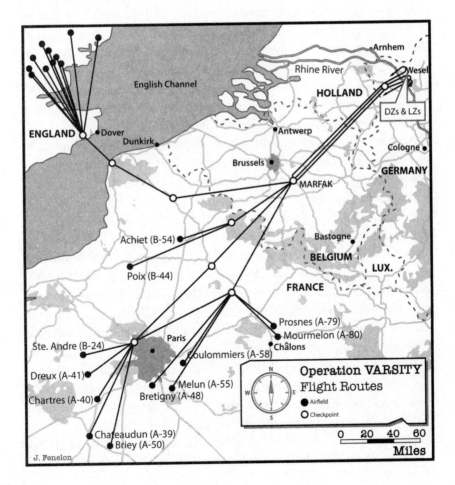

Since it was a daylight flight, navigational challenges figured to be minimal—but both radio beacons and visual markers would be set up at key checkpoints with colored smoke and panels marking each lane's crossing point over the Rhine. Flight leads for each serial would have navigators on board; for those behind them, it was more a case of following the leader. Pilots were to maintain radio silence during the flight in; there'd be no asking for navigation assistance.

In glider pilot Bill Knickerbocker's briefing, the operations officer noted a final navigational checkpoint: "Now this is a small town called 'Wesel,' right on the river bank. But I wouldn't try to use it as a landmark, because when you fly over—it won't be there."

Harder than staying on course would be maintaining the proper airspeed. Rather than attempting to hit their LZs at a specified time, the pilots were instructed to fly a steady course. The daisy-chain effect of lead serials reducing or increasing speed to adhere to their timeline would create havoc for the pilots behind them, who might react by climbing to avoid collisions. The stacked-up formations would result in gliders being released at higher altitudes, exposing them to prolonged enemy fire. Preventing that pandemonium would be more important than releasing the gliders over the LZ at a precise time.

According to the math, and if each flight lead followed the plan, it should take two hours and thirty-seven minutes from the moment the first paratrooper jumped until the last glider cut loose from its tug. Tight formations and proper airspeeds would be critical.

Approach routes and obstacles on the landing zone were pointed out next: fences, tree heights, bomb craters, and houses all needed to be avoided. Each glider pilot received an eight-by-ten, black-and-white overhead reconnaissance photo of the LZ for further study. If he followed the manual, each pilot should "have a definite part of the area assigned to him in which to spot [land] his glider. Such a procedure . . . will eliminate 'jockeying for position' on the approach as is the case when no particular plan is followed."

But Bill Knickerbocker, staring at the big maps through the haze of cigarette smoke, scoffed at the idea of a neat and orderly landing. In his experience, once they cut loose from the tugs the sky would be filled with gliders trying to get to the ground first.

He later wrote, "You could give odds that a large number of gliders would head for the obvious fields." He preferred "to pick a field that looked too short or had other undesirable qualities; then there'd be less competition for the landing space."

But what about the enemy? Despite their tremendous losses, intelligence estimated that the *Luftwaffe* had nearly 900 available offensive aircraft. The mention of approximately 500 single-engine fighters and 75 twin-engine jets got the most attention. The Messerschmitt 262s, in particular, made everyone nervous. Just a week prior almost thirty had swarmed an American formation, downing seven B-17 bombers in just eight minutes. If the 262s pounced on the lumbering unarmored troop transports and gliders, they could wreak absolute chaos.

To mitigate the threat the Air Force had spent the last three days bombing every enemy airfield within flying range of VARSITY's objectives. What they gave away in surprise, they equaled in brute force. Air Force planners hoped that between the damaged airfields and Allied fighter cover the *Luftwaffe* would be kept at bay. Escorting the American column would be over 300 Air Force P-47 Thunderbolt and P-51 Mustang fighters; the British would have another 200 fighters for their column.

Everyone liked fighter cover, but to the pilots sitting in the briefings, the bigger threat was enemy anti-aircraft guns. Almost the entire flight route, except the last five or six miles, would be over friendly territory; but that brief exposure could get plenty hot, thought the pilots.

Pointing at the map, an operations officer said, "Those orange pins represent flak positions, but [we] expect to clean out most of them before Saturday."

The pilots erupted in laughter and jeers at that one. They knew that for every AA gun spotted in an aerial photograph plenty more went undetected. Indeed, the senior operations officer at Troop Carrier Command warned that "antiaircraft fire might inflict losses such as the command had never before encountered." And the RAF's tactical air commander, Air Marshal Arthur Coningham, called flak his "chief anxiety."

Indeed, the Germans kept moving in more guns. They may have been running short on tanks and armored vehicles, but they had plenty of antiaircraft guns. Unknown to the Allies at the time, Germany had committed one-third of its industrial artillery production to building AA guns.

Intelligence officers had been dutifully keeping their maps updated as the guns poured into the VARSITY area. Estimates varied, putting the number of 37mm and 20mm AA guns around Wesel anywhere between 300 and 400, plus another hundred or so of the heavier 88mm guns.

The Allies would be using artillery and fighter-bombers to neutralize the flak threat before the troop transports and gliders arrived. The lighter 20mm four-barreled guns posed the biggest challenge. They were easy to move, hard to locate, and could shred attacking aircraft. In MARKET GARDEN anti-flak attacks nearly decimated two fighter groups. Attacks on identified batteries were being held off until the next morning so as not to spook the AA crews into hiding. Artillery and aircraft would have to cease their attacks before the armada arrived, both to avoid hitting the descending aircraft and to allow the smoke and dust to dissipate.

The briefer concluded his section with sage advice: "Don't forget to wear GI shoes," a reference to possibly having to make a run for it after getting shot down. The quip served as the cue for the next officer, who reviewed escape and evasion procedures. He warned the pilots not to expect help from the locals as they had in previous missions—this was an invasion, not a liberation. If they crashed in enemy territory, they should evade capture and link up with advancing friendly forces. If capture seemed unavoidable, they should surrender to uniformed military personnel. Reportedly, civilians had recently taken to hanging downed airmen or beating them to death.

The biggest news for the pilots going into LZ S was their ground mission: assisting the 194th glider riders in perimeter defense. The glider pilots were being organized into a provisional battalion composed of four companies, each formed by pilots from the same squadron. The senior squadron pilot would serve as the company commander. Like their infantry brethren, the pilots were subdivided into squads and platoons.

Given that Colonel James Pierce's 194th would be a battalion short— Miley had designated his 3rd Battalion as divisional reserve—the 875 glider pilots would bring his regiment almost back to full strength. After the pilots landed, the 194th troopers were to assist in unloading their cargo and move out to their squadron assembly points. From there, having formed into their company-sized elements, they'd occupy their designated positions: two of the companies, including Bob Casey's, would plug gaps in the perimeter; a third would provide protection for one of the field artillery units; the fourth would guard POWs and civilians.

To ensure there were enough copilots to fly CHOKER II, the VARSITY glider pilots needed to get back for flight duty as soon as the tactical situation allowed. Briefers reminded the pilots they were "responsible for reporting promptly to their Group assembly area and will be held strictly accountable for their actions if they fail to report as instructed." Command was serious this time. Any pilot unaccounted for in a timely manner would be reported as missing in action. Pilots would have to weigh their desire for thrill seeking against putting their families through the anguish of receiving a Western Union telegram.

Clutching their black-and-white photograph of the LZ, the glider pilots departed with a lot on their minds. There were those orange pins sprinkled all over the map, each indicating an AA gun. Weapons needed to be drawn from supply; maps needed to be studied; there was a great deal to accomplish before takeoff. And the briefer's closing comment weighed on many minds: "Well, here we go again! May your dog tags never part!"

While the pilots got their brief, Dillon and his platoon sat through a final briefing of their own. Aerial photographs, taken that morning, revealed freshly dug defensive positions on the LZ, and intelligence had confirmed enemy anti-airborne units had moved into position. Dillon knew everyone had the same question, *Do they know we're coming?*

One trooper remembered, "Most of the men were on edge and that news didn't help any."

Word was passed around that, after chow, movies would be shown for those unable to sleep. The films would start at 21:00 and end around 02:00 the next morning. Dillon made the rounds to check on his men and noticed that those not at the movies "spent the last few hours before going to bed writing a last letter, oiling their weapons, putting a razor-edge on their trench knives . . . or going over and over with their buddies the plan for tomorrow."

Clyde Haney, also at A-55, attended a Catholic service to take Communion. Outside in the open air, the men knelt on the grass. One attendee observed, "It was mighty solemn. . . . During that Mass they knelt and bowed their heads more reverently than I'd ever seen it done before. They were going over the Rhine the next morning, and they weren't all coming back."

Corporal Melvin Manley, a glider rider, remembered all the activity as "exciting and thrilling and yet the undercurrent of danger was there." Not everyone, however, found the events exciting or thrilling. To some they were overwhelming—a portent of certain doom. One of Manley's comrades, Private Rocco, shot himself with his carbine. Wounded, he was evacuated to a hospital.

The division's medical unit would be using 53 of the division's 900-odd gliders to carry in their equipment and personnel, including two attached surgical teams. These medics and doctors had the responsibility of triaging and caring for the wounded until such time as they could be evacuated back across the Rhine to field hospitals. The medics loaded jeeps, adorned with red crosses on white backgrounds, into twenty-five of the gliders; another twenty-six would carry the trailers stuffed with medical supplies; and two gliders carried the larger, bulkier medical equipment. There were enough supplies to treat the estimated number of casualties for two days.

The plan called for three of the teams, each consisting of a doctor and three assistants, to join each regiment as soon as they could get their jeep unloaded and find a trailer. The division surgeon had put the medics and doctors through their paces, overseeing a dry run of setting up tents and conducting mock operations to ensure all of their equipment was accounted for and operational.

Also going into LZ N would be six gliders of the division's quartermaster unit. Flight Officer Don Pinzel climbed into the back of his glider to see what he'd be transporting: a jeep trailer filled with body bags. He found such a stark omen unsettling.

One of the quartermasters' duties would be to set up the division's collection point for the dead. The Graves Registration Collecting Point, as it was officially called, would be sited in the southern section of DZ W and close to the area designated for corralling POWs. If timely evacuation of the bodies wasn't feasible, prisoners would dig the temporary graves.

At airfield A-40 near Chartres, Sergeant Thad Blanchard's squad rode out to the flight line in the back of open cargo trucks. Each chalk had crowded into an olive-drab truck; twelve troopers sat on the folding benches along each side, with several others standing in between, holding on to whatever or whomever they could. Each trooper was fully kitted up: helmet, parachute, field equipment, and weapon.

Jumping from the tailgate, Blanchard's men made their way to the

C-47 chalked "41." A line of paratroopers waiting to jump was referred to as a "stick," and each man was assigned a place in the stick order. There'd be no confusion; everyone knew his place.

The troopers assigned to Chalk 41 split up to prepare the aircraft. With the help of the crew they removed the cargo door. The hinges on the trailing edge of the door were taped over with copious amounts of duct tape. Any offending protuberance perceived to be sharp enough to potentially fray a jumper's static line as he went out the door was smothered by tape. Inside the cabin Blanchard inspected the installation of the steel-braided anchor line cable to which the parachute's static lines would be attached, ensuring there were no frayed or broken strands.

The men worked together to rig their five external equipment bundles under the plane. The canvas bundles were big and bulky and, at an average of 200 pounds, awkward to handle. Four of the five bundles contained 940 pounds of 60mm mortar rounds and ammunition for the belt-fed machine guns.

Each bundle required a cargo parachute, which in the case of Chalk 41, were all red-canopied chutes. Colored, twenty-four-foot canopies were used to help identify the contents once on the DZ. The SOP required red and yellow be used for ammunition and explosives, green for signal gear, white for medical supplies, and blue for rations. Those were the standards, but sometimes the troopers had to use whatever color they had available.

Raff's Ruffians also packed up their allotment of M18 recoilless rifles. Following Miley's plea, Airborne Army had managed to procure thirty of them for his division, and each regiment received ten. Troopers constructed wood crates for the recoilless rifles so they could be dropped as external loads; they were too big to jump with individually.

Idle troopers loaded ammo belts and automatic-rifle magazines while others took a break to flip through their recently issued *Pocket Guide to Germany*. The forty-nine-page pamphlet, small enough to fit in the breast pocket, provided troops with an overview of the Nazis' rise to power and some guidance that Mom back home would have agreed with: "Respect property rights, vandalism is inexcusable. . . . Unauthorized appropriation of food stores is contemptible and punishable by court martial." It also contained sage advice: "Be on guard, stay vigilant . . . trust no one but your own kind . . . be fair, firm, aloof and aware."

Others studied their maps. Due to their potentially scattered landing patterns, paratroops required more maps than ground units, who went into battle with their leadership structure in place. Ideally, each trooper got a map. The advancing Allies' demand for paper was such that maps were often printed on the reverse side of captured enemy stocks. Many troopers discovered German invasion maps of England on the back of their Allied invasion maps of Germany.

At the Ruffians' other airfield, A-79, Staff Sergeant Bill Consolvo listened as his company commander, Captain Bill Miller, went over their plan one last time.

Consolvo, a Normandy veteran, recalled, "I thought we were pretty well prepared as long as everything went as planned. . . . What made it interesting was the fact our portion of the sector contained historic old Diersfordt Castle, which we knew would be strongly defended."

Before dismissing his men, Miller held up a folded, worn American flag. Ensuring everyone could see it, he announced, "Before the sun goes down tomorrow night, this flag will fly on high over Diersfordt Castle!"

The troops filed out and returned to their tents. Lying on his cot, Consolvo thought, *Wouldn't it be a thrill to run that flag up the pole tomorrow!*

Sergeant John Chester and his crew at airfield A-80 muscled the crated components of their 75mm howitzer into the racks underneath their C-47. Their six bundles had the added complexity of being daisy-chained together—linked by canvas straps long enough not to interfere with the parachutes while ensuring they didn't separate during descent.

They used a forklift to load the door bundle, an unwieldy combination of the howitzer's two big rubber wheels, the breech assembly, and ten rounds of high-explosive ammunition. Chester sent one of his crew over to the supply tent to procure what they called "broom handles"— thirty-inch dowel rods over which they could roll the 720-pound monster.

Chester kept busy focusing on the task at hand, double- or triple-checking the little details. The big stuff was out of his control anyway, and focusing on specific tasks distracted him from dwelling on his chances of getting injured or killed. He repeated the mantra, *There is a job to be done and I am going to do it!* He suspected his fellow troopers felt the same: "They may have been a lot of things, but they weren't cowards."

Even if they were scared, and certainly many were, they wouldn't have given voice to it. In their 1945 study of combat stress, Drs. Grinker and Spiegel noted that paratroopers almost uniquely adopted an air of "belle indifférence" in the face of fear. The report described the culture that Miley's early efforts to build esprit de corps had helped produce: "These men, who face the highest casualty rates and the most difficult situations in combat, have a group attitude which does not permit free expressions of anxiety and fear. In an atmosphere where everyone is tough, rough and ready for the worst, anxiety cannot be verbalized or socially accepted."

No one volunteered to be a paratrooper so he could serve with guys who wanted to talk about their feelings. Obviously, no topic was off-limits between close buddies—but as a group they wanted to fight alongside the best, and that meant those who concentrated on the job. Competence and trust were their most valued qualities. Discussions of fear and uncertainty were a waste of time and dangerous. No one wanted to go into combat alongside a doubter.

After spending the day preparing their equipment at airfield B-54, the Thirteeners of the 513th Parachute Infantry Regiment now turned to preparing for the next day's jump. Borrowing a warrior tradition from Native Americans, they psyched themselves up by shaving one another's heads, leaving a narrow tuft of hair in the style of a Mohawk.

Life magazine photographer Robert Capa loved it, capturing the ritual with his ever-present camera. A lean paratrooper, with a lathered head and a cigar butt clamped in his teeth, obliged Capa by striking a dramatic pose while shaving his own Mohawk. A Signal Corps photographer caught another group of eleven troopers sitting one in front of another shaving one another's heads with their razor-sharp fighting knives.

Capa later wrote, "Before their battles, the old Huns and Greeks used to sacrifice white horses and other expensive animals. That afternoon, the U.S. airborne soldiers sacrificed most of their hair, shaving it off in Indian fashion."

Over in Able Company's cluster of tents, Texan Lendy McDonald and Ben Scherer spent the evening with their comrades talking and playing cards. They were a tight group, having served together since May 1943—they'd fought leg tankers at Fort Benning; broiled under the merciless sun in North Carolina and Tennessee; braved U-boats while crossing the Atlantic; and to a man had almost frozen to death in the Ardennes. And of course they'd all lost buddies. Who better to jump into Germany with than someone who'd gone through all of that with you? The next day they'd be heading back to a world where everything would be against them—the enemy, the weather, the very ground itself would try to resist them. But today they bonded with those willing to stand beside them. They were a fortunate bunch indeed.

As the sun went down, a deep shade of purple consumed the sky, and Bud Hutton, a reporter for *Stars and Stripes*, stumbled on a curious ritual. A group of Thirteeners had tied one of their own to a fence post, started a fire at his feet, and with their rifles raised over their heads begun whooping and hopping in circles around him. With their Mohawks and emotion on display, Hutton later admitted, "You had to look pretty hard to be sure it was a mock dance." Looking on with interest, Jim Coutts, the regimental commander, nodded to his executive officer and said, "They're ready."

Later that evening the Thirteeners of Easy Company gathered in the mess tent to polish off a few beers. The twelve-ounce cans had to be punched open with a church key, and the contents were low on both taste and alcohol, but that didn't bother the boisterous crowd. At one point Private First Class Stuart Stryker from Oregon jumped up on a table and declared that tomorrow "he was going all out and that he wouldn't be coming back." Whether it was the beer talking or a gift for prophecy, Stryker was right.

Helmut Steltermann and fellow OSS agent Robert Staub, along with Team Poissy, arrived at airfield A-58 under the cover of darkness after having navigated back roads from their safe house in Paris.

Team Algonquin had split up that morning: Team Alsace, with their radios packed in a parachute container, left for airfield A-40 near Chartres, and Team Student proceeded to A-41. Steltermann's team, wanting to avoid unwanted attention during their journey, had covered the hood of their Volkswagen with tarps and stuffed their German uniforms and weapons into duffel bags. A separate vehicle with an OSS colonel on board led the small convoy in case they were stopped by curious MPs. Captain Vinciguerra and wireless operator Leo Jungen, who'd arrived earlier to coordinate their arrival, met them at the gate and escorted them through security. Once onto the airfield, they drove down the flight line to the last glider, Chalk 80.

Their two pilots had been waiting for them and after brief introductions helped the team properly secure the Volkswagen inside. When they were satisfied that everything was in order, the agents retired to their assigned tent for a few hours of rest.

✶   ✶   ✶

It had been a busy day for the senior Allied commanders as well. Brereton was in Brussels settling into his forward HQ from which all of the air operations were being coordinated. Ridgway had moved farther forward and closer to the Rhine to establish his command post. To get a better view of tomorrow's battleground he folded himself into a two-seater light observation plane for a reconnaissance flight along the river's west bank. Cramped next to the pilot, Ridgway prayed that his Novocain treatment would prevent his back injury from flaring up again. The shot did the trick, and he completed his reconnaissance without incident. While Ridgway took care of last-minute details, his former boss, Omar Bradley, held a press briefing.

Whereas American generals had more or less heaped their joint disdain on Field Marshal Montgomery, Bradley served as the British bête noire. He'd elicited the wrath of no less than Winston Churchill, who referred to him as a "sour faced bugger who would not listen."

Almost as if pulling a trick from Montgomery's own playbook, Bradley issued a statement to the correspondents gathered at his 12 Army Group HQ: "Without benefit of aerial bombardment, ground smoke, artillery preparation and airborne assistance, the Third Army at 22:00 hours Thursday evening, March 22, crossed the Rhine River."

Patton, who'd launched a second American crossing some eighty miles downstream from Remagen, at Oppenheim, had egged Bradley to do it. Patton had implored him the night before, "Brad, all the world must know that the Third Army was able to cross before Monty in the north!"

In his memoirs Bradley, recalling the final push into Germany, captured the prevailing American sentiment at the time: "Had Monty crashed the river on the run as Patton had done, he might have averted the momentous effort required in that heavily publicized crossing. Fourteen days of preparation had given the enemy sufficient time to dig in with artillery on the far shore."

He just couldn't resist rubbing it in. The announcement, intended to needle Montgomery the day before his own crossing of the Rhine, clearly juxtaposed the Americans' hasty crossing with the Brits' more deliberate and yet-to-be-executed operation. By referencing four components of Montgomery's plan, three of which were already in progress, and mentioning airborne troops, Bradley displayed a lapse in professional judgment and a flagrant breach of security.

He wasn't alone, though. If the Germans needed any more confirmation of the pending airdrop, they got it from no less than General Eisenhower himself. Later that same day, a commentator at Radio Luxembourg—the Allied propaganda station—read a proclamation addressed to the entirety of the German armed forces:

> *The Supreme Commander of the Allied forces has come into possession of a secret order issued by the German High Command on October 18th, 1943, and supplemented by another order dated October 1944. This secret document orders the execution of Allied airborne soldiers.*
>
> *The Supreme Allied Commander therefore addresses to you the following strict warning:*
>
> *One: You may encounter large or small formations of Allied paratroopers or airborne troops in the course of the war at any time. These units may be dropped behind your lines.*
>
> *Two: You are expressly warned that these units are no "terrorists"— they are soldiers who are doing their military duty in accordance with their orders.*
>
> *Three: The execution of uniformed airborne troops and parachutists is therefore an offense against the recognized laws of warfare.*
>
> *Four: All persons—officers, soldiers, and civilians who have any part in the ordering or carrying out of the above-mentioned order issued by the German High Command will be severely called to account and punished according to military law.*
>
> *The same applies to any order which may meanwhile have been issued or may be issued in the future. The excuse of having "only carried out orders" will not be recognized.*

Sergeant John Chester, a section chief and gunnery guru in the 466th Parachute Field Artillery Battalion. Courtesy of John Chester

Helmut Steltermann, OSS agent and member of Operation VARSITY's Team Algonquin. Courtesy of the Steltermann family

American OSS agents, Helmut Steltermann and Robert Staub, stand in their German uniforms beside their captured Volkswagen *Kübelwagen*. Courtesy of the Steltermann family

Twenty-one-year-old Gene Herrmann, mortarman in the 194th Glider Infantry Regiment, outside his tent near Châlons-sur-Marne.   Courtesy of Gene Herrmann

A squad of Thirteeners use their razor-sharp combat knives to shave each other's heads while waiting in their staging camp near Achiet, France.   Courtesy of Army Signal Corps

American CG-4A gliders on a landing zone in Germany; note the chalk number (34) on the nose.   Courtesy of Don Pinzel, Glider Pilot

Thirteener Jim Conboy, kitted up with his parachute, rifle, and demolitions, waits to board his plane for the flight into Germany.   Robert Capa/Magnum Photos

General William "Bud" Miley at the airfield prior to boarding his C-47 transport for the flight into Germany. He will jump with the Ruffians on Drop Zone W.   Courtesy of Army Signal Corps

Thirteeners boarding their double-door C-46 at Achiet, France.   Courtesy of Army Signal Corps

A platoon of Thirteeners waiting for the green light to exit both doors of their C-46 cargo plane.   Robert Capa/Hutton Archive/ Getty Images

Paratroopers of the 17th Airborne on their way into Germany. This trooper has his static line ready to attach to the anchor line cable.   Courtesy of Army Signal Corps

The Thirteeners landing in Germany; this photo was taken by Robert Capa as he lay on the drop zone.   Robert Capa/Magnum Photos

On the ground in Germany; dead glider troopers cut down by enemy machine guns as they stormed off the landing zone.

American glider troopers search a German field desk for anything of intelligence value.   Courtesy of Army Signal Corp

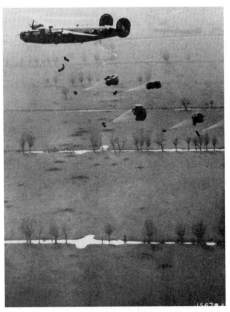

B-24 Liberators flew in on the tail of the massive airdrop to make low-level supply runs.   Courtesy of Army Signal Corps

The cost of defeating the Third Reich: dead paratroopers on the drop zone, killed while getting out of their parachutes.

One of the Ruffians' VARSITY objectives: Diersfordt Castle, as it appeared in the 1930s. The tower in the middle provided sanctuary for stubborn German defenders.

The burnt hulk of a C-47 transport near Drop Zone W; all of the crew perished in the crash.

Several Thirteeners head to their assembly point as a British Horsa glider silently swoops in to land. Robert Capa/ Hutton Archive/Getty Images

A 17th Airborne anti-tank team loading their M18 57mm recoilless rifle. The M18 was far superior to its predecessor, the bazooka. Courtesy of Army Signal Corps

A trooper carries his wounded comrade past a supply container with the bundle's parachute entangled in overhead wires. Robert Capa/Hutton Archive/Getty Images

One of Miley's Thirteeners killed by the Germans before he could disentangle himself from a tree.   Courtesy of Don Pinzel, Glider Pilot

Paratroopers of the 17th Airborne Division taking a break during their advance into Germany.

One of the Thirteeners on a requisitioned enemy bicycle showing off his newly liberated top hat.

His *Werwolf* guerillas largely existed in his imagination, but the Allies didn't know that. Instead they now believed they'd be the targets of fanatical hit-and-run attacks. Goebbels' speech imprinted a more sinister structure on what up until then had seemed, and in reality were, isolated, emotional attacks by foolish civilians.

Any GI unsure of how to react to being fired at by civilians would quickly get over his hesitation. Incoming bullets could kill regardless of who pulled the trigger, and the GIs would shoot back—with overwhelming firepower. All Goebbels had really accomplished was to turn German civilians into Allied targets.

Montgomery's retort came a few hours later. At 20:00 his 21 Army Group instigated PLUNDER with an earth-shattering artillery barrage fired from over 3,400 howitzers. Described as "breathtakingly fearful but, at the same time, exhilarating," the salvos would continually pound the far side of the Rhine with shells and rockets for the next thirteen hours. It was an unprecedented display of Allied might; in some cases the howitzers were so densely packed the gunners had aligned them wheel-to-wheel for over a hundred yards.

An hour into the bombardment the first assault wave of Montgomery's redcoats crossed the Rhine, released with the code words "Two if by sea." Earlier that afternoon Montgomery had received confirmation from Brussels that Brereton had given formal approval for VARSITY. There'd be no postponement of the airdrop. His plan unfolding as designed, the field marshal went to bed at 22:00 as per his custom—it was just another day in a long war. Thirty minutes after he was tucked into his personal caravan, complete with a bathtub and a porcelain sink, a deep and steady droning cut through the cacophony of the artillery barrage. The RAF had arrived.

Over 200 bombers roared over Wesel and dropped payload after payload, pummeling the town for the second time in twenty-four hours. (They'd dropped 1,090 tons of explosives on the town the previous evening.) Reporter Howard K. Smith, witnessing the second raid, said, "It was the single most terrifying spectacle I have ever seen. The entire town was smothered in red and yellow flame, and smoke billowed thousands of yards up in the sky."

Lurking in the shadows of the Rhine's west bank, and occasionally illuminated by the flames from the far side, stood Tommies, Canucks,

From Berlin, *Reichsminister* Joseph Goebbels radioed a broadcast directed at Germany as well, but with quite a different call to action:

The terror raids have destroyed our cities in the West. Our starving women and children along the Rhine have taught us how to hate. The blood and the tears of our brutally beaten men, our despoiled wives and murdered children in those areas occupied by the Reds cry out for revenge. Those who are in Werwolf declare in this proclamation their firm, resolute decision; sealed with their oath, never to bow to the enemy, even though we suffer the most terrible conditions and have only limited resources. But to meet the foe with resistance, to defy him, despising bourgeois comfort and [we] shall face possible death with pride and we shall revenge any misdeed which he commits against our race by killing him. Every means is justified if it helps to damage the enemy.

The Werwolf has its own courts of justice which decide the life or death of our enemy as well as of those traitors among our people. Our movement rises out of our people's desire for freedom and is bound up with the honor of the German nation whose guardians we consider ourselves to be. If the enemy feels that we are easy game and that the German people can be driven like slaves; as he has driven the Rumanian, Bulgarian or Finnish people to deportation, to hard labour in the tundras of Russia or the coalmines of Britain or France, then let him know that in those areas of Germany from which the German Army has been forced back, there will arise an adversary with which he had not reckoned, but who will be more dangerous to him, who will fight without regard to so-called, old-fashioned, concepts and bourgeois methods of war, which our enemies adopt only when these are of advantage to them, but which they cynically reject if these bring no such advantage. Hate is our prayer. Revenge is our battle cry.

As part of his total war stratagem Goebbels had revealed the existence of a Nazi guerilla army and encouraged the populace to join them in terrorizing and assassinating Allied soldiers as they advanced into Germany. Propaganda radio echoed the rallying cry, attempting to ignite a shadow resistance movement hungry to "drown the enemy in a sea of blood."

Goebbels had again demonstrated his adroitness for twisting reality.

and Yanks gazing at the spectacle of shellfire and madness, bitterly hoping that by dawn every German on the other side would be dead.

Airfield A-40, Chartres, France. After midnight.

"Are you awake?"

Sergeant Thad Blanchard wanted to pretend that he wasn't, but instead rolled over on his cot to face Private Harry Pinson, a twenty-three-year-old replacement who'd joined his squad in Châlons.

Blanchard had heard the uncertain tone before and knew what was coming next.

"Sergeant, I'm not coming through this," said Pinson.

Blanchard tried to convince him otherwise, but Pinson remained unsettled by his premonition of death. Blanchard asked if he should go get the chaplain. Pinson shook his head no and asked Blanchard to pray with him.

While Pinson quietly cried in the dark, Blanchard prayed aloud for both of them and suppressed his desire to run screaming from the tent. Blanchard, quietly consoling Pinson, looked down the row of cots and wondered how many of his sleeping men would still be alive the same time tomorrow.

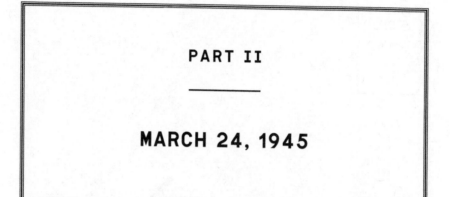

PART II

————

MARCH 24, 1945

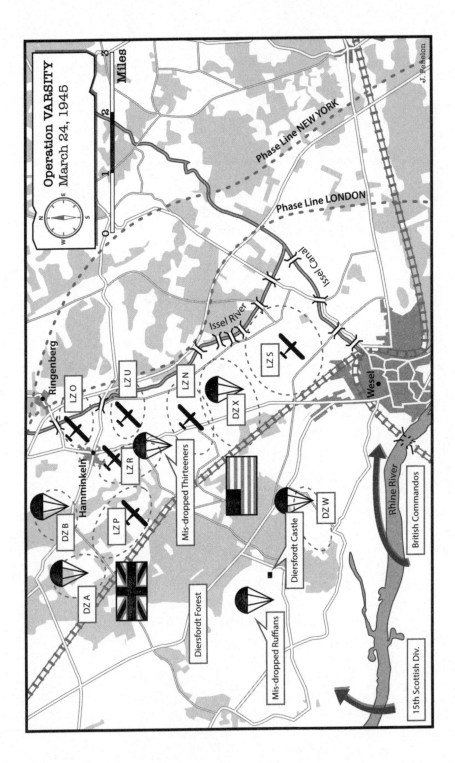

Operation VARSITY
March 24, 1945

Miles

Phase Line NEW YORK

Phase Line LONDON

Issel Canal

Issel River

Ringenberg

LZ O

LZ U

LZ N

LZ S

DZ X

Hamminkeln

LZ R

Mis-dropped Thirteeners

Wesel

DZ B

LZ P

Diersfordt Castle

DZ W

Rhine River

DZ A

Diersfordt Forest

Mis-dropped Ruffians

British Commandos

15th Scottish Div.

J. Fenelon

CHAPTER 11

"GOOD HUNTING"

Allied Glider Airfields, France.
Saturday morning, March 24, 1945.

It was still dark when the sergeants began waking their men: "Okay, off and on. Chow in ten minutes. Fallout, column of twos." Sitting up in their cots, the troopers blinked the sleep from their eyes. For those who'd managed to grab some shuteye the wakeup call came too early; for those who hadn't, it was the end of a long anxious night. Most had slept in their combat uniforms to stave off the cold and save time.

Under the clear night sky they gathered in front of their tents—smoking and waiting. Up above, a nearly full moon hovered over the horizon as if waiting to witness the day's spectacle.

At the mess tents the cooks had outdone themselves. There were fresh eggs. Fresh eggs! None of the usual blue-green instant stuff. There was steak too! And thick slices of fresh bread with plenty of butter. For dessert there was apple pie and ice cream. Hot coffee with a slice of apple pie and ice cream? Any hope the mission would be scrubbed vanished.

Jokes about consuming their last meal wore out quickly. But some, like Sergeant Ted Velikoff, found they didn't have much of an appetite. "I couldn't eat much of my eggs for some reason and threw them away," Velikoff said. "Fresh eggs is something you don't get much of over here." Medic Joseph Moscar, on the other hand, relished his: "The best part of it was we could take all that we wanted and I had six of them. I was thinking that this might be my last one so I ate all that I could."

Opinions varied on the merits of a full stomach. Many troopers believed eating helped ease the dizzying side effects of the motion-sickness pills during their flight. The contrarians preferred to keep an empty stomach until the hard part of the day was done.

After breakfast the troopers returned to their tents to don their equipment. Everyone wore combat boots and the same field uniform: olive-drab cotton-sateen trousers with the Airborne's signature oversized canvas cargo pockets on each thigh. The pockets bulged with grenades, rations, or extra socks. The field jacket, the same Olive Drab No. 7 color as the trousers, was worn over a button-up flannel shirt or wool sweater, and had another four pockets, each stuffed with personal items such as gloves, Army-issued ID card, cigarettes, silk escape maps, candy bars, chewing gum, and squares of toilet paper. Personal items often included photographs of loved ones, a rosary, a pocket Bible, or a lucky rabbit's foot.

Most troopers strapped a fighting knife to the outside of their right leg, below the knee, making it readily accessible. Over the coat each GI wore his webbed equipment or cartridge belt and suspenders. What a trooper attached to his belt varied widely, but ubiquitous items included a metal canteen in its canvas cover and a folding field shovel. Additionally, a man might attach his bayonet, or even a machete, multiple ammunition pouches, a compass, wire cutters, an additional first-aid kit, or a pistol. The suspenders, necessary to support the weight, were a popular place for clipping one or two grenades. Riflemen draped themselves with additional bandoleers of ammunition.

Each man also had a musette bag—a small canvas backpack stuffed with extra socks, underwear (optional), rations, an aluminum mess kit, a small towel, shaving articles, a toothbrush, a rifle cleaning kit, a rain poncho, a sweater, or maybe some extra ammunition.

Around every man's neck dangled his two metal dog tags. Stamped into each were his name, serial number, and blood type. Troopers could also include their religious preference if desired. The savvy taped theirs together to eliminate the clanking. If a man was killed, one tag was to remain with the body and the other was to be collected for reporting. Contrary to popular myth, the tag left with the body *wasn't* to be wedged between the dead man's teeth.

Last was the steel helmet, covered with a camouflage net to which each trooper had tied his parachutist's first-aid packet.

At airfield A-55 Frank Dillon's platoon sergeant called the men to attention and ordered, "Right, face! Forward, march!" The sergeant followed the commands immediately with "Route step, march!" Route step kept the men in formation but allowed them to walk to their own cadence and carry their weapons however they wanted; there was no need for "Left, right, left" parade drill this morning.

Silhouetted against the predawn horizon were long columns of armed platoons walking the mile and a half out to the flight line. Rifles were slung over shoulders, along with plenty of Thompson submachine guns, carbines, and M3 grease guns. Some carried the heftier Browning Automatic Rifles or .30-caliber belt-fed machine guns balanced on one shoulder. A few troopers carried bazookas.

All the men in Dillon's platoon also carried a wool blanket, a common practice among the glider riders. Placed on top of the glider's hollow wood troop benches, the folded blanket provided comfort and several precious inches of layered protection from flak.

As the platoons walked to their assigned gliders, the rising sun chased away the dim gray light of dawn and played off the silent rows of dew-covered aircraft. The formations came to a halt in front of their gliders for a final formality: roll call. The troopers' long shadows spiked across the grass as they stood waiting for their names to be called. With all accounted for, the sergeants ordered them to "Fall out."

The pilots received a last-minute briefing at the control tower before they headed out to the flight line. At the gliders, they found troopers sprawled on the grass, napping, smoking, chewing tobacco, or horsing around. Some had scrawled names on the side of their crate with chalk—monikers such as "Purple Shaft No. 2," "Is this trip necessary?" and "The Towed Target." Some added their hometowns—"Chattanooga," "Texas Rebels," "Brooklyn Bums"—or the names of wives or lovers—"Mabelle," "Josie," "Lady Hellen," and "Ruth-less." Some scurrilous soul scribbled "suicide" in small, tight letters on the engine cowling of a tug transport.

Many of the glider pilots now had to play catch-up. By the time they'd emerged from the previous night's briefing it had been well after dark. The intrepid had climbed over loads with flashlights and made adjustments with their copilots. Others had rousted their passengers to make corrections earlier that morning. As a pilot noted, "There was little margin for error in the loading of a CG-4A; a shift of as little as four inches in the position of a jeep or a cannon would send the glider and its cargo into a dive from which there could be no recovery."

The pilots climbed into their cockpits for final inspections. From the interior it looked like they were sitting in a metal cage, surrounded by a web of exposed pulleys and cables that originated in the cockpit and snaked their way back to control the aircraft's spoilers, flaps, rudder, and ailerons. The pilots ensured that the nose locks had been engaged, verified that the instruments functioned, and checked for a solid feel of the brakes. Copilots helped test the controls for responsiveness and freedom of movement.

Glider rider Frank O'Rourke eyed his pilot, noting that he "looked like a typical glider pilot. Wearing a wool knit cap, an old flight jacket and dress shoes, he was not outfitted for combat. His appearance was so casual that it gave me a sense of security to be in his hands." O'Rourke found the copilot, a reluctant "volunteer" power pilot, "not so inspiring. . . . He looked nervous."

O'Rourke's chalk had agreed that if their pilots got hit on the way in it would be up to their lieutenant, Herman Clausen, to land their crate. Everyone liked Clausen, but they had little faith in the infantry officer's ability to master the fundamentals of flight in an emergency. Still, they agreed Clausen was their best Plan B.

Frank Dillon, over at Chalk 155—now christened *Just One More Time*—noticed his men easing the tension by cracking jokes or horseplay. "There was no outside sign of fear. It was strange to think of fear on such a peaceful, sunny spring day in France with the fighting many hundreds of miles away."

Farther up the flight line, Flight Officer George Buckley and his copilot introduced themselves to the men of Chalk 86. Buckley assumed his passengers were all combat GIs who'd fought in the Ardennes. One of the troopers informed him, however, that most of them were replacements who'd just arrived in France a few days ago and that they all sure hoped Buckley knew what he was doing. Buckley assured the private that both he and his copilot had flown into Normandy and Holland; they expected today's mission would be a "piece of cake." Buckley later admitted, "Little did I know that this was going to be the toughest mission for the Glider Pilots to date."

Lieutenant Zane Winters also readied his glider at A-55. Winters, as one of the "volunteer" power pilots, had been paired with Smokey Ellington, a veteran glider pilot, who warned him against traveling light. Winters heeded the advice—but now he felt like a "walking ammo dump." He carried a .45 automatic pistol with several spare magazines, a carbine with 200 rounds, a satchel of grenades, and an additional 200 rounds of ammo for Ellington's M3 grease gun.

Ellington, after confirming Winters could actually fly a glider, tasked the novice with piloting up until they cut off from the tug, at which point Ellington would take over to land. Winters agreed "100%" with Ellington's plan.

Field Marshal Montgomery had dictated a few words of encouragement to be read to all the troops before departure. In part they read, "Having crossed the Rhine, we will crack about in the plains of Northern Germany, chasing the enemy from pillar to post. The swifter and the more energetic our action the sooner the war will be over, and that is what we desire, to get on with the job and finish off the German war as soon as possible."

The message closed with "Over the Rhine, then, let us go. And good hunting to you all on the other side." The men paused to listen; if they were inspired by Montgomery's sporty metaphors, few showed it. Such bravado from someone not going in with them meant little.

By 07:00 the sounds of engines coughing to life engulfed the airfield. With a belch of exhaust, first the left propeller and then the right burst into full rotation. The cacophony of seventy-two C-47s warming their engines filled what had been a quiet morning with the racket of angry buzz saws. It was time to load. Before climbing into his glider, one flight officer passed around a flask of Cognac for each passenger to take a good luck slug.

The eleven troopers riding with Dillon in *Just One More Time* filed in, stepping around the 600 pounds of equipment, including twelve 60mm mortar shells, secured to the floor. Each trooper positioned his folded blanket on the wooden bench before taking his seat. They'd heard, but didn't bother confirming, that the pilots had steel plates under *their* seats; weight restrictions made such luxuries for passengers impracticable anyway. Dillon loaded last so he could sit as far forward as possible; a view out of the cockpit would help keep him oriented during their run into the LZ. As the platoon leader he wanted to know exactly where they were landing.

The ground crew had staged the gliders for double tow, positioning them at forty-five-degree angles in the direction of flight on each side of the runway so the C-47 tugs could line up and taxi head-to-tail down the middle. Under the supervision of the line chief, crews began the complex orchestration of getting the armada into the air.

Inspectors ensured towropes were properly S-rolled in front of the gliders, while two-man crews took turns hoisting each other onto the nose to secure the towline and give the pilots a thumbs-up before disappearing from view. Maintaining the takeoff tempo of a double-tow combo every sixty seconds meant moving quickly and efficiently.

Dillon, hearing the engines change pitch, leaned into the cockpit, watching from behind the pilots as their tug edged forward, taking up the slack of the S-rolled towrope. All eyes turned to the signalman off to the left of the runway. Tug pilots, unable to see behind them, especially relied on his signal to know when the slack had been taken out of the towropes. As the ropes became taut, the signalman flashed his panel down the runway in a rapid chopping motion — "cleared for takeoff."

Straining under the weight of two gliders, the twin Pratt & Whitney engines whined to full throttle. The initial jolt nosed the glider down onto its front skids as they were dragged down the runway. The pilot trimmed the glider back onto its wheels, and as they hit a speed of about seventy-five miles an hour, he pulled back on the controls to get them off the ground.

Dillon looked to his right, watching as the second CG-4A on double tow took to the air as well. Settling into his seat, he reminded his men not to unfasten their seatbelts until they landed. They'd strapped themselves in for the same reason they strapped down their equipment: turbulence and the potential of a violent landing. Dillon wanted to avoid any needless injuries before they got into the fight.

Behind them hundreds of additional gliders took to the sky, laboriously circling their way up to altitude and sliding into place in the growing invasion armada.

Not all takeoffs went smoothly. Lumbering down the runway, Franklin Dentz noticed the glider next to his was already airborne while his continued scraping along on the wood skids. Even the C-47 had taken off. Realizing what was happening, Dentz and several others unbuckled and scrambled to the rear. The shift in weight sent the tail down and the nose up, creating lift and allowing the pilot to pull up just in time to clear the hedge at the end of the runway.

Pilot Bill Knickerbocker, waiting his turn to take off, pondered the towrope laid out on the ground in front of his glider and daydreamed about nylon. Manufactured by DuPont, the towropes were just one reason why ladies' stockings had become a rare commodity during the war. Nylon's strength and elasticity for stretching a third of its length without snapping made it perfect for towropes. In 1944, *National Geographic* reported that a single 350-foot towrope was equivalent to 1,620 pairs of ladies' stockings. Knickerbocker contemplated the same number of women, holding hands in their stockings, linking his glider to the tug.

Allied Parachute Airfields, France.
Saturday morning, March 24, 1945.

Just after sunrise at airfield A-40, Thad Blanchard and the stick of Chalk 41 arrived at their aircraft; the aircrew weren't there yet. The mood was relaxed but organized. A small group of troopers stepped to the side for a game of craps, throwing more than rolling the dice across the grass airstrip.

When time came to chute up, they divided into pairs for the intricate ritual of donning their parachutes. What ordinarily would have been a straightforward process was now complicated by having to route the harnesses around or over canteens, shovels, weapons, medical aid bags, maps cases, and demolition kitbags. During the chute's opening shock, a misrouted strap could damage equipment or injure the jumper. Special care was taken when tightening the leg straps; no one wanted to ride a pinched testicle on the way down.

It often took a buddy, if not two, to help a trooper into his chute as he struggled to get the chest buckle closed over all of his equipment. The last item snapped into place was the chest-mounted reserve parachute.

Once each trooper was kitted up, a jumpmaster inspected him and made any necessary adjustments. Each aircraft had a designated jumpmaster: an officer or sergeant who'd received specialized training. The jumpmasters were responsible for the stick—inspecting their chutes and controlling their actions during the flight. The final inspection ensured the jumper had properly secured his equipment and that none of it would interfere with the chute's deployment. The last point of the inspection verified that the static line was properly stowed; if misrouted it could prevent a chute from opening and leave a jumper dangling from the aircraft.

Complicating the process was the special equipment Raff insisted his men carry on the jump. Raff had made Blanchard and several other squad leaders jump with the thirty-one-pound machine gun on their last training drop, to prove it could be done. Now Blanchard's squad rigged up Rexford Bass with a chest-mounted satchel for his belt-fed machine gun, clipping it to each shoulder of his parachute harness. It was awkward and so long that it dragged the ground as Bass waddled toward the plane. Glenn Lawson strapped on a British leg bag to carry the squad's light mortar. The bag, attached to his right leg, allowed heavier equipment—like the 60mm mortar or its ammunition—to be jumped rather than dropped in an equipment bundle. Lawson would release it after his main chute opened, lowering the equipment on a twenty-foot suspension line to dangle below him during descent.

Not far up the flight line from Blanchard was Chalk 37, flown by Lieutenant Langland Van Cleef, who'd skipped his breakfast in favor of just a cup of coffee. Chalk 37 was in good hands. Van Cleef, a twenty-five-year-old from New York's East Side, had flown jump operations in Sicily, Salerno, Normandy, and Holland. When he and the aircrew arrived, the stick was already chuting up. As the troops went about their business, they traded insults and cursed their equipment, the time of morning, and one another with the casual profanity of GIs. Several made wisecracks offering their willingness to serve as life insurance beneficiaries. Better a buddy should get the money over their girlfriend's boyfriend back home, right?

As his paratroopers donned their equipment, Colonel Edson Raff drove up the flight line. He stopped at clusters of troopers to stand in his jeep and deliver a short but direct sermon of violence: "Give the goddamned bastards hell, men! You know what to do. Cut out their goddamned guts!"

Raff understood the nature of his profession and the benefits of direct communication. His combat experiences in North Africa and France only served to reinforce his perspective: "Forget good sportsmanship on the battlefield. War is not a refereed football game but the dirtiest game yet devised by human minds. And, if for one moment you feel soft towards that Nazi shooting at you, remember he's trying to kill you and, if he had the chance, he'd drive your dad into slavery, cut your mother's throat, and rape your wife, sister, sweetheart or daughter. You'll get no quarter from him. Give him none!"

Raff's aircraft, Chalk 1, piloted by Colonel Joel Couch, would be the first in the serial of forty-six departing from A-40. Couch, a veteran pilot who'd flown lead missions into Italy, Southern France, Normandy, and Holland, wagered a case of champagne that he'd drop the Ruffians right on target. Raff, who suspected everyone of incompetence, took the bet.

Underneath Raff's aircraft, the stick had strapped two bundles carrying 150 pounds each of radio equipment, another with 175 pounds of medical supplies, and a bundle with 200 pounds of anti-tank rounds for the M18 recoilless rifles.

Sergeant Harold Barkley would be jumping after Raff, who'd be the first to exit over Germany. Barkley, like many others, skipped the issued airsick pills, which tended to induce drowsiness. "We had no time for [that] at the moment, especially at a time when we must be at our best physically and mentally."

By 07:00 the troopers had pulled themselves up the short ladder and into the cabin. Some, saddled with too much equipment, were pushed ungracefully through the cargo door. Jumpmasters stood by, checking each man's name off the loading manifest as he boarded. The pilots revved their engines, letting them idle while waiting to taxi.

Blanchard was unimpressed with his pilot, who, based on the single camel painted under the cockpit window of Chalk 41, had only completed a single supply run. There was no parachute insignia indicating an operational drop. The kid was green.

We'll be lucky to even get to Germany, thought Blanchard. The stick had just strapped into their seats when the pilot cranked the engines and started to roll forward.

Dear GOD! Isn't he even going to warm this thing up? Blanchard almost yelled. He leaned out the jump door to confirm that their pilot really intended to take off, just in time to catch a cloud of exhaust in the face as the left engine sputtered and coughed in protest.

Raff's aircraft rolled down the runway at 07:25, and within minutes the other forty-five planes of the first serial had climbed into the clear blue sky. They would soon rendezvous with the Ruffians' other battalions flying in two serials out of A-79.

As the planes turned toward Germany, Bill Consolvo noted that his fellow troopers were quiet, but looked confident. He glanced over at medic and Normandy veteran Henry Lysek, who gave him a wink and grin—*We'll be fine, buddy.*

•   •   •

At 08:12 the cannon cockers of Branigan's Bastards, Raff's artillery support, lifted off in forty-two C-47s from airfield A-80 to rendezvous with
the Ruffians.

The Bastards were already one man down after a trooper shot himself in the leg. He claimed he had accidently pulled the trigger on his
carbine when placing it in its canvas scabbard, but everyone knew better. He was removed quickly. When courage often hung by a thread,
any sign of weakness or lack of aggression could be infectious—best to
remove the cancer before it spread. Of course, the troopers had heard of
such cases before, and perhaps in more desperate moments a few may
have even contemplated such a scheme themselves. One of the division's most notorious self-inflicted exits from combat occurred in the
Bulge when a trooper pulled a pin on a grenade and wrapped his arm
around a thick tree. The trunk sheltered him from the shrapnel, but his
hand evaporated in the blast. His screams could be heard up and down
the line before morphine dulled his misery.

Within Branigan's serial there were three aircraft carrying a small
divisional headquarters group, including General Miley himself. With
his parachute harness covering the two stars on his epaulettes, he looked
like any other officer in the division. He wore the same olive-drab combat uniform and had tied his first-aid pack onto the front of his helmet
and safety-pinned a large oilcloth US flag on his right shoulder. He wore
a standard-issue khaki cotton tie and binoculars slung across his chest.
He'd donned a kit cap under his helmet against the morning chill. With
a cigarette dangling from one corner of his mouth, he exuded a noncha-
lant calm. But he had plenty on his mind.

Miley had decided to establish his command post on the edge of
Diersfordt Forest, bordering the Ruffians' DZ. He knew that the initial
pandemonium would likely delay by hours his ability to directly influence his units. Unlike ground divisions, whose commanders controlled
events from a relatively safe distance, Miley would be surrounded by the
enemy and fighting for his life along with every trooper on the DZ. It
would be up to the division's junior officers and sergeants to take charge
until wider command could be established.

Since it was possible that Miley's plane would get shot down, the division's chain of command was split up, with the rest of the headquarters
group, commanded by Miley's chief of staff, headed into LZ N on glid-

ers. Landing first, Miley would command from his temporary CP and move to the LZ once local resistance had been overcome.

Next to take off were the Thirteeners at B-54, on their way to DZ X. As the engines of the massive C-46s coughed to life, the troopers in back were engulfed by the smell of oil, gasoline, and hot metal. At 08:00 the first of seventy-two C-46s lumbered down the runway. But after a dozen of the transports took off, the Thirteeners' flouting of superstition finally caught up with them. The pilot of Chalk 13, with thirty-four troopers on board, lost control of his plane when a strong gust of crosswind pushed him off course. The aircraft careened off the runway, just missed the control tower, and plowed through several parked trucks and jeeps. Undaunted, the pilot of Chalk 14, his path clear, thundered down the runway past the wreck, followed seconds later by Chalk 15.

Transports continued to roar down the runway as medics attended to Chalk 13's injured, including the jumpmaster, who'd been thrown out the cargo door. The remaining twenty-three able-bodied troopers loaded onto a truck and sped off to board a standby aircraft. With no time to rig the equipment bundles under their new C-46, they stacked them inside the cargo doors to be shoved out over the DZ.

The C-46s flew in wide, lazy circles over Achiet's airfield while the pilots eased their aircraft into formation. After thirty minutes one of the navigators peered out his glass astral dome and yelled to the passengers in back, "We're on our way."

Troopers squirmed into pockets for cigarettes or gum; some wanted both. The noise discouraged conversation, and the crowded conditions made reaching for canteens or turning to look out the small windows next to impossible. Some managed to nod off for a bit of sleep, or at least pretended to, while others read issues of Stars and Stripes or stared straight ahead, focused on nothing.

Their stoic demeanor masked a natural fear. They were well-trained and disciplined troops who knew that the unspoken rules of their brotherhood required they ignore any misgivings. Some feared they might surrender to self-preservation or fail their comrades through inaction. The most common fears were more immediate: snapping an ankle or breaking a leg in a bad landing. The wisest course was to focus on the task at hand, but that was hard to do when sitting for hours in the back of an aircraft with no distractions.

The men in platoon leader Dean Bressler's plane occupied their time by unsnapping their reserve parachutes and passing them forward to be piled out of the way. Bressler later wrote, "No one needs a reserve chute at 500–700 feet—you only get one chance at that altitude." The troopers in several aircraft didn't bother with stacking their reserves; they simply passed them back to be thrown out the open cargo doors.

Many of the Thirteeners were still leery of the C-46's double doors. In spite of the obvious advantage of facilitating a faster exit—and hence, landing closer together—nobody wanted to jump from what they called the "fucked-up door." The unfamiliar starboard door required routing the static line over the right shoulder instead of the left and making a left turn to jump rather than the customary right out of a C-47. In short, it required split-second thinking at a moment when a trooper was rushing for the door and didn't want to think; rather, he wanted to rely on muscle memory.

Others could care less what door they went out. Sitting in one of the C-46s was twenty-four-year-old Lieutenant Stanley Galicki from Cleveland. He'd joined the Thirteeners after having instructed them at jump school. Described by one of his men as "a killer and an instructor of killers," Galicki had reminded them what they'd volunteered for. His blunt words stuck with many of his awestruck pupils: "In case you gentlemen have forgotten while engaged in the glamorous business of learning how to be a parachutist, you're being paid to be killers. That is your primary, your only function in life: to be *killers*! The parachute is only a means of transportation by which you are delivered to the ground. And once you're there, you do what?"

"Kill!" they yelled.

"What?" Galicki taunted them.

"Kill!" they roared back.

Flying in behind the Thirteeners and headed into the same DZ would be John Chester's 466th Parachute Field Artillery Battalion's serial of forty-five C-47s departing from A-80.

On the back of Chester's helmet, like those of all combat sergeants, was a three-inch-wide, horizontal white stripe—officers' were vertical—to help identify leaders in the heat of battle. Chester, who likened it to "wearing a bull's-eye target on our back," did his best to blot it out with a black marker.

Before boarding, several of the men observed their battalion commander, Lieutenant Colonel Kenneth Booth, in an animated conversation with a circle of pilots, pounding his right fist into the open palm of his left hand as an exclamation point. As the group broke up, one of the artillerymen asked a passing pilot, "What was that all about?"

"Your Colonel wants us to drop you from four hundred feet."

*   *   *

As the troopers had been finishing their breakfast, both the RAF and the US Air Force were already at work, continuing one of the most wide-ranging aerial interdiction campaigns of the war. The raids flown on the morning of D-Day were the climax of an already staggering three-day effort to distract, decapitate, isolate, frustrate, and hamper the enemy surrounding PLUNDER/VARSITY's target area.

To counter the threat of German jets, RAF fighters arrived above enemy airfields at dawn, circling overhead and daring the jets to come up to meet them. They kept the 262s buttoned up until the heavies arrived. The heavies came in the form of 1,430 four-engined bombers who dropped over 4,000 tons of ordnance on the sixteen enemy airfields within range of VARSITY. The Air Force lost eight bombers on the raids, which followed attacks that had upended the same airfields three days ago. The airfields were hit again in case the Germans had repaired them.

Another wave of almost 3,500 bombers hit communications centers within fifteen miles of Montgomery's crossing sites. By targeting the Germans' ability to disseminate information and coordinate the movement of their reserve troops, the Air Force hoped their attacks would improve VARSITY's chances of surprise. Another sortie of 2,090 bombers dropped 6,600 tons of bombs on other military facilities, while fighter-bombers swept in, attacking anything that moved on highways or rail lines. Targets within VARSITY's actual assault zones, however, were excluded from heavy bomber raids for fear of cratering the LZs and DZs.

Adding to the bedlam, a stream of US B-24 bombers flying from their Italian bases made a round-trip of 1,500 miles to pound Berlin, sowing confusion and further hampering communication. The RAF also made diversionary attacks, hitting several oil facilities in the Ruhr area as well as a major rail center fourteen miles southeast of Wesel.

The Allies intended their air raids to overwhelm the German defense system. By striking everywhere at once they planned to stretch the system to the breaking point, rendering it mute.

Over Wavre, Belgium (MARFAK).
Saturday morning, March 24, 1945.

Two hours into their flight American transport pilots watched the long string of British aircraft approach from their left. The 6th Airborne Division had departed from eleven airfields in England at 07:09 and slipped into the air route's western lane for their run into Germany.

Reveille for the British troopers had come early that morning at 02:45. Their serials carried over 7,000 airborne troops and rendezvoused not far from the coastal town of Dover before heading across the English Channel. Their route took them over Waterloo, where their ancestors had fought to turn back Napoleon's conquest of Europe in 1815.

The British flight hadn't been without incident—they'd already lost thirty-five gliders en route, owing to snapping towropes or structural failures. Several witnesses watched in horror as one of the massive Hamilcar gliders folded in on itself, with the light tank it was carrying and all those on board pitched into the air as the glider cartwheeled to earth. Like their American counterparts, neither the British glider pilots nor their passengers had parachutes.

Those on the ground in Wavre had a front-row seat as the two air columns came together to form the war's largest single-day airborne armada. Close to 500 British and American fighters, darting about like angry hornets on all flanks, added to the impressive display. Drawn outside by the reverberating sound of droning engines, the populace gazed skyward as the aircraft passed overhead at a thousand feet. Those who wanted to watch the entire spectacle would have to wait over three hours for the armada to pass.

First in the American column came the parachute serials. Organized into tight groups of nine aircraft, known as a V of Vs, each group was subdivided into elements of three transports. The lead aircraft of each Vee flew forty feet in front of his two wingmen, who'd positioned themselves fifty feet or so off his wingtips. Behind and flanking the three lead aircraft were the other two Vees, trailing by approximately 160 feet and offset on each side by just 250 feet. A tight formation ensured a tight drop pattern. The next Vee of nine aircraft trailed by a thousand feet, and so on. As one witness observed, "The troop carriers looked sleek and well fed, bobbing up and down in the air currents and propwash like fat men in a gentle surf."

After the parachute transports came the glider serials. The double-tow formations were first, formed into small elements of two tugs with the lead sixty feet in front of the second, who followed behind and to the right. Carrying the gliders into LZ S, the eight double-tow serials—made up of approximately forty tugs—were spaced ten minutes apart to provide a buffer for the varying speeds.

The single-tow gliders going into LZ N were last in the column. They flew in "pair of pairs" formations: four tugs, staggered to the right. The lead pair, flying slightly offset from each other, led the second pair in an identical formation. The seven single-tow serials of forty to forty-eight aircraft flew with a seven-minute gap between each.

In the gliders, the men watched the parachute serials overtake them. Most had been quiet during the flight due to the overwhelming racket. At a tow speed of 110 miles per hour, with the howling wind slapping at the gliders' canvas sides, the cacophony made anything but a yell impossible to hear.

Communication between glider pilots and tugs fared little better. The technology was simple enough: a closed-loop intercommunication system, the wire for which was stretched between the two aircraft, attached at points along the towrope. It gave pilots a secure and interference-free method of plane-to-glider communication. But of course it was never that easy.

"To us they were a joke," said Bill Knickerbocker of the communication systems. As the taxiing C-47 dragged the towrope along the runway, the sets would often short out due to abrasions in the commo wire. If the wire survived takeoff, the noise in the glider's cockpit made most transmissions inaudible anyway. The setup also required a headset, which prevented wearing a steel helmet against flak. The intercom, when working, allowed tug pilots to communicate their position along the route and advise on distance to the LZ—information any situationally aware glider pilot should have been noting for himself. If the system went out, a member of the tug's aircrew would stand in the astrodome and flash colored lights back to the glider: steady red for approaching the LZ and green for release. Blinking red meant *Do not cut loose, we'll go around for another pass.*

In Private Seymour Tuttle's glider, the copilot turned back into the cabin and yelled for him to remove the troop door and take a look at the wing—the flaps were not responding as they should. Tuttle did as requested, but his visual inspection failed to reveal the cause. Now Tuttle had his own problem. The outside airstream prevented him from locking the door back in place, so he had to prop it up with his right arm for the rest of the flight. Occasionally, Tuttle's buddy, buckled in across from him, would express the sentiment of everyone on board by yelling, "Son of a bitch!"

Turbulence jostled the gliders, causing strain on the pilots and discomfort among the passengers. Rough air could buck or drop a glider several feet in an instant, keeping all on board alert and nervous.

Reporter Howard Cowan wasn't enjoying the flight either. He kept eyeing nearby crates of anti-tank mines and wondering if the bumpy ride could set them off. His apprehension had started before boarding when one of his fellow passengers looked at the graffiti on the side of his CG-4A and observed, "We ought to paint 'V-3' on the side of it, it's so full of explosives."

Peering out the port window, Cowan saw the glider on short tow drift uncomfortably close to his own, causing him to worry about a midair collision and the resulting sensation of tumbling into the fields below. His unease shifted into a higher gear when a sudden downdraft sent the trooper next to him cracking into the steel framework; the man had made the mistake of taking off his helmet and now blood poured down his face.

To relieve the physical stress of trying to tame their bucking gliders against the turbulence, many pilots alternated flying to give each other a break. In Flight Officer Paul Swink's glider, his "volunteer" copilot wanted to do most of the flying, which Swink thought was great. He'd never had the luxury of a copilot, having flown his other operations solo.

Swink periodically yelled over to see if he could relieve the other man, to which he always got the same reply, "No!"

As they got closer to the Rhine, Swink asked him if he was getting tired. "Hell yes, I'm tired, but I want you rested enough to land this thing!"

For many passengers the turbulence became unbearable, unleashing waves of vomit. Luckily in Chalk 155, only one of Dillon's men barfed. Those next to him passed the trooper's helmet, full of vomitus, back to the last man, who dumped the mess into the glider's rear.

The misery in Private Charles Knight's glider was more widespread. One trooper's airsickness set off a chain reaction. Then Knight, already feeling queasy, threw up, followed by the rest of the squad. "That glider was one big stinking mess," said Knight, recalling the sickly, sour odor.

A formation of 240 B-24 bombers took up a trailing position behind the transports and gliders. Having lumbered into the sky from their air bases in England at 09:10, they'd crossed the English Channel at 1,500 feet before turning northeast toward Brussels. Their route was nearly identical to that flown by the serials delivering the British 6th Airborne who had preceded them. With virtually every C-47 in Europe towing gliders or dropping paratroops, an aerial resupply would either have to wait for returning aircraft to be loaded, which would take hours, or use another type of aircraft. The four-engine B-24 Liberators got the job.

The timing of the Liberators' supply drop had to be as close on the heels of the personnel drop as possible. Three factors contributed to this: Montgomery's artillery units along the Rhine were still on cease-fire until all of the low-flying aircraft had cleared the airspace; dropping supplies immediately allowed the airborne troops to collect what they needed while assembling rather than waiting on the DZ; and, finally, planners wanted the bombers-turned-supply-aircraft to enjoy the benefits of the same anti-flak operations that the VARSITY transport aircraft did. Tragically, everyone overestimated the effectiveness of the Allies' efforts to eradicate enemy AA positions.

The B-24 crews had been briefed the day before on their unconventional cargo mission. Typically, their behind-the-lines missions stretched hundreds of miles, but their target on this trip would be a mere 8,000 feet into enemy territory. Also different: instead of cruising over Germany at 25,000 feet, they'd be dropping supplies at less than 300. It would be a novel experience for aircrews that considered 13,000 feet an unusually low-level run.

The briefer had left no doubt as to the urgency of the mission: "This is it! Tomorrow will be the most important mission you will have flown. In importance and preparation it rivals the landings of June 6, for tomorrow, 24 March, is another great assault against Germany across the Rhine. . . . Our part in this assault is the dropping of vital equipment and supplies to the boys who have already crossed. The accurate dropping of these supplies is absolutely essential for the success of the boys on the ground."

With its cavernous bomb bay, some creative thinking, and a few modifications, a B-24 Liberator could carry 2.5 tons of supplies. The cargo, divided into twenty or twenty-one bundles per aircraft, consisted of fuel, food, signal equipment, medical supplies, and a cornucopia of ammunition ranging from .45-caliber tommy gun bullets to 75mm howitzer shells. In each bomber the heaviest and bulkiest of the supplies were loaded into twelve A-5 equipment bundles and shackled into the bomb racks. To facilitate even more cargo the ball turret was removed, along with the escape hatch in the aircraft's rear. The additional bundles placed near the open, five-foot hole of the ball turret, and those clustered around the escape hatch would have to be pushed out manually.

Like the supplies dropped from under the C-47s, each bundle was attached to specific color parachutes to aid identification of the contents. The chutes' static lines were attached to various anchor points within the bomber, and the crew had to navigate the spiderweb of lines and cargo straps carefully to avoid entangling them. If properly jettisoned, all twenty-one bundles could be out in six seconds.

Up front in the lead serials, the Ruffians witnessed the changing terrain as they neared Germany. The view below shifted from colorful villages and idyllic farms to an ominous gray landscape of shell craters, splintered trees, and burnt fields. Olive-drab convoys congested the roads, bringing forward tanks, engineering equipment, sections of pontoon bridges, and countless other supplies.

As they pushed closer to the Rhine, the pilots passed back the ten-minute warning. The troopers' solitude was interrupted by the jumpmasters who stood to face their sticks, bellowing, "Get readddyyyyy!"

"Get ready!" the stick shouted back.

CHAPTER 12

"LET'S GO!"

09:48–13:00. Drop Zone W, Germany.
Saturday, March 24, 1945.

At the Rhine, PLUNDER was in full swing. British landing craft slogged across the thousand-foot-wide river, coxswains straining to steer their craft in the choppy water. Artillery shells whistled in, sending geysers exploding skyward, rocking the boats and showering the soldiers crouched against the gunwales. The odd bullet pinged off the closed steel exit ramp. Volleys of friendly shells sailed overhead seeking targets on the far bank.

German *Fallschirmjäger* used interlocking fields of machine gun fire and mortars to keep Allied troops pinned to the riverbank in Montgomery's northern sector. Until the vigorous defense could be broken, no help could reach the British airborne troops from that quarter. The delays irritated one of Montgomery's commanders, who later wrote, "It says a lot for the morale of those German parachute and panzer troops that with chaos, disorganization and disillusion all around them they should still be resisting so stubbornly."

Farther south, in Wesel, the British Commandos—who'd entered the town on the heels of the previous night's plastering by the RAF—also struggled. The Germans there had dug into the rubble, using it for cover and forcing the Commandos to fight their way forward block by block. Subsequently, they too were behind schedule in seizing their side of the Issel Canal where they intended to link up with Miley's glider riders.

Progress *was* being made, however, in the center sector. British regiments spearheading the assault there had secured their objectives along the banks and were poised to take advantage of the VARSITY landings farther inland.

• • •

197

Gathered on a small balcony overlooking the Rhine, Winston Churchill, Eisenhower, and Montgomery observed the full grandeur of the crossing.

Churchill, who was seated and wearing a light overcoat, scoped the far bank with a pair of binoculars while Eisenhower and Montgomery stood to better survey events downriver. From their vantage point they would have seen assault craft chugging across the Rhine and, in the skies above, British and American fighters pirouetting into German flak positions on the far bank.

But the fighter pilots circling overhead at 4,000 feet were having trouble spotting their targets. Montgomery's smoke screen and clouds of dust from the artillery barrage had partly obscured the ground below. The reduced visibility forced the fighters to lower altitudes so they could get a better bead on their targets. A few made passes at treetop level to draw enemy fire so their circling comrades could spot the muzzle flashes.

Once the American pilots in their P-47 Thunderbolts located a target, they made attack runs in serial fashion. Flying in groups of twelve, the first pair dove at a flak position dropping bombs, which exploded into large mushroom clouds of smoking tentacles. The second pair of Thunderbolts then swept in, firing their wing-mounted rockets into the resulting inferno. The final pair made a low-level strafing pass to gun down survivors.

As one P-47 pilot recalled, "When you're flying 20 feet off the ground and hitting infantrymen with eight .50-caliber guns, [it becomes very obvious] that war is a very messy sonofabitch of a business."

Inevitably, several of the Thunderbolts were hit. Pilot Charles Bennett's aircraft took several rounds coming out of a strafing run. With his aircraft trailing smoke, Bennett climbed to make a turn for home but quickly lost airspeed as his engine died. Just as the plane started to roll, Bennett slid back the canopy and threw himself out. Drifting under his fully deployed parachute, he watched the corkscrew smoke trail of his aircraft as it crashed into the Rhine. He landed in the river soon after and treaded water, edging his way to the friendly bank from which a small rescue boat headed toward him.

From their balcony vantage the assembled Allied leaders directed their attention back to their side of the Rhine as the booming British howitzers fell silent. Filling the void was the deep, unrelenting drone of overhead engines rising from behind them.

Churchill jumped to his feet. Clasping his cigar between two fingers he pointed skyward and announced the arrival of VARSITY's armada, "They're coming! . . . They're coming!"

A correspondent just upstream witnessed the same wave of aircraft: "There seemed no end to the lines of planes which streamed slowly in from the west." His fellow journalists and groups of nearby soldiers all stared upward, "none speaking, enthralled with one of the greatest spectacles of this or any war."

In the armada's vanguard were the C-47s carrying the paratroopers of the 507th Parachute Infantry Regiment into Drop Zone W. Raff's Ruffians had arrived eight minutes early, cutting short the Allied artillery barrage that had shifted to target known anti-aircraft positions.

After hearing the command "Get Ready!" the troopers had opened the gates of their static lines' snap hooks.

"Staaaand up!" shouted the jumpmaster over the throbbing engines and rattling airframe. The troopers struggled to their feet and formed a single line. Holding the static lines in their left hands and bracing themselves with their right, they faced the rear of the aircraft where the jumpmaster stood by the open cargo door, wind ripping at his uniform.

"Hoooook up!" he bellowed. With a metallic click, the troopers snapped their static lines onto the anchor line cable and yanked down to engage the gate's safety button, locking it closed. They fought for balance as they used their right hand to insert, then bend the safety pin into place, making sure the snap hook couldn't come undone. The jumpers were now engaged in the mechanics of a familiar ritual, and the activity achieved exactly what was intended—establish order and provide a distraction from racing hearts and nauseous stomachs.

The jumpmaster's fourth command—"Check equippppppment!"— sent the stick into the motion of each man inspecting the man in front of him. A tug of the chute on his back confirmed the trooper behind was doing his job; he verified that the static line was routed correctly and the risers were still tucked in. Sitting and shifting in cramped quarters for hours could loosen straps or unbuckle snaps. After each man was satisfied with the trooper's equipment in front of him, he inspected himself: Helmet fastened? Reserve ripcord accessible? Weapon case still secured? Static line over the left shoulder?

Once the stick had completed their inspections, the jumpmaster gave them the fifth command: "Sooooound off for equipment check!"

The last man in the stick started the count by yelling "Eighteen OK!" and slapping the man in front of him on the right leg. "Seventeen OK!" "Sixteen OK!" and so on. The first man stomped his right foot onto the metal deck and yelled to the jumpmaster, "All OK!"

At this point the jumpers were worked up and ready. Wanting to capitalize on their adrenaline, a jumpmaster might inquire, "Is everybody happy?" The entire stick would shout back in unison, "YES!"

With a nod, the jumpmaster skipped the next command of "Stand to the door." Instead, he slid his static line past the open door and pivoted into the position himself. With his left foot forward, he gripped each side of the door frame, ready to propel himself out.

The second and third jumpers crowded forward, sliding their static lines past the door as well, ready to follow the jumpmaster. Those at the end of the stick craned to see what was going on up front or focused on the pack of the man in front of them, waiting to surge forward.

Over the steady pitch of the engines the troopers heard the muffled *crumps* of exploding flak getting closer. From the far side of the river German anti-aircraft gunners targeted the incoming transports. Several near misses burst between the planes, showering the thin skin with what sounded like gravel. The concussions jarred the aircraft and buffeted the men inside.

Sounds like heavy flak, but not as bad as we expected, thought many. Despite the nerve-rattling experience, they were right—it could have been worse. As the lead serial they benefited from being first in, and most of the enemy gunners were still recovering from the air attacks. The following serials would have it much rougher.

In the cockpits pilots scanned for visual checkpoints. Yellow smoke drifted up from a clearing on the west bank, marking their crossing point.

"Rhine!" yelled the jumpmasters leaning back into the plane. Pilots toggled the jump light on. It glowed red: the two minute warning.

Flying the lead aircraft, Colonel Joel Couch crossed the Rhine at a sharp bend near Xanten and began his three-mile run into DZ W. Flying parallel to the river, Couch kept looking for his main checkpoint: a narrow lake formed from the old riverbed. But he was having difficulty spotting it through the haze. Although the generators for Montgomery's smoke screen had been turned off the day before, the smoke hadn't dissipated and had drifted inland, reducing visibility to less than a mile.

As the pilots descended to 600 feet, the troopers in back felt the planes reduce speed to 110 mph for the jump. They could smell the smoke from the battlefield below. They were anxious and wanted out—anything was better than being tossed around in the back of a flak magnet.

Couch, flying over open farm fields, flipped the jump light to green at 09:48.

"Let's go!" shouted Raff, launching himself out the door. Wide-eyed troopers rushed forward to the sound of shuffling boots on metal decking and static lines scraping along the overhead anchor line cable. Less than ten seconds later, all eighteen jumpers were airborne.

Sergeant Harold Barkley followed Raff out the door. After his chute opened, he narrowly avoided colliding with an equipment bundle that had drifted toward him; getting entangled would have likely collapsed both chutes. Drifting backwards, Barkley peered over his shoulder. He was heading directly for a barn with a large section of the roof blown off. He floated into the loft, landing safely on several hay bales.

Keying off Couch's plane, the other pilots flipped on their jump signals as well. Most troopers tumbled out rather than jumped, snapping their chins down onto their chests to keep their heads clear of the chute's deploying risers.

Forty planes behind Raff's, Thad Blanchard stood next to the jumpmaster in the open cargo door. Blanchard was desperate for fresh air. The plane reeked of vomit; most of the stick had thrown up, and he was gagging to keep his breakfast down. Passing over the Rhine, Blanchard watched plumes of shellfire chase assault craft as they shuttled back and forth.

In less than two minutes they were over the DZ, and Blanchard's assistant squad leader yelled words of encouragement to the stick as they crowded toward the door. But something was wrong; they hadn't reduced speed.

Blanchard finally felt the pilot cut back on the throttle. "Go! Go!" he yelled, just as the jump light flashed green. The men shuffled past Blanchard, tumbling out one by one. Rexford Bass waddled along, trying to keep up with the man in front of him while not getting his bulky machine gun chest bag caught on anything. He should have been the first man to exit; placing him in the middle of the stick slowed them all down. Blanchard slapped Harry Pinson on the back as he went past, "I'll see you on the ground!"

As the last man, Blanchard slid his static line past the door and followed Pinson out.

Fighter pilot Wallace King watched in horror as anti-aircraft guns unleashed into the lumbering transports. He dove his Thunderbolt between two C-47s to make a low-level gun run, hurtling below the transports at just a few hundred feet above the deck. When he pulled back up to break away at the end of his attack, he almost clipped a paratrooper descending under a full canopy. King recalled, "It was obvious we could do no more without putting our guys at risk. The sky was filled with flak. . . . But the wave of cargo planes continued like giant caterpillars crawling toward the raging inferno. From my position, it seemed like a horrendous failure."

Blanchard's opening chute jarred his fall to a near stop. His stick's delayed jump and sluggish exit had put him out over the far end of the DZ. Bullets snapped past him, cutting holes in his parachute canopy. Realizing he was drifting over the trees, Blanchard abandoned his Hollywood daydream of returning fire with his tommy gun. In less than twenty seconds he would be crashing through the branches.

A jumper could steer his chute only in the most rudimentary sense. Pulling down on one of the four risers long enough could influence the direction of drift, if the trooper had time and good upper-body strength—a prayer didn't hurt either. Blanchard reached up, grabbed two of the chute's risers, and pulled them deep into his chest, attempting to collapse the canopy to increase his rate of descent. But he was already too low.

Smashing into the branches, he crossed his ankles and covered his face, hoping to fall all the way through the tall trees. The top branches snagged his chute, leaving him dangling just a few inches off the ground. He didn't have long to marvel at his luck. A German machine gun crew had spotted him. As he struggled to undo his harness, bullets chewed up the tree around him. With a twist and a punch, Blanchard's quick release dropped him to the ground. Racking the bolt on his Thompson, he fired a quick burst in the direction of his unseen enemy.

"Get me down!"

Rolling over, Blanchard saw Sergeant James Lyons from Chalk 37 caught high up in a nearby tree. Blanchard, firing another burst toward the machine gun, yelled, "For God's sake cut yourself down before that gun blows you away!"

When hung up in a tree, a jumper had few options: attempt to climb down with all of his combat equipment, pull the ripcord on his reserve and lower it as a means to climb down, or use a length of rope carried for the purpose. But with machine gun fire getting closer, Lyons' choices were limited. He popped his quick release and fell to the ground in a heap.

The two sergeants each heaved a hand grenade in the direction the bullets were coming from and dashed back through the trees toward the DZ. They found most of the platoon waiting. Raff's insistence that they jump with their heavy weapons had paid off. Blanchard's squad already had Bass' belt-fed machine gun and Lawson's 60mm light mortar ready for action.

Sergeant Robert Vannatter, jumping with Chalk 26, had a completely different experience when he hit the ground. He landed not far from a German soldier who ran toward him. Before Vannatter could get to his rifle, the German embraced him warmly, helped him out of his parachute, and surrendered. Vannatter may have bagged VARSITY's first POW.

Just as they had been briefed, the nearly 500 Ruffians of the first serial moved north toward the tree line. The murky haze reduced visibility to 300 yards and obscured landmarks, but the fields crossed with irrigation ditches and hedgerows appeared to match the sand tables and maps they'd studied. As frustrating as the smoke was, it worked both ways—the Germans had a difficult time identifying their shadowy targets. Incoming fire from the same high ground the Ruffians were heading toward snapped by high and wide.

Officers and sergeants gathered troopers and formed them into squads and platoons as they moved. While a few men had landed in the trees, most had dropped in concentrated groups, allowing them to organize rapidly.

Raff herded 200 men toward the closest wood line. He knew that the next serial should be dropping in four minutes, and it never hurt to clear the DZ as fast as possible.

Four or five entrenched enemy machine guns opened up on them

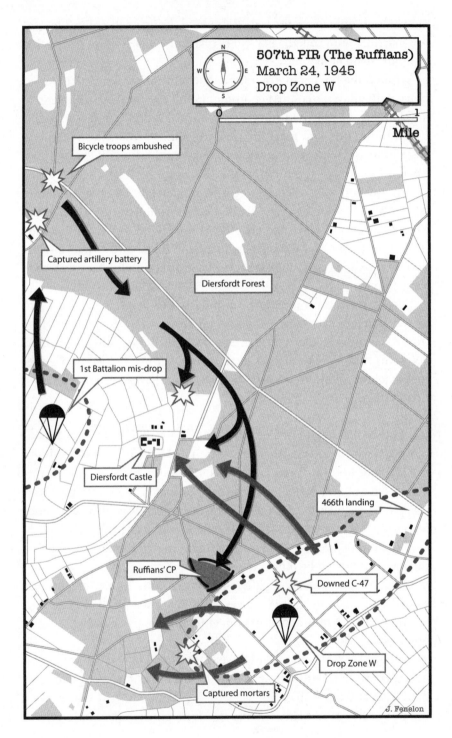

507th PIR (The Ruffians)
March 24, 1945
Drop Zone W

0   1
Mile

Bicycle troops ambushed

Captured artillery battery

Diersfordt Forest

1st Battalion mis-drop

Diersfordt Castle

466th landing

Ruffians' CP

Downed C-47

Captured mortars

Drop Zone W

J. Fenelon

as they advanced. The German machine gun, known to GIs as "Hitler's buzz saw" for its high rate of fire—twenty rounds a second—made a distinct sound, almost like ripping fabric. The veterans instantly recognized the terrifying stutter.

Squads of troopers went to ground while others bounded forward. This was Infantry Tactics 101; there was no swagger about it. Its choreography was simple: sprint forward in full kit, throw yourself to the ground, fire a few rounds while your buddy dashed forward—roll to your feet to repeat it all over again. Someone was always shooting and someone was always moving. If everyone did his job, the tactic overwhelmed the enemy by keeping their heads down or making them traverse too quickly to be accurate. It was effective, deadly, and exhausting work. The Ruffians closed with the Germans and swept into their positions. They suffered some casualties, but killed more of the enemy and captured their first prisoners.

Raff's group, organizing in the wood line, could hear a battery of German heavy artillery firing from the northwest. The guns would have to be dealt with; but with less than half the serial accounted for, Raff wanted to finish assembling his men and confirm his location.

When the planes of the second serial came over, they were flying farther south and dropping troops on the far side of the forest. Something was off. Map study and information from a POW confirmed that the first serial had been dropped almost a mile and a half away from the DZ. Raff was disgusted to have won Couch's champagne bet.

Another 200 Ruffians had assembled under the command of Major Paul Smith, Raff's 1st Battalion commander. Before they could move to the assembly area, they were fired on by a squad of German infantry barricaded in a farmhouse. Surrounded and refusing to give up, the Germans were all killed by hand grenades and rifle fire.

Smith soon came to the same conclusion as Raff. He realized they'd dropped off target when he noticed the hazy silhouette of Diersfordt Castle a half mile to their east. Smith got Raff on the radio and informed him of his discovery; they agreed to rally in the northern wood line already occupied by Raff. Smith's group, however, was still fighting their way off the DZ. They assaulted forward, overtaking enemy trenches held by well-armed infantry and knocking out several anti-aircraft guns whose crews had cranked their barrels down to engage the advancing Americans.

With roughly 400 men of the first serial assembled, Raff focused on the two immediate targets: the artillery battery firing from the northwest, and the castle. Raff understood the value of aggressive action and calculated risks. Seizing these objectives, even with a portion of his still-organizing troops, would pay off. They must exploit the initial pandemonium; delays would only favor the enemy, giving him time to muster stronger defenses. It was important to keep the Germans back on their heels, reacting to events rather than dictating them.

Since no radio contact had been made with the 3rd Battalion—which was supposed to attack the castle—Raff gave Smith's group the job. The situation called for improvisation and they'd now be going into the attack.

While Smith and Raff worked on a plan for the castle, the mission of silencing the guns fell to First Lieutenant Murray Harvey. It didn't matter to Raff that the artillery battery was in a section of the forest assigned to the Thirteeners; the heavy howitzers were firing into the British and had to be dealt with.

Harvey led a group of troopers through the woods to creep up on the artillery position. It looked like a horse-drawn battery of five towed guns. The crews were thoroughly engrossed in their task of firing until the Americans unleashed their barrage from the protective cover of the trees. The first volley dropped several of the artillerymen; their surviving comrades either threw their hands up in surrender or fled into the woods. It was a complete rout, and the troopers took the position without the enemy firing a shot.

Because Harvey knew they wouldn't be occupying the position for long, he organized several parties to fan out and spike the guns. They dropped white phosphorus grenades down the barrels to fuse the breeches into hunks of useless metal. Other troopers searched the dead and segregated prisoners by rank. They patted down the survivors too, turning out pockets and packs looking for weapons and souvenirs. Anything of little interest was tossed aside. Among the sixty POWs was an *Oberstleutnant* and a *Hauptmann* (captain). Not a bad haul.

Harvey left a group behind to guard the prisoners then led a patrol to clear out the woods between the captured battery and the main road cutting through the forest. There they intercepted a squad of enemy infantry pedaling bicycles toward the DZ. This might have been one of *Kampfgruppe Karst*'s anti-airborne groups scrambling to counterattack the airdrop. With their rifles slung across their backs, the cyclists were sitting ducks. The troopers raked the formation, killing or wounding all.

So far the Ruffians estimated they'd killed fifty-five of the enemy, wounded another forty, and captured close to a hundred.

09:53. Drop Zone W, Germany. Saturday, March 24, 1945.

Five minutes after the first Ruffians dropped too far west, the forty-five aircraft of the second serial arrived over the intended DZ. The pilots flipped the jump lights to green as they passed over the edge of the Diersfordt Forest, dropping Raff's 2nd Battalion right on target.

Unfortunately, this was also where the Germans expected them. As the troopers floated down, tracer rounds arched past. Shells from 20mm cannons ripped through whatever was in the way. Bursts from the heavier 88mm were the most terrifying, exploding into thick, black clouds of shrapnel.

Four aircraft were hit by anti-aircraft fire, one fatally. The pilots were most likely killed by a flak burst, which sent the aircraft into a steep dive. The jumpmaster escaped, but the other seventeen troopers and all of the aircrew died when the plane plunged into a large stone barn.

Once on the ground, troopers hugged the furrowed fields of the DZ and inched along. It seemed as if enemy fire came from every direction. The woods to the north and west sparked with muzzle flashes from dug-in machine gun positions. Fire poured in from several houses turned into fortified bunkers; heavy mortars and artillery peppered the DZ.

The plan for the troopers of the second serial was to assemble and attack a small spit of high ground on the DZ's southern perimeter. Orders were unnecessary as groups organized by proximity bounded forward, firing as they moved. They ran past the twisted dead bodies of their comrades, many still buckled into their parachute harnesses. They got their light mortars and belt-fed machine guns into action, pushing the Germans back, house by house, and in some cases, tree by tree.

On his way to the assembly area, Private Richard Boe found a lone German shot in the chest. There wasn't much Boe could do, but he paused long enough to open his first-aid packet and give his wounded adversary a shot of morphine to ease his pain.

Rifle fire crackled in all directions, punctuated by the occasional *FOOM!* of exploding grenades. Taking their small bit of high ground, troopers overran a section of German heavy mortars, capturing all four of the 81mm beasts intact. The dead crew's range card confirmed suspicions: targets had been designated throughout the DZ. Clearly they had been expected.

As the troopers of the second serial pressed south across the DZ, the next forty-five planes of the third serial—Raff's 3rd Battalion—roared overhead at 600 feet. The lead pilot gave the jump signal five seconds late, putting several sticks 500 yards farther east than intended. These groups dropped into an area well covered by the Germans. They'd have to fight their way out to get back to the DZ. Among them was the Ruffians' unarmed chaplain, Captain Paschal Fowlkes, who was shot to death while caught in a tree.

Sergeant Earl Westcott, descending with the rest of Chalk 99, drifted toward a farmyard full of Germans shooting troopers as they landed. Westcott had jumped with his Thompson at the ready, and despite the oscillation of his chute he took aim. Witnesses claimed that, squeezing off several bursts, he killed five Germans before he hit the ground. The remaining three retreated into the house pursued by Westcott and another sergeant. They threw a British Gammon grenade through a window, which erupted in an earth-shattering explosion that ended the skirmish.

Floating under his full parachute, Private Bob Baldwin was rocked by the sudden explosion of his platoon sergeant, who disintegrated into mist when shrapnel ignited his satchel of demolitions. The sergeant's empty parachute canopy collapsed like a discarded blanket.

If any of the troopers had bothered to look up, they'd have seen the plight of Technician Fourth Grade Charles Rushing, whose jump came to a jolting halt as his misrouted static line left him dangling behind the aircraft. Luckily there was only one jumper behind him in the stick, saving him from getting slammed by equipment or other bodies. As he hung helplessly behind the plane, several rounds of flak burst nearby, but the shrapnel missed him. The turbulence didn't jar him loose, nor was the crew chief able to haul him back inside. Pulling his reserve chute might have jerked him free, or it might literally have torn him in half. The pilot made another pass over the DZ, hoping they could free their stubborn cargo. But one pass was all they could manage before the next inbound serial forced them to turn for home. A thousand feet over Holland the crew chief decided to cut Rushing's static line. As Rushing tumbled away from the plane, he pulled his reserve's ripcord and landed safely.

Private George Peters, who'd celebrated his twenty-first birthday five days prior, crashed to earth near the edge of the DZ along with the rest of Chalk 108. A German machine gun, seventy-five yards away, had the area well covered. Bullets zipped overhead and kicked up dirt. No one moved for fear of getting stitched.

Sergeant Cleo Hohn landed close to Peters. "I was lucky enough to land in a fold of ground that protected me from the gun. . . . Peters was halfway between me and the machine gun, trying to wiggle free of his chute harness while ducking the hail of bullets. We were all forced to hug the ground."

Peters was no stranger to the vicious hammering of German machine gun fire. He'd first witnessed their buzz saw rate of fire in Normandy. He knew what the men of Chalk 108 were up against, and he knew what would happen if they just lay there.

Lieutenant Edward Keehan watched as Peters ditched his chute, grabbed his rifle, and charged, firing as he ran. Peters closed the distance by half before the German crew turned their attention on him. Hit by a burst, he fell. Getting back up, he continued onward. Peters made it to within twenty yards of the machine gun before a second burst hit him, sending him to the ground in a crumpled heap. Badly wounded, but still alive, he clawed his way inch by inch closer to the gun. Rolling onto his side, Peters lobbed two hand grenades into the position—the explosions ripped through the crew, killing them instantly.

With the machine gun out of action, the Americans poured fire into the woods and bolted forward through the blue smoke of gunfire. The remaining Germans fled. A few troopers went back for Peters. He was an unconscious, bloody mess, already turning greenish-gray. They carried him into the shelter of the woods for first aid, but his pulse stopped a few minutes later. The nation's highest honor for gallantry, the Medal of Honor, would later be presented posthumously to his parents. One of seven children, George was the youngest of their four sons.

At 10:03, just twelve minutes after Raff landed, the fourth serial passed over DZ W. By then the ground was littered with hundreds of abandoned parachutes and unopened equipment bundles. Black smoke billowed from a farmhouse where the downed C-47 had crashed. Gun battles raged in every direction. Despite the melee, enemy anti-aircraft gunners were still at it, raking seventeen of the serial's aircraft. They all managed to make it back over the Rhine, but several carried wounded crew. One aircraft, with an engine shot out, force landed in France.

In one of the riddled C-47s, two wounded troopers staggered toward the door trying to follow their stick out. The first man had a bleeding head wound; the trooper behind him—with lacerated fingers—fumbled with his static line's snap hook. He wanted to unhook so he could get to the door. But it was too late; the pilot gunned the engines and turned back across the Rhine. The troopers pleaded with the crew for another pass, but the pilot held his course.

General Miley and his command staff, landing near the center of the DZ, found themselves pinned down. Spread in a prone position as bullets whizzed just a few inches over his head, Miley spotted three troopers hunkered down in a small depression. An equipment bundle, whose red parachute and stenciled markings indicated it contained a belt-fed machine gun, lay between the general and the men.

Above the staccato of the battle, Miley yelled and gestured, "Meet me over at that bundle!"

Staying as low as possible, the men wormed their way to the bundle. Together they removed the parachute harness and assembled the machine gun, mounting it on its tripod and racking the first round of the belt into the chamber. Most likely, it was one of the three heavy machine guns dropped by the fourth serial. Miley's impromptu crew lashed out at the barricaded Germans. Firing in short bursts, the men poured down .50-caliber bullets on the closest enemy positions, splintering doors and windows.

With Germans in the immediate area scrambling for cover, Miley left his three new best friends in search of his staff. As the two-star general scurried away, one of the troopers told his comrades, "We sure as hell had some goddamned high-priced hired help today."

Miley eventually arrived at the designated assembly point, one of the last to do so, and found his security detail establishing a perimeter around their temporary command post. A head count revealed that two of Miley's intelligence officers were missing. They'd been killed on their way to the assembly point.

• • •

Branigan's Bastards—the Ruffians' artillery support—jumped in the same serial as Miley. Most of the sticks landed accurately, but several jumped late, putting them out over the trees. Three of their howitzers' chutes malfunctioned; the massive bundles tumbled through the sky in a tangled mess, thudding into the ground. Useless.

One of the jumpmasters, Lieutenant George Hawley, was so focused on his stick that he forgot to hook himself up. It was his thirty-first jump, and when his count hit "Four thousand!" without the opening jolt, he unhesitatingly yanked his reserve ripcord. He had a rough landing, but lived.

Lieutenant Colonel Branigan landed unscathed, but his map case took a bullet. He landed close to the farmhouse that he'd preselected for his command post. Unfortunately, the Germans had also chosen it for a strongpoint.

Branigan rounded up five troopers, including First Sergeant Ed Kissinger. The six of them laid down a base of fire and started maneuvering on the house. As they closed on the target, Kissinger sprinted past Branigan to pitch a hand grenade. Just as it left his hand, he collapsed, fatally shot in the head. The five troopers stormed in, killing several of the defenders and taking as prisoners a handful of the more quick-witted, who dropped their weapons.

One of the troopers rushed up to the second floor with his bazooka. From an elevated window he engaged nearby enemy positions.

Once the Germans realized that the house had fallen to the Americans, they targeted it with mortars and an 88mm anti-aircraft gun. After several near misses and a mortar round through the roof, Branigan realized that the house would offer scant protection until the 88 was dealt with. One of the war's most versatile weapons, the German 88 was an effective anti-aircraft gun that could also be leveled for use against ground targets. It was known for its lethal accuracy and the whip-crack sound of its high-velocity shells.

Small groups fought their way out to the bundles, and the Bastards soon had two more of their heavy .50-caliber machine guns in action. The methodical *chug-chug-chug* of the belt-fed machine guns could be heard raking the tree line along the eastern edge of the DZ. Their overwhelming firepower provided essential cover for the crews crawling out to assemble their guns. The welcoming boom of friendly artillery rose above the fracas. Crews leveled their 75mm howitzers in direct fire on the German positions and in some cases targeted individual enemy riflemen, too stubborn, or too well dug in, to be taken out by more patient means.

With the initiative shifting in their sector, the Bastards fought to establish a perimeter on the northeast end of the DZ. One of the artillerymen scrambling to join them was William Pandak, who skirted the enflamed skeleton of the downed C-47. Bullets whizzed out of the conflagration as fire set off the dead troopers' ammunition, and the smell of burning flesh hung in the air. It wasn't a place to linger.

Several shell bursts sent Pandak diving into a ditch already occupied by troopers with the same idea. As a designated grenadier, Pandak had a rifle loaded with blank ammunition. It wasn't a role he relished. The blanks were the mechanism that allowed him to launch grenades from a device attached over the barrel of his rifle; the blank provided enough pop to hurl the four-ounce grenade 200 yards.

Pandak crawled to the end of the ditch and, with a buddy calling out adjustments, started arching the grenades toward the Germans firing at them from a farmhouse hedge. After three misses he found the right range; the last three projectiles exploded on impact in the hedge and the shooting stopped. Out of grenades, Pandak ditched the launcher and loaded his rifle with live ammo.

While the Ruffians on DZ W mopped up resistance, those who had misdropped with Raff prepared to seize the Diersfordt Castle complex. The task fell to Thad Blanchard and the rest of Able Company. Advancing through the woods single file, Blanchard's squad came under fire from the front. They'd stumbled on several dug-in positions along the edge of the woods, surprising the German infantry. The first several troopers formed a quick skirmish line while the squads behind them fanned out to each flank. The troopers killed nine of the Germans before the remaining fifteen surrendered. The biggest prize, however, was a captured 81mm mortar. It would prove to be fortuitous booty.

The brisk firefight hadn't gone unnoticed by the defenders in the castle, who barraged the tree line with mortar and machine gun fire. With a few men left behind to man the heavy mortar and enemy trenches, Able Company began a wide flanking move through the woods to approach the castle from the east. The terrain on that side provided better concealment.

As Able advanced on the castle, Blanchard spotted a group of Germans sprinting to their Mark IV tank idling at a crossroads. Blanchard yelled at Rexford Bass to hit them with his machine gun. But the tankers won the race, pulling the hatches shut behind them as bullets ricocheted off the six-inch steel plating.

The tankers rotated their turret to line up the main gun for a shot at Bass' chattering gun. The first round exploded right in front of Bass; miraculously, he survived with only minor injuries, but his machine gun was a twisted piece of junk. The spraying shrapnel killed Lieutenant John Sterner, one of the company's most popular officers.

The tank fired its 75mm main gun again and again, blasting the American line. Blanchard watched in horror as Private Albert Ballon, who'd been perforated with shrapnel wounds and was covered in his own blood, calmly collected his machine gun and walked away.

Blanchard screamed, "Set the gun down!"

Suffering from severe shock, Ballon grinned and said he was leaving with his mother, his left hand out as if holding hers. As he turned to continue the conversation with his maternal hallucination a machine gun burst ripped through him. He was dead before he hit the ground.

Having taken eight casualties in a matter of seconds, the platoon gave up the attack. Blanchard ran back through the woods to retrieve a working machine gun. As he did so, he passed one of Able Company's tank hunters, armed with the new M18 recoilless rifle, who was moving forward.

As Blanchard and Able Company struggled to get the upper hand in their sector, the Ruffians' 3rd Battalion departed their assembly area on the edge of the DZ. As they advanced toward the castle, they entered the thick woods of the Diersfordt Forest.

The trooper on point stepped lightly, his eyes scanning for movement. The smoky haze hugged the ground, turning the trees into dark silhouettes and limiting observation to a few feet. Behind him, the rest of the troopers kept their rifles at the ready. The woods were quiet, but the men could hear the sounds of battle echoing from the castle. Experienced troopers would have been eyeing the terrain for small folds in the ground or good, thick trees—cover to take advantage of should they stumble into a gunfight.

As they neared the castle a dug-in tank fired into their right flank. Several troopers went down injured and a lieutenant was killed. Yells from the flank brought a mortar squad forward. With only the tank tur-ret visible, they used the high-angle fire of the mortar to bracket their target. It took them several rounds before a 60mm shell dropped directly on the turret top's thin armor plating, killing the occupants instantly.

All the while, Raff coordinated his units over the radio, ordering Blanchard's Able Company to hold their position and provide covering fire as the 3rd Battalion organized for their assault.

To Ruffians with any imagination the castle had probably proven a dis-appointment. It was nothing like what they might have seen in a Holly-wood movie. There were no rounded turrets and there was no wooden drawbridge. The foundations of the castle had been laid more than 700 years ago and had seen a fair share of action, having been sacked and looted multiple times by Spanish soldiers, most notably in 1621 when the original castle was believed to have been destroyed. Rebuilt in the late 1700s as more of a residential palace, the compound now consisted of several freestanding buildings with a shallow moat on three sides; the water was probably no more than two feet deep.

The most formidable structure was on the compound's east side: a three-story brick building with a gable roof. Built in 1432, the walls of the massive blockhouse rested on parts of the original castle's perime-ter. From the Ruffians' view the back of it would have appeared to be a thirty-foot sheer wall of brick with three rows of tiny windows.

The compound also contained a church large enough to accommo-date 120 worshipers. Built in the late Baroque style, it sat atop a large underground vault, which had in recent days served as a bomb shelter. Eight steps led up to its two tall front doors, flanked on either side by stone columns. Above the door a coat of arms cast in concrete had ded-icated the church in 1776; its copper spire held a bell forged in 1747.

The largest structure, though, was the main building, erected in 1931 after its predecessor had burned down. The replacement was an L-shaped, four-story brick building with dormered windows along a squat roofline. At the foot of the L sat a square, five-story tower. Covered in ivy, it was the most imposing structure of the complex and provided the defenders with an elevated position.

Determining the best route to attack the castle was crucial. Open fields bordered the north and west sides of the complex; approaching from

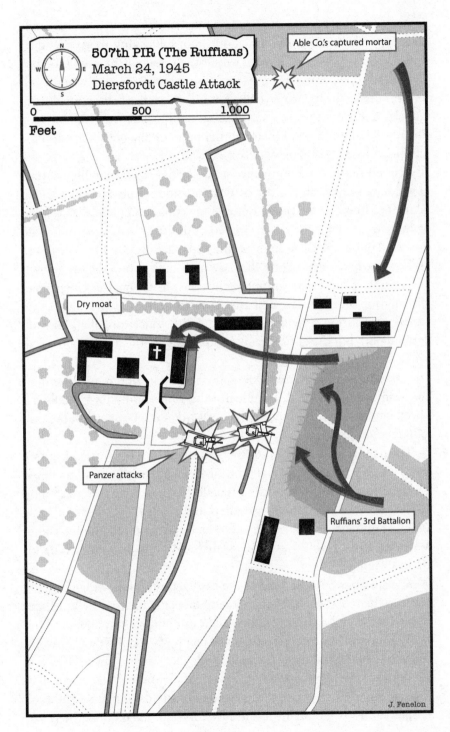

507th PIR (The Ruffians)
March 24, 1945
Diersfordt Castle Attack

0   500   1,000
Feet

N
W   E
S

Able Co.'s captured mortar

Dry moat

Panzer attacks

Ruffians' 3rd Battalion

J. Fenelon

either would have been suicide. The moat on the south side was made deeper by the eight-foot foundation; troops attacking there would be funneled over a narrow bridge, which the Germans undoubtedly had well covered. That left the east side, closest to the protection of the forest, dominated by the massive blockhouse. It was the best option, but an attack there would require suppressing the blockhouse while crossing the moat to storm the northeast corner between the old stables and the church through a section of collapsed wall.

Around noon, two companies of the Ruffians' 3rd Battalion formed a wide, half-moon arc on the castle's east side, using an embankment along the tree line for cover. Before they could completely set up, the volume of fire from the castle swelled. A distinct clanking sound could be heard under the cacophony of rifle and machine gun fire. The troopers knew what it was before they saw it: a tank. The German panzer rolled out of the castle grounds and down a narrow tree-lined road, directly for the troopers' embankment. Rounds from the main gun sailed in, injuring several troopers. The radio operator called for artillery support, but the guns remained silent due to the low-flying aircraft still coming in.

From their position Able Company used their captured 81mm mortar to thump out several rounds. But the white phosphorus shells fell short, landing in the compound's courtyard and setting one of the outbuildings on fire.

The panzer continued its advance. Ruffian Ivey Hutchinson leapt up from his position and sprinted down the embankment toward the tank. He heaved a British Gammon grenade baseball style; the deafening explosion rocked the tank. It appeared undamaged, but the dazed crew had had enough. Not knowing what had hit them, they pulled themselves out of the hatches and ran toward the Americans with their hands up in surrender.

A second panzer rolled out of the castle grounds following the same route as the first, which sat abandoned, blocking the road. The panzer blasted at the embankment, killing and wounding several troopers. One of the Ruffians' two-man recoilless rifle teams worked their way forward, stalking the tank and using trees alongside the road for cover. Their first shot made a direct hit, punching a perfect hole through the armor plating and showering the crew with white-hot shards of metal. The tank erupted into a ball of flame as the survivors scrambled out of the smoking hatches. They opted to run back toward their comrades in the castle, but were picked off one by one by the Americans.

Having blunted the armored counterattack, the Ruffians resumed their siege. With Blanchard's Able Company providing mortar and small arms cover, the Ruffians along the embankment launched their attack on the northeast corner. However, as soon as the advancing troopers crossed into the open field, they were pinned down by withering fire. The assault commander was wounded and the attack stalled. The men withdrew back to the shelter of the berm—they would have to try again.

Regrouping, the battalion commander came up with a new plan: at 13:00 every trooper along the perimeter would unleash his weapon, firing rifles, machine guns, and mortars to keep the Germans' heads down and give the attack on the northeast corner a better chance of success.

While the men at the castle waited, a deafening roar at treetop level caused a momentary distraction. The men stared up as waves of B-24 bombers screamed overhead with their bomb bay doors open, on their way to DZ W to drop supplies.

CHAPTER 13

"THE YANKS ARE COMING!"

10:09–13:00. Drop Zone X, Germany.
Saturday, March 24, 1945.

Flying in six minutes behind the Ruffians were the seventy-two C-46s carrying the Thirteeners into DZ X at the far end of the bridgehead. Their mission was to seize the remaining section of high ground in Diersfordt Forest and to set up blocking positions along the Issel River. Supporting the Thirteeners were John Chester and his fellow artillery-men, bringing up the rear in forty-five C-47s.

Pilot Gordon Wood recalled seeing, from the cockpit of Chalk 9, the Ruffians' C-47s on the way back from their drop: "We could see planes coming out of the first drop zone all in formation and it looked like a piece of cake. The picture soon changed with the second serial coming out. They were all over the sky and I can remember at least two going down in fire." Now it was their turn and things were looking a lot more uncertain.

The planes flew in over the Rhine at 1,000 feet and began their descent to jump altitude. As they flew over the Diersfordt Forest, the pilots scanned for their primary checkpoint—a double-track rail line. From the shelter of the dense woods the Germans fired small arms and light flak up at the C-46s passing overhead.

In Private Tom Funk's aircraft, the platoon medic led the stick in singing several songs during the flight. Belting out *"Over there! Over there! Send the word, send the word over there! That the Yanks are com-ing!"* kept the stick's spirits up. Until the flak started.

Funk had joined the regiment in Châlons and he had learned that his comrades valued humor almost as much as hard work. Ever the comedian, he yelled to his buddy Doug Lawson, "What's that noise I keep hearing?"

"Well, it isn't firecrackers," Lawson yelled back.

Realizing that his joke had fallen flat, Funk grabbed Lawson's shoulder and wished him luck. The two men turned their attention to the jumpmaster's bellowed commands.

The first serial came in too fast. It was here that the pilots' inexperience with the C-46 became obvious. The lead pilot chopped his power back belatedly, reducing speed from 170 to 100 mph. The sudden deceleration had a domino effect, forcing pilots higher to avoid collision. The jostling broke up the formations, and several pilots throttled down to as little as 80 mph. It was close to stalling speed for the large twin-engine transports. And one, seemingly undamaged by flak, dove into the ground, killing everyone on board. In an instant over thirty men were gone, consumed in an explosive inferno as the formation screamed overhead on their final approach into the DZ.

As the planes cleared the forest at 600 feet, 20mm anti-aircraft guns opened up from their left, and heavier flak cannons peppered them from the right. The German gunners on DZ X had had more time to collect themselves after Montgomery's artillery barrage. They were almost gleeful in their retaliation.

Black and white puffs of exploding flak scarred the sky; streams of tracer fire crisscrossed through the formation. The glowing tracer rounds, designed to help gunners track the trajectory of their bullets, created an optical illusion: from a pilot's view the rounds appeared to lazily arc upward until they got close enough to reveal their true speed, zipping past with hair-raising lethality.

At 10:09 the pilot in the lead aircraft flipped on the green light. With the plane already hit by multiple AA rounds and the left engine in flames, the shrill ringing of the bailout bell added to the bedlam. The C-46 pilots supplemented the jump signal with the bell so troopers at the back of the stick knew it was time to jump. Just after Chalk 1's troopers cleared the cargo doors, several of the crew bailed out too, but the pilots didn't make it, as the aircraft nosed over and augured into the ground. Off the right wing, Chalk 2 burned in as well, taking most of the crew with it. Fortunately, the troopers had jumped in time to escape.

On the run in, flak burst on the right side of Chalk 11, killing Sergeant Tom Harvey, who was standing in the jump door. With no time for options, First Sergeant Royal Donovan slid Harvey's shrapnel-torn body out of the plane, letting the static line deploy his chute. Within seconds the clanging of the bailout bell and the glow of the green jump light sent the troopers rushing for the doors. The sticks of thirty-odd jumpers cleared the double doors in less than twelve seconds.

First Sergeant Dick Carter candidly recalled his deepening anxiety: "I'll admit that when we stood up in the plane I was damned frightened, and when the bell rang for exit I was scared, but when we jumped and I heard the flak, I was terrified, I saw two of my buddies get hit while in the air. I'll always remember how they slumped in their chutes, silent and sinister."

Trooper Sid Laufner was more direct, if less eloquent: "I was scared shitless." He jumped anyway. The fear of going down in a flaming coffin far outweighed anything that might await on the ground.

In his aircraft, Mac McKirgan was the last man in his stick. He rushed to get out as flames consumed the fuselage, filling the cabin with smoke. The plane rattled horribly, and a jolt threw McKirgan flat on his face just short of the open jump door. He grabbed the edge and pulled himself forward, tumbling out headfirst. He twisted as he fell, and his chute opened with a backbreaking shock, but he made it.

The trooper jumping in front of Private Harry Deaton was struck by shrapnel, which ignited the phosphorus grenade in his cargo pocket. "He was just a sheet of flames, screaming and trying to get out of the harness, and the phosphorus burned him up," recalled Deaton. "It was horrible, and I'm sure he was dead by the time he hit the ground."

In Chalk 46 combat photographer Robert Capa braced himself against the turbulence. He secured his cameras, verified that his parachute harness was tight, and made sure his flask was snug in his breast pocket. Capa later remembered that, with the red light on and standing at the rear of the stick, "I started to think over my whole life. It was like a movie where the projection machine has gone crazy, and I saw and felt everything I ever ate, ever did. . . . I felt very empty." In front of him thirty men, including the Thirteeners' commander, Colonel Jim Coutts, stood poised to jump.

Braced in the right door, Coutts felt the plane lurch as it took a hit. Pieces of the engine fell away as it was consumed in flames. Several more rounds ripped through the plane's belly. As he leaned back into the aircraft, Coutts spotted blood running down the deck, a clear sign someone had been hit. With the C-46's future in doubt, he and a sergeant dragged the wounded trooper up front and pushed him out the door. Seconds later they all followed.

• • •

Texan Lendy McDonald, hooked up and waiting, had a narrow escape when a shell sliced up through the seat he'd just vacated. Green light on, he rushed for the door but found it blocked by bright sheets of orange flame wicking back from the wing. He turned to William Trigg and yelled, "Jump the other door!"

"No time!" Trigg yelled back. The plane was going down.

They both leapt through the inferno. McDonald was terrified the heat would melt his nylon canopy. As the chute popped open, he estimated his altitude to be 300 feet. Twisting, he looked over his shoulder to see the aircraft explode on impact. The entire crew was lost.

Landing hard, but in a well-plowed field, McDonald shed his chute and loaded his carbine. By hacking at the camouflage canopy with his combat knife he was able to cut out a big section to use as a battle blanket. While he stuffed the nylon into his pack, McDonald recoiled from a sickening thud. A trooper had slammed into the ground just a few yards away.

McDonald sprinted over, but there was nothing he could do. The trooper's chute had failed and he was clearly dead. Because the man had landed on his left side his face looked like a macabre mask: the left side was a deep purple and the right an alabaster white.

Several pilots coaxed their stricken aircraft back across the Rhine to bail out over friendly territory. One pilot recalled, "Our right wing tank was opened up and on fire. We tried to get back over the river, but when the skin of our wing started to peel, I said 'Get Out!' I trimmed the plane as much as possible so I too could get out. All you can do at a time like this is get up out of your seat and run like hell for the door."

Bad luck continued to plague Chalk 13. Their replacement aircraft flew in on the tail end of the formation, never having managed to catch up. They were hit by flak on their pass over the DZ and the plane caught fire. Several troopers jumped before the pilot banked hard to get back over the Rhine. The rest of the stick, refusing to abandon their comrades, jumped on the west side of the Rhine. They planned to make their way to DZ X as soon as possible.

Out of the 2,000-odd Thirteeners only a few refused to jump. In Noah Jones' plane the stick watched an unwilling trooper shed his chute. The man, a veteran of the Bulge, had been given the option to skip the

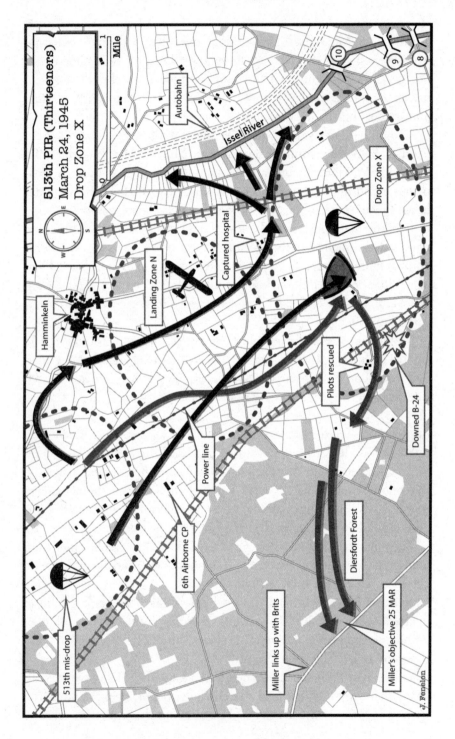

513th PIR (Thirteeners)
March 24, 1945
Drop Zone X

Autobahn

Issel River

Drop Zone X

Captured hospital

Landing Zone N

Hamminkeln

Pilots rescued

Downed B-24

Power line

6th Airborne CP

Diersfordt Forest

Miller links up with Brits

Miller's objective 25 MAR

513th mis-drop

J. Fenelon

mission—due to his still-healing wounds—but had said that he wanted to go. Jones never learned why the trooper lost his nerve. Just after the men jumped, the aircraft went down in flames, taking the crew and the frightened jumper with it.

It took approximately nine minutes to drop the Thirteeners along with their sixty-four tons of mines, demolitions, medical supplies, ammunition, and radios. The cost to get them over the Rhine was staggering. In what a troop carrier historian would later call a disaster, fourteen of the seventy-two C-46s were shot down, five crash-landed in friendly territory, and another thirty-eight were damaged. One crew, lucky to make it back, gave up counting the number of holes in their aircraft when they hit 200. The aircrews suffered accordingly, with more than thirty killed and twenty-two wounded.

Hitting the ground like a rag doll, Robert Capa rolled onto his stomach to fish out his camera. "We lay flat on the earth and nobody wanted to get up," he recalled. "The first fear was over, and we were reluctant to begin the second."

Ten yards from Capa, fellow jumpers drifted into the tall trees and their chutes entangled in the upper branches. Before their feet touched the ground, they were riddled by a German machine gunner. Capa erupted with the frustrated rage of a useless bystander, letting out a long string of Hungarian profanities.

"Stop those Jewish prayers," a trooper lying nearby yelled at him. "They won't help you now."

Capa rolled onto his back and waited for the firing to die down before he risked moving. A silver B-17 circling above the DZ caught his attention. He thought about his friend and fellow correspondent, Chris Smith, who was aboard the plane. Brereton had arranged for the Flying Fortress to serve as a platform for reporters so they could capture the operation's grandeur from the air.

The newsmen in the B-17 knew they'd been pushing their luck. Having flown in on the armada's flank, the pilot, Lieutenant Colonel Benton Baldwin, had taken them down to almost 700 feet so the photographers could get favorable shots of the Ruffians' drop. With its aluminum skin catching the sun, the big, four-engined bomber proved too tempting a target. The first shell hit with no noticeable damage, so Baldwin continued his course, circling back to follow the Thirteeners into DZ X.

Then the B-17 took another hit, on the left wing. The big bomber was already near stalling speed and it shuddered with the blast. Flames engulfed the inboard engine and spread along the wing to the second engine as well as toward the main fuselage; smoke poured into the cabin through the open waist gunner window. The reporters dropped their cameras, ditched their flak vests, and donned their parachutes. Baldwin had already turned back toward the Rhine, and just as they cleared the friendly shore everyone bailed out.

On the ground, Capa watched the smoking plane lose altitude and was relieved that "just before the plane disappeared behind the trees, I saw seven black dots—seven black dots transforming into seven silken flowers. They had jumped; their chutes were open."

One of the reporter's chutes malfunctioned, but Capa would learn later that his friend Chris had made it.

Back on the DZ troopers were chased by bursts of bullets from every direction, so they sought refuge wherever they could find it: in irrigation ditches, behind fence posts, among hedgerows, and even behind dead cattle. The *fumping* sound of mortars mixed with the blasts of rifles, machine guns, 20mm cannons, and high-velocity 88s.

One man recalled his first minutes on the ground: "Two bullets hit the dirt not three feet from my head. I did a hundred and fifty yards on my stomach to a nearby mortar crater in nothing at all. A burp gun opened up on me as I rolled in and hit bottom in a shower of stones and dirt. I cautiously raised my head to look out and was treated again to a burst from the burp gun fired from a farmhouse 50 yards away. Rifle fire from the opposite direction began throwing dirt around my hole. Every time I raised my head I received burp fire from the other."

Unknown to the troopers, civilians were also trying to stay out of the crossfire. Fourteen-year-old Wilhelm Westerfeld sheltered from the pandemonium with his mother and little sister in their cellar. His mother had placed a white pillowcase near the entrance to signal no harmful intent should be expected from the occupants. After several low-flying transports had passed over, Wilhelm risked peeking from the shelter. Not far away he spotted a camouflage parachute draped over a pear tree, at the foot of which lay a dead American. As the family emerged for a closer look, the trooper jumped to his feet and brandished a pistol.

"*Soldat? Soldat?*" he asked, gesturing toward the shelter.

"Nix Soldat, Nix Soldat!"

The trooper stepped into the cellar and fired a few rounds to make sure. As he emerged, a squad of Germans came into the yard. Caught in the crossfire, the family stood helpless with their hands over their heads, afraid to move. Wilhelm's sister, Hani, cried out, a finger on her left hand having been severed by a bullet.

Drawn by the firing, more troopers arrived, and the Germans threw down their weapons. The Westerfelds along with the POWs were herded toward a temporary aid station set up alongside the railroad embankment.

While medics attempted to save Hani's finger, Wilhelm watched as troopers escorted in more prisoners. The POWs had their hands over their heads, and most appeared happy to still be alive. One, however, wearing a long camouflage smock, refused to keep his hands up. Instead, he stood at attention with his right arm raised in a Nazi salute. In the middle of his loud diatribe about the Führer, a paratrooper gunned him down with a burst from his tommy gun.

John Magill, the forward artillery observer who jumped with the Thirteeners, landed close to his equipment bundle where he was to rally with the rest of his four-man section. He wanted to get his radio set up; the artillery support would be dropping in five minutes, and when the first 75mm howitzer was assembled, he needed to be ready to relay fire missions.

Almost ten minutes later it became apparent that the howitzers had dropped elsewhere.

They'll be shot to pieces trying to put their howitzers together under direct enemy fire, thought Magill. *Where have they landed?*

Led by Captain James Cake, Magill and the other two artillerymen tried to keep up with the advancing Thirteeners, but the weight of their bulky radio equipment slowed them down. They soon found themselves caught in the open with only one pistol per man to defend themselves. Enemy rifle fire from a nearby barn reinforced the absurdity of their situation. Desperate calls on the radio for artillery support went unanswered.

They agreed to take turns leapfrogging to better cover. Magill went first. He made it a few feet before being knocked to the ground by a bullet ricocheting off the radio on his back. The captain made his bound successfully, but the third man was hit. Before Magill and the captain could reach him, the nineteen-year-old had bled out. They stripped him of his radio and left his body; it would have to be dealt with later.

A squad of Thirteeners, seeing their predicament, came on line and advanced to within bazooka range of the barn. The explosion brought out eight Germans with their hands over their heads. Magill wanted to kill all of them in retaliation for his dead friend, but cooler heads prevailed.

10:24. Drop Zone X. Saturday, March 24, 1945.

Magill was right. The forty-five C-47s of serial A-7 had accurately dropped the artillerymen and their howitzers onto DZ X. But because the Thirteeners had been dropped two miles off target, the artillerymen were alone. The serial's aircraft made it out comparatively well; sixteen had been damaged, with just one shot down. But what happened on the ground was a different story.

While keeping his feet and knees together, John Chester crashed into a heap fifty yards from his howitzer. With the deftness of a rattlesnake, he slipped out of his parachute harness and slithered across the field toward the equipment bundles, his crew's rally point.

Lying prone, Chester tugged at the straps of the bundle containing the howitzer's tail section. A few seconds later a bullet smacked into a discarded packing board just inches from his head. A German in the upper window of a nearby house had spotted him. Chester realized the rifleman "had friends and plenty of ammunition up there too," so he decided to abandon the howitzer for the moment.

He grabbed his carbine, rolled to his feet, and serpentined to a nearby hedgerow, diving behind a pile of lumber. In midair he realized he was about to land on a German. He tried to change course, but it was too late. He crashed next to the man, who thankfully was dead.

Chester searched the corpse and got his hands on arguably the most prized of GI souvenirs: a semiautomatic Luger pistol. Chester tucked it into his combat jacket, along with several extra magazines of 9mm ammunition.

Twang! Chester had tried to peek out of the woodpile, but the piece of lumber in front of him splintered in his face. He hadn't escaped the attention of the rifleman after all. A third shot got Chester moving again. As he followed the hedge to a stand of trees, he gathered up members of his crew as he ran. That's when he found his section chief, Sergeant Ralph Foulk, hit by shrapnel just above the knee.

Chester examined the wound. It didn't look too deep, but it was bad enough that Foulk would be down for a while. Chester told him, "I'd better get on with the fight but I'll send the first medic I can find your way." Chester's crew was now down to five men, and whether he wanted the responsibility or not, he was back in charge.

Chester's A Battery had been hit hard. Their commander, Captain Charles Duree, had taken a bullet in the stomach while leading an attack. Duree's second in command was killed, along with several others, as they dashed out to assemble a howitzer. And inexplicably, one entire planeload was missing. It was later reported they'd dropped early—on the friendly side of the Rhine.

The battalion commander, Lieutenant Colonel Kenneth Booth, landed just twenty yards from the farm complex designated for his command post. But heavy rifle fire from the main house wounded several troopers before it could be stormed. Two of the enemy were killed before the other twenty-three surrendered. The buildings were then occupied, with radios set up in one and an aid station in another.

Two troopers crashed through the roof of a barn. The botched landing probably saved their lives, and they instantly set upon the defenders who were firing at descending paratroopers. Their surprise attack from within the strongpoint bagged them sixteen prisoners.

One wounded trooper—shot in the thigh—was found still lying in his harness. Twenty-five feet away lay the body of a farmer missing half his head. "I got hung up in this goddamn tree," the trooper explained, "and while I was struggling to get out of the harness this old bastard rushed out of the house and shot me. Then I plugged him."

Meanwhile, from the protection of the trees, Chester and his small group sporadically shot back at Germans in a stone farmhouse, but their small-caliber carbines had little effect. Private Gene Buswell spotted an equipment bundle lying in the open area between them and the enemy. Based on the markings it contained a bazooka, but they all agreed it would be suicide to attempt its recovery.

As the men strategized their next move, a trooper dashed past them and into the kill zone. Chester didn't know the man's name, but knew he had a reputation as an "8-Ball, who spent half his time in the guardhouse." As the tinny *burrrrrrp, burrrrrrp* of German machine pistols erupted from within the house, bullets kicked up dirt all around 8-Ball as he dragged the bundle back to the group. Buswell assembled the bazooka, while 8-Ball darted back out, zigzagging his way across the open ground to a crate of rockets. The troopers, in awe, poured suppressing fire at the house as 8-Ball once again miraculously avoided getting hit and returned with the rockets.

Buswell's first shot missed, the rocket soaring over the roof with a loud *whoosh*. As he waited for his assistant gunner to load the next round, he took a deep breath to settle into his aim. The second round exploded inside a third-story window, sending smoke and debris out of the gaping hole. Buswell's plan was simple: put a round through every window of the building. His next shot exploded in a room on the second floor. The effect was immediate, as the volume of fire from the farmhouse dropped significantly. Before Buswell could fire again, the defenders waved several white rags and pillowcases from the windows. They'd had enough.

Troopers advanced cautiously as coughing Germans filed out of the smoking building with their hands up. They pushed past the Germans to clear out the building and deal with any stragglers.

Trooper Anthony Moon, making his way alongside the structure, was surprised by an old man coming at him with a double-barreled shotgun. Chester raised his rifle, but Moon was faster. The farmer slumped to the ground, shot twice.

All over the DZ the devastating ground fire was taking its toll. Once the transports had picked up speed and banked away, German anti-aircraft gunners lowered the barrels of their 20mm cannons to rake the assembling artillerymen. The quad-barrels skipped thousands of rounds across the DZ, ripping apart whatever they hit.

The Germans had the area well covered. There were at least eight 20mm guns dug into shallow pits surrounded by infantry foxholes. Additionally there were ten of the heavier 76mm guns protected by at least twenty machine gun positions.

The American artillerymen, who were now fighting as infantrymen, abandoned the idea of assembling their howitzers. They'd have to push the Germans back before pinned-down crews could get to the equipment bundles.

An unexpected respite came in the form of British gliders released over the DZ. The Germans shifted fire to engage the slow-circling Horsas, which gave the momentum back to the Americans, who took advantage of the distraction to press their attacks. Rifle grenades eliminated one 20mm position. Another was taken out by deft marksmanship as troopers picked off the gunners one by one. A captured gun was pressed into action and used against other enemy positions.

Finally, an hour after landing, Chester and his men heard the sweet sound of booming artillery fire from one of their own howitzers on the far side of the DZ. A crew in B Battery had assembled one of their guns and leveled it in direct fire at enemy strongpoints. The 75mm, ten-pound projectiles, with a forty-five-yard kill radius, gave them the firepower they desperately needed.

With enemy fire waning, the troopers were able to piece together more howitzers. But some German zealots remained stubborn. A crew led by Sergeant James Guy wheeled their howitzers into position to engage a German-held building. Over a dozen rounds exploded in the building, and still the defenders refused to give up. Troopers dashed out to get more ammunition from equipment bundles. It took several more shots before a surrender flag waved from a window. Over two dozen battered but defiant Germans came out with their hands up.

As the artillerymen mopped up resistance on the DZ, they wondered: Where in the hell were the Thirteeners?

10:35. Two miles north of Drop Zone X.
Saturday, March 24, 1945.

One of the first to realize he'd been dropped in the wrong place was the Thirteeners' 2nd Battalion commander, thirty-three-year-old Colonel Allen "Ace" Miller.

Miller had jumped with the lead echelon and landed in a fenced pigpen on the side of a farmhouse. From the racket of ripping concussion waves he knew the Germans had a machine gun set up just around the corner. He peeked quickly and confirmed that four Germans had a sandbagged position in the cellar door. Miller rushed in from the flank, killing all four with slugs from his automatic pistol. Pushing past the dead bodies, he entered the house through the cellar to clear the strongpoint from the inside. He tossed a fragmentation grenade into the dining room and rolled a thermite grenade into one of the bedrooms. The two detonations tore through the remaining defenders and destroyed most of the house.

Outside, Miller looked for checkpoints. He spotted the double-track railroad he'd expected to find on the leading edge of the DZ, but the power line his battalion planned to use as a reference for assembly was too far west. The high-tension line, notable for its hundred-foot-tall metal pylons spaced about 230 yards apart, ran on a northwest-by-southeast axis. Miller checked his map and confirmed that the regiment had landed too far north by almost two miles.

Following the power lines south would lead to the correct DZ. Miller gathered troopers as he moved, yelling and reportedly even firing his pistol to get their attention. The group swelled to almost 300 men. Ideally, Miller would have used a radio to establish control, but both of his radiomen were unaccounted for. Those two troopers—along with Miller's two runners, his operations officer, and his operations sergeant— had been killed. Miller was one of only four or five jumpers who'd survived from his aircraft.

He ordered three lieutenants to organize the growing group into three elements for better control. The first group formed into skirmish lines and led the trek back to their DZ, gathering up more troopers as they moved.

For all his snap in the opening moments of VARSITY, Miller had his share of detractors. His entry as a combat commander in the Bulge had been rocky, even described as "erratic at best." Just over five feet tall, Miller was shorter than most of the troopers he commanded, and behind his back they referred to him as "Boots and Helmet." When he was dressed for combat, they joked, "one tended not to see the middle of him."

Back in Châlons one of the pluckier men had placed a helmet on top of a pair of combat boots and leaned a pistol holster against the effigy. The men thought it hilarious and took turns saluting the diminutive colonel. Another running joke was that Miller's aide—who dug the colonel's foxhole every night—let the colonel lie on top of him so he wouldn't have to sleep on the ground. Most troopers found Miller, a 1936 graduate of West Point, to be brash and unnecessarily loud.

One of Miller's subordinates, Major Irwin Edwards, described Miller as "a gutsy little bastard. He had that same type of guts that a lot of little men have." However, Edwards cautioned, "He would do some horribly irrational acts. . . . He was irrational, not crazy, but very irrational."

Along their route south Miller's group ran into multiple enemy strongpoints, each engagement requiring that they fan out and bound forward. It was exhausting and dangerous work. At one farmhouse machine gun fire sent the troopers into the dirt yet again, and the movement invited a hail of bullets. From his position behind the cover of some trees, Miller grew impatient with his men's lack of aggression.

"Get that damn machine gun," he yelled at a group of troopers concealed behind a haystack.

No one moved.

"I said get up and get that damn machine gun!"

The troopers held their positions and kept their heads down.

Incensed, Miller screamed, "I wish I had the old 2nd Battalion, I'd show you how to get that machine gun."

One of the nearby troopers, unimpressed with Miller's tantrum, yelled back, "If you hadn't got the old 2nd Battalion all killed in the Battle of the Bulge, you'd have the old 2nd Battalion to take that machine gun nest."

Fuming, Miller jumped to his feet. "Who said that?" he demanded. "Who said that?"

No one gave up the culprit, but troopers did start bounding forward. The German gunners, realizing their predicament, surrendered without much more of a fight. Dusting themselves off, Miller's group, with POWs in tow, continued down the power line.

Not far away, Lieutenant Dean Bressler, one of Miller's platoon leaders, had hit the ground hard. His aircraft had been damaged, and while it was losing altitude a trooper paused in the cargo door, shaking his head and yelling, "I can't, I can't." When the jump light turned green Bressler tackled the man out the door. The two men tumbled down together until their deploying chutes snatched them apart. Bressler's quick thinking had probably saved the stick.

After he'd ditched his parachute, Bressler loaded his Thompson. He noticed that the wood handle of his folding shovel had been shot off. A close call. He was thankful for the ground haze. It was his only protection from the bullets zipping overhead, but the haze also prevented him from identifying checkpoints.

"Over here! D Company, let's go!" Bressler began collecting his men. He didn't know it yet, but he was one of the few officers from his company still alive. His commander, First Lieutenant Ed Tommasino, had been gunned down while hanging from a tree, as had Bressler's assistant, nineteen-year-old Second Lieutenant Jerry Schmid.

Curt Gadd, the Ohio troublemaker, had already killed his first German of the day before joining up with the group. Gadd had crashed to earth under fire. With the snap of bullets getting closer, he rolled onto his back to undo his chute. As Gadd unlimbered his carbine, a German sped past in a horse-drawn cart. Still on his back, Gadd whipped his carbine up and aimed between his feet. He fired several rounds at the fleeing German; after the fifth or sixth shot the man spilled off the cart.

With bullets getting closer, Gadd resumed squirming out of his chute. In his panic he forgot he was in a quick-release harness. Unable to find his leg strap buckles, he drew his knife and started cutting. Halfway through the second strap he remembered the quick release; in a flash he was free.

Meanwhile, Bressler was still rallying the company when an alert trooper yelled, "Look out! Gliders coming in!"

Heeding the warning, Bressler turned to see the shadowy form of a large British glider headed right toward him. To Bressler the silent monstrosity appeared to be as big as a C-47. The group sprinted out of its path as it plowed into the field. Other gliders followed it in, the next one on fire.

Trooper Ken Eyers watched another glider crash into a farmhouse and tear the roof off as it spewed men and equipment as far as fifty yards. The gliders became more hazardous than the enemy. All over the DZ troopers scrambled to get out of their way.

The British area should be well north of our DZ, or this could be their LZ and we're not on our DZ, thought Bressler. Certain his group was in the wrong place, he rallied his men and headed southeast, not far behind Miller's group.

As the gliders continued to swoop into their LZ, British airborne troopers, sporting red berets and camouflaged smocks, soon joined in the fray, rushing through the haze to help attack German positions.

For Jim Coutts, the Thirteeners' commander, the arrival of the British confirmed what he'd begun to suspect—his regiment was in the wrong spot. After shedding his chute and loading his tommy gun, he'd been heading north per the original plan. But when he realized the error, Coutts steered his group back toward the original DZ. In what would later be attributed to a lack of combat experience, Coutts and his battalion commanders led their growing groups of troopers toward their original assembly areas rather than directly to their objectives. Though they'd been dropped off target, the Thirteeners' concentrated landing pattern had put them in position to organize where they were. Assembly was merely a means to organize before attacking. The choice to rally at the DZ before moving against the objectives delayed their primary mission by hours.

The delay was further compounded by a series of bitter skirmishes as strongpoints held up the troopers' advance at every opportunity. In one such scrap Coutts assisted an M18 recoilless gunner. Several fields away they'd spotted German crews removing camouflage nets from their tanks, preparing them for action. Coutts and the gunner concealed themselves in a hedge to engage them. Coutts slapped a round in the chamber and locked the breech closed. Tapping the gunner on the helmet to let him know he was loaded, Coutts estimated the range, "Try 250 yards!"

Coutts ducked aside to escape the tremendous back blast just as the gunner squeezed the trigger. The rocket screamed downrange, exploding against the closest tank. The rumbling shock wave shook the hedge and the two men celebrated their success. It appeared that the round must have ignited shells stored on the deck of the tank. It was the only explanation for such a devastating detonation. The other tanks buttoned up and clanked away in the opposite direction.

Another German tank crew, concealed in a barn, had spotted Miller's group still working their way south along the power line. The German Mark IV rolled out of the farmyard firing into Miller's left flank. Several men had been hit and lay sprawled in the fields before Miller's men could fan out to become less of a target.

As the brawl started to unfold, an immense British Hamilcar glider careened to a stop on the far side of the tank. To the amazement of the troopers the glider's nose swung open and a small, three-man M22 Locust tank rumbled out. The Tommies didn't hesitate—they charged straight at their opponent. One man fired the machine gun to put the

Germans off-balance, while the gunner frantically loaded the Locust's 37mm gun. But the Germans fired first and true. The M22's 25mm armor was no match for the Germans' 75mm main gun, and the explosion engulfed the small British tank, killing the crew.

The Tommies' bravery distracted the Germans long enough for Miller's tank hunters to get into position. Their first shot fell short, throwing up an impressive but harmless cloud of dirt. The second round was low as well, but it detonated against the tracks, immobilizing the tank. When the crew piled out of the hatches, Miller's troopers cut them down with several bursts. After the Thirteeners had regained their feet and dusted themselves off, they resumed their slog.

Mac McKirgan, who'd clawed his way out of a doomed C-46, was lost. He would roam for the next several hours looking for his platoon. Not finding them or any of the expected landmarks, he joined a group of troopers heading south.

Along the route a German machine gun opened fire on the group. From the safety of a ditch McKirgan waited for a trooper to line up his bazooka. The rocket *whoosh*ed out of the tube and took the enemy gunner's head clean off. McKirgan admired the marksmanship.

A short time later McKirgan's group paused to follow the action of several British fighter planes chasing a lone German aircraft. The British got their quarry and the German's engine spewed flames and oily smoke. The *Luftwaffe* pilot slid back his canopy and jumped, but his chute malfunctioned. The troopers cheered as the pilot tumbled through space. They watched him fall until he hit with "a meaty sort of thump and lay very still."

McKirgan stopped to help some troopers organize a group of POWs. No one relished the idea, but they'd have to drag the prisoners with them as they moved. One of the Germans, an officer with an arrogant demeanor, refused to get in line with the enlisted prisoners. As the officer walked away from the group, McKirgan ordered a fellow trooper to "keep that son of a bitch in line."

Ordered to "Halt," the prisoner stared at his captor and took another two steps forward. The trooper, apparently in no mood to be tested, shot the officer through the head. There was no more trouble keeping the other prisoners in line.

From there McKirgan joined an attack in progress. Germans in a fortified farmhouse were putting up a staunch defense and had support from another group dug into a hedgerow behind the house. Dead and wounded troopers littered the yard. Several camouflage chutes were draped over the trees around the barn.

The enemy strongpoints were often tough nuts to crack, with the defenders well barricaded and well armed. Each attack was a small drama, with the troopers often having to go in, as the enemy—dug in like ticks—only came out when blasted out. These particular Germans were no different, and they certainly knew their business.

The steady pop of bolt-action rifles combined with the burp of machine pistols kept the troopers' heads down. A wire fence a hundred feet from the house was the last obstacle. A lieutenant who recognized the stalemate jumped to his feet and shouted, "Come on you bastards!"

He got one leg over the fence before a bullet hit him in the forehead, leaving his corpse grossly entangled in the fence.

A bazooka team crawled forward and launched three shells into the house. The blasts tilted the initiative in favor of the attackers, and McKirgan followed fellow trooper Al West in for the assault. West had a phosphorus grenade at the ready. He arched it toward one of the shattered windows but missed. The grenade bounced off the façade and rolled back toward McKirgan. The duo made a hasty retreat. Safely clear of the blast, they resumed the attack but were quickly sent back to ground by incoming mortar fire. Troopers unaware of the attack's progress were thumping out 60mm mortar rounds to blast the defenders into submission.

McKirgan was lying in the open and drawing fire from the hedgerow. He snapped his carbine up to return fire just as a bullet slapped into his weapon, taking off the carbine's rear site. Before he could squeeze off a shot, another bullet glanced off his helmet. In quick succession two bazooka rockets *whoooooooshed* over McKirgan and exploded in the house. The troopers surged forward and the defenders finally started to surrender.

As Gene Ackerman approached the house, one of the enemy riflemen in the hedge snapped a shot at him then threw down his rifle, putting his hands over his head. The bullet had missed, but barely. Ackerman punched the *Soldat* in the face several times before accepting his surrender.

Ackerman wasn't alone, as Robert Capa later observed: "And much as I hate to make primitive statements, the Germans are the meanest bastards. They are the meanest during an operation and afterwards they all have a cousin in Philadelphia."

Jim Conboy, a nineteen-year-old private, had joined members of his demolition platoon heading south; together they attacked another tough nut. Conboy advanced toward the farmhouse at a brisk walk, firing from the hip. Two troopers ran past, forcing him to cease fire. A burst cut the two men down and sent Conboy diving behind a metal water trough. Using it for cover, he fired at the windows. A German ran from the house aiming his bolt-action rifle at Conboy, but Conboy shot him down first.

One of the two troopers who'd been shot called out in agony for help, but his buddy didn't respond. He was dead.

Conboy yelled for the trooper to give himself a shot of morphine. He'd been hit in both arms and begged Conboy to come help him. Getting to the trooper would be risky as he was splayed out in the open and a lot of lead still zipped back and forth.

The man continued screaming.

Conboy sprinted toward him. He had gotten within a few feet when he was tossed into the air by an explosion that shredded his right leg. Now he was down too and couldn't move.

The pleas for help continued: "Can you crawl? Please come help me."

Conboy tried. But the pain from the shattered bones in his leg was too overwhelming.

Conboy called out again, but got no reply. The trooper had bled out.

Fumbling with his first-aid kit, Conboy gave himself a morphine shot and passed out. His fellow troopers left him for dead and abandoned the attack.

By this point the artillerymen on DZ X had seven howitzers in their designated positions and were lugging in two more. They'd largely secured their sector but were still under sporadic small arms fire. The artillerymen had killed 50-odd Germans and taken over 300 prisoners. By their count they'd captured ten 76mm gun positions, eight 20mm positions, and had knocked out eighteen machine gun nests.

As the Thirteeners got closer to DZ X, they were able to establish

radio communication. The situation was made clear, with both elements of the combat team understanding for the first time where the other was. With their radios now within range, the Thirteeners could call for artillery support as needed. It was a delicate arrangement, as the artillery would be firing toward them rather than over their heads.

John Chester moved confidently, leading his crew out to their equipment bundles. As a Christian he knew he couldn't lose—he'd either survive or, if killed, go somewhere much better.

The crew heard an American yelling an impressive series of profane insults as they moved toward their howitzer. They recognized the voice of Charles Crow, a private from another section in A Battery notable for being the smallest trooper in the battalion. He was shepherding a dozen prisoners through the woods—using his rifle and verbal tirades to keep them moving.

Crow asked Chester, "I've not got time to fool around with this bunch of 'square heads' Sarge. Can I shoot them?"

Chester thought about it.

"No, better not do that," he replied. "They would just stink up the place. Herd them over to your right flank; looks like there is another bunch over there and they are trying to make a pen for them."

Chester continued along the wood line and happened upon a dead trooper hanging from the trees, shot multiple times. Chester had spoken to him yesterday; he'd been upset about a letter from his wife threatening to divorce him if he didn't "unvolunteer" from the paratroops. She was afraid of raising their two kids alone, and he'd confided to Chester that he planned to request a transfer after the mission.

It was just one of many tragedies Chester witnessed that day. Like all GIs, he had to choke back his emotions and bury them. There wasn't time to mourn. Maybe he'd process them later, maybe he wouldn't. The seeds of such trauma would eventually lead many veterans to solitude, alcoholism, divorce, or even suicide. But all that would come later. For now, there was still a war to be fought and more death ahead.

Chester's attention was drawn to the sudden eruption of German anti-aircraft guns. The B-24 Liberators were coming in low for their supply run.

CHAPTER 14

"NOW IS WHEN YOU PRAY"

10:26–13:00. Glider Landing Zones, Germany.
Saturday, March 24, 1945.

Trailing the paratroopers were the glider riders of Miley's 194th Combat Team on their way into the northern landing zones. The first eight serials of 592 gliders headed to Landing Zone S, while another 314 gliders in seven serials navigated to the second landing zone, LZ N.

For three hours the gliders had pitched and yawed behind the tow planes as the pilots strained to keep them steady against the turbulence. Despite the pilots' efforts, the fully loaded—and in some cases overloaded—gliders were nevertheless buffeted about in the armada's agitated prop wash. It was exhausting work with pilots and copilots swapping turns at the controls to reduce fatigue. Many veteran pilots complained it was the worst turbulence they'd ever experienced.

In the back, passengers braced themselves against unpredictable updrafts and downdrafts. Private Jim Lauria had tied a rope the length of the cargo area to give himself a handhold as he periodically worked his way around his 75mm howitzer to inspect its tie-downs during the bumpy flight.

Another gun crew hadn't been so diligent, and their 105mm howitzer worked itself loose. Staff Sergeant Jimmie Taylor screamed over the racket of the wind slapping at the canvas fuselage to get his crew into action. As the big gun threatened to upset their center of gravity, Taylor and another trooper muscled it back into place. Vomit all over the plywood floor made their work more precarious; they kept slipping in it.

In addition to holding their gliders steady, pilots on double tow had the added responsibility of preventing their towrope from drifting into the neighboring glider. There was little in the way of instrumentation to help a pilot prevent drift. The rudimentary instrument panel consisted

of an altimeter, a compass, and indicators for airspeed, rate of climb, and bank and turn. The instruments were designed for use in powered aircraft where the engine vibrations prevented the gauges from sticking. Many a glider pilot developed an obsessive tic of tapping the instruments' glass to ensure they registered correctly.

Pilot George Buckley focused on the glider in front of him, keeping well to the right of it. Without warning, a wing snapped off of it and the glider whirled down through the sky like a wounded bird, spilling a jeep and several men as it tumbled. Buckley glanced back, hoping his passengers—most of whom were replacements experiencing their first glider ride—hadn't seen the tragedy. He was shaken by the sight and, in a cold sweat, asked his copilot to take over for a few minutes so he could collect himself.

All told, twenty-one gliders were lost on the way over the Rhine. Some succumbed to poorly balanced loads, others to towrope entanglements, and a few, like the one in front of Buckley, to "structural weaknesses." Most managed to land safely while others fell out of the sky like olive-drab comets. The accidents reduced the glider riders' strength by a hundred men, several jeeps, and seventeen tons of equipment, including six mortars and howitzers.

Troopers spotted hints of what lay ahead as they neared the Rhine. Major Carl Peterson caught a glimpse of the war correspondents' damaged B-17 as it limped by in the opposite direction, left wing on fire and reporters bailing out. Several glider riders in trailing serials made note of the big silver bomber's crash site as they passed overhead.

First across the Rhine was glider "*Kansas City Kitty-Mary Lou,*" named after pilot Hugh Nevins' hometown and wife.

In his glider, Lieutenant Colonel John Paddock popped the cork on a bottle of champagne he'd smuggled aboard. He passed it around to his troopers and then made a small ceremony of tossing it into the Rhine as they officially crossed into Nazi Germany. "I figured the dice were cast, might as well enjoy ourselves," he recalled.

The route from the banks of the Rhine to LZ S was about six miles and passed over the southern edge of the Thirteeners' DZ. Despite the murky fog from Montgomery's smoke screen, the tow pilots' slower speed gave them time to pick out landmarks and, for the most part, stay on course.

The serials going into LZ S consisted of thirty-six to forty transports each, all double towing gliders. The plan called for them to split on their way into the LZ. The first serials veered south while the rest headed north, creating two distinct landing patterns to prevent congestion. It was an ambitious plan. Unlike previous missions, where success had been defined as simply landing in the designated zone, the VARSITY planners had assigned pilots specific sectors within the two-mile-long, one-mile-wide LZ.

The gliders in the lead serial were to land in the southeastern portion of the LZ; their troops would seize the bridges along the Issel Canal. The second serial was to land along the LZ's eastern boundary so their troopers could seize and hold the crossing points over the Issel River. The third serial of infantry, along with supporting artillery and anti-tank guns, would aim for the center of the LZ.

Pandemonium struck when the aircraft of the middle serial came in too fast and overran those ahead of them. To avoid collision the serial of thirty-six tow planes and seventy-two gliders climbed to over 1,000 feet and slowed down. The stack-up caused the following serial to climb even higher, up to 2,000 feet. The whole SNAFU was subjected to profane verbal abuse from the glider pilots who were helplessly dragged up to a more exposed altitude. They were supposed to be released at 600 feet.

The ack-ack started as they crossed the Rhine. It would take four more minutes to cover the six miles to the LZ. Red lights flashed from the navigator's glass astrodome, signaling back to the gliders that they were almost there. Stand by.

Normal procedure for aircrews flying into anti-aircraft fire was to start evasive maneuvers three minutes out, but that wasn't an option for the transport pilots. There could be no twenty-degree changes of course or shifts of 500 feet in altitude to frustrate enemy gunners. The transports had to hold a steady heading and stay in formation. The Germans' heavier guns, the big 88s and 105s, got the range first. The coal-black clouds of bursting flak exploded and drifted past as the gliders were towed relentlessly onward. In their fabric-covered gliders the pilots could smell the "rotten egg stench" of exploding ack-ack shells.

To the German gunners, whose weapons were designed to engage Allied bombers flying 5 miles up at 300 mph, the lumbering transports coming in at a thousand feet on a predictable course at 110 mph were easy targets. The heavier guns just had to get their shells close; the bursts of shrapnel would do the rest. They were very effective against the thin-skinned tow planes and fabric-covered gliders.

The two lead aircraft were shot down a mile short of the LZ; the glider pilots cut loose to avoid being pulled into the ground. Out of the first 40 aircraft, 36 were hit. In the next sixty minutes German gunners would down 10 more C-47s and damage another 140.

As the serial reached the edge of LZ S, green lights blinked from the planes' astrodomes, replacing the red stand-by signal. Once over the LZ the glider pilot determined when best to release. It was this decision that earned them the "G" on their flight wings. They preferred to release later rather than too soon. Overshooting their landing point could be corrected by the judicious use of flaps, spoilers, or the arresting chute; there was no way to compensate for not having enough altitude. Ideally they'd approach into the wind from a ninety-degree turn to dissipate speed, which for a glider was a major nemesis. A pilot had very little control once he committed to landing. Momentum, weight, and ground conditions determined the distance the glider traveled. Reducing speed before touching down was critical. Arresting chutes helped; pilots deployed them at a hundred feet to reduce their speed by almost half, then cut them away before landing.

Pilots on double tow had to coordinate their release with the other pilot. Protocol called for the short tow pilot to dive, while the long tow pilot allowed the first to clear the area before following. Rarely did that plan work in combat.

The first glider pilot released at 10:36, sending the towrope snapping forward and his glider into descent. In the space of the next hour, 591 gliders did the same at the rate of almost one every six seconds.

The reporter Howard Cowan had his eyes glued on his pilot. He wanted to cast off as soon as possible; the flak was loud and close.

After what seemed like hours the pilot shouted over his shoulder, "Going down!" With a flick of the release toggle the glider pitched forward into a steep dive. No longer under tow, the passengers heard the howl of the wind decrease, only to be replaced by the din of the raging battle. Seconds later, Cowan was startled by the *POP-POP* of shrapnel puncturing the taut canvas skin of the glider on one side and slicing its way out the other.

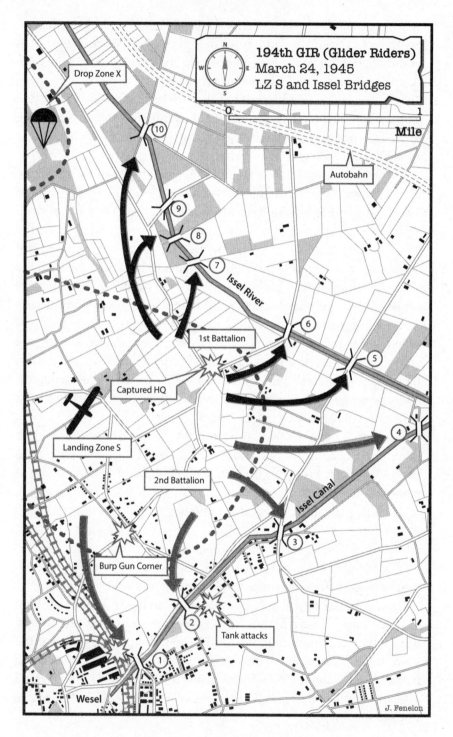

194th GIR (Glider Riders)
March 24, 1945
LZ S and Issel Bridges

0   1
Mile

Drop Zone X

Autobahn

Issel River

1st Battalion

Captured HQ

Landing Zone S

2nd Battalion

Issel Canal

Burp Gun Corner

Tank attacks

Wesel

J. Fenelon

The sergeant sitting across from Cowan advised, "Now is when you pray."

Their pilot banked hard right to avoid another glider. The troopers racked a round into the chambers of their rifles and braced for landing. Not wanting to waste time or worry about a crash jamming the exit door closed, troopers pushed them open and let them fall away; others waited for the exact moment of impact before chucking them.

In at least one case a pilot, unaware that a fouled towrope had damaged the glider's wing, went into a nosedive as soon as they cast off— killing everyone on board.

Inadvertently, a number of pilots released above other serials, forcing the gliders below to cut loose early to avoid collisions. Soon the sky filled with gliders trimming their flaps to spill as much air as possible so they could get on the ground as fast as possible. Pilots threaded their gliders through a congested airspace and jockeyed for a landing spot.

Down on the ground, *Kanonier* Peter Emmerich's three-gun battery of 883rd *Flakabteilung* had been finishing their breakfast when the unmistakable rumbling of aircraft filled the sky. There appeared to be no end to the staggered formations; they stretched as far back to the horizon as Emmerich could see. As he stared for a few dread-filled moments at the spectacle, his gunners swiveled their 20mm Flak-38s into action. The *Flakvierling*, a vicious quad-barreled anti-aircraft gun capable of firing over 800 rounds a minute, could traverse 360 degrees and elevate in excess of 100 degrees, allowing it to easily track the lumbering aircraft. Its effective range of over 7,000 feet put the transports and gliders well within reach.

The rapid booming of the guns snapped Emmerich back to reality. He followed the trajectory of tracer fire as the rounds chewed through the wing of a C-47, vaporizing its left engine.

There were so many aircraft, Emmerich recalled, "We did not have to aim anymore; just point our guns in the air and fire. We would have always hit something."

The crews hustled. At the gunner's command of "*Laden!*" they swapped out the empty magazines for four fresh twenty-rounders. Emmerich's battery commander liked to stagger the types of ammunition for maximum damage: armor-piercing, incendiary, high-explosive. Repeat.

When the gliders released overhead, section chief *Unterfeldwebel* Bosse ordered the gunners to ignore the tugs. "Aim for the gliders!"

As the first glider neared Emmerich's position, the gunner gave it a full burst, emptying all four barrels into it. The right side of the glider shattered, losing the wing and rear stabilizer. It crumpled into the ground.

All three guns in the battery were firing at their full cyclic rate of 1,000 rounds a minute. At such sustained rates of fire, the crews rotated barrels frequently to prevent them from melting. At the command of *"Den Lauf wechseln!"* Emmerich put on his asbestos gloves, removed the smoking barrels, and replaced them with cold ones.

"I can no longer turn the gun!" yelled the gunner.

Emmerich spotted the issue: empty shell casings had blocked the traversing mechanism. Together he and the crew threw the empty 20mm shell cases over the side of their gun pit to clear the jam.

The surrounding field was littered with dropped towropes and heaps of twisted metal-framed gliders on fire. Two dead bodies, presumably pilots, lay nearby; the air was heavy with a sick burning smell.

During a lull the crew swapped barrels again and oiled each gun's bolt. The battery commander, an officer named Kruckenberg, was in a panic; Emmerich thought he'd gone mad. As Kruckenberg moved between gun positions, he shot at anything that moved, not bothering to verify if his target was friend or foe.

Unterfeldwebel Bosse told Emmerich to go get more ammunition. As he scurried the thirty yards to the ammo point, Emmerich hoped he didn't get shot by his own commander.

While Emmerich was grabbing ammo cans, a *Kanonier* from another battery told him that a call to one of their gun pits, via the landline telephone, had been answered by a man speaking English. The *Amerikanisches* were getting close.

In the opinion of nineteen-year-old pilot George Buckley, a veteran of multiple combat operations, the flak was the heaviest he'd seen yet.

"A C-47 in front of us with one engine out and with flames streaming back over its wing held to a steady course, determined to get its two gliders to the LZ," he recalled. "All through this hell in the air, formation discipline was fantastic. They all tucked in closer and bored straight on towards the landing zones with no attempt at taking evasive action."

When Buckley and his copilot scanned the terrain below, they were horrified by the lack of visibility. The ground was bathed in a murky fog; landing in it would be tricky; obstacles would be hard to spot. Some pilots reported that the haze reduced visibility to as little as an eighth of a mile. Many hoped it also degraded the Germans' accuracy, but others were afraid it silhouetted their gliders against the bright sky.

In Lieutenant Colonel John Paddock's glider any residual buzz from champagne would have evaporated with the first burst of machine gun fire ripping through both their cockpit and their pilot. Copilot Lieutenant Harry Dunhoft took over, yelling for help, urging one of the troopers in back to hold the wounded pilot away from the controls so that he could bring the glider in to land. The German gunner had them in his sites, riddling the cockpit twice more but missing Dunhoft.

Dunhoft managed to land the glider in one piece. He dragged the wounded pilot from the cockpit while Paddock and his men fanned out after, throwing themselves out of the exit doors. Dunhoft bandaged the pilot's wounds as best he could and injected him with morphine.

The four-man OSS team sat in the back of the first serial's last glider. Two of the agents, "Easy" Steltermann and Robert Staub, had removed their GI coveralls to reveal their German uniforms. Of concern to both men was getting shot by their own troops. The glider riders had been briefed about them, and their pilot planned to get them as close to the edge of the LZ as possible. But when lead was flying, two Germans racing a *Kübelwagen* off the LZ could easily become the victims of trigger-happy GIs. They'd already survived one close call when a dozen bullets sailed through the glider—startling all, but injuring none.

They hit again fifty feet off the ground. Shells from a 20mm shredded the tail's starboard elevator and cut through the cargo bay. Captain Vinciguerra, Steltermann, and the copilot were all hit. The team's *Kübelwagen* was mortally wounded: three punctured tires and a damaged radio. Their mission was over before it started.

The pilot managed to keep the glider in one piece as they plowed to a stop. More bursts of machine gun fire punched through the back of the glider. Steltermann and Staub wanted out, but dressed in German uniforms, they hesitated. Realizing their plight, Leo Jungen, the fourth member of the team, scrambled through the blood-splattered interior to toss them their coveralls. After they were dressed, Jungen covered their escape.

Steltermann, dazed and clutching his German submachine gun, made it to a ditch before passing out. Coming to, he could only see out his right eye; the left was filled with blood. He'd been hit multiple times by shrapnel—twice in the left thigh, once in the right knee—a laceration on his chin revealed the bone, and blood poured from a wound above his eye; he also had a bullet in his left shoulder. As a medic worked on dressing his wounds, Steltermann watched dozens of gliders from the second serial swoop out of the sky one after another.

In one of those gliders, copilot Zane Winters, the well-armed "volunteer" power pilot, felt like a sitting duck. He and the pilot, Smokey, had divided the labor: Smokey was responsible for getting the glider down while Winters called out flak and monitored airspeed.

"Four birds at three o'clock!" yelled Winters as several bursts of 88mm shells blossomed off the right wing.

Smokey jerked left and sent the glider into a diving turn. Winters cautioned him that the airspeed indicator was needling into the red.

Smokey growled that he'd "rather chance the wings coming off, over being shot down." As a more experienced glider pilot, Smokey knew the position of the glider's pitot tube exaggerated their speed by at least eight miles per hour.

Seconds into the diving turn a burst of 20mm tracer fire arched past the right wing. Winters credited Smokey's quick action with saving their lives: "If we had been in a normal turn, they would have had us dead center."

The pilot in front of them wasn't as fast. His glider took several rounds from a high-velocity 88—the glider was there one moment, and then just a big ball of lingering smoke.

The airspeed indicator read 120 mph: too fast. Smokey, using a combination of the flaps and the arresting chute, got it down to 70 mph as they careened across the LZ, coming to a stop only when they hit a fence post. Winters kicked his way out of the cockpit through the side window.

Small battles erupted across the LZ as troopers ran from their gliders and the chaos shifted from sky to ground. It was a 360-degree battlefield of barking sergeants, cracking guns, snapping bullets, coughing mortars, and screaming wounded.

To Major Carl Peterson, one of the glider riders' staff officers, the unfolding scene seemed beyond horrific. He reckoned that at least a third of his regiment lay dead on the LZ.

Mortar fire proved devastating to the stationary gliders. The CG-4As were easy targets—even for inexperienced German crews. Hitting a glider with incendiary rounds often set it on fire. A favored tactic was to withhold fire until the pilots or troopers began unloading. With everyone focused on lifting the glider's nose the Germans opened up with machine guns, raking the assembled group.

For the Germans it must have been a scene of hellish anarchy as more and more gliders swooped in. They came from every direction, plowing into the open fields, knocking down telephone poles, bowling through fences, and toppling trees. Germans firing at a glider were often surprised by another landing behind them. Several gliders ran over foxholes, and in at least one case a copilot fired his tommy gun through the nose of his glider, scattering an enemy machine gun crew as the CG-4A crashed into them.

The plan of organizing the landings into specific sectors paid off. Enough pilots overcame the challenges of stacked formations and congested patterns to get their cargo to the right area, facilitating a rapid assembly of organized fighting units. There was no doubt the glider pilots had earned their pay. In the battle for LZ S, the concentrated landing patterns saved the day. The platoons of the first serial were assembled and attacking within minutes, taking ground and prisoners as they advanced toward the Issel Canal.

Trooper Harry Ellis, first out of his glider, exited in a crouch and sprinted for a nearby road embankment. On the other side of the road a German anti-aircraft position was firing in the opposite direction. Two of the *Kanoniers* crouched in front of a bunker facing away from Ellis. Ellis, his rifle at the ready, hesitated to shoot his enemy in the back.

A trooper flopped down next to Ellis and pulled his trigger twice. First one, then the other German tumbled over.

A *Soldat* from inside the bunker emerged waving a white rag of surrender. He ran to the Americans and explained to Ellis—who spoke fluent German—that his battery would surrender if an American came over to accept the offer. Ellis agreed and sprinted back with his prisoner. Together they convinced the remaining sixteen Germans to give up. The negotiation took four anti-aircraft guns out of the fight.

Glider rider Bud Dudenhoeffer and his squad landed safely but came under immediate small arms fire. They kicked out the doors and evacuated as fast as possible, sprinting for the protection of a ditch at least a hundred yards away.

It wasn't until the squad was bunched shoulder-to-shoulder, all trying to fit into the same ditch, that they realized they'd left all of the belt-fed machine gun ammunition back in the glider. Dudenhoeffer volunteered to fetch the ammo if the rest of them would increase their rate of fire to keep the enemy's heads down while he made a run for it. Somehow he reached the glider and collected four of the metal ammunition boxes. His return now gave them real firepower, and they unleashed the .30-caliber machine gun.

With the machine gun in action, half the group darted to the next position. Once set they provided covering fire so the machine gun crew could join them. In this manner they leapfrogged their way off the LZ and toward their assembly point.

At 10:46 the first glider in the third serial cut loose, followed closely by seventy others. All angled for the same real estate: the eastern edge of the LZ. They dove into a maelstrom. Four exploded as they came in to land, their cargo detonated by ack-ack. Burning men and materiel cartwheeled across the furrowed fields. Another twenty-one gliders were raked by small arms fire or the vicious quad-barreled 20mms.

While most troopers emerged from their gliders brandishing a myriad of rifles, submachine guns, and pistols, one plucky corporal, Nick Bakarich, had a baseball at the ready. On it he had scribbled, "To Hitler from the 194 . . . we're a tough gang!" He promised he'd throw it at the first German he saw, and his swagger lightened the mood. His squad was more worried about his sanity than their own safety.

Frank Dillon, peering between his two pilots, scanned the terrain below for landmarks. The haze blanketed everything, and the occasional break revealed only featureless fields. The pilot cut loose, banking hard left to avoid a glider edging in on them. Off tow, Dillon and his men could now distinctly hear the bursting flak and the rattle of German machine guns. Shrapnel hit one of Dillon's men, but the fragment embedded itself in the man's pack, leaving him startled, but uninjured.

As they descended, ground details emerged. Dillon spotted his pla-

toon's assembly point—a triangular patch of woods bordered by a dirt
road along the eastern perimeter. They were right on target.

He called out the distance and direction to his men as they all braced
themselves for a rough landing.

A power line loomed up out of the fog. The pilot pulled above it
in time, but the tail struck the wire, pitching them forward until he
leveled it back up. The quick maneuver kept them from crashing but
increased their speed. Coming in too fast, the glider slammed into the
ground and skidded across the field. Trees ripped off both wings. The
fuselage continued forward, mowing down a row of fence posts before
a large tree brought them to a bone-jarring halt. The tree trunk creased
the cockpit between the two pilots, but neither was injured. Before the
dust settled, Dillon and his men tumbled out into a nearby ditch. They
left the 619 pounds of ammo and equipment in the glider for someone
else to recover.

In the wood line their squad joined others and assembled into an
organized platoon. The pilots had their own assembly plan, and Dillon's
platoon sergeant, Forrest Saffeels, conducted a head count, readying the
troopers to move out. Among their number they already had their first
prisoner, a lone German caught by surprise.

Their sector on the east side of the LZ was relatively quiet. Before
moving to the company assembly area, Dillon's men helped other platoons round up POWs and civilians and left them under guard at a
farm.

By 11:10, 75 percent of the battalion had assembled, and Dillon's
unit joined the exodus of troopers headed toward their assigned bridges
over the Issel River.

Meanwhile, a few hundred yards to the west, the fourth serial had
released another seventy-two gliders. Clyde Haney felt his pilot bank
right as they commenced their run into LZ S. They were hit almost as
soon as they cast off. A shell exploded against the wood floor, sending
splinters and shrapnel into the legs of the men riding in back. Haney
slumped forward against his seat restraint.

Sergeant Henry Dorff could see Haney had been hit in the neck.
The wound didn't appear grievous, but Haney had either been knocked
unconscious or had passed out. The glider's jarring landing interrupted

Dorff's visual assessment, and before they came to a stop the *POP-POP* of bullets puncturing the glider chased the troopers out. The landing jolted Haney back to consciousness, and he stumbled out after the rest of his squad, then collapsed a few feet from the fuselage.

As the squad crawled to better cover, a medic darted over to treat Haney. The air was thick with heavy fire, and the medic worked feverishly as bullets snapped overhead. Despite his best efforts, he couldn't stem the bleeding and Haney bled out on LZ S. The medic scurried off in search of other patients.

George Buckley's load of troopers jumped out of their glider while it was still skidding to a halt. Buckley and his copilot joined them in a ditch, where they huddled together trying to determine their location by comparing tactical maps and the pilots' aerial photograph. Still unsure where they were, they agreed to head toward the sounds of the heaviest fighting.

The group departed up a narrow dirt road and was soon targeted by a German rifleman in the upper story of a farmhouse. They ran forward to take shelter behind a low stone wall surrounding the yard.

Bullets whined off the masonry as they plotted their course of action. The clatter of stampeding hooves shifted their attention to a surreal raid. Six troopers with guns blazing from atop "captured" horses encircled the farmhouse. Each of the troopers fired into the windows as he wheeled his horse around for another pass. One of the cowboys broke rank long enough to fire a rifle grenade through a second-story window. The detonation terminated the enemy fire. Seemingly satisfied with their handiwork and oblivious to having rescued the group behind the rock wall, the six rancheros galloped off.

The following three serials aimed for the center of the LZ. They brought in more men and heavier firepower: 57mm anti-tank guns and the howitzers of the 680th and 681st Glider Field Artillery Battalions. A battery of German howitzers pulverized glider after glider as they skidded to a halt. Artillerymen of the 680th unloaded a howitzer and lugged it out into the field to duel with the enemy guns. They fired first, but missed. The German crew didn't. A second group of Americans wheeled their howitzer into position, splattering the enemy battery with flanking fire. It was enough to take out several of the guns and bag twenty-five prisoners. Short but nasty little gunfights erupted throughout the 680th sector. The troopers gave better than they got, but it cost them dearly: two battery commanders were killed within a hundred yards of each other, along with seventeen troopers, in addition to more than fifty wounded in the melee.

Jim Lauria's 75mm howitzer—one of twelve brought in by the 681st—was trapped inside the glider; the aircraft had hit a wire fence on landing and the collision had fouled the nose so badly the men couldn't open it.

After enlisting the help of some glider riders with wire cutters, Lauria finally got out his gun. At the same time, one of the troopers spotted muzzle flashes coming from a hayloft, where a German machine gunner was methodically spraying the LZ. Lauria and crew nudged the howitzer into alignment and aimed down the tube like it was a rifle. When satisfied, Lauria jerked the lanyard. The 75mm shell whined across the field and flashed into the barn. From Lauria's position it looked like the explosion lifted the roof off the barn. No more firing came from the hayloft.

In little more than an hour the gliders had delivered into LZ S 3,492 troops and 637 tons of cargo—including 202 jeeps and 78 mortars and artillery pieces. Like an oil spill, the combat team spread in all directions, drowning German resistance.

11:55. Landing Zone N, Germany.
Saturday, March 24, 1945.

The armada's last seven serials—all single-tow gliders—headed into Landing Zone N. LZ N, sandwiched between the British sector and the Thirteeners' DZ, served as the destination for Miley's supporting units of combat engineers, anti-tank gunners, signalers, medics, and additional artillery. In total the final serials would deliver 1,321 more troops and almost 400 tons of medical supplies, jeeps, communication equipment, anti-tank guns, mortars, ammunition, and body bags. The Thirteeners should have already secured LZ N, but due to their mis-drop, it was still full of Germans.

By the time the single-tow glider serials passed over Diersfordt Forest, the Ruffians were pushing back or overrunning much of the resistance in that sector. The British glider assaults and the artillerymen engaged on DZ X also reduced the anti-aircraft fire directed at the final serials.

However light the ack-ack was, the remaining gunners were still determined. One of the first gliders released over the LZ exploded in midair when tracers ignited its cargo of demolitions. A later count determined that 293 out of the 345 gliders were hit before landing. The Air Force lost another three transports over the LZ, with forty-four more damaged. What the German gunners couldn't do, excessive speed accomplished: over 50 percent of the gliders came in too fast and were damaged in crashes.

Flight Officer Wes Hare's glider smacked in hard, injuring almost everyone on board. Hare's spine was fractured; one of the troopers in back had both of his legs broken while another soldier sustained severe internal injuries and two broken arms; three of the other troopers got away with minor injuries. With two men from his glider already shot, Hare hunkered down to stay below the flying bullets. From the shallow pit he'd scraped out with his hands he watched a trooper shepherding five prisoners across the LZ. As the trooper got closer, a squad of Germans took a few potshots at him. In a single movement the trooper mowed down all five of his POWs with a full magazine from his Thompson submachine gun and dropped to the ground, slithering into a ditch.

On his way into LZ N, George Holdren, the twenty-year-old Midwesterner with good teeth, couldn't see much from his position in the back of the glider. He'd taken a seat on a stack of ammunition cases in front of his 57mm anti-tank gun while two fellow crew members occupied the only available seating.

But Holdren could see well enough to know that the pilot had released higher than he wanted to. What Holdren didn't realize was that his pilot had also released too early. The fluctuating airspeeds had disrupted the formation, forcing the tow pilots to climb to avoid overrunning the preceding flights. Holdren's pilot, recognizing the danger, disengaged the towrope early rather than risk being towed even higher. The decision made it difficult, if not impossible, for the glider to reach its designated landing sector.

Holdren ducked instinctively as machine gun bullets popped a row of neat holes through the tail section of the glider. The rounds clattered off the metal frame "like a string of firecrackers going off." Tiny, precise rays of sunlight beamed through the bullet holes.

The pilot saw several gliders on the ground already getting hammered by enemy guns and pulled up to land farther away. The glider bounced a few times before slamming into the edge of a shell crater. The gun held, but Holdren didn't. He woke up a few minutes later with a dent in his steel helmet and a concussion. Shaking it off, he scrambled out to join his crew and the two pilots peering over the edge of their crater.

They had front-row seats as more gliders dove in to land, including one that burst into flames after hitting a power line. There was no discernible landing pattern, and it appeared to be "every man for himself." The accuracy of the release was commendable, but the landings were all over the place, which delayed assembly. Considering the poor visibility and that gliders from both British and American divisions were already cluttering the LZ—along with the burning hulks of several twin-engine transports—it was a tribute to the pilots' skill that they landed on the LZ at all.

Gunfire poured in from every direction, and Holdren debated who had whom surrounded. Attempts by him and his fellow crew members to unload their glider proved futile as the frame was too mangled to surrender the gun. Holdren and one of the other troopers left in search of a jeep to pull the glider apart. Dodging bullets and running from glider to glider, they had no luck finding a jeep. The two troopers continued deeper into the LZ looking for their comrades.

They'd managed to find some members of their unit to help when they stumbled across a badly wounded German not far from the LZ. The back of the *Soldat's* head had been blown off, exposing his brain. He weakly called out to them, *"Hilfe"*—"Help."

"We were sure that moving him would certainly prove fatal," recalled Holdren. "No one knew of anything else to do, so we just left him crying plaintively. Several fellows suggested that the kind thing to do would be to shoot him to end his suffering, and, while many agreed that it was probably the kindest thing to do, no one would actually do it."

Several of the gliders landed on the southern perimeter, which overlapped with DZ X, where John Chester had landed. He watched two of the CG-4As circle on their final approach to land. Plumes of German mortar fire surrounded both gliders as they skidded across the furrowed field. The first was hit before it stopped moving, killing everyone aboard. The second was hit just as it nosed to a halt, and the whole contraption burst into flames.

From a hundred yards away Chester saw two troopers stumble from the wreckage, both engulfed in flames and trailing smoke as they ran for their lives. Chester raised his carbine to put them out of their misery, but before he could fire they fell to the ground out of his line of sight. As he later admitted, "Fate had just delivered me from a hard thing to do."

Once on the ground many glider pilots felt outgunned. Joseph Shropshire and his load of two troopers took shelter near their glider, digging shallow pits to get under the incoming fire. The bullets hummed and whined overhead with such ferocity that medic Thomas Helms decided his best chance for survival was to give up. He crawled to the edge of their tiny perimeter, waving a rag in surrender. Sergeant Jesse Twitty, a paratrooper none too happy to have arrived by glider, yelled that he'd shoot Helms himself if he didn't stop it.

Shropshire's carbine jammed and Twitty crawled over to provide covering fire. A bullet hit him in the side and tore out through his back. Shropshire and his copilot dragged him to the most protected spot they could find, a deep ditch four or five yards in front of the glider. A few minutes later Twitty called for help as the pain was excruciating. Though he was nearly petrified with fear, Shropshire crawled back through the murderous crossfire to give Twitty a shot of morphine.

In an attempt to reduce the incoming volume of fire, the two pilots stopped shooting at the enemy after Twitty was hit. By Shropshire's estimate they were drawing four times more fire than they could dish out, and their carbines didn't have the range in such open terrain to be effective. Their ploy didn't work.

The mini-Alamo that Shropshire's glider had become was a study in handling fear. Being shot at from every direction with only a peashooter to defend yourself would terrify any sane person. For Helms it was almost too much to bear, freezing him into inaction. Shropshire, on the other hand, although certain he would be killed, had overcome his fear enough to render first aid to someone in need.

Helms still doubted they were going to make it. He crawled back into the glider to call for help on the jeep's radio. Whoever replied told him to get off the radio. Helms might have had a premonition—he was killed the next day.

In the same LZ, Bill Knickerbocker and his copilot ran from ditch to ditch trying to get off the LZ. Their plan required patience, since each crouching sprint attracted bursts of enemy fire. Near a farmhouse,

Knickerbocker heard a shout from inside, "What's that Goddamned kid doing out there?"

Americans were inside. Out front a young German boy had stripped down to his underwear and was herding cows into the barn. The boy's logic was sound; neither side would mistake him for a threat. He successfully got his herd out of the crossfire and disappeared with them into the barn.

Knickerbocker waved his yellow signal scarf toward the house, wanting to be recognized as a friendly. A few seconds later a trooper in a second-floor window waved his scarf back in acknowledgment. As the two glider pilots zigzagged toward the farm, the front door opened for them while the troopers provided covering fire. The pilots tumbled in, out of breath, but safe.

Fifty-three gliders going into LZ N carried medical teams and equipment. Despite bullets chewing up dirt all around them, the medics went to work almost immediately. Jeeps fanned out to collect casualties and bring them back to surgical teams erecting the division aid station.

As the casualties arrived, medics divided them up by severity. In a process referred to as triage, the wounded were segregated into priority cases—with the more serious treated first. Those expected to die were made comfortable rather than operated on. It was a difficult decision, but the medical teams had to focus on saving those they could rather than try to perform miracles while others bled out. Evacuation to rear-area hospitals wasn't expected for at least twenty to forty-eight hours, and the field teams stabilized their patients as best they could until such time as evacuation was feasible.

Many troopers would later accuse the Germans of intentionally targeting the medics, who had red crosses over large white circles painted on their helmets. Glider pilot Robert Staub later reported that "four medics in my glider were shot thru the head by deliberately aimed fire." Medic Joe Leonardo had been machine-gunned in half. "His lower extremities were missing," recalled one of his buddies.

Sergeant Paul Totten dashed out into the open fields multiple times to rescue the wounded. His actions attracted the attention of a determined German rifleman who singled him out. As Totten dragged a wounded trooper to cover, the rifleman shot him once and his patient twice. Totten managed to get them both to safety, where he treated the wounded man first—saving his life—then patched himself up before running back out to recover more casualties.

One ingenious medic had had enough: at pistol point he ordered a POW to sit on the hood of his jeep while he drove across the LZ collecting the wounded. He made several trips in this fashion, avoiding enemy fire each time.

The medical teams paid a heavy price for their bravery. Sixteen medics were killed and thirty-nine wounded. In spite of their condition, more than a dozen of the wounded medics refused to leave their station, continuing to attend casualties as they were brought in.

German POWs were put to work digging trenches to shelter the wounded from incoming fire. They also served as litter bearers, shuttling the casualties as needed.

11:45. *Landing Zone S, Germany.*
Saturday, March 24, 1945.

Back on LZ S, the glider riders had struck out toward their objectives: the bridges over the Issel. Planners had numbered them for easy reference. Starting in Wesel and moving counterclockwise, the bridges over the canal were numbered 1 through 4 and were to be seized by the 2nd Battalion. Bridges 5 through 10—over the river—were to be taken by the 1st Battalion.

Members of George Company fought their way across the LZ, dodging gliders and bullets, to attack Bridges 1 and 2. Their destination was the far side of the canal, where they were to set up a perimeter and prevent any German attempts to occupy or blow up the bridges.

On the outskirts of Wesel, still 600 yards short of Bridge 1, the troopers went to ground in an open field. Squads of well-armed Germans had barricaded themselves in a cluster of industrial buildings bordering the railroad tracks, and they quickly pinned down the Americans. The buildings were little more than shells of heaped bricks, but the defenders made the most of the crumpled urban redoubt. Squads of glider riders scratched forward block by block to reach the bridge.

Two tanks clanked toward the bridge, trying to sweep the Americans off their objective. The rubble and splintered beams of Wesel were a tank hunter's playground. Private Robert Geist let the first tank get within fifty feet before firing a high-explosive rocket from his bazooka into the metal monster. The round impacted with an orange flash and tremendous shock wave. Private William Paliwoda took out the second tank from close range as well. The enemy's first counterattack ground to a halt.

Farther up the sixty-foot-wide canal, troopers of Fox Company assaulted Bridges 3 and 4. The company already had two coups to their credit that morning. Several of their gliders had landed under fire from a German 75mm howitzer positioned in front of an ornate two-story split-wing estate. The well-positioned howitzer had obliterated multiple gliders as they came to rest. But despite suffering casualties, two squads from Fox Company attacked the gun and swooped into the estate. It turned out to be a regimental command post, and the forty-five-member staff surrendered. The haul included an *Oberst*, the commanding officer himself. In a similar attack, another platoon from Fox Company sacked the headquarters of *Artillerieregiment Elbe*, again capturing the commander and his staff.

Within thirty minutes of landing, Fox Company had bagged two regimental command teams and vital intelligence, including maps marked with gun positions surrounding Wesel. As the 2nd Battalion's after-action report later noted, the "consequent disorganization amongst the Germans was tremendous."

By 11:45 Fox Company was back en route to their bridges. The large formations of troops cutting across the open terrain proved a tempting target for a German Mk V Panther tank. It opened fire with its 75mm main gun from 500 yards. Private Robert Weber unlimbered his bazooka for a Hail Mary—at that distance the tank would have been difficult to hit, let alone scratch. But with what was later described as a "miraculous hit," the round either ignited ammunition carelessly stored on the tank's exterior, or if some witnesses are to be believed, arched into an open hatch. What was not in dispute was the result: the tank "all but disintegrated," bursting into flames and engulfing the trapped crew in an inferno.

After knocking out several German outposts at Bridges 3 and 4, Fox Company crossed the Issel Canal and captured the bridges intact. With heaving shovels and flying dirt, they dug defensive positions to fortify their perimeter on the far side.

An hour later, at a blocking position 800 yards northwest of Bridge 2, German infantry, led by two Panther tanks, attempted to storm through the glider riders' flank. The situation was precarious. The glider riders' anti-tank guns weren't yet in position and they were on the verge of being overrun.

In a desperate "the ends justify the means" decision, the troopers prodded several of their POWs up onto the road at gunpoint, forming them into a human shield. The gambit paid off and the German attack stalled, allowing one of the anti-tank crews to wheel their 57mm gun into position.

The Panthers spotted them and cranked their turrets around for a shot. Shells shrieked back and forth; it was a race for the first hit. The troopers scored first, knocking out one of the forty-four-ton Panthers. They reloaded and ricocheted a round off the second tank. The Panther's muzzle barked, and the round splattered into the anti-tank gun with a devastating crash, wounding all four of the crew.

The surviving tank and German infantry fell back, withdrawing toward Bridge 1, where George Company lay in wait. Heavy rifle fire and the *whoosh* of a bazooka greeted the Panther as it approached. The rocket disabled the tank, scattering the remaining infantry, who were cut down by rifle fire as they fled.

Farther north along the river, elements of Able Company had taken control of Bridges 5 and 6 within fifteen minutes of landing. But they were having trouble keeping their perimeter secure. They'd clear a house only to have it later reoccupied by lone snipers. After chasing them out a few times, the troopers simply blasted away with bazookas to burn the houses down.

Gene Herrmann and Phil Snow were two of the first mortar troopers to arrive at Bridge 6. Gliders were still coming in, landing on both sides of the river. Together, the two troopers crawled up the levee to observe their target: a farmhouse already under attack across the Issel. They watched a trooper slink along the façade to throw a grenade through an octagonal window, which silenced the sporadic gunfire from within.

After a salvo of German artillery rounds crashed fifty feet short of the bridge, Herrmann and Snow sprinted across. They found that section of the Issel was only a foot deep due to a closed sluice on the other side of Bridge 5.

They got to their position, and Herrmann went to work laying out the firing points. By the time the others arrived with the heavy mortars, all was in order. One of Herrmann's fellow troopers had had most of his teeth knocked out in his rough landing. The medics told him his injury wasn't severe and sent him back to the line.

Frank Dillon's platoon and the rest of Baker Company went into reserve, setting up positions back behind Bridges 6 and 7. The battalion occupied a shallow, two-and-a-half-mile front along the river. Baker Company would be on call as a quick reaction force in the event of a German breakout at Bridges 5 through 10. Dillon moved between his squads checking on the men and verifying the position of crew-served weapons and individual foxholes.

The troopers tasked with seizing Bridges 7 through 10 found them well protected by dug-in German infantry armed with prodigious numbers of machine guns and automatic weapons. Particularly stubborn defenders held Bridge 7, firing volley after volley of devastating mortar and artillery barrages.

By the time the B-24s started their supply run, the glider riders had a tenuous grip on Bridges 1 and 2. George Company was strung out and pinned down, and the status of their forward platoons was unknown. Attempts to reinforce Bridge 1 were stopped by lacerating machine gun and small arms fire. Bridges 3 through 6 had been secured, while those farther north remained heavily contested and in enemy hands.

CHAPTER 15

"I SHALL FEAR NO EVIL"

13:10. Drop Zone W, Germany. Saturday, March 24, 1945.

The formations of supply-carrying B-24s, aligning for the target run, had tightened up into nine-plane V of Vs as they passed east of Brussels. First Lieutenant Tom Shafer, flying B-24 *Ole King Cole*, followed his three-ship formation as they tucked in just behind and to the left of the lead flight. This was the seventeenth mission for Shafer's crew; two days prior they'd dropped bombs on the German jet airfield at Giebelstadt, which unknown to them had been part of the plan to isolate VARSITY's battlefields.

Montgomery's smoke screen had drifted inland on the friendly side of the Rhine as well, bathing the landscape in monochromatic grays and making navigation—already a challenge at low level—even more difficult. Once the pilots were engulfed in the haze, their visibility was reduced to a mere half mile. Stress levels escalated when two high-tension electrical towers emerged out of the smoke.

Shafer had already been flying his ship below a hundred feet, so he reacted to the apparition by going under the power lines; other crews broke high right or left to go above them. The evasive maneuver jumbled the formation, and the pilots steered back into position as they bore down on the Rhine. The lead formations veered south to line up for their approach to DZ W, while behind them the last 120 Liberators peeled off to drop their cargo farther west for the British airborne troops.

As *Ole King Cole* crossed the Rhine at 150 mph, Shafer passed control to his copilot so he could snap a photograph of their bomber's shadow skidding across the water. Below them signs of battle flickered past: Allied artillery positions, assault craft traversing the river, and a pontoon bridge under construction. Radio operator Darrell Reed's brief amusement at seeing cattle stampeding away from the B-24s was replaced by the sobering sight of crashed gliders and dead paratroopers: "We saw the US Army in action. . . . Tanks, guns and all sorts of heavy equipment. . . . Saw homes and buildings, fields entirely burned and blown up." Ground troops waved or raised their rifles in a jubilant salute.

Off their port wing, *Ten Gun Dottie*—flown by First Lieutenant Raymond Schultz, a flight school classmate of Shafer's—nudged in closer for a tight drop pattern. On starboard, *P-for-Peter* did the same. Ready in the back, the crew waited for the signal to jettison supplies. *Ole King Cole*'s two waist gunners, Sergeant Thomas Paone and Staff Sergeant Horace Meacomes, traced static lines to ensure they were routed correctly. They'd have just twenty seconds to jettison the cargo within the boundaries of the supply drop point.

The Ruffians were supposed to have marked the drop point on DZ W with colored panels and red smoke. But unknown to the inbound B-24 pilots, the team of Ruffians assigned to the task had mis-dropped and were unable to get to the DZ in time. Fortunately the navigator in the lead aircraft recognized the DZ and salvoed the bomb bay supplies. The crew in back cursed and pushed out the bundles clustered around the open ball turret and escape hatch.

Taking his cue from the lead aircraft, Shafer raised *Ole King Cole*'s nose to slow its airspeed, and his copilot hit the bailout alarm to signal the crew. As the A-5 containers dropped from the bomb shackles, Staff Sergeant Edward Cassinari inched out onto the narrow catwalk spanning the open bomb bay to jettison the static lines. In the rear of the aircraft, the three gunners cut the retaining cords and dumped the supplies. Once all were clear, Shafer dropped the nose and increased power as the bomb bay doors rolled closed.

As the four-engine bombers roared past, paratroops watched and noted that some were too low, leaving the chutes insufficient time to open. To avoid the expected flak and small arms fire, many of the pilots had dropped below 300 feet, and some as low as a hundred, forcing them to climb as they approached the drop point. Not all made it back up to 300 feet in time. As a result some of the containers plummeted into the ground, bursting open on impact and littering the field with supplies.

As the first B-24s finished their run and banked right, they flew into a hornet's nest of enemy small arms fire. The lead navigator later recalled, "The air was filled with an intense storm of 20mm cannon, machine gun and small weapons fire. From my position in the nose, I was sure that the tracers were going to cut my legs off."

Shafer brought *Ole King Cole* back down to fifty feet, while his copilot surveyed the instrument panel for the slightest hint of trouble. Behind them stood their navigator, Second Lieutenant Bob Overstake, calling out obstacles. The rest of the crew were now merely observers as Shafer evaded the venomous ground fire. Tracer rounds crisscrossed up from all directions.

Ten Gun Dottie disappeared off their port wing, flaming into the ground like a comet, killing all nine of the crew instantly. The explosion's huge ball of flame was so close that tail gunner Dick Howell felt the heat from inside *Ole King Cole*.

Holding into the turn, Shafer kept his bomber just off the wing of *P-for-Peter*, both ships hugging the ground at fifty feet. Suddenly anti-aircraft fire peppered *Peter's* cockpit, slumping both pilots over the controls. From his vantage point Shafer watched helplessly as one of his bunkmates, navigator Eugene Golub, struggled to get out of *Peter's* nose turret as the plane pitched into the ground. Just behind *Ole King Cole*, the bomber *Silver Wolf*, flown by Second Lieutenant Arthur Keith, raced through the crash's enormous fireball. From *Ole King Cole's* waist window, the last thing gunner Horace Meacomes saw of his friends was "four engines rolling across the field and through the hedgerows in balls of fire." Burning debris spilled across the ground for nearly half a mile.

In a decision later hailed as lifesaving by his crew and reckless by his chain of command, Shafer cut his turn short. Keeping the plane low, he barreled along at treetop level, cutting through a section of burning forest, which subsequently required the removal of charred twigs from the engine cowlings.

Shafer later explained, "Because of ground fire and the loss of two planes that were flying near me, I decided I was too high to be comfortable. So I went down to less than fifty feet." Egressing just above the rubble-strewn streets of Wesel, Meacomes admitted, "everybody was scared to death." Though Shafer was threatened with a court-martial for breaking formation and flying too low, his crew adamantly defended his decision. Meacomes later wrote in his diary, "It is almost certain that if he had not done so, we would never have made the return across the Rhine."

• • •

Behind them, a group of bombers had drifted too far out of position to make an accurate drop. Instead of jettisoning the supplies somewhere on the east bank of the Rhine as instructed, they circled for a second, more accurate pass.

With three bombers already downed by enemy fire, the remaining twenty-three made a wide turn to roar back over the DZ. They lost another aircraft, and a second flown by Captain John Hunter was mauled badly. Despite the severing of the aircraft's elevator trim tabs and the freezing of its rudder, Hunter and his copilot wrestled the bomber back over the Channel to England for an emergency landing with three wounded aboard.

Nose gunner Jack Young remembered his crew's ordeal: "Tracers flashed up from 20mm cannons. The first shots hit the aircraft to our right, blowing the number two engine completely off. They veered left 20 feet above in an almost vertical left bank and disappeared from view. The cannons next hit the lead aircraft, blew off the entire left fin and rudder . . ."

Crews had strict orders against shooting at ground targets, for fear of fratricide, but Young had seen enough. "I flipped on my gun switches, swung the turret toward the cannons. Suddenly my turret shattered. I will always remember two tracers coming slowly like Roman candles slashing into my turret, the Plexiglas shattering, the metal bent and torn as the projectiles entered the bombardier's compartment behind me. The pilot was shouting over the intercom, 'We're crashing!'"

After forcing his way through the turret's hatch and squeezing into the main compartment, Young found the bombardier, Lieutenant Don Huelsman, uninjured. Their happiness at being alive was replaced by the desire to stay that way.

The tracers had set the supplies, still in the bomb racks, on fire — singeing the two men as they pressed their way up to the flight deck. The Number 1 engine was nonresponsive, Number 2 was on fire, Number 3 appeared to be spinning out of control, and the fourth was rotating only due to the forward momentum of the wounded bomber. Young took up his crash position behind the copilot and waited. He felt the bomber jerk and then everything went black.

When Young regained consciousness sometime later, his eyes were swollen shut and someone was cutting off his flight jacket. Before he passed out again, he heard explosions, shooting, and English-speaking voices. The plane had crashed on the Allied side of the Rhine! Young later learned that of the nine-man crew, only he and two others survived.

Second Lieutenant Donald Potter, flying *Southern Comfort III*, watched the B-24 on his right take a round through their Number 1 engine. "The wing dropped and the pilot lost about 25 feet of altitude. With a beautiful piece of handling, he managed to bring the wings level. His bomb bay hit the ground and the craft seemed to give a little bounce, and was flying again. The pilot would have made it, but immediately ahead was a string of telephone or power poles and wire. As I recall, he had to bank left in order to lift his right wing over a pole. In doing this, his left wing dug into the ground and the plane started cartwheeling and exploded. In a great black and crimson flash, the crew and plane were gone, nothing left but scorched earth and debris. I felt empty!"

Kanonier Peter Emmerich got caught out in an open field when the bombers cut overhead. He was on his way back to his crew's four-barrel *Flakvierling* with more ammo when two of the B-24s roared toward the German guns.

"Gun ready!" yelled one of the gunners.

Emmerich remembered the incident vividly, "Over the tree tops the first monster arrived. It flew approximately some 40 meters above the ground. . . . The second plane flew a little more to the right of us and a little higher, maybe 60 meters."

All three guns opened fire.

"I saw how the tracers found their way to the aircraft," Emmerich continued. "The first aircraft caught fire in both engines and his left stabilizer broke off. . . . Parts of the wing came down. The aircraft went straight up for about 200 to 300 meters, stalled and turned to the ground. We only heard two loud explosions and saw two smoke piles going up some 80 meters above the crash sites."

One of the gunners shouted "Hurray!" as the bombers went down.

Another two B-24s soon followed the same course.

Unterfeldwebel Bosse ordered the gunners to wait, "Easy, let them near us! Fire!"

"I saw nothing," admitted Emmerich, who earlier dove to the ground. "I kept my head in the soil! When I heard the screaming noise of the engines I looked up and saw these two were also on fire. They also exploded with two big explosions."

Bosse was proud of his crew's work. By his calculations they'd hit more than a dozen gliders and four of the bombers. He shook each man's hand, encouraging them to "Continue till victory."

Emmerich couldn't tell if Bosse was a patriot or a blind fanatic, but he began to feel that he'd be sacrificed for a lost cause. As he looked at the surrounding carnage, Emmerich worried what the Americans would do to them if captured. The airborne troops were still a few hundred yards away, but Emmerich could feel the storm getting closer.

Flying *E-for-Easy*, Second Lieutenant Jack Hummel dropped his Liberator's altitude back down onto the deck immediately after making their drop. Several shells riddled both wings. Copilot Jim Reynolds surveyed the instrument panel and yelled that he was shutting down Number 3. He flipped switches to feather the propellers, cut the gasoline, closed the cowlings, and cut the electrical. Despite his quick reaction, the engine continued to burn. Hummel reported that on his side Number 2 was losing oil pressure.

In the bomb bay Corporal James Deaton was making his way along the narrow, nine-inch catwalk when the aircraft lurched from the shellfire. He lost his balance and fell out. The cramped conditions of the bomb bay prevented him from wearing a parachute.

With two engines out and having reduced airspeed for the supply drop, Hummel fought to get the B-24 up to at least 500 feet. Reynolds hit the bailout alarm to get the crew out. The nose gunner and the navigator jumped out of the front escape hatch just in time.

The rest of the crew, recognizing they were too late, scrambled into their crash positions. The pilots knew there was no way they could jump before the plane crashed. Reynolds mumbled a quick prayer—"Lord, it is all up to you now"—and worked the rudders with Hummel to keep the bomber level. They headed for a spot of open ground on the western edge of DZ X.

Below them, the bomber's plight was witnessed by a glider pilot who just minutes before had survived his own aircraft getting shot out of the sky, "[The B-24] just missed the high-tension lines, flew over us and crashed in the field on the other side of the tracks," he recalled. "I could feel the heat of the engine on fire when it passed over our heads!"

Reynolds woke in the cockpit when Hummel asked if he was hurt. Both pilots had superficial head wounds, but the gashes bled profusely. Together, they crawled out through a large hole in the side of the cockpit and staggered twenty feet from the wreck. Dazed and likely in shock, the two men needed a few seconds to realize the dirt kicking up around their feet was from German bullets.

Inside the aircraft top-turret gunner Sergeant Herbert Finney was still stunned. He and Sergeant Elmer Milchak, one of the waist gunners, decided to exit from one of the waist windows. Milchak stuck his head out to survey their position. He jerked once and slumped over the open sill, dead from a head shot.

Hollis Powell and Paul Keagle pulled themselves out of the twisted fuselage through a hole in the side. The five airmen were desperate to get away from the wreck, fearing it would explode any second, but the fuselage was their only shelter from enemy rifle fire. Powell recognized that all potential escape routes were cut off and pulled out the canopy of his unused parachute and waved it in surrender.

German infantry surrounded the crew and allowed them to remove Milchak's body from the burning bomber. In all of the confusion, no one knew what had happened to the missing crew members; they couldn't find their bodies so figured they must have made it out. Before herding them away, the Germans waited for Reynolds to recite the 23rd Psalm over Milchak.

The Germans ushered the crew 200 yards across the field to a small complex of buildings where they were segregated by rank. The pilots were sent to a large château for interrogation while the three enlisted men were held in a basement.

After Reynolds had his head bandaged by a German medic, he was presented to a *Hauptmann* and an *Obergefreiter* (corporal). The *Obergefreiter* began by asking for the standard name, rank, and serial number. Reynolds complied.

While the *Hauptmann* flipped through a small Bible taken out of Reynolds' breast pocket, the *Obergefreiter* continued his questions.

"Do you speak German?"

"No," replied Reynolds.

The *Obergefreiter* then wanted to know if Reynolds spoke French.

"No."

"What languages do you speak?"

"Only English," said Reynolds.

Exasperated, the Corporal said, "You are an officer in the American Army and can speak only one language, and I am a Corporal in the German Army and I can speak five languages fluently. What do American schools teach?"

Reynolds gave his name, rank, and serial number. Which he repeated in response to every question thereafter.

Growing tired of the game, the *Obergefreiter* threatened, "We have ways of making people talk."

The comment spurred the *Hauptmann* into action. He put the Bible back in Reynolds' pocket and in perfect English said, "Lieutenant, he is not going to harm you."

Reynolds was led away to a room filled with dozens of wounded Germans. A medic, who perhaps sensed the inevitable, befriended the American pilot, confiding that he hoped to be sent to the United States if captured.

The three-story château where Hummel and Reynolds were being held appeared to be serving as a German headquarters. The two pilots heard several soldiers address an officer as "General," and there was a soldier peddling a stationary bicycle attached to a generator. The contraption apparently produced enough juice to power a bank of radios. Other soldiers stood around a metal barrel tossing papers into the growing flames. As far as Hummel and Reynolds could tell, the complex consisted of the château and several brick outbuildings. It was manned by an estimated 200 soldiers and ringed by multiple machine gun nests. There were two sections of 105mm light artillery guns, three facing north and another three pointed east.

As they sat on the floor of the château's basement, the three enlisted crew members sensed increasing anxiety within the headquarters. Gunfire could be heard outside; Allied troops must be getting closer. Finney, the top-turret gunner, became more afraid of getting killed in the growing crossfire than of being executed by his captors.

Their German guard, glancing nervously at the basement windows, flipped over a large wooden table, telling Powell to get down behind it.

"Why?" he asked.

"Americans might run by and toss a grenade in the window." The airmen complied.

CHAPTER 16

"ARE THEY GOING
TO SHOOT US NOW?"

*13:10. Diersfordt Castle, Drop Zone W, Germany.
Saturday, March 24, 1945.*

At Diersfordt Castle the defenders were still putting up a worthy fight from behind thick brick walls. The Ruffians had laid siege to the castle for several hours. The burning tanks spewed black clouds of diesel fire, and one of the building's roofs crackled with flames. Dead from both sides lay sprawled throughout the compound.

The new plan was to cross the moat and storm the compound from the northeast corner. It would be a textbook drill: in a coordinated effort, one element would unleash fire at the castle, aiming at windows to keep the enemy's head down; the other element would use the covering fire to maneuver across the moat between the blockhouse and the church. It *would* have been routine except for the fact that attacks rarely go according to plan and the enemy always gets a vote.

As the second hand of their watches ticked up to 13:00, the troopers cut loose. Bullets from rifles and belt-fed machine guns chipped away at the brick façade. Able Company got their captured mortar into the act once more, lobbing shells into the compound. A few plucky sharpshooters clanged the bell in the church spire, which soon collapsed under the impact of the Thirteeners' mortar barrage. The east wall of the church collapsed with it, destroying the organ. Frightened civilians sheltering in the church basement could hear the swell of incoming fire and the *crumps* of grenades.

The assaulting troopers surged forward, splashing across the moat and clearing the outer buildings room by room. They ran past the bodies of their buddies who'd died in the first attempt to storm the castle. Grenades echoed in the large blockhouse as the attack became a series of individual battles, with troopers scurrying across the complex for cover and shooting at anything not in olive drab. Faced with the paratroopers' full fury, pockets of defenders started to surrender.

After two hours of mopping up, the Ruffians had corralled almost 300 prisoners. But a group of diehards barricaded themselves in the castle's square tower, refusing to give up.

The castle's owner, Count Bolko Graf von Stolberg-Wernigerode, attempted to negotiate their surrender. He approached the tower waving a white rag. One of the diehards opened fire from a tower window to chase him away. As the count ran for cover, the Americans blasted the upper floor with bazookas and set the roof on fire. Still the zealots stood fast.

The Americans tried once more, ordering Herr Tinnefeld, a local farmer sheltering in the basement, to act as a negotiator under a flag of truce. Again the offer was rejected. The Ruffians would have to pursue another option to evict the holdouts.

★   ★   ★

As the Ruffians at the castle pondered their next move, three amphibious landing craft churned across the Rhine. General Ridgway, unmistakable with his 1903 bolt-action rifle and camouflage helmet with two white stars, waited to land. He'd watched the airdrop from the Allied side of the river and now crossed with a small element of his staff to establish his corps command post.

The British crew was hesitant to drop the general onto a hostile shore. To ensure no threats lurked nearby, they raked the bank with a Browning belt-fed machine gun, shredding vegetation that could conceal anything bigger than a bread box.

Satisfied by the lack of return fire, the Brits guided their tracked vehicles up onto the shore. The crew dropped the rear ramp to let Ridgway, his aide, and their three tommy gun–wielding bodyguards disembark onto the east bank. They also unloaded several jeeps.

The initial destination was Miley's command post. The group split up, with most of the staff loaded into the three jeeps and proceeding ahead. For reasons unknown, Ridgway opted to continue on foot with his small retinue. Perhaps he liked the idea of a walk in the brisk weather, or maybe he wanted to get a better feel for the terrain. Regardless of the reason, he knew it would still be several hours until his corps staff could coordinate action between the two airborne divisions.

Ridgway's group headed inland, moving cautiously down a small path through the tall, thin trees. They passed signs of the fighting. The general noted a dead but otherwise unscathed German soldier in his foxhole, the victim of an artillery concussion.

When a blur of movement appeared through the trees followed by the sound of thumping hooves, the small group dashed off the trail. From his concealed position in the undergrowth, Ridgway later recalled, "I saw one of the strangest sights I ever observed in war. Down that little trail came a big, heavy-footed farm horse. On his back was an American paratrooper. On the paratrooper's head was a high silk hat. He had his rifle slung on his back and a look of smug contentment on his face."

Ridgway stepped out onto the trail. The stars on his helmet caught the cavalier's attention, and he almost fell off his mount trying to simultaneously salute and present arms.

Ridgway laughed at the man's comical discomfort.

The trooper—one of Raff's Ruffians—explained that he'd "found" the horse and hat in a farmhouse. After getting directions from the trooper, Ridgway motioned his entourage to continue inland.

Ridgway arrived at the Ruffians' command post to find the situation well in hand. Raff had already established radio contact with his three battalions, and he provided a comprehensive briefing to Ridgway.

The initial confusion of the mis-drop had been quickly replaced with orderly execution. The regiment's perimeter had been established and at least 80 percent of the troops accounted for. Raff estimated the Ruffians' losses at ninety-nine casualties, with several men still missing.

Though the mopping up at Diersfordt Castle was still under way, the defenders had been buttoned up and no longer posed a threat to PLUNDER. Roadblocks had been established along the southern sector. A patrol sent toward the Rhine had made contact with a reconnaissance unit of the 15th Scottish Division who were probing their way up from the riverbank. German units sandwiched between the two Allied units were considered under control.

The B-24 drop had gone well, with the Ruffians witnessing the spectacle from their perimeter. Several of the troopers who'd scampered out to claim a few bundles discovered that some of the containers should have been dropped farther north as they were filled with British ammunition along with tea and biscuits. The supplies had been welcome. Raff's battalion at the castle was running low on ammo.

Despite his professional and deferential posture toward his corps commander, Raff actually harbored a deep disdain for Ridgway. His list of grievances ran deep: he blamed Ridgway for bringing politics into the airborne community and believed Ridgway's Distinguished Service Cross—an award for valor—was a sham. Raff felt that if the criteria for Ridgway's award were applied equally, every man in the 82nd Airborne Division who'd jumped into Normandy should have gotten one. Equally egregious, Ridgway had elected to cross the Rhine in a boat rather than jump in with his troops.

Raff's criticism failed to recognize Ridgway's role as the corps commander. His influence on the battle would only commence after the two airborne divisions had accomplished their initial missions. Raff's disgust was so vitriolic that had Ridgway actually jumped, most likely Raff's criticism would have been redirected at the misappropriation of valuable aircraft at the expense of the division's combat power.

Ridgway was unaware of Raff's resentment and soon departed the Ruffians' perimeter in search of Miley's command post. But not before Raff, cognizant of the surrounding skirmishes, assigned two squads to escort the general's group.

Ridgway and his entourage found Miley exactly where they'd expected him, on the western edge of DZ W. The cluster of officers was set up in a shell crater, gathered around maps and radios. Miley's radio operator, who'd jumped with a SCR-300 in his leg bag, was in communication with each of the three regimental combat teams. The thirty-pound SCR-300 backpack radio allowed voice communication within a 2.5- to 5-mile range, depending on which antenna the operator was using.

Miley also had radio contact with his chief of staff, who'd landed via glider with the main headquarters team on LZ N. The two teams were to rendezvous at a pond located equidistant between them—in the center of the division's zone of responsibility. But due to the Thirteeners' mis-drop, the section of the forest Miley's group needed to cut through hadn't yet been cleared.

A plan to send a security patrol to reconnoiter a trail through the dense woods was scrapped due to concerns of an enemy ambush. An alternate route through a reportedly secure area was identified, but an hour later members of Miley's defense platoon returned with bad news: Branigan's Bastards were still fending off the Germans, and there was no way to get through to the pond.

Still under heavy small arms and mortar fire, Branigan's artillerymen were fighting as infantry to blunt German counterattacks into the DZ. By this time three of the Bastards' 75mm howitzers had been assembled, and troopers were eyeballing shots down the barrels to blast enemy positions.

The German 88mm that had forced the Bastards out of their command post still had them under direct fire. The 88 was cunningly concealed behind a screen of trees near a farmhouse, and the Bastards were having a hard time spotting it. One of Branigan's crew muscled a howitzer several hundred yards through the woods to get a better shot at it. Finally, a lieutenant got a bead on the 88 and over the radio guided a few artillery rounds into it, destroying the big gun along with the house next to it.

At least two enemy StuGs—self-propelled guns—clanked their way into the northern perimeter, blasting at Branigan's howitzers with their own 75mm guns. The StuG, similar to a tank in appearance, had a gun built directly into the casemate-style hull, which gave it a lower profile than a tank. The compact design lacked the lateral movement that a turret would have provided.

As the enemy armor loitered on the perimeter hurling shells into the Bastards, a forward observer called for fire. Several rounds rattled in, bracketing the tracked vehicles before making direct hits. The counterattack was over.

Miley was sufficiently concerned about Branigan's precarious position to radio the Ruffians for infantry support. Raff's 1st Battalion, standing by for just such a need, sent two companies: one to reinforce the Bastards' perimeter and another to clear the woods north of their position.

Thad Blanchard's squad in Able Company had set up on the edge of the DZ, scratching out shallow fighting positions with their shovels. They now packed up to assume the vanguard in the effort to clear the woods from which most of the harassing fire emanated.

After crossing over the main road through Diersfordt Forest, they used the woods for cover to get closer to the enemy positions. Just after leaving the concealment of the tree line, they were driven to ground by the *rat-tat-tat tat-tat* of two German machine guns protecting an 81mm mortar crew. They knew what to do: cover the other squad with rifle fire as they bounded into the enemy. Blanchard later recalled the chaos of the attack: "Everywhere was a grey uniform, shoot, run, shoot, throw a grenade."

Once he'd emptied his Thompson, Blanchard reloaded by flipping the magazines he'd taped back-to-back for the assault. He released the bolt, but the first shell mis-fed in the chamber. He took a knee to clear the jam just as a young German emerged from a dugout with his rifle and bayonet pointed at him. Fumbling with his submachine gun, Blanchard yelled incoherent words as the German charged. The *Soldat* yelled back, presumably calling for Blanchard to surrender. Gaining speed, the German sprinted forward with his bayonet at the ready. Blanchard cleared his jam. With just a few feet separating the two men, Blanchard unleashed a full burst into the German's face, virtually severing his head from his body. Momentum carried the headless corpse forward and Blanchard parried the bayonet with his tommy gun.

"That bastard sure didn't want to die, did he?" asked a passing trooper who'd witnessed the dead man's final charge.

The question snapped Blanchard out of his daze, and the two men rejoined the attack, which had surged past them.

Blanchard yelled over his shoulder to Harry Pinson, "Toss me a grenade!"

Pinson leaned against a tree with a grenade in his hand, but he didn't move. He was dead.

Blanchard sprinted back to Pinson and slid down next to him. A bullet tore the epaulette off Blanchard's shoulder. He grabbed the grenade from Pinson's lifeless hand and hunkered down, figuring what to do next. A heartbeat later, Private Wyman Martin spotted the German who had Blanchard pinned down (and who'd likely killed Pinson) and shot him. Another burst of machine gun fire sent Blanchard ducking behind the tree.

Now the rest of the platoon bounded forward, assaulting the position. The two German machine guns and the mortar had been set up on the flank of an artillery battery. The howitzers were dug into the front gardens of two farmhouses; trenches and foxholes surrounded the entire emplacement.

The first house, a two-story stone structure with the barn attached, had already been the scene of heavy fighting. Several of Branigan's dead troopers—many still in their chutes—were scattered around the farmhouses. From the way some of the bodies were positioned it appeared that at least six paratroopers had been executed. The second farmhouse was on fire from the Bastards' artillery duel with the 88. The two guns located there had been destroyed and abandoned. As the Ruffians flushed the trenches, the Germans retreated, leaving behind their dead and wounded.

A few hundred yards up the road a group of Germans scurried across the street. Several bursts from an American machine gun cut through the flurry of gray-clad figures. Tragically, only two of the group were soldiers—the other three were civilians, including a woman and her daughter.

After a radio message confirmed that the Ruffians had secured the area, Miley's command group moved along the eastern edge of the woods, dodging periodic artillery fire as they made their way to the pond. With Ridgway tagging along, Miley's linkup with the glider-borne headquarters element officially established the division command post.

Meanwhile, the Ruffians at Diersfordt Castle still surrounded the Germans barricaded in the tower. Twenty-one-year-old Private Robert Watson finally lost patience with the stalemate and dashed from his position to chuck a white phosphorus grenade through a shattered window. The blast severely burned the *Oberst* in charge of the garrison and deflated his men's appetite for further resistance. The diehards filed out with their hands up.

Troopers formed the prisoners into three ranks and patted them down, emptying the contents of their pockets onto the ground.

Staff Sergeant Bill Consolvo was hailed by his executive officer, "[See] if you can get that damn Kraut flag down and put this one up!"

Consolvo ran up the tower's staircase to replace the red-and-black Nazi flag with the Stars and Stripes. He later recalled, "I sure got a warm feeling when I saw it fluttering in the breeze!"

With their objectives secured and resistance reduced to minor skirmishes, the Ruffians sent out patrols to sweep the area. One bumped into a squad from the British 9th Parachute Battalion out looking for the Thirteeners. The good news was passed back by radio. A staff officer confessed in the regimental diary that the event "[relieved] the feeling that we were all alone on this mission."

The patrols searched houses and collected civilians, herding them to holding points under guard. Rounding up civilians was the safest option for all concerned as it would get them out of the crossfire and ease the minds of punchy troopers wanting their perimeter cleared before sunset.

Troopers evicted Vicar Heinrich Müller from his house, holding him at gunpoint while they searched the cellar. He had to be relieved his wife had discreetly burned their portraits of Hitler before she evacuated. Downstairs they found his sister, Marianne, who was escorted outside with her hands up.

"Are they going to shoot us now?" she asked her brother.

No, but the troopers would be taking them to a civilian collection point at a farm on the southern end of the DZ.

The vicar wanted back inside to fetch his Bible and shaving razor, but either his broken English was misunderstood or his escort didn't care. Whichever case, he wasn't allowed back in. When he returned a few days later, he found his Bible and razor but not his gold pocket watch or any of the family's sterling silver.

The vicar and his sister joined several other groups of civilians in their exodus to the collection point. The group grew as the Ruffians went door to door, clearing homes and barns. Families shuffled down the dirt roads under armed escort, women carrying their babies.

Having passed the carnage of burning farms and dead bodies, the civilians were relieved to be reunited with neighbors they'd assumed were dead. They learned of tragedies: several families had lost loved ones to the artillery barrage. Americans shooting through the window of their cellar had inadvertently killed Herr Büttner's wife, Laura. Rumors circulated that everyone sheltering in the castle's cellar was dead. They could all see the smoke from the burning castle and had heard the furious battle. Relief swept through the collected crowd when that group arrived a short time later.

The troopers segregated the civilians from the *Wehrmacht* prisoners, whose numbers had swelled to an estimated 700.

The local English teacher, Frau Bruns, became the civilian ambassador. Farmers were concerned about their livestock and requested to go feed their animals. Chaperoned by Ruffians, the women were allowed to return briefly to their farms.

At some point during their clearing operation the troopers recovered the body of Major Gordon Fowler, a P-47 Thunderbolt pilot who'd bailed out of his damaged aircraft earlier that morning. He'd landed not far from the DZ, but the troopers found him murdered, his throat cut.

At the division command post, the radio crackled to life informing Miley and Ridgway that the Thirteeners hadn't yet secured the northern perimeter. The generals departed in a three-jeep convoy to see what could be done; on the way they would stop by the canal to check up on the glider riders' progress. Miley rode in the lead jeep with his radio operator while Ridgway's vehicle brought up the rear. Two tommy gun–toting MPs with a pedestal-mounted machine gun occupied the middle jeep.

CHAPTER 17

"A VERY DIRTY BUSINESS"

Mid-afternoon, Drop Zone X, Germany.
Saturday, March 24, 1945.

Lieutenant Colonel Kenneth Booth, commander of the 466th Para-chute Field Artillery, took stock of his battalion. His artillerymen had slugged it out all morning as infantry on the heavily fortified DZ, and the Thirteeners were still missing. By 11:30 the medics, led by Captain Loran Morgan, had set up their aid station in the same building as the command post, after taking out the machine gun position the Germans had barricaded in the front door.

Booth knew from the number of casualties pouring in that his men had taken a beating. Add in the wounded Tommies and the number of patients doubled. Many of the British gliders had overshot their LZ, crashing nearby on the edge of the American zone. Morgan's medics treated their broken bones, burns, and shrapnel wounds with the same urgency as they did their American patients.

Medics divided the casualties into four large rooms by severity: the walking wounded, the serious but stable, the seriously wounded, and those needing evacuation to the division's aid station, where surgical treatment was available. Medic Steve Miladinovich moved between rooms monitoring the patients' condition, upgrading or shuttling the wounded as necessary.

A timely supply of plasma and bandages arrived when Private James Lefler rolled up in one of the unit's jeeps. To deliver his cargo Lefler had landed by glider and single-handedly navigated off the LZ, over double railroad tracks, and across the DZ, all while under fire. Once the sup-plies were unloaded, Lefler rigged his jeep with litters and ranged the DZ, looking for more casualties.

While the medics worked, Booth counted. It had been a devastating morning. The numbers were still coming in as the batteries regained order, but in addition to the hundred-odd wounded, they had nearly fifty dead—a staggering 25 percent casualty rate. In exchange for those losses, the artillerymen had littered their section of German real estate with more than four dozen German corpses; bagged over 300 prisoners; and captured or destroyed eighteen machine guns, ten howitzers, and eight anti-aircraft guns.

Booth arrived at John Chester's A Battery to find all of their officers dead or wounded. He directed one of his staff officers, First Lieutenant James Nammack, to take command. Chester had worked with Nammack since before leaving the States and respected him as an artilleryman. Perhaps most appealing, his new CO "had a highly desirable trait called common sense."

A Battery, in addition to losing their officers, had lost two of their enlisted men and suffered sixteen wounded. Nammack's first duty was to reassign five men to the gravely mauled C Battery. They'd suffered forty-one casualties. Their drop had started badly, with an entire stick of twelve jumpers mowed down as they landed, including Donald Stanford, who, despite his medic armband and the large red crosses adorning his helmet, had been machine-gunned while sprinting to aid a comrade.

While the artillery crews collected themselves, an officer—an observer from Fort Benning's Parachute School—took advantage of the lull to recover an important personal item: his teeth. As the forty-two-year-old Ridgely Gaither later recalled, "Before the jump, I'd removed my plate of two upper front teeth and placed it in a matchbox, packed in a canvas bag. When I hit the ground, I lost the bag. Without my plate, I was unable to pronounce the password, 'Hither-Thither,' and was worried that some blood-crazed paratrooper would shoot first and ask questions later. So I crawled to the spot where I landed, found the bag, reinserted my plate, and then crawled back."

BLAM! BLAM! Chester's crew scrambled for cover. The shots rang out from what they thought was a secured area. Two men were hit, one dead before he fell. More bullets sang overhead as the crew scanned for telltale muzzle flashes. With the near misses getting closer, someone spotted the assassins and yelled, "In the Horsa!"

As the crew rushed toward the abandoned British glider, two German bolt-action rifles were thrown out of it. What followed surprised everyone: two teenage girls emerged with their arms raised. The troopers, boiling with anger, crowded around the girls. The lieutenant asked for volunteers. The implication was clear.

Chester could tell "none of the boys wanted any part of it," but after an awkward silence, two spoke up. The gathered artillerymen watched solemnly as the girls, with hands bound, were marched away. A few minutes later two gunshots cracked from the tree line. When the volunteers returned, no one asked for details. It was later rumored they'd let the girls go, but stories claiming the opposite persisted.

Armed civilians, despite the common misunderstanding throughout the ranks, were not to be summarily executed but rather treated in accordance with the laws of land warfare. According to the 1940 field manual, "The inhabitants of a territory which has not been occupied, who, on the approach of the enemy, spontaneously take up arms to resist the invading troops without having had time to organize themselves . . . shall be regarded as belligerents if they carry arms openly and if they respect the laws and customs of war." In other words, they could be shot in the course of a battle, but once captured they were to be protected as prisoners whose fate would be decided by a military tribunal. But not all soldiers bothered with manuals or cared what lawyers thought about war's finer nuances.

However repugnant, the troopers served as judge, jury, and executioner, believing they were acting within the limits of their trade. Chester had long ago resigned himself to the fact that "war can be somewhat beyond a very dirty business, very ugly." A very dirty, very ugly business indeed.

They were rescued from any deeper contemplation of the incident by an order to lug their assembled howitzers over 2,000 yards to their designated firing position. Until they could find some horsepower, manpower served as the mechanism of conveyance. They muscled the 1400-pound howitzer across the tilled fields through a sweat-inducing combination of pulling and pushing. Two men, tethered like mules, used harnesses to pull it tail first. The others pushed, keeping the barrel down so the tail stayed up. The crews rotated positions to minimize grumbling. Forty-five minutes later, after a lot of huffing and puffing, they completed the move.

B Battery, already in position, had been firing in support of the Thirteeners making their way to the DZ. The first groups filtered in just after one o'clock that afternoon. Their numbers had grown as they moved south, cutting across fields littered with wrecked British and American gliders. Small groups and individuals continued to wander in for the next twenty-four hours.

The Thirteeners' commander, Colonel Jim Coutts, and his staff had been leapfrogging southeast as the regiment advanced out of the British sector. Upon reaching the DZ, they set up their command post in a farmhouse on a spot of high ground a mile short of the Issel River. The disorientation of their mis-drop had cost the Thirteeners time. Even with the arrival of the British glider troops to help flush the enemy, it took three hours to overcome local resistance so they could move to their assembly areas.

Some troopers, despite the urgency, paused to collect spoils of war. Lieutenant Peter Scotese from Philadelphia and two of his men had routed a German unit that left their payroll behind. The three agreed to split the 40,000 *Reichsmarks*, stuffing the bills into their packs between grenades and ammunition.

Coutts had met up with his 1st Battalion on the march and was informed that both the commander and executive officer were unaccounted for. A proactive lieutenant, who'd assembled almost 80 percent of the battalion, was leading them. Coutts put his intelligence officer, Captain Gates Ivy, in charge of the battalion. He led the troopers to an orchard, where they set up a defensive position and awaited further orders as Coutts' quick reaction force.

Texan Lendy McDonald's squad, having followed Ivy, dug into their section of the perimeter that included an observation point along the main road, down which the 116 *Panzer-Division*'s counterattack was anticipated. The latest intelligence indicated that the Germans' armored reserve was still in Bocholt, seven miles north of Hamminkeln.

Coutts' 3rd Battalion, with arguably the Thirteeners' most important mission, was behind schedule too. They were responsible for occupying a mile-long gap along the Issel River that would tie together the British 6th Airborne's line of defense and the glider riders' perimeter farther south, at the twelve-foot-wide Bridge 10.

During the exodus south the 3rd Battalion had formed several groups. A group of fifty troopers led by Lieutenant Eugene Crowley was the first to the assembly area. They'd collected 158 prisoners, one of whom had obligingly confirmed their location and got them moving toward the DZ.

Next to arrive was a group of 150 troopers led by the battalion commander, Lieutenant Colonel Edward Kent. Kent, a thirty-six-year-old lawyer by trade, had mistakenly led his group west before bumping into British paratroops seizing the village of Hamminkeln. Kent turned his columns around at that point, heading back the way they came.

Kent's group, while en route to the DZ, found the battalion's aid station already in operation not far from the planned location of their command post. Captain Arthur Young, Kent's medical officer, had the situation well in hand. Set up in a grand manor house with several out-buildings, the Americans found the complex already in use as a *Wehrmacht* field hospital. The German medics surrendered without a fight, and the former adversaries agreed to work together on treating their American, British, and German patients.

"The Krauts had some stuff we couldn't bring in by chute and we had some stuff they didn't have, so we worked together," said Young. "[They] did a good job, we gave them the basement for their wounded and we took the first floor," he added.

Whenever other groups from Kent's 3rd Battalion trickled into the assembly area, they were directed to positions along the river, where they seized the lone footbridge in their sector. Lieutenant Dean Swem's platoon was one of the first to get into position.

One of Swem's troopers on outpost duty spotted a squad moving toward them in a skirmish line. He couldn't positively identify them as either friend or foe—they wore camouflage smocks—they might be Germans or they might be British paratroopers.

Swem alerted the rest of his platoon and instructed a trooper to wave his yellow identification panel.

"Are you friendly, are you friendly?" yelled Swem.

A spatter of small arms fire was the reply, followed by shouts of *"Hände hoch, Hände hoch!"*—"Hands up, hands up!"

Swem's platoon shot back, scattering the Germans. A few escaped, disappearing into a cluster of trees, but the rest were gunned down. The wounded called out, *"Kamerad, Kamerad."* But Swem, aware the survivors might be lurking in the woods, refused to send any of his men to assist them.

Not long after Coutts' headquarters group set up their command post, an American pilot wandered in. He'd bailed out of his stricken C-46 and was still carting his bundled-up parachute over one shoulder.

"What in God's name are you lugging that parachute for?" Coutts asked him.

"Colonel, in the Air Force, if you parachute out of a plane and don't bring it back, you get your paycheck docked $32.84," he replied.

Coutts thought that hilarious. He relieved the Air Force officer of his burden, trading him a handwritten receipt and a carbine for the chute. Coutts assigned the pilot to a nearby foxhole until he could be evacuated.

Miley and Ridgway's jeep convoy pulled into Coutts' command post shortly after 18:30. They'd come from the glider riders' sector, where fighting for several of the canal bridges was still under way; now they wanted to know how the Thirteeners were faring.

The paratroopers had created a holding area off to one side of the CP to corral several hundred POWs. Coutts gestured toward his caged prize, bragging that he'd left just as many with the British glider troopers. Ridgway jestingly rebuked him for failing to get a receipt from the Brits. Prisoner count aside, both generals were more interested in Coutts' progress along the river.

By the time Miley and Ridgway arrived, Coutts' 3rd Battalion had two companies along the Issel. Their detailed planning in Châlons had paid off. Having carefully studied maps and aerial photographs, the troopers quickly found the predesignated positions for their heavy weapons: belt-fed machine guns, 60mm mortars, Browning Automatic Rifles, and bazookas. But they'd recovered only fourteen out of the thirty-five machine guns dropped in equipment bundles, and they were also running low on ammunition.

Attempts to recover equipment bundles from the B-24 drop had been frustrated by German mortar crews successfully chasing away search parties. Ransacking the gliders yielded some crates of ammo, but not enough. Resourceful troopers forced some of their prisoners out into the open to recover more supplies. When the POWs complained about possibly getting shot by their own men, the paratroopers gave them a choice.

Squads continued to dig in and distribute the recovered ammunition. Several patrols had been dispatched across the river to determine what opposition they might be up against. As far as Coutts could tell, his 3rd Battalion alone had suffered over 160 casualties, with 38 killed, and at least 24 men still missing.

As Coutts briefed the generals, intermittent artillery rounds scudded overhead, crashing on the far side of the Issel. The Thirteeners were calling in harassing artillery fire on targets of opportunity; British guns back across the Rhine answered their requests.

With the 3rd Battalion tucked in along the river, Coutts' right flank still had an exposed break of 200 yards between them and the glider riders at Bridge 10. Coutts deployed elements of his 1st Battalion to plug the gap. Captain Ivy had relinquished command to Lieutenant Colonel Harry Kies, who'd rejoined his unit. He and his executive had been captured but negotiated their own release as glider troops closed on the building in which they were being held. With the 1st Battalion in position, Coutts' Thirteeners were shoulder-to-shoulder with the glider riders along the Issel, forming a defensive barrier to repel counterattacks from outside the bridgehead.

But it wasn't all good news. No contact had yet been made with the British glider troops who were to tie into Coutts' left flank; nor had Coutts' 2nd Battalion, commanded by "Ace" Miller, seized their objective. Miller knew the Ruffians had cleared the high ground of the Diersfordt Forest north of the castle, but the objective was still susceptible to reoccupation by the enemy. Perhaps the delay was due to having lost two company commanders or only recovering nineteen of their thirty-one belt-fed machine guns. Regardless, Miller sat in his assembly area for hours. By late afternoon he'd collected more than 50 percent of his battalion—over 300 men.

Not all of Miller's men waited. Lieutenant Dean Bressler led his small group of troopers toward the forest. But they were held up by barricaded *Soldats* in two houses on the edge of the wood. They radioed back to Miller for artillery support, which brought Chester's 466th into action. White phosphorus shells arced into the yards, blossoming around the houses and setting them on fire. The stubborn Germans streamed out with their heads down and their hands up.

Miller ordered Bressler, who assumed the battalion was already moving, to hold up and wait for the rest of them. This perplexing demand only compounded the delay. Finally at 19:00, after further unexplained postponements, Coutts—no doubt urged on by Ridgway and Miley—ordered Miller to seize his objective. After more than seven hours, Miller finally got his assembled battalion on the move. The slowest record in the division.

Miller's men, moving in a skirmish formation, came under fire as they crossed over the railroad tracks skirting Diersfordt Forest. The fire was coming from a cluster of brick buildings protected by multiple machine guns and several large 105mm field guns. Before the Thirteen-ers could enter the forest they would have to deal with this complex of German-held buildings, which included the large three-story château serving as an enemy HQ.

Among the paratroopers preparing for the assault was Stuart Stryker, a dark-haired, twenty-year-old former welding machine repairman from Portland, Oregon. Still suffering from the lingering symptoms of dysen-tery, he'd kept his condition quiet so he could make the jump. Stryker was so keyed up for his first combat jump that he'd announced the pre-vious night—from atop a table—that he'd be going all out, and he was as good as his word.

Stryker's platoon made their attack directly across open ground, com-ing in under the protective fire of two other platoons set up along the railroad embankment. They made it about fifty yards before blistering machine gun fire sent them to ground. The buzz saw's ripping rate of fire was too much. The platoon sprawled in the dirt with 200 yards yet to go. Every attempt to move drew more fire. No one dared to even shoot back.

Stryker, from his position at the rear of the formation, saw the attack collapsing. He'd seen it happen too many times in the Bulge—if they didn't move, they'd be picked off one by one. He shrugged off his pack, rolled to his feet, and ran toward the gunfire. Sergeant Clinton Lynch watched as Stryker rushed forward from trooper to trooper, urging them onward. Lynch heard Stryker yell what he thought was "Follow me!" as he charged past the prone troopers.

Simultaneously, one of the platoons from the railroad tracks shifted to the right, maneuvering through a wooded area to flank the compound.

Firing his carbine as he ran, Stryker's one-man assault inspired his platoon into action. One by one they started returning fire. Stryker, slowed by a shot in the leg, continued moving forward while bullets snapped past him. About twenty-five yards from the Germans' perime-ter, a machine gun burst took him down. He crumpled into a heap. For his critical role in spearheading the assault, Stryker would later be post-humously recognized with the Medal of Honor.

His comrades, their blood up, bolted forward. Bob Patterson and his mortar squad set up a hasty position near the railroad tracks to provide additional covering fire. They dropped several shells into the cluster of brick buildings while the flank attack came in through the woods. A bazooka team took a knee to blast several rounds into the large château.

The enemy 105mm howitzer crews fired vainly at the Americans. One stray round whistled overhead, hitting the chimney of a nearby house. The German crews all died at their guns, surrounded by empty brass shells, relics of their day's work. An *Unterwachtmeister* (artillery sergeant), his section's lone survivor, spiked one of the guns before falling in a hail of bullets. Paratrooper Robert Gill stared at the body of a dead gunner and was struck by the realization that the human skull is only about a quarter inch thick.

The Thirteeners laid siege to the Germans wherever they found them. Entering the château, they fired up through the ceiling with Browning Automatic Rifles and Thompson submachine guns. The splintering floor chased the upstairs defenders.

The three captured American B-24 airmen crouched behind the overturned table in their basement sanctuary. Hollis Powell watched one of his captors take up a firing position at a window halfway up the stairs. With a dull splat, the dead man tumbled back down, shot in the head. An unsettling quiet enveloped the compound.

An American voice yelled from the top of the stairs, "Anyone in there?"

Herbert Finney hollered back, "Yes we're in here, come in and get us!"

Powell, afraid the answer was too ambiguous, added, "We are Americans, we are in here."

A paratrooper cautiously descended into the basement. The airmen noted his baggy olive-drab pants and the casual manner in which he kept his M1 Garand at the ready. "Did they hurt you?" he asked.

Shaking his head, Powell assured him, "No."

The airmen emerged into the sunlight with dozens of paratroopers milling about the compound, smoking and reloading weapons. Medics were already treating the wounded in one of the outbuildings. A gaggle of over 200 enemy prisoners were being searched and organized.

A shot rang out, and a bullet thudded into the brick wall near Finney's head. The three airmen scrambled under a German half-track for protection. Powell longed for his B-24 and the high-altitude anonymity of flak and enemy fighters.

The amused paratroopers ignored the shot and continued smoking and joking, but after a few more bullets ricocheted off the building, an officer gave the order to "go get that son of a bitch."

Two troopers reluctantly peeled themselves away from the group to walk around the corner. Two shots were followed by one of them hollering, "I got him!" Powell hoped the dead sharpshooter was the same German who'd shot Milchak.

It would be several days before the rescued B-24 crew made their way across the Rhine and back to England. Only then would they learn the cost of their mission: 16 B-24s had been shot down, 4 were scrapped, and 126 needed repairs. The human cost, as always, eclipsed the aircraft losses: 109 killed, at least 5 taken as POWs, and scores more wounded.

Miller had secured the German HQ, but he now made another questionable decision, opting to dig in a mile short of his objective. Not wanting to risk a night movement through the forest, he left the Diersfordt road unsecured, exposing a gap in the perimeter between the Ruffians and the British airborne troops. It was a tactical mistake for which he'd later be criticized.

Mid-afternoon. Landing Zone S, Germany. Saturday, March 24, 1945.

Back on LZ S, the OSS agents were set up in a barn licking their wounds. Leo Jungen powered up his suitcase radio to report back to Paris while the agents replaced the damaged tires on their *Kübelwagen*. Unfortunately, its radio was beyond repair.

With the team occupied, Steltermann and Vinciguerra left to get their wounds properly treated. They found an aid station bustling with activity. Bleeding and moaning men lay everywhere, and medics moved with intensity to save lives. The dead were laid out to the side of one tent, their brown paratrooper boots sticking out from under gray-green Army blankets stained with dried blood. The two agents took in the scene, glanced at each other, and left. They could wait.

Overall it had been a frustrating day for Team Algonquin. Vinciguerra's primary team, Steltermann and Staub, had been taken out before they landed. Steltermann had a bullet through his shoulder, and their *Kübelwagen* radio was *kaput*. Team Alsace, the other uniformed agents, had dropped with the Ruffians, and thus far, no one had heard from them. Team Student, as Vinciguerra later put it, "proved itself thoroughly incapable." Upon landing they simply crawled into the closest undergrowth and didn't move.

His only remaining hope was Team Poissy. They'd arrived in the same glider serial, but had been unable to move far enough fast enough, and were rounded up by American glider troops. Vinciguerra rescued them from their internment. The two unarmed agents, Frenchmen in civilian attire, were willing to give their mission another try.

Vinciguerra and the others agreed that an attempt should be made to infiltrate Team Poissy closer to their original objective: the village of Hünxe, six miles northeast as the crow flies. As the OSS agents drove off the LZ in their *Kübelwagen*, followed by a second captured enemy jeep, two armed Germans fled into a nearby house. Vinciguerra and Steltermann dismounted to fire a few shots at the windows. Steltermann zigzagged closer, yelling for the occupants to surrender. Thirty-one *Soldats*, including two *Leutnants*, filed out. While Steltermann and Staub interrogated the prisoners, Vinciguerra escorted Team Poissy to a point along the railroad tracks leading into Wesel. They didn't know it yet, but the likelihood of getting across Bridge 1 and through town would be slim.

By midday the glider riders entrenched along the canal were strengthening their positions as more men trickled in. Crews positioned their heavy machine guns and anti-tank guns to cover the bridges' far approaches. They'd taken all of their objectives with the exception of Bridge 1, which was still contested by an undaunted German battle group.

The German units trapped inside the Americans' perimeter reeled from the initial surprise and violence of the airborne assault, but those outside organized for a counterattack. To break the Americans' hold they needed at least one bridge capable of bearing the weight of armored vehicles. Elements of *Kampfgruppe Karst* prowled the banks across from Bridges 1 through 4, probing the glider riders' defenses for a weakness.

Responsibility for stopping that counterattack fell on the shoulders of Lieutenant Colonel Harry Balish, who took over the glider riders' 2nd Battalion after the commander was injured on landing. Given the tenuous situation at Bridge 1, Balish ordered a platoon from his reserve company forward to bolster the defenses.

Ten minutes later three German tanks attempting to get out of the airborne perimeter stormed Bridge 1 from behind. Troopers repelled the attack, knocking one tank out with a bazooka and another with a 57mm anti-tank gun. The third panzer retreated.

At 16:00 *Kampfgruppe Karst* launched a concerted counterattack against Bridges 1 and 2. Determined to keep a route open, they pounded George Company's sector with showers of mortar and artillery shells. The glider riders dug their foxholes deeper and waited.

Forward observer Lieutenant Herman Lemberger moved toward the attack as more panzers lurched toward the bridges. Lemberger needed a better view, so he climbed to the top of the canal bank to call back instructions to British artillery batteries. One of the panzer crews must have spotted his radio. The bark of their main gun rocked the tank, and Lemberger disappeared in the explosion of a direct hit. But he'd sent the coordinates, and the British gunners had the range. They dropped shell after shell into the enemy formation, chopping the attackers to pieces with salvos of high-explosive rounds. It was close. One of the panzers clanked within ten yards of the main line before Andrew Adams knocked it out with a shattering shot from his bazooka.

Simultaneously, German infantry attacking Bridge 3 with two Mark IV tanks in the lead threatened to overrun Fox Company. Again British artillery from the far bank disrupted the attack. The shells splashed viciously into the German columns; shrapnel whizzed through the ranks of infantry and sent the tanks scurrying in retreat. Thank God for the artillery, but the troopers' relief was temporary. They figured it was just a question of time before the Nazis would try again. After the dust settled, both George and Fox Companies radioed Balish to report they'd lost contact with their forward squads at Bridges 1, 2, and 3.

While the line companies sweated out the status of their missing men, farther to the rear the executive officer of a glider field artillery battalion ordered those men not manning howitzers to take care of the livestock of the farm they'd occupied: twenty-five cows were milked, while eleven pigs and two horses were fed. They also dispatched scrounging parties to canvas the LZ in search of ammunition. From crashed gliders and supply bundles dropped from the B-24s, the artillerymen obtained an additional seven hundred 75mm shells, bringing their inventory up to 1,000 rounds.

In an attempt to reach the cut-off squads, George Company sent a patrol across Bridge 2 to maneuver along the east side of the canal down to Bridge 1. But stout, well-armed German defenders stopped them cold.

Next up was Lieutenant Thomas Wittig, whose platoon had been whittled down to nine men. He volunteered to lead them along the west side of the canal in a second attempt to reach Bridge 1 and hopefully the British Commandos in Wesel as well.

Unfortunately, Wittig didn't have any better luck. As the sun dipped below the horizon and a light mist formed over the canal, a breathless runner from Wittig's patrol stumbled back into Balish's command post: the patrol was taking fire and were all pinned down. He'd escaped only because he was the last man in the file and could crawl away.

With the situation at the far end of Bridge 1 uncertain, Balish flung in another of his reserve platoons. They were to set up a blocking position on the west side of the railroad bridge, and if they could, extract Wittig's patrol. Lieutenant John Robinson eyed the graying sky and organized his men to depart as soon as it was fully dark.

The isolated troopers at Bridge 1 caught fleeting glimpses of green berets in the fading light as the Commandos attempted to flush out a group of Germans occupying a redoubt near the railroad bridge. The glider riders couldn't raise the Commandos over the radio despite being just 400 yards apart, nor did they have the numbers to overwhelm the defenders' strongpoints and force a linkup.

A group of approximately 300 obstinate German youngsters held the area east of the railroad bridge. Those troopers who'd been trading shots and flicking grenades at them estimated that none were over twenty years old. Regardless of their age, the Germans took advantage of the rubble and their numerous machine guns to keep the Americans at bay. With the Commandos' location uncertain, the glider riders couldn't yet rain down artillery on the holdouts.

✶   ✶   ✶

Not long after dark, Miley's radio operator received a message that nine British infantry battalions had crossed the Rhine, clustering along the riverbank near the British airborne's sector of the bridgehead. There was still no word, however, on the disposition of the British airborne troops themselves. Had they secured the left flank? Had they seized their bridges near Hamminkeln? At 20:00 Ridgway and Miley departed Coutts' command post to find the answers.

Coutts warned the generals to "be careful." There were still plenty of Germans running around out there. They declined Coutts' offer to lead them back, and the column of jeeps nosed through the gloom and out into no-man's-land.

While the two generals made their way northwest to find the British, Miley's intelligence section sifted through reports and radio logs to stitch together an overview of the day's battle. All of the division's objectives had been taken—except that of the Thirteeners' 2nd Battalion. The Ruffians were in full possession of the western defensive line but running low on ammunition. Raff had a battalion arrayed to block the sporadic enemy units squirting up from the river. The glider riders' stalemate along the canal was still touch and go, with *Kampfgruppe Karst* actively probing and attacking to gain possession of a bridge. Thus far, the division had collected prisoners from a number of German units, including infantrymen, *Fusiliers*, *Grenadiers*, engineers, signalers, antitank gunners, medics, *Fallschirmjäger*, staff officers, artillery gunners, *Volkssturm*, and several hostile civilians.

☆   ☆   ☆

John Chester's artillery crew was hungry. With the task of relocating their howitzer completed, their rumbling stomachs reminded them that they hadn't eaten since before dawn. Their dining options were limited, since they'd elected to carry ammunition and grenades in lieu of rations. Chester gestured at a farmhouse and suggested it be searched for gun cleaning material. His message understood, two of the crew sauntered over to see what they could find.

The scroungers returned with two bulging gunnysacks. The kitchen had been well stocked, yielding two smoked hams, bread, fresh eggs, milk, cans of fruit, and a skillet. In short order they were enjoying fried ham sandwiches.

Their final order of business was to dig in for the night. Before sending their prisoners to the holding area, Chester's crew made the Germans dig them foxholes. The troopers then lined the holes with parachutes to make their stay a little more pleasant. Commo wire had been laid from the gun position to the fire direction center, and each man took a turn on watch, keeping his eyes peeled and his ear to the field phone, waiting for the call that would spring the crew into action.

CHAPTER 18

"WE HAD LUCK WITH US"

20:00. Ridgway's jeep convoy. Saturday, March 24, 1945.

The convoy of blacked-out jeeps inched their way through the dark. For the two American generals navigating to the British airborne's command post, the veil of night added another dimension of complexity to the still-active battlefield. Ridgway later confessed, "We didn't know where our own people were, much less the enemy, so we had to move with a moderate degree of caution."

The glow from the moon's nearly full orb combined with the still-lingering haze to blanket the landscape in an eerie monochromatic palette of silver and deep shadow. Winding along dirt roads flanked by wrecked aircraft and burning farmhouses, every man in the small convoy squinted into the dark for signs of trouble. It was still very much a 360-degree battlefield. Sporadic gunfire and the *crumping* of grenades echoed from unexpected quarters as bands of Germans bumbled around the battlefield trying to find a gap in the Allied lines to escape the bridgehead.

It took the generals almost three hours to creep their way the two and a half miles to the 6th Airborne's command post. The Americans finally arrived at 22:45, having passed through a cordon of sentries and roadblocks.

The command post—established in the single-story brick farmhouse owned by the Köpenhof family—served as a headquarters, communications center, aid station, and mortuary. Cows and chickens wandered past foxholes and the dark hulks of splintered Horsa gliders. A group of civilians huddled together under a large chestnut tree; in their company were a few *Soldats* stripped down to their underwear to discourage escape. Signs of the fighting lay all around. In the pig barn was a dead American parachutist hung up in the rafters where he'd broken his neck; in the cowshed was the graying body of ten-year-old Heini Quartsteg, a victim of crossfire.

A small bulldozer, brought in by glider, had dug a large trench for the division's signal unit just outside the front door; it was deep enough to leave nothing but a few antennas sticking out aboveground. The signalers had lined it with cargo chutes to make it more luxurious. Their hushed whispers could be heard as they made inquiries for status out on the perimeter.

The kitchen had been converted into a surgery; blood stained the dining table and dripped onto the floor. Wounded troopers, lying on stretchers, lined the walls of every room. A British officer, attempting to get a few minutes of sleep, stretched out next to another napping figure in a dimly lit hallway. Only later would he discover he'd been snoozing next to a dead American paratrooper. The farm complex had initially been conquered by the Thirteeners, and many of their dead and wounded had been left behind.

British General Eric Bols greeted Ridgway and Miley in the front room. Since Ridgway was the first emissary to arrive from the west bank of the Rhine, he was particularly welcome.

The forty-year-old Bols wore the distinct red beret and camouflage smock unique to the British airborne troops; like the two visiting American generals he dressed the same as any soldier under his command. Bols briefed the Americans on the disposition of his own division. Between drags on his cigarette and pointing to a map for reference, he explained how he'd anticipated his men would be "fighting like stink for the first day." The Germans hadn't let him down. His division of 7,000-odd troops had landed on two DZs and four LZs. Bols himself had landed by glider, touching down within a hundred yards of the farm.

Within four hours of their landing, the three bridges over the Issel River had been seized by glider troops and the village of Hamminkeln cleared as per their plan. The Germans were relentlessly attacking the bridges, desperate to seize a crossing point. Bols' men had repelled multiple German counterattacks—so far. Close air support had been a great help in staving off German counterattacks. A Forward Visual Control Party landed via Horsa glider and radioed in four air strikes from RAF fighters circling overhead. The British fighters would be credited with destroying sixteen German tanks within the first two days of the operation.

Reports were incomplete, but it appeared that Bols' division had suffered almost a thousand casualties with another 300 still missing.

The three generals crowded over the map to coordinate tying up the two divisions' perimeter along the Issel. Ridgway issued his orders for the next day's expansion of the bridgehead: Bols would hold his current positions another twenty-four hours to await his relief by Montgomery's ground forces; Miley's 17th Airborne would move east to secure Phase Line LONDON, which was the first in a series of predetermined phase lines radiating out from the airborne perimeter.

All told, Montgomery's 21 Army Group had established their crossing on a twenty-two-mile-wide front. There was still heavy German resistance on the left flank, but engineers had commenced bridging the Rhine. In turn, German engineers farther upstream floated several large mines down the river in an unsuccessful attempt to disrupt the effort. Allied engineers strung chains across the river to stymie a repeat attempt.

For *General der Fallschirmtruppen* Alfred Schlemm, the commander of the I *Fallschirmjäger-Armee*, little had gone right that day. Still feeling the effects of the concussion he'd suffered earlier in the week, he'd been bedridden for the last three days drifting in and out of consciousness. His vision had returned just that morning, and his first action was to immediately load into the back of his staff car for a tour of the front. As per his custom, he wanted to appraise the situation firsthand.

Montgomery's staggered attacks throughout the night had thrown Schlemm's commanders off-balance, and he was concerned the British were about to drive a wedge between the seam of his two *Korps*—II *Fallschirmjäger* and LXXXVI *Infanterie*.

While Schlemm had been unconscious, his boss, Johannes Blaskowitz, had ordered their reserves into the fray: the 15 *Panzer-Grenadier-Division* against what they thought was Montgomery's main attack at Rees, and the 116 *Panzer-Division* to destroy the airborne troops at Wesel.

Schlemm's luck remained horrible. Allied fighters strafed his staff car off the road multiple times. To the general it seemed that his driver was careening into a ditch every 200 meters to dodge another air attack. Indeed, the Allies' patrolling of the road networks was so aggressive that *General* Eugen Meindl, commander of Schlemm's II *Fallschirmjäger Korps*, later complained that he could only maintain contact with his divisions by motorcycle couriers traveling over back roads or cross country.

Once Schlemm had confirmed that Montgomery's attack was not a feint, he returned to his HQ, where his condition continued to deteriorate. He spent the next two days feebly coordinating the battle from his bed before a temperature of 104 degrees forced him to relinquish command.

Ridgway and Miley, with their plan set, departed the British command post at midnight. The column of jeeps nudged their way over dirt roads, picking their way forward with only enough moonlight to see a hundred yards. Artillery whistled overhead and they could hear the sound of distant gunfights—the deep *chug, chug, chug* of heavy American machine guns resonated from multiple directions.

Riding in the lead jeep, Ridgway peered ahead as his driver detoured off-road to navigate around the charred remains of a German truck. Once he bumped back onto the road, Ridgway noticed a scurried movement twenty yards in front of them just as a burst from a German machine pistol cracked overhead.

Ridgway jumped from the jeep to fire a few shots over the hood from his bolt-action Springfield. He hit at least one man, who squealed before falling. Meanwhile, Miley, who was lying off to the side of the road, aimed at muzzle flashes and fired his carbine into the mass of shadows. The bodyguards in the security jeep held their fire for fear of hitting the generals in front of them.

Each side hurled profanities as well as bullets and grenades. Ridgway flopped down beside the jeep's passenger-side front wheel for cover while reloading. An explosion shook the jeep with an earsplitting roar. Ridgway caught some of the burning grenade shrapnel in his shoulder, but his jeep was the main casualty—the cracked crankcase bled oil.

The Germans took advantage of the grenade blast to melt into the darkness. After the sudden pandemonium of the skirmish, the silence was uncanny.

Ridgway still wasn't sure who was where; he heard movement all around him. Then he spotted the vague silhouette of a man concealed in a clump of vegetation and yelled, "Put up your hands, you son of a bitch!"

A distinctly American voice answered, "Aaah, go sit in your hat."

Ridgway later complimented the concealed paratrooper's sangfroid: "The man in the willows could have killed me easily. . . . But the paratrooper is not trigger-happy. He's so used to being alone and surrounded, not knowing where his friends are, nor the enemy, that he's very, very careful about firing until he's sure he knows whom he's shooting at."

The group picked themselves up to assess the damage. Ridgway's wound would need attention, but it was nothing serious. One of the bodyguards got behind the wheel of the damaged vehicle while the other jeep pushed it back to Miley's command post.

As per their assembly plan, the LZ S glider pilots had organized themselves into four infantry companies, with flight and squadron commanders assuming the role of platoon and squad leaders. Three of the pilot companies fanned out to establish roadblocks along the southwest perimeter of the LZ while a fourth dug in around the howitzers of the 681st Glider Field Artillery to bolster their defenses.

The four platoons of the 435th Troop Carrier Group dug in around the intersection of Holzweg and Hessenweg Roads, the latter of which led down to Bridge 2. The seventy-odd pilots of the 77th Platoon centered themselves on the intersection, blocking Holzweg, while the 76th Platoon took the right flank and the 75th the left. The 78th was located to the rear, near the group command post, where they'd be on standby as the reserve platoon.

The four corners of the intersection were vacant lots, giving the glider pilots clear fields of fire. A few troopers lugging a 57mm anti-tank gun and a heavy, belt-fed .50-caliber machine gun joined them. They were welcome company to the lightly armed pilots.

Several of the "volunteer" power pilots grumbled that they hadn't been trained for this type of work, but they grudgingly grabbed shovels to help dig foxholes. Many of the pilots lined their foxholes with straw or blankets, and at least one pilot dragged a feather mattress out of a nearby house to make himself more comfortable. The pilots quickly realized that the qualities of a senior aviator didn't necessarily translate into being a competent ground combat leader.

"The rank didn't necessarily denote leaders," recalled Flight Officer Richard Barthelemy. "Lieutenant [Floyd] Hand was good; Lieutenant [John] Love was good; they both took orders willingly from Flight Officer Robert Campbell who is a soldier's soldier." Campbell, though junior in rank to the lieutenants, had landed in enemy territory multiple times and had served in the Marine Corps before the war; he was comfortable on the ground and knew his weapons. The trouble, as Barthelemy saw it, was that the more experienced man could only make suggestions. Fortunately for the pilots of the 77th, common sense prevailed and the senior ranks heeded Campbell's advice.

Upon arrival at the intersection, the squads fanned out to clear the handful of surrounding houses. Civilians were ushered out of their homes without incident, and several wounded *Soldats* were found hiding in the houses. In one house a squad of pilots rescued four members of a downed C-47 crew, bagging the nine *Volkssturm* who'd been their captors. Other pilots strung communication wire back to the group command post since field telephones and runners would be their primary forms of communication.

A few German stragglers approached the roadblock to surrender. A pilot escorted two of them back to the command post but was told by an airborne sergeant not to bother with taking prisoners. With the sun setting and the cacophony of tanks, mortars, and heavy machine guns drifting back from Bridge 2 to fray nerves, the pilot heeded the advice. He ushered the Germans a little farther down the road before executing both prisoners with his pistol.

At 23:15, a snub-nosed German JU-88 night fighter, festooned with an array of radar antenna and six machine guns, buzzed in low over the battlefield. It was chased by tracer fire and apparently hit the same power line that had claimed multiple gliders earlier in the day.

Several of the glider pilots from the group command post raced across to where the JU-88 had plowed into a field. The *Luftwaffe* pilot was dazed and his copilot was pinned in the crumpled cockpit. The other two members of the crew were dead. In a gesture of unnecessary chivalry, the pilot surrendered his pistol. The crash served as a portent of what was about to break loose back at the roadblock.

The grinding of gears and the clatter of a tracked vehicle clanking toward them focused the glider pilots' attention. They nervously fingered the safeties on their rifles and fidgeted in their foxholes, scrutinizing the darkness. Whoever was coming toward them had the advantage of approaching up the reverse slope of a small hill, masking both their approach and their identity. The pilots held their fire. Waiting.

It wasn't until the advancing unit was almost in the intersection that the pilots could see them. They were Germans! The first shots rang out almost simultaneously, each side opening up on the other.

Everyone fired what he had. The pilots snapped off shots at figures scurrying through the crossroads or plinked at the tank with rifles, praying to hit the vision slits or unsettle the crew. The airborne troopers' heavy machine gun opened fire, its deep cough cutting over the clatter of carbines and rifles. Rounds zipped overhead as German infantry swarmed forward on each side of the tank.

Several of the pilots' guns jammed. The flow of adrenaline made clearing the unfamiliar weapons difficult. Second Lieutenant Raye Niblo set his aside to throw grenades. He heaved them as hard as he could into clusters of Germans setting up machine guns and maneuvering a single-barreled 20mm anti-aircraft gun into position. From his foxhole Valton Bray steadily snapped off shots with his automatic pistol.

The Germans pushed up a second 20mm. The incendiary tracer rounds sliced overhead like deadly glowing golf balls. A glider immediately behind the platoon was set alight by a burst from the 20mm. Two pilots who'd dug in under one of the glider's wings waited as long as they could before the flames got too close and they had to abandon their foxhole.

The pilots' volley of fire and the steady beat of the .50-caliber drove the attackers back down the road. The heavy machine gun rounds pinged off the tank's armor and sliced through the infantry.

Just when the pilots thought the attack was faltering, the tank pivoted and blasted the Americans' .50-caliber position. The gun was destroyed and the two crewmen fell wounded.

On the other side of the road, pilots Chester DeShurley and Albert Hurley knew their .30-caliber belt-fed machine gun might be next. Assistant gunner Hurley later admitted, "We were afraid to open fire immediately for we saw the 50 cal. go out."

The German infantry regrouped for another lunge. As they advanced behind the tank, they started howling like a pack of wolves. The bellowing was intimidating and increased the perception of their true numbers.

"There must have been about a hundred or more Germans, but between their concentrated fire and yelling their heads off, it sounded like a regiment," thought Flight Officer Elbert Jella. With his bazooka shouldered, he waited a few more seconds before squeezing the trigger; the high-explosive rocket *whooshed* out from his foxhole on the left side of the intersection.

"I held my fire until they were just about 15 yards off," he said. "You see, I didn't want to miss."

The round hit just above the tracks. The explosion was tremendous, sending a hot concussion wave rolling back at Jella. But the blast appeared to have only damaged the tank. It lurched once and reversed course, backing over one of the 20mm guns. Momentarily entangled, its treads ground the gun into scrap. The tank crew opened up with their stubby machine gun as they retreated. The gunner reloaded and the cannon roared.

The shell threw up a geyser of dirt twenty feet in front of DeShurley and Hurley's machine gun position, pelting them with debris. The pilots continued to fire back, peppering the tank and supporting infantry with their .30-caliber despite the unwelcome attention. They squeezed off short bursts to conserve their ammo as they only had a single ammo can of 250 rounds.

The tank fired again. The shell cracked two feet over the pilots' heads, hitting the house behind them. The interior of the two-story brick structure burst into flame. The tank clanked away, backing out of sight between two houses, where the crew abandoned it.

Bullets were still flying back and forth, preventing the pilots holding positions in front of the burning house from evacuating. Fortunately, the brick façade contained the flames, but there were civilians sheltering in the cellar. A group of pilots, most likely from the 78th Platoon, worked their way around back to free the civilians. They rescued an elderly couple and a young pregnant woman before the structure was engulfed in flame.

The German infantry, with their armor out of the fight, lost their momentum and retreated back down Holzweg Road. Their machine gunners on their flanks kept up a steady stream of fire to protect the retreat.

Several pilots, taking advantage of the lull, jumped out of their foxholes and ran back to the command post for reinforcements. The Germans might come back, and almost all the pilots were running low on ammunition.

"Things were plenty SNAFU," admitted Hurley. "No one knew how strong the attacking force was and no one knew who was still there or who had pulled out."

Plenty SNAFU it was. During the confused battle the group command post had withdrawn. Most of the 77th Platoon, if not all, were unaware of the departure, including Floyd Hand, the assistant platoon leader. Claims would later be made that the platoons had been informed, but given the number of bitter accusations, it's clear any communication to that effect never reached them. Additionally several pilots took it upon themselves to leave their positions during the fight. Some went to get reinforcements; some went in search of more ammo. Some just went.

"During the attack five of our squadron deserted their post and returned to the command post," noted Flight Officer William Bruner. "It left seven of our squadron in a bad spot."

But most of the 77th Platoon held their ground, repulsing the attack. "We had luck with us," said Albert Hurley. He was right; for all of the flying lead, the platoon had sustained minimal injuries: just two superficial head wounds.

The "Battle for Burp Gun Corner"—as it would later become known—petered out after thirty intense minutes. The Germans left their dead scattered in the street. The survivors fled across the fields or sought refuge in nearby houses. Some harassed the pilots with the occasional odd, angry shot. The lurking enemy kept the pilots on their toes for the rest of the night.

The brick house continued to smolder, and occasional anonymous shots rang out from both directions. Three *Soldats* stumbled into the intersection, wanting to surrender. A jumpy pilot shot one of them before their intentions were understood. Confusion and doubt continued to course though the pilots' veins. Two more Germans approached, presumably to give themselves up, but either they didn't hear the command to halt or had other intentions. A burst from the .30-caliber cut them down.

00:10. Issel Canal: Bridges 1, 2 and 3.
Sunday, March 25, 1945.

Five hundred yards due east, at Bridges 1 and 2, the situation was still very much touch and go. No further word had been received since Lieutenant Thomas Wittig's runner had made it back to the command post. Lieutenant John Robinson's patrol had moved forward just after dark, making their way to a point 200 yards short of Bridge 1. The only sign of Wittig's patrol they could find were empty shell casings and a dead GI. Robinson's platoon hunkered down for the night and ambushed groups of enemy troops attempting to infiltrate via the railroad bridge.

Reports coming in from George Company weren't encouraging. The platoons were spread thin trying to hold Bridges 1 and 2. Their forward squads remained unaccounted for and German patrols were taking advantage of the darkness to scout their lines. The mist rising up from the canal further hampered visibility; gray-clad Germans moved like specters through the gloom, more apparition than man.

Lieutenant Colonel Harry Balish dispatched another platoon from his reserve company. Led by Lieutenant John Anderson, the patrol's progress was held up by the steady flow of German infiltrators. The patrol bumped into three groups of Germans in less than an hour, capturing thirty-six of them. The number of prisoners became too unwieldy, and Anderson returned to the command post to off-load them. It was a good haul but didn't account for the suspected number of Germans who'd broken through the lines. Where were they?

At midnight German gunners yanked the lanyards on their howitzers, sending shell after shell arcing into the American lines. It was the opening salvo of yet another concerted counterattack against the glider riders at Bridges 1, 2, and 3. After a few miserable minutes, the shelling lifted, shifting back to the vicinity of Balish's command post. Clearly German scouts had plotted their position.

The field phone crackled to report Fox Company had ambushed twelve Germans snooping along their right flank, near George Company. A few minutes later they called back to report they'd lost contact with George altogether.

But the field telephone lines were still intact between George and the command post. They were calling back for artillery support, requesting fire all across their front. The sound of small arms fire and grenades swelled from George's positions. The firing diminished briefly only to flare again. Almost simultaneously both wire and radio communication went dead. George was now on their own. From the ruckus drifting back from the canal, they were still in the fight, but how long could they last?

Balish ordered a small contact patrol to suss out what was happening. They didn't get far. A burst of fire spit out of the darkness, cutting down the squad leader and wounding another man as the Germans swept past them.

Less than three minutes after George Company had been overrun, the Germans swarmed up to Balish's command post from the two roads leading up from Bridges 1 and 2.

One of Balish's staff managed to blurt out a message on their field phone, "Firing 310 degrees . . ." The line went dead before he could fin-

ish his sentence. Every clerk, officer, radio operator, and supply sergeant rushed to a defensive position. They joined the troopers of the defense platoon whose withering fire lashed out at running shadows. It did the job. The German assaulters had either shot their bolt or had their ranks thinned by George Company to such an extent that they couldn't muster enough firepower to overwhelm the command post. The scattered German formations fell back in all directions, leaving several dozen corpses behind as evidence of their failed attempt.

Balish reorganized the defenses after the melee and tried to ascertain the extent of the incursion. Repeated attempts to raise George Company went unanswered, and contact with two of the 57mm anti-tank gun crews near Bridge 2 had also been lost.

Balish feared that George Company had been overrun and that Bridges 1 and 2 were now back in German hands, so he sent out a two-man scouting party to confirm the situation. Creeping up on the bridges, the two men spotted an idling German panzer with an estimated sixty troops marshaling near the canal.

Back at the command post, Balish received the scouts' report and again tasked Lieutenant John Anderson's platoon: stop the German infiltration and find George Company. Another lieutenant, Robert Sheehy, who'd led the scouting party, would join Anderson to guide the platoon back to where he saw the tank. Anderson's troopers loaded up with extra bazookas and departed the command post at 02:00. Sheehy led them to Bridge 2 in search of the tank. They found it soon enough. It sat astride the road, hurling high-explosive shells straight across the bridge, and the number of Germans had grown to almost a hundred. It was obvious to Sheehy and Anderson that another breakthrough was imminent.

Outnumbered three to one, the lieutenants agreed it was wise to lie low and avoid giving their position away. Instead they radioed back for artillery. Anderson carefully plotted the coordinates. With the Germans almost in George Company's lines, the danger of fratricide was high. Five interminable minutes later the rounds from the far side of the Rhine warbled overhead and crashed into the enemy formation. The platoon watched in silence, holding their fire, as the explosions blossomed in a tight pattern and cut the Germans to ribbons.

Anderson and Sheehy made it back to the command post at 03:00 with a full report. They could find no trace of GIs at Bridge 2, and as far as they could tell George Company's left flank had folded, leaving an

undefended gap between George and Fox Companies. They did hear a firefight raging farther southeast across the canal: a crackle of American machine guns dueling with the buzz saw bursts of enemy guns. Somebody was alive out there and still fighting. The platoon moved toward the sound of the battle, only to engage a sizeable band of Germans that forced them to withdraw.

Balish rousted his reconnaissance platoon as a final measure. They were the only reserve he had left to fill the gap. Before they could reach the broken lines, the recon troopers bumped into the displaced George Company command group. They'd retreated after being pummeled by an enemy counterattack, which confirmed that the Germans held Bridge 2.

The two groups attacked together, "firing everything from 45 pistols to bazookas" and forcing the Germans to flee. Ten prisoners were bagged in the process. The combined units restored the line, and the recon men took up positions to defend Bridge 2. George Company's commander, who'd been out of contact with his forward platoons for hours, couldn't shed any light on what was happening over at Bridge 1. No one had been able to reach the positions there or hail the men by radio.

At the same time George Company was fighting for its life and possession of Bridges 1 and 2, the Germans prepared another counterattack against Bridge 3. The first indication that something might be brewing was a solitary *Luftwaffe* night fighter streaking overhead to strafe Fox Company's lines. The low-level gun run was ineffective, but ensured everybody was awake.

A few minutes later, at 02:45, the glider riders heard the Germans marshaling for their attack. At least four tracked vehicles—tanks or self-propelled guns—lumbered into position. Trucks pulled up, and the clang of their tailgates dropping to unload troops reverberated.

Fox Company's forward observer crept to the edge of the canal to get a better bead on all the activity. Squinting at the distant shadows milling around in the moonlight, he guessed there were 400 troops on the far side of the canal. He used his own location to plot an azimuth and estimated the distance to the noise at 300 yards before whispering his request into the radio's handset.

On the far side of the Rhine British artillery tubes belched flame once more, spitting out the first volley of shells. The FO, seeing the rounds land on target, relayed the command, "Fire for effect!" The

order unleashed salvos of high-explosive rounds. They tore into the German ranks, inducing panic. Desperate to escape the slaughter, many ran toward the canal in blind confusion. Fox Company's machine gunners were waiting. All along the canal American muzzles flashed, downing the Germans or driving them back into the eviscerating shrapnel.

22:00. Issel River: Bridges 7–10.
Saturday, March 24, 1945.

At Bridges 7 through 10, Charlie Company fought off several attacks, ranging from platoon to company in size. Frank Dillon and the rest of Baker Company rushed in for support. As the battalion's reserve fire brigade, they'd been withdrawn and deployed multiple times along the canal to reinforce and fill gaps between the line companies. At 22:00 the Germans broke through at Bridge 7 and held it for thirty minutes before Baker Company pushed them back.

The field phones rang at the forward positions just after 23:00 to warn of a new enemy tactic: women were pretending to be wounded and using moans to attract the Americans' attention. Concealed Germans would ambush any GI coming to a woman's aid. It worked once, with the bait shot down in retaliation.

Five minutes later the radio crackled again to deliver an intelligence report from the British. A reliable source indicated that the lead elements of the Germans' 116 *Panzer-Division* were moving south against the canal, and were reportedly just a few hours away.

At one in the morning a small group of Germans attempting to escape the bridgehead bumped into Charlie Company's rear security near Bridges 9 and 10. The attack was brushed off with the help of mortars and Baker Company. There'd be no rest for Frank Dillon's platoon that night.

Skirmishes continued to erupt all along the river. In one such engagement, Sergeant William Wolf, not wanting to reveal Charlie Company's position, grabbed a 60mm light mortar and moved forward to disrupt an attack. Opting to leave the bipod and sight behind, he spiked the mortar into the ground and leaned it forward. With a well-practiced eye and some Kentucky windage Wolf accurately dropped six rounds on the advancing horde, unhinging their attack. Satisfied, he hoisted the sixteen-pound tube and hauled it back to the safety of his lines before the Germans retaliated by lobbing shells into the area where they'd seen the flash of his mortar.

Grenades had to be used when the Germans got too close. Private Levert Smith, Jr., apparently fumbled his. He was found severely wounded in his foxhole, the victim of his own grenade. It had either gone off prematurely or he'd dropped it. His comrades rushed him back to the aid station, sliding him onto the kitchen table for immediate attention. But it was too late, and within a few minutes the aspiring baseball player and avid Yankees fan bled out. He'd celebrated his nineteenth birthday three days before the drop.

Misfortune came in all sizes for Charlie Company that day. A forward observer called for British artillery to hit some Germans sheltering in a copse of trees. "We heard the shells coming," recalled Frank O'Rourke, "but instead of passing over us to their target in the woods, they began exploding on our side of the canal." Fortunately, the short rounds only maimed the observer himself. The troopers were happy to see him go. "We didn't need his kind of help."

21:35. Ruffians' Sector. Saturday, March 24, 1945.

Formal contact had yet to be made with the Commandos in Wesel. Radio communication was finally established, but there were still several pockets of resistance keeping the Yanks and Tommies apart. The Commandos had been fighting house-to-house all day, pushing the Germans around Wesel. They'd killed the garrison commander, *Generalmajor* Friedrich-Wilhelm Deutsch. Deutsch had vowed to fight to the last man, and in a display of fanatical leadership he charged out of his bunker spraying lead. He was promptly cut down by a burst from an unimpressed Commando machine gunner.

Because Ridgway was concerned about the inability to contact the Commandos in Wesel, he ordered Raff to dispatch a combat patrol to probe east, skirting the riverbank to determine if that route was open. Fifteen minutes later the command was relayed to Lieutenant Joseph Kormylo.

Planning and coordination took several hours since Kormylo had to pick his patrol's route wisely. He took several factors into consideration, including that they'd have to stay south of the railroad tracks to avoid the unfriendly fire of the glider riders' perimeter. This put them out in the open moving east across flat farmland, the same spit of land that undoubtedly concealed enemy units bumping around to find a way out of the bridgehead. Twenty minutes before midnight Kormylo's lead scouts walked out of the perimeter and led the way east.

Kormylo was a Normandy veteran and knew to take his time. There was no need to rush into anything, and the Commandos weren't going anywhere. The patrol snaked its way through no-man's-land, taking over two hours to traverse the two and a half miles and reach the rubble-strewn outskirts of Wesel. The scouts stumbled on a lone German hoping to go unnoticed in an abandoned trench. He surrendered, but the commotion attracted attention. Shots erupted from Wesel, and Kormylo went down, hit in the gut. The Ruffians spread out, snapping off rounds at the hostile muzzle flashes.

Private Richard Boe launched rifle grenades at the enemy from the bottom of a muddy shell crater and yelled for his squad to pull back. The enemy firing stopped.

"It's OK Yank, it's OK Yank, come on in."

Hearing the Americans shouting orders, the Commandos had realized their mistake. They'd fired at a friendly patrol. Because Kormylo's scouts had flushed several Germans in front of them as they moved, the Commandos mistook the Ruffians for another group of befuddled Germans.

Kormylo was rushed into the Commandos' perimeter for medical treatment. He survived and was later awarded a Bronze Star and a Purple Heart. Contact with the Commandos was officially made at 02:00.

The moon dropped below the horizon a little after 04:00, taking what visibility it provided with it. The fighting along the canal petered out as the belligerents, bathed in almost complete darkness, settled in to wait for sunrise. Sentries stared into the blackness for the smallest hint of movement. The temporary peace, which allowed men on both sides of the canal to ponder the fate of their missing comrades, was broken at 04:45 when the Commandos radioed the glider riders to let them know they were attacking. They should expect escaping enemy troops to drift their way.

CHAPTER 19

"ORGANIZED RESISTANCE HAS NOW CEASED"

Dawn. Issel Canal: Bridges 1 and 2.
Sunday, March 25, 1945.

The sun began its climb out of darkness on that Palm Sunday at 05:45. The gray of early dawn revealed the toll of the night's work. Scattered around the glider riders' positions were hundreds of dead and maimed Germans. Black smoke curled up from still-smoldering tanks and gutted half-tracks. Competing smells wafted over the battlefield: the fresh earth of churned artillery craters and the acrid odor of gunpowder.

Daylight brought a sigh of relief but also the need for each trooper to swallow his fear once more and rediscover his courage. What a man did one day was no guarantee for the next. No one knew when his fount might run dry, and he hoped he had enough to keep going.

A lone, weary messenger made his way back from Bridge 1, picking his way through the rubble and dead bodies. A survivor from one of George Company's lost platoons, he panted into Balish's command post with welcome news: despite being cut off and sustaining heavy casualties, two platoons had held their positions on the far side of the canal. Efforts to reach them had failed because they'd unknowingly fought 400 yards past the bridge and had gotten trapped on the outskirts of Wesel.

The two platoons had launched an attack at first light to secure their sector and retake Bridge 1. Lieutenant John Robinson's patrol joined them. Having hunkered down during the night near the canal's railroad bridge, his platoon joined the beleaguered troopers in their attack. Thirty minutes later they'd beaten down what remained of the enemy's will to fight, adding 200 more POWs to the regiment's growing tally.

Lieutenant Thomas Wittig, who'd been given up for lost, also wandered in with seven of his men and a British guest. Wittig's men had wiggled their way into Wesel and spent the night with a group of Commandos, one of whom Wittig brought back with him to coordinate the day's mopping-up.

Despite the successful counterattack, the situation around Bridge 1 was still very fluid. While the bridge itself had been secured, the surrounding area was not. German shells streaked in randomly; snipers and machine gunners dug in like ticks, hampering any attempt at movement. Balish was still unable to coordinate attacks with the Commandos. It wouldn't be until mid-afternoon that commo men would be able to get wire laid between positions, giving the two units a reliable field phone connection.

Farther up the Issel, twenty-six-year-old Private Ben Roberson stood up in his foxhole to ditch the flak jacket he'd obtained from a dead glider pilot. Having appreciated its snug protection through the night, he now found it heavy and cumbersome. A German corpse lay a few feet from Roberson's foxhole. "I don't know who killed him," Roberson said, "but he was wearing an Iron Cross that I wanted so I took it off him." A practical man, Roberson understood that the dead were beyond caring for such trinkets.

Daylight also revealed the toll on the bridges themselves. A number had fallen victim to the back-and-forth contests for possession. While Bridges 1 through 4 remained intact, Bridge 5 had been badly shelled, knocking out the far abutment and its center section. The thirty-foot span of Bridge 6 was still intact and capable of supporting armored vehicles. But Bridges 7 through 9 had been damaged by artillery, making them either impassable or limited to foot traffic. Bridge 10 was still intact. Combat engineers found and defused previously unnoticed demolition charges on its forty-foot span.

Gene Herrmann's crew was instructed to grab their 81mm heavy mortar and move into position near Bridge 5. The troopers in that sector needed their help. There was a stubborn enemy machine gun set up in a house about 900 yards away, and its harassing fire needed to be dealt with. Fixing their aim on the house, they dropped a round down the tube, and it sailed over the Issel to explode a hundred yards behind the target. They adjusted their site—and the second round exploded with a geyser of mud just short of the house. One more tweak and they

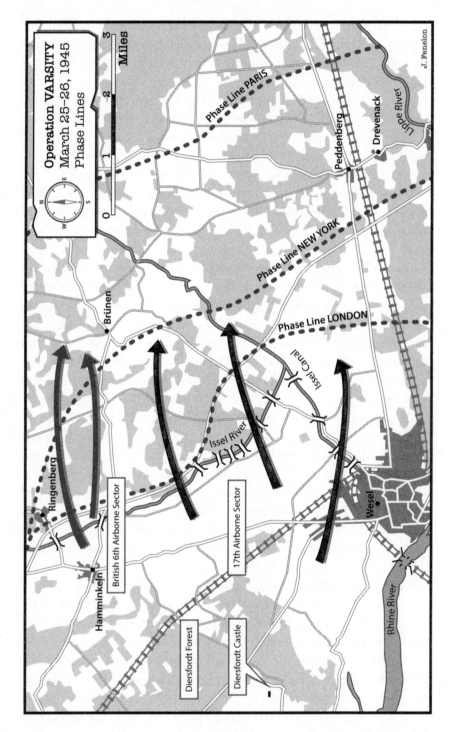

Operation VARSITY
March 25–26, 1945
Phase Lines

Miles

N
W   E
S

Phase Line PARIS

Phase Line NEW YORK

Phase Line LONDON

Peddenberg

Drevenack

Lippe River

Brünen

Issel Canal

Issel River

Ringenberg

British 6th Airborne Sector

17th Airborne Sector

Hamminkeln

Wesel

Diersfordt Forest

Diersfordt Castle

Rhine River

J. Fenelon

sent four accurate rounds raining down. The explosions threw roof tiles everywhere and silenced the machine gun.

For the glider riders at Bridge 10, the morning's tranquility evaporated almost instantly. The Germans still wanted their bridge. Its ability to support the weight of armored vehicles made it particularly attractive. A company of gray-clad infantry and two tanks advanced with the rising sun to their backs. A lone unarmed woman was in the vanguard. Her presence in the front rank had its desired effect: the glider riders hesitated.

Medic Joseph Moscar witnessed the drama from his foxhole. One of his officers, clearly wrestling with his conscience, aimed and lowered his rifle multiple times. As the assault drew near, the officer raised his rifle, squeezed the trigger, and killed the woman with a single shot. She pitched into the dirt, and the previously squeamish banged away, unleashing a blistering volley. Supporting artillery helped swat the German attack aside. More bodies littered the riverbank, and two more smoldering enemy tanks gushed greasy smoke like funeral pyres.

If the Germans had had any hope of breaking into the bridgehead, it would have been the previous night. Forward observers now had the visibility to call down a wall of steel anywhere along the perimeter, and Allied fighters darted overhead, greedy for something to shoot.

Miley's plan for the operation's second day called for securing and expanding the bridgehead. From the division command post he radioed his combat teams their orders for the day: spend the morning mopping up their sectors and prepare to seize positions along Phase Line LONDON at 15:00. LONDON started in the Thirteeners' sector and roughly followed the under-construction, 150-foot-wide autobahn until it dropped due south approximately two miles east of Wesel where the Lippe River flowed into the Rhine.

As those closest to LONDON, the Thirteeners would hold their positions in the morning and send a few companies across the Issel River toward the autobahn later in the day. The Ruffians would have the longest trek since they needed to move over four miles east, cutting across the Rhine's floodplains and pushing through Wesel to relieve the glider riders at Bridges 1 and 2.

Dawn. Burp Gun Corner. Sunday, March 25, 1945.

Half a mile northwest of Bridge 2 the glider pilots at Burp Gun Corner counted over a dozen enemy dead strewn in the street; scores more lay wounded. Moving among them was a lone German medic, easily identified by his white tunic with a large red cross emblazoned across the front and back. He ignored the Americans, and they left him to carry out his work, some even giving him their first-aid kits.

"I still remember today very vividly how this fellow worked to save his wounded comrades," recalled one of the pilots. "He struck me as a very compassionate attendant and went about his task in a very professional and caring manner."

While the medic treated the suffering, several of the pilots dragged the dead over to one of the vacant lots for burial. Shallow pits would do for now as Graves Registration teams would collect them later. The pilots weren't sure how long they'd be there and opted to clean up before the bodies started to smell.

Since the pilots realized the Germans hadn't retreated far, they searched nearby dwellings and rousted another thirty-odd wounded.

A four-pilot patrol party left in search of two missing comrades. They scoured all of LZ S for them, stopping at aid stations and hoping to discover them among the wounded, but found no trace.

Those pilots not patrolling or rousting out prisoners improved their position and prepared to stay another night. The undamaged 20mm anti-aircraft gun now supplemented their defenses, and a few pilots added German 9mm machine pistols to their personal arsenal. Many pilots dug their foxholes a bit deeper, having learned their lesson from the previous night's excitement.

At 14:00 word came down from the group command post that they'd start for the Rhine shortly since they were being evacuated. They got the order to move out three hours later.

The Burp Gun Corner pilots joined an exodus of their peers heading back to France. Zane Winters and Smokey had been in the middle of a gunfight when they were ordered to pack up.

"I only used fifteen rounds from my M-1 carbine, plus two grenades, trying to get some Germans out of a house," recalled Winters. They departed leaving a group of troopers to deal with the barricaded Germans. "I don't know how it turned out," he added. When he left, they "were telling them they were going to burn the house down if they didn't come out."

The glider pilots evacuated against a continuous stream of personnel and vehicles surging into the bridgehead. The pilots made their way down the congested lanes, frequently jumping to the side of the road so advancing convoys could pass. In the vanguard of the supply columns were seventeen amphibious trucks loaded with 38 tons of ammunition. They formed part of a larger effort organized by Miley's ordnance company, which, all told, would move 157 tons of ammunition over the Rhine.

Dozens of pilots riding bicycles with rifles and tommy guns slung across their backs weaved in and out of the traffic. Apparently, the bikes had originally been confiscated from the locals by *Wehrmacht* flak troops, who'd abandoned them in a warehouse near Burp Gun Corner.

As Miley's troops prepared to attack, they handed over their POWs to the evacuating pilots for escort to the Rhine. There they'd be corralled by MPs for formal processing. The herds of shuffling prisoners were a menagerie of defeat: unbuttoned gray overcoats splattered with mud, torn camouflage smocks, and the faded black tunics of panzer crewmen. Their headgear also varied wildly: field caps, visors, sometimes nothing at all. To a man they'd ditched their helmets. They were drained and dirty. For every stoic Nazi attempting to retain his delusional dignity, there were many more smiles. For the rational, the war was finally over.

The prisoners were herded into fields and made to sit or lie down. Just one or two well-armed glider pilots wielding their tommy guns in a breezy manner was enough to control large groups.

Once they handed off their prisoners, the pilots would await transportation back across the Rhine via amphibious vehicles. The pontoon bridges over the Rhine were still only open to one-way traffic. From a reception station on the far bank the pilots would be trucked the remaining forty miles to an airfield in Holland. Cots and rations were provided while they waited for the trucks.

Flight Officer Howard Schultz was impressed with the organization. It contrasted with his experience in MARKET GARDEN where pilots had been left to their own ingenuity to find a way back to England. But not everyone appreciated the Army's bureaucratic attempt to wrangle them back so soon. Schultz overheard one of his peers lamenting, "These missions are no longer any fun when we have to come back by the numbers." The sentiment was practically unanimous; the pilots' sense of wanderlust remained strong.

A few still tried to buck the system. Taking leave of their comrades, Flight Officers Wes Hare and Tom Lochard slipped out to hitchhike to Brussels. Their glee at having made a successful escape was dampened by a sign on the outskirts of town: "Any Glider Pilots picked up in Brussels will be subject to Court Martial." They arrived back at their airbase in Poix one day after everybody else.

Despite transportation delays and evasion attempts, within seventy-two hours close to 500 glider pilots had returned. And within six days, almost all who were fit for travel were back.

Bill Knickerbocker returned to his unit in record time but found little had changed in regard to the lack of respect his profession garnered from his superiors. His first post-mission paycheck contained a $25.00 debit for his combat uniform and boots and an insulting fine of $75.00 for being AWOL.

In the wake of the glider pilot migration Miley's troops readied themselves for the push. Salvage teams picked through wrecked gliders for unclaimed supplies and ammunition. Jeep teams raced to DZ W, where the division's quartermaster troops stockpiled supplies from the B-24 drop. Combat engineers tinkered with captured vehicles to get them running. Idle squads collected the dead—both friend and foe—and separated them into grim piles for easier recovery.

09:05. Drop Zone X—The Thirteeners.
Sunday, March 25, 1945.

Generals Ridgway and Miley returned to Coutts' command post at 09:05 to check in on the Thirteeners' readiness for the day's mission.

Coutts' men had already been busy that morning. The Thirteeners' 2nd Battalion, led by Colonel "Ace" Miller, had moved out before dawn to finally seize their objective. In hushed tones Miller had ordered his men to advance through the woods in a single column.

Stepping carefully to avoid snapping twigs, the lead scouts dove for cover as rifle and machine gun fire cracked through the still air. The enemy muzzle flashes set the machine in motion: squads bounded forward, forming loose skirmish lines. The *POP! POP! POP!* of suppressing rifle fire was quickly drowned out by the steady bursts of belt-fed machine guns. The Americans' superior firepower swelled, overwhelming the Germans, who, faced with the inevitable, gave up. Two platoons of *Grenadiers* were added to the division's cages, and the Thirteeners' final D-Day objective fell at 07:30.

Miller's battalion would stay in place to link up with British airborne troops—a task he should have completed eighteen hours before. While Miller awaited the Tommies with a flask of whiskey brought to celebrate the occasion, Coutts' other two battalions along the Issel would mop up any remaining resistance within the combat team's sector.

The clearing operation netted sixty-three more prisoners and a battery of 105mm howitzers. The paratroopers also rescued a group of C-47 and B-24 crewmen who'd barricaded themselves in a farmhouse. Numerous liberated vehicles were duly pressed into service. Bicycles and horses became popular means of individual conveyance, and several troopers pushed their mortar ammunition down the road in captured baby carriages.

Personal trophy taking was rife as many paratroopers accessorized their combat uniform with fashionable accoutrements such as formal top hats, stylish monocles, and flashy striped ties. The pirates did little to hide their plunder. Embracing one of history's most pervasive rules, "to the victor go the spoils," they took what they wanted.

For all the frivolous pillaging, there was still work to do. That morning Tom Funk's platoon leader asked him to volunteer for a six-man patrol.

"I didn't want to go," Funk admitted. "But I also didn't want to be thought of as being afraid, so I agreed to go." Funk had worked hard to overcome the stigma of being a replacement and didn't want to jeopardize his growing status as a veteran trooper, so he pulled himself out of his foxhole to join the others.

Crossing an open field, he admired the beautiful weather, thinking that back home it would have been a perfect day for a picnic. The daydream shattered as six Germans leapt up and dashed into a house under covering fire from the windows. The first shots killed Funk's friend Frank Burton instantly, and the other five paratroopers flopped to the ground.

Several of the Germans made a break for it. "One ran behind a crashed glider that lay behind the house," recalled Funk. "All I could see was his feet, but I started firing my M-1 through the glider at a height that I thought should be about belt high. After a few rounds I saw him topple over."

"That's for Burton!" Funk yelled.

The patrol flushed the Germans out, capturing a wounded *Soldat* and taking a few "suspicious looking" civilians into custody. They took one of Burton's dog tags and made note of his body's location for later retrieval. Leaving the corpse behind, they headed back to report but found the unit had already pulled out for the attack.

Lieutenant Dean Swem's platoon of Thirteeners still occupied their positions overlooking the Issel River. They'd been kept on their toes all night. Their company had captured sixty-three enemy POWs and killed an undetermined number of Germans trying to escape over the Issel. They continued to eye the patch of woods suspected of containing the Germans who'd fled yesterday's shoot-out. Maybe they were still in there, maybe they weren't. Everyone kept his head down just in case.

Sergeant Bob Cull approached Swem and pointed to a crashed British glider. "I think I see a jeep sticking out of the end of the ramp inside," he said.

Both men knew what a prize that could be. Parachute infantry regiments had only 15 of them compared to the 149 allocated to "leg" regiments. Getting their hands on a jeep would give them much-needed transportation.

Cull was confident he could get the jeep back to their lines.

"Like hell you will," said Swem, "you'll get your ass shot off for sure."

But Cull was adamant; *he needed* that jeep to haul supplies.

"OK," agreed Swem, "we'll give you some covering fire to keep any Krauts down. But you haul your ass across that clearing like a turpentined cat."

Cull did just that, blitzing across the field and into the British glider. He had to work his way around several dead Tommies, but soon had the jeep out. Cull tore across the field as the platoon fired into the wood line. Screeching to a halt with his arms raised in triumph, Cull announced, "Now we've got it made!"

They had it made for just a few hours.

Word of the jeep soon spread, and Coutts' headquarters requested it be delivered for use by the staff. Cull was incensed. He'd risked his neck to steal the jeep from the British—it was a fortune of war. He ignored multiple orders to hand it over. Finally, an officer dispatched someone to fetch it.

"It will be ready, all right," mumbled Cull.

Swem, who empathized with Cull's disgust, stood by as Cull popped the jeep's hood and heaved the distributor cap as far as he could. Next, Cull slashed all four tires with this bayonet and stabbed the spare for good measure.

"Now they can have the goddam thing!" declared Cull. If he couldn't keep his booty, certainly no brass hat would get it.

John Chester and his fellow artillerymen had a restless night as well. The sounds of battle had ebbed and flowed all around them, and at 02:00, a small German patrol had blundered into their perimeter. A spatter of carbine fire dispersed the enemy, who fled leaving three wounded behind.

The 466th's batteries rotated their guns to support the day's eastern advance after Miller's battalion of Thirteeners occupied the main Diersfordt road. Unless the situation was dire, fire support missions would continue to be serviced by the British howitzers back across the Rhine, allowing the airborne artillery units to conserve their shells. By one o'clock that afternoon, Chester's battalion had all fifteen of their howitzers ready for action, the only airborne battalion in the division to have all its tubes in firing order.

The Thirteeners moved forward later that afternoon. Two platoons from Coutts' 3rd Battalion crossed the Issel, seizing a section of woods that bordered the autobahn. While some troopers used the lone footbridge, most opted to wade across the four-foot-deep river with their rifles lifted over their heads. Scrambling up the far bank, the paratroopers occupied the wood line and started shoveling out their fighting positions.

Initial opposition was light, but they soon came under fire from a group of occupied houses. Incoming artillery rounds silenced the German machine gunner, set the houses on fire, and scattered the defenders. The men took advantage of the lull to organize a shuttle system and passed much-needed ammo crates across the river.

It didn't take long for German mortars and artillery to retaliate. Two hundred–odd rounds crashed in, methodically ranging back and forth across the American lines. The retreating Germans had pre-plotted the target for their gun crews; thirty-two more of Coutts' troopers were cut down in the barrage.

Closer to Bridge 10, Texan Lendy McDonald had spent the night in a foxhole with two buddies wrapped in a parachute for warmth and munching on ham and cheese from their K-rations. The trio, reflecting on their time in Belgium, were grateful: "No snow, no ice, no howling wind." But their reverie couldn't last, and soon they, along with the rest of Able Company, were on the move.

They were to occupy LONDON between 3rd Battalion and the glider riders at Bridge 10. Having crossed the Issel, the troopers went to ground under bursts of ripping German fire from at least two entrenched machine guns. Large explosions from a dreaded 88 mixed with fountains of enemy mortar shells. The troopers fanned out and returned fire. The mortar squad couldn't unlimber their tube due to the trees; the overhead branches would detonate the projectiles.

Not far from McDonald, Ben Scherer's squad was trying to get a bead on the machine gun emplacements. Scherer was close to Hal Leathers, who stuck his head up to take a peek. He jerked once and slumped back down, dead with a bullet through his forehead. Scherer was next. An explosion peppered his left thigh, torso, and shoulder with shrapnel. He limped back to a house they'd passed to wait for medical help.

Nodding in and out of consciousness, Scherer awoke to find two Germans in their field-gray uniforms staring at him from the door. He recalled, "I knew that if I reached for my carbine, they may have reacted. One could speak some broken English and I could speak some broken French, so we could communicate. They took my watch and some money and my carbine. They put one of their own sulfa-type packs on my hip area and left."

Back near the autobahn the two stubborn German machine gun crews held up the advance for hours. It took several lucky artillery rounds from across the Rhine to finally destroy the bunkers.

Darkness caught up to the Thirteeners before all of them made it to LONDON. Lendy McDonald's platoon came to a large field through which they'd have to pass to get to the autobahn. They were assessing their options when the radio crackled with orders for them to clear the far woods and keep moving. McDonald didn't like the look of it, nor did his scouts.

One of McDonald's buddies understood his leadership burden: "A squad leader who makes a wrong decision would lose men, men who trusted him. . . . [They] test their expertise in immediate action; at the point of the triangle, the chances are that the [squad] leader will make no more than one mistake." McDonald thought it would be folly to cross the field as "it was too dark with poor visibility and with no idea of what we might run into, we should wait until morning."

His men agreed and so did their platoon leader, Lieutenant Beckett, who was concerned they'd shoot one another in the chaos of a firefight; he decided to hold tight.

The radio again repeated the order to keep moving. Beckett informed the caller of his decision and told him to relay the message.

The radio was insistent: cross the field and clear the woods on the other side.

Beckett grabbed the handset, identified himself, and said, "You tell General Miley that if he wants those woods cleared tonight, he better hurry on down here." There was no reply.

05:15. Drop Zone W — The Ruffians. Sunday, March 25, 1945.

The Ruffians' day started with the disconcerting sound of tracked vehicles clanking toward one of their roadblocks. Alarm gave way to relief as the morning's gray gloom revealed olive-drab American half-tracks crawling up the dirt road. As one of the embedded reporters put it, the sight of half-tracks towing M5 three-inch anti-tank guns was "as welcome as Betty Grable in a bubble bath." The gun teams of the 605th Tank Destroyer Battalion had crossed the Rhine downstream near Xanten on barges at two o'clock that morning. The first twelve guns were assigned to the Ruffians, each of Raff's battalions getting four. The other twenty-four guns would cross later in the day via the completed floating pontoon bridge and would then fan out to Miley's other combat teams.

The M5s fired a three-inch (or 76.2mm) shell and weren't ideal for anti-tank warfare. Weighing in at close to 5,000 pounds, the gun was heavy and unwieldy, making it a beast to manhandle into position and slow to traverse around against moving targets. These lumbering weapons did, however, provide infantry with a substantial bunker-busting capability. On the move, though, the guns had to leapfrog one another so they could be well positioned for fire support and keep up with the advancing GIs.

Despite assault crossings on either flank of the 17th Airborne's sector, formal contact had yet to be made with any ground troops. At 10:50 the British started another wave of crossings just south of the Ruffians' perimeter. Raff sent a patrol out to the Rhine to confirm the landings and establish contact. Moving in a wedge formation, the patrol threaded through the protective cover of the Diersfordt Forest toward the river, trudging over plowed fields and tributaries on their way to meet the British. The patrol radioed back at 12:50, reporting that the British had landed in six assault boats and contact had officially been made with Montgomery's 21 Army Group.

After getting the report, Raff ordered his regiment to attack toward the east. With one battalion on their left flank and another on the right, the Ruffians would cut across the open fields before hitting the Wesel railroad tracks.

The approaches to Wesel were cluttered with pockets of die-hard snipers and machine gunners fighting a lost cause. And die hard they did.

The Ruffians to the rear of the formation hoped their platoon leaders would let the situation develop before rushing them into the attack. The veterans knew it was often best to size up the situation, to understand what they were up against, before reacting. Moving by bounds, leapfrogging one another, and using a base of fire to fix the enemy until they fled, surrendered, or died was effective; but it was also exhausting and took time to re-form the unit. The men wanted their leaders to assess and observe, then leverage the best weapon at their disposal to destroy the enemy—if that meant an infantry assault, so be it; they would do it. That was the job.

Branigan's Bastards tagged along. They'd Frankensteined together a working howitzer from parts of the three that had been damaged during the drop, giving them ten tubes for supporting fire. They moved their guns with the help of five jeeps and five horse-drawn carts they'd collected from farmers. The crews shuttled the howitzers forward, firing them to support Raff's infantry as they moved east. The plan worked. The Bastards fired four "fire missions," lobbing 279 high-explosive 75mm rounds to help the Ruffians take LONDON.

Thad Blanchard's company trudged along in a column behind Baker Company on Raff's right flank. They split up when they crossed the railroad tracks about a mile from Wesel. Blanchard's squad shifted up to the left flank.

It was getting dark by the time they approached the outskirts of Wesel. Muzzle flashes and the ubiquitous buzz saw of a heavy machine gun greeted the lead squad. Tracers from the Americans' machine guns zipped back to ricochet and whine off the houses, keeping the Germans' heads down while the big guns were brought up. It took the combined firepower of the Ruffians and the Bastards' pack howitzers to reduce the resistance.

The paratroopers had trouble maintaining contact with one another in the dark. As they padded through the decimated town, puffs of chalky dust coated their jump boots. One of the troopers noted, "The city had been pulverized and there were absolutely no streets whatsoever, making progress difficult because of the mounds of rubble and craters."

When the Ruffians crossed over the canal to take up their positions, the glider riders shifted north, reducing the size of their front by several hundred yards. They held Bridge 3, while the paratroopers passed over Bridges 1 and 2 to push out to LONDON.

Thad Blanchard's worn-out troopers stumbled into the phase line after eleven hours of slow movement. They were famished, not having eaten since they landed. They'd have a few hours of rest before moving out again at daylight to occupy the next phase line, NEW YORK.

Thirty minutes before the clock ushered in March 26, Miley's command post broadcasted over the division's radio net: "Organized resistance has now ceased."

Approaching Midnight. Issel River: Bridges 6 and 10. Sunday, March 25, 1945.

If organized resistance had ceased, no one had bothered to inform the Germans massing to attack Bridge 10. Using nightfall to their advantage, they again pressed an attack forward. Supported by tanks and self-propelled guns, they successfully crossed over the autobahn and pushed through the thinly defended lines held by Frank Dillon's company.

The Germans barreling toward the bridge had come within seventy-five yards of crossing it when the glider riders leveled every weapon in their arsenal to repel them: massed artillery barrages, mortars, machine guns, and rifles.

A second wave from *Kampfgruppe Karst* wedged into the line between the Thirteeners and the gap created by the first assault. They were too close to repel with artillery, and one of the glider riders' platoons was almost enveloped by the swarm. A quick deployment of reserves saved them. At Bridge 6, the German attack forced troopers to abandon the far bank, scrambling back over a makeshift bridge of wagons they'd pushed into the river to ease their crossing earlier in the day.

The Germans regrouped and attacked Bridge 10 multiple times. Artillery fire saved the day—again. Forward observers called in salvos at "danger close" range all across the front to keep the hordes at bay. By the next morning, having committed all hands, the battalion's reserve consisted of a mere eight commo men, five enlisted staffers, and three officers.

CHAPTER 20

"THIS IS A PURSUIT"

Wesel, Germany. Monday, March 26, 1945.

Miley's objective for Monday was Phase Line NEW YORK: a line on the map that started in the British Airborne's sector at Ringenberg and arced through Brünen before ending at the banks of the Rhine, seven miles east of Wesel. The plan called for the 6th Airborne to swing north of the Americans as they made another leap due east.

Miley's combat teams would have the benefit of armored support for the push. The tankers of the 771st Tank Battalion, with over fifty lumbering M4A3 Shermans, had crossed the Rhine under the cover of darkness using both barges and pontoon bridges. Like the 17th they were relatively new to the war, having cut their teeth on the front lines only days before the Battle of the Bulge. Since their baptism they'd earned a reputation of working well with the infantry. Nonetheless, Miley greeted their commander, Lieutenant Colonel Jack Childers, with only mild enthusiasm.

Childers found Miley "dubious" about the tankers' willingness to provide effective close-in support, citing his division's "sad experiences with tanks" in the Bulge. His troopers were skeptical, not of tanks, but of the men who drove them. The trigger pullers, with only their rifles to hide behind, wanted the armored tanks up front. Tankers, on the other hand, wanted the infantry out front clearing the way of enemy anti-tank gunners. Miley told Childers he expected to see his tanks up front. Childers assured him he'd see just that.

Childers knew the deal. It was "easy for the infantry to blame its lack of success on the attached tanks and I don't think we ever permitted this to happen," he recalled. "No inference, however slight, of a lack of aggressiveness on our part ever went unchallenged." With the mutual understanding in place, he dispatched a tank company to each of Miley's combat teams.

321

The eighteen tanks under the command of Lieutenant Vince Cochrane rumbled off to find Coutts' command post. Cochrane, a leader known by his peers for his "swashbuckling" style of leadership, liked to lead from the front. His dashing aggression had earned him several awards for bravery and just as many Purple Hearts.

As the tanks clanked through the dark, they passed under the riddled corpses of paratroopers hanging from trees and by dead Germans lying in roadside ditches. Blackened gliders with the charred skeletons of buckled-in passengers made an even more vivid impression on the new arrivals. The carcasses of cattle, horses, sheep, and goats added to the portrait of carnage.

Cochrane's tankers found the Thirteeners at 03:30. They were preparing to attack a few hours after dawn, and Coutts wanted Cochrane to hold his tanks back in reserve. Coutts explained that the assault companies were being issued extra ammunition and rations for a 09:00 kickoff. The autobahn would be their line of departure.

Coutts had his plans. And the Germans had theirs—they still wanted a bridge. At first light, a quaking barrage of German artillery pounded the paratroopers' positions, and dawn gave enemy observers the visibility they needed to accurately range the American lines. The Nazis' ground attack commenced against the Thirteeners at 07:00 with a company of German infantry directing their assault on Able Company's lines.

A mortar shell killed Able's radio operator, exploding directly in his foxhole. Shrapnel cut down several others. Without the tanks up front, holding the line was in doubt. Lieutenant W. C. MacFarlane hurried over to a .30-caliber machine gun position manned by three privates. Sliding down beside their foxhole, MacFarlane ordered them to hold tight and cover the retreat with suppressing fire. They could fall back once everybody else was across the river. In mid-sentence a mortar round exploded at MacFarlane's feet, showering him and the crew with dirt, but miraculously nothing else. Eyes wide, MacFarlane nodded and scrambled back across the canal. The crew chugged out a few bursts then made a run for it, shouldering their machine gun and sprinting back over the canal with gray-clad infantry close on their heels.

German artillery peppered both sides of the canal. Private Noah Jones found himself out in the open as several 88s crashed in. He ran for cover, throwing himself into a shell crater and landing on a woman's corpse. Recoiling in revulsion, he crawled away and headed back to his mortar crew. Jones found them just as the Germans poured across Bridge 10, and he fell in with a group of troopers to hold them back. It was a vicious little firefight, with the enemy mortar crews lobbing in rounds to support the assault.

Coutts released Cochrane's Sherman tanks, urging them forward to counterattack. The sight of tanks alone was almost enough to unhinge the German infantry, and their attack soon collapsed under the weight of advancing armor. Coutts' combat engineers estimated the bridge could support the 66,800 pounds of a Sherman but just barely. Six rumbled across, one at a time, fanning out upon reaching the far bank.

Another wave of Germans advanced on the right flank, well armed with machine guns and anti-tank *Panzerfausts*. Cochrane's Shermans plastered them with 76mm cannons and their .30-caliber Browning machine guns. Meanwhile, paratroopers moving under the supporting fire captured one of the dreaded 88mm guns before it could be brought to bear against the tanks. Two audacious *Soldats* managed to crawl close enough to pummel the lead tank with *Panzerfausts* before another tank cut them down.

Noah Jones, along with his mortar squad, followed the attack in while hauling their forty-two-pound 60mm mortar up a small hill. The crest was littered with the dead and abandoned equipment jettisoned by the fleeing enemy. With a good vantage point they set up.

Their target was a fortified farmhouse from which Germans were engaging the advancing troopers. As the three-man mortar squad watched the action unfold below them, they dropped a high-explosive round down the tube. The shell arced through the air before crashing through the roof of the farmhouse, exploding inside. The survivors bolted from the burning building and attempted to escape across an open field. None made it. A volley from the prone paratroopers saw to that.

Lendy McDonald's platoon, having stopped short of the autobahn the previous night, still needed to get to the line of departure. Daylight confirmed what they'd suspected: Germans were milling around bunkers on the other side of the clearing. While they felt vindicated—attacking that position at night would have been "hopeless chaos"—they had to attack it now.

Bent double, McDonald and one of his scouts sprinted across under the covering fire of belt-fed machine guns. They collapsed behind one of the bunkers and opened up on the Germans, giving the following man covering fire as he ran to join them.

McDonald motioned for Private Carol Clausen to cross over next. As the lanky Clausen started his run, the distinct POOMPH of a *Panzerfaust* flashed from the wood line. The warhead exploded at his feet. But Clausen didn't miss a beat, leaping through the cloud of dust and debris to make it safely to the bunker. Behind him, his bright yellow identification scarf floated to the ground, ripped from his neck by a piece of shrapnel.

After the skirmish to secure their sector of the autobahn, McDonald learned that two of his good friends, Sergeants Alfred Morton and Harlan Leathers, had both died in the assault.

On Coutts' left flank, his 3rd Battalion opened their attack with a fusillade from their supporting tanks and three British self-propelled guns. From the banks of the Issel they shelled clusters of enemy-held houses on the far side of the autobahn. Scouts estimated that a company of *Grenadiers* held the buildings. The troopers moved under protective tank fire to get close enough to rake the buildings with rifles, machine guns, and their M18 recoilless rifle. The tanks ceased fire at 08:00 and the troopers surged in to rout the enemy. While the counterattacking Able Company occupied the enemy on their right flank, their left was exposed. The Germans opened fire on them from the left as they ran toward the buildings. Fifteen troopers were cut down, with four killed before they knew what hit them.

Lieutenant Dean Swem's platoon advanced on their assigned cluster of houses, barns, and sheds. They were bounding up a dirt lane with grazing cattle on both sides when small arms fire from their front pinned them down.

The troopers returned fire, and Swem called his bazooka team forward. As he did, panicked cattle bolted back and forth trying to escape the melee. In their frenzied, terrified state they voided their bowels as they loped through the prone Americans, pelting them with warm shit.

The white phosphorus bazooka rockets exploded into the thatched roofs, which burst into flames, setting the buildings ablaze and showering the dug-in troops with white-hot embers. Flanking fire now poured into the enemy from the platoon on Swem's right, who emerged from the wood line just as the American fire peaked for the assault. Swem's men charged forward in what he later described as a "maniacal frenzy." The troopers threw themselves into the German positions, shooting and bayonetting them in their foxholes.

Clearing the buildings, the troopers discovered three ammunition supply dumps and a German aid station overflowing with wounded. The Thirteeners pressed their attack farther east, where the terrain opened up with the only defensible points being more fortified farms. Tanks, bazookas, and the recoilless rifle reduced those in short order.

The last remaining obstacle on their route was a well-defended, 200-foot hill about 700 yards short of Phase Line NEW YORK. To crack it the Thirteeners called in a fifteen-minute artillery barrage, most likely from John Chester's battalion of 75mm howitzers. The shells rained down on the target, but the requested smoke rounds, intended to mask the assaulters, never materialized. Supported by overhead fire from the tanks, the troopers went in anyway.

George Holdren, who'd been advancing behind the infantry with his anti-tank gun, watched the drama unfold from the protection of a farmhouse. His section had set up their two 57mm guns on either side of the house to take out any machine gun positions on the hill. But the machine gunners spotted them first, peppering the 57mm guns with bursts of bullets that sent the crew scrambling inside the building and under the jeeps.

The two infantry companies, using marching fire, walked forward, firing from the hip or shoulder every two or three steps to keep the enemy's heads down. No one paused to aim, making the firepower of the automatic rifles and tommy guns critical; the rest of the battalion supported them with suppressing fire from the flanks. The tactic created a wall of lead and worked well against the skittish German infantry already shredded by artillery.

The entrenched Germans appeared to not have any artillery or mortar support, and the reason soon became apparent: they were *Volkssturm* troops, old men and adolescents armed with bolt-action rifles and plenty of machine guns. From Holdren's position the Thirteeners' tactic appeared "very effective" and decimated "the poor Germans."

It was all over an hour after the first artillery shell crashed into the hilltop. At the cost of three wounded troopers, the 3rd Battalion took their final objective of the day, killing twenty-eight of the defenders and bagging eighty more shell-shocked POWs. Many were wounded, and indifferent troopers carried them down the hill for evacuation. By Holdren's estimate, "there were only about fourteen or fifteen left walking."

The Thirteeners continued their advance, occupying NEW YORK by early evening. It had been a rough slog. The bridgehead had been expanded by two miles and more than 200 prisoners had been taken. Coutts had suffered thirteen KIA and scores more wounded to seize Phase Line NEW YORK.

Holdren's section, passing through a knot of farm buildings, eagerly took jelly sandwiches from an elderly woman handing them out from her back door. With an exchange of smiles Holdren took the gift, wondering what lay behind the gesture. Was she a frightened German woman trying to appease the terrible enemy, just being friendly, or perhaps someone from Eastern Europe who'd been forced into slave labor?

It had been two days of firsts for Holdren. He'd seen his first jet aircraft the day before when a dappled-gray German Me-262 screamed past at fifty feet, and earlier that morning he'd witnessed his first and only aerial dogfight of the war. He craned skyward as *Messerschmitts* and Spitfires swooped and circled after each other. It appeared the *Luftwaffe* won: a Spitfire was shot down and another trailed smoke as it beat a hasty retreat.

A little farther on the troopers found a farmhouse in which to spend the night. They arrived just in time to douse the flames starting to consume the hay barn. The fire must have been started by a passing group of Thirteeners embracing the scorched earth policy of their Civil War ancestors. Holdren had seen many such blazes, but never understood "the necessity of that sort of thing." He and his anti-tank gunners were quite happy to spend the night indoors.

A search of the house produced an enticing distraction: a locked safe. The troopers took turns pressing their ears to the metal surface while slowing rotating the dial. Closing their eyes, they strained for the sounds of a tumbler falling into place. No dice. The finesse of cat burglary gave way to blunt force; they butt-stroked the dial, trying to knock the locking mechanism askew. That failed too. Finally they dragged it outside, backed away, and fired a bazooka rocket into it. The explosion sent the safe tumbling and the door flew open. It was empty.

Boys were being boys, but the brass at Miley's HQ had had enough looting and mayhem; they issued three warnings in seventy-two hours, each more stern than the last. The division's chief of staff issued the first on March 25, calling on officers to take disciplinary action to stop the looting. The memo read in part, "There is evidence of considerable looting—bicycles, radios, quilts, and numerous other articles have been seen. There is no objection [to] requisitioning transportation for movement of equipment and supplies. However, the taking of other articles is strictly forbidden." Another memorandum was issued two days later observing that despite the previous order, "personnel of this command are ransacking, pillaging and looting private homes and leaving them in a deplorable condition." The document again called on the troopers and officers to "cease immediately." The third appeal came less than twenty-four hours later, this time directly from General Miley: "I have personally seen and stopped many cases of looting of civilian houses. This will not be tolerated and any officer failing to take adequate measures to prevent looting will be disciplined to the full extent."

The troopers' lack of reverence for military professionalism rankled the career officers in Miley's staff. Despite the warnings from HQ though, vandalism and petty theft continued to be a problem. Enforcement was halfhearted in the front line units as it was difficult to convince a soldier who might be dead tomorrow that it was wrong to take from a population that had upended the entire world. A lieutenant colonel summed up the feeling of many troopers when he wrote, "This part of Germany wasn't hurt much until we came along. I think we ought to burn it to the ground."

Miley's glider riders arrived at Phase Line NEW YORK having swept aside minor resistance and were in position by two o'clock that afternoon. Using tanks and artillery they knocked out several anti-aircraft positions, including a battery of 20mm guns captured by Frank Dillon's company. All told they bagged 250 prisoners at the cost of two of their own killed in action.

Not everything they seized was of military value. Captain George Streukens and his men captured a creamery, allowing them to load up with sausages, canned fruits, duck eggs, bread, and butter. They settled in for the night and ate like kings.

The Ruffians, despite constant shelling from artillery, made short work of their objective as well, occupying NEW YORK by noon in exchange for three dead. Thad Blanchard's squad was part of the group that made contact with their fellow Americans at the phase line. On Montgomery's right flank, the US 30th Infantry Division had crossed the Rhine farther upstream as part of the American Ninth Army's assault. With the linkup of the two American units, the Ruffians reported, "assigned objectives for operation 'Varsity' had been accomplished."

Midday. Landing Zone N. Monday, March 26, 1945.

Captain Ernest Carpenter needed a drink. After two days of almost no sleep and nonstop work, he and his team of medics were worn out. He wanted to quench their thirst and find them a comfortable place to bed down. As the medics set up their aid tents in an open field, Carpenter grabbed Sergeant Edmund Wienczak to serve as his translator.

The civilians in the first house readily surrendered the only bottle of liquor they had. While rooting around their kitchen, Wienczak noticed a stockpile of canned goods, wryly observing that starving them out would have taken forever.

Jetzt! They told the family in the next house to leave.

Off-duty medics filed in, huddling around sinks to wash up and, also, searching for a place to crash. Wienczak meanwhile trudged back to the aid station to take care of the wounded; he would catnap on a litter as opportunity allowed. One of the patients was a Ruffian from Wienczak's hometown of Cleveland who'd lost his small finger in a gunfight to take NEW YORK. He'd be patched up and returned to the line.

The medics had been ferrying the most urgent cases back to the Rhine via jeep since the day after the airdrop. Braving stray artillery rounds and occasional potshots from insolent Germans, the medics gingerly navigated their littered patients to evacuation points. The bridges were still limited to one-way traffic, with priority given to tanks, ambulances, and tarp-covered cargo trucks toting in troops and supplies. As such the wounded were lifted onto barges and amphibious trucks for the ride over the Rhine: 270 casualties, including 53 seriously wounded, were evacuated this way.

Several of the ambulances and trucks crossing the pontoon bridges belonged to the 643rd Clearing Company, the unit responsible for stabilizing and evacuating critical patients. They brought in well-equipped surgical teams armed with sulfa powder, battle dressings, splints, morphine, and plasma. They arrived at the 17th Airborne Division's aid station to find surgeon Lieutenant Colonel Edward Sigerfoos still tending to the wounded. He had medical tape over his broken nose and moved with a distinct limp, both injuries sustained when his glider crashed. His team had been operating shorthanded since landing: one surgeon was dead, another still missing, and a third had broken his leg.

Miley's medics handed over their charges to the newly arrived medical teams and joined the push east. The clearing medics loaded up their ambulances and evacuated an additional 500 cases, including over 200 POWs, for transfer back across the Rhine on barges.

When the Rhine bridges opened up for two-way traffic two days after the airdrop, ten ambulances evacuated a further 108 casualties, along with two wounded civilians.

Once the patients reached the west side of the Rhine, they were transported to the 113th Evacuation Hospital, established prior to D-Day in a former German medical facility. It was a large, imposing three-story building of institutional brick, divided into two wings with multiple wards and topped with a severe mansard roof.

The patients' first stop was a large olive-drab receiving tent set up just in front of the grand portico at the end of the long driveway. Here they were again triaged; those not expected to make it were left to drift away as quietly as possible. Care stations had been organized to minimize carrying the wounded up and down staircases. The more serious cases were on the first floor; the walking wounded made their way up to the third.

The medical staff also tended to the wounded POWs. Captain Quinn Whiting, head of the hospital's trauma unit, later said, "There was no discrimination in the treatment and care of the enemy, except our American soldiers were always treated first."

The patients weren't segregated while awaiting attention. A grievously wounded paratrooper, lying on his stretcher in the receiving tent, drifted into consciousness. Blinking at the man lying next to him, his eyes focused on the SS runes stitched to the collar of his field-gray tunic. The paratrooper threw himself on top of the German, wrapping both hands around his throat to choke the life out of him. It took three medics to restrain the trooper who, despite his wounds, was still spoiling for a fight.

★ ★ ★

Surprisingly, Joseph Goebbels' propaganda ministry announced the crossing of the lower Rhine over the radio, accurately comparing it in scope to the landing in France. The announcer declared that while the Allied invaders had broken through the main defensive line, they were suffering heavy casualties at the hands of the *Wehrmacht* counterattacks. The commentator further softened the distressing news with vivid accounts of German bravery and confidence.

But hyperbole couldn't stop the inevitable. The German losses were staggering. The two airborne divisions' three-day tally alone cost the enemy 3,246 prisoners and more than 1,200 dead. And Allied mechanized might continued to flow across the Rhine, bringing more tanks, artillery, and troops than the Third Reich could ever hope to repel.

Mixed into the congested traffic crossing the pontoon bridge at Xanten was a jeep ferrying General Lewis Brereton over the Rhine River. As the First Allied Airborne Army commander bumped through Wesel's streets he saw that "there is nothing left in the city's main section except rubble and a few burnt-out brick shells."

Brereton, who'd elected to make an uncharacteristic visit to the field, spent the night at Ridgway's command post, but complained the next morning about his poor sleep due to the racket of *Luftwaffe* night fighters fruitlessly attacking the pontoon bridges.

Sleep deprivation aside, Brereton must have been pleased. Ridgway had the operation well in hand, the airborne troops had accomplished their mission, and just as important, the press corps was behaving admirably, reporting VARSITY with Brereton's name at the top of the press release. That positive news coverage was critical to Brereton was made ridiculously clear on D-Day, when he sent an urgent message to Ridgway's command post at 23:15 requesting an update: "Have not received any copy from correspondents. Can you check the units to which they were attached and find out what has happened? . . . Request you reply immediately." That Brereton dedicated more diary pages to the performance of embedded reporters than his two airborne divisions confirmed his priorities.

Before departing back to the peace and quiet of his Parisian HQ, Brereton took a short jeep tour to witness Miley's advancing glider riders. As the escorting squad of MPs cleared a path through the marching infantry, a dust-covered trooper yelled: "Okay, fellows, unload your rifles, here come the MPs. The war is over. Here comes the big brass!" Unfortunately, the war wasn't over.

•   •   •

While Brereton had been tossing and turning to the sounds of strafing aircraft and rattling anti-aircraft fire, British General Eric Bols was dispatching patrols from his 6th Airborne's sector to reconnoiter Phase Line PARIS. They found it lightly held. Ridgway sensed an opportunity to advance aggressively and ordered his legions to "disregard" PARIS and push farther east, "to obtain maximum exploitation with minimum delay." Miley echoed his commander's intent, issuing clear instruction for the day: "Advance to Dorsten. This is a pursuit."

Miley's troopers, wanting to maintain their momentum, continued to plunder any form of available transport they could find: horses, carts, wood-burning trucks, cars, bicycles, and in at least one case, a wheelchair. As one observer noted, "Their columns sometimes resembled gypsy caravans."

To take advantage of what Montgomery's Second British Army commander General Miles Dempsey called a German collapse, Miley's division was split up and attached to units surging up the left flank of the Ruhr's envelopment. The Thirteeners served as infantry for a British armored brigade, and the Ruffians went to the village of Haltern to relieve another British armored unit, while the glider riders were farmed out to an infantry division. Simultaneously, American units having crossed the Rhine south of Cologne swept up the Ruhr's right flank as part of the encirclement campaign.

For Miley's scattered combat teams, the next several days became a blur of clanking forward on tanks and dismounting to clear out stubborn pockets of resistance. One of the Thirteeners remembered the skirmishes as "sporadic and rang[ing] from several highly intensive, costly encounters to almost unopposed dashes down major highways and roads."

The rapid progress, represented by sweeping grease-penciled arrows on map boards, belied a series of nasty scraps. "Moderate resistance" to a general back at HQ was often something quite different to a sergeant and his squad of trigger pullers on the ground. Closing with the enemy to conquer villages and farmhouses still often required spilling blood. And lots of it.

Private Noah Jones and his platoon of Thirteeners jumped off the tanks to clear out one such enemy position. He recalled, "They [the Germans] were in the woods and when we got there, they really put up a fight. We thought we had them whipped good when we got orders to return to our unit. When we started back, they came out of the woods after us. That was their worst mistake, coming out in the open. We went back and clobbered them good. I think we shot some of them twice to be sure they were dead. We killed all of them. They had decided they wanted to die for Hitler so we gave them the privilege."

It was the same all across the front. On March 28, as the glider riders advanced into the village of Lembeck, the lead platoon went to ground under sweeping machine gun fire from two entrenched positions. Sergeant Clinton Hedrick sprung into action, charging the positions while firing his Browning Automatic Rifle from the hip.

One of Hedrick's platoon mates described the BAR as "a long, unwieldy weapon, a cross between a rifle and a machine gun, highly effective, but designed to rest on a bi-pod and be fired from ground position." Hedrick, a lanky twenty-six-year-old, preferred to wield it like a submachine gun. He knew his business; he'd enlisted in 1940 and had been fighting since 1942, when he landed in North Africa. VARSITY was his second glider assault, having flown into Southern France before being reassigned to the 194th Glider Infantry Regiment for the Battle of the Bulge.

Hedrick's platoon was reorganizing when six well-armed Germans attempted to flank them. Hedrick again leveled his automatic rifle and cut them all down with a twenty-round burst. Wanting to avoid a direct attack, he led his squad in a sweeping maneuver to get around the enemy positions. Hedrick's squad, according to one witness, flushed more than a hundred of the enemy before them.

The aggressive assault was typical of Hedrick, who was known for plunging forward. When asked why he never took cover, he replied, "It makes no difference. I'm six feet standing up and lying down. If I'm going to get it, I'm going to get it."

The Germans fell back as the glider riders advanced. They retreated through the grand portico of Lembeck Castle, sprinting across its low stone bridge over the wide moat. Hedrick, well in front, led a handful of troopers in pursuit.

A German with his hands up waited for the Americans inside the gatehouse. He said the garrison wanted to surrender. Hedrick, with four troopers close on his heels, entered the courtyard to accept the surrender. An explosion ripped through Hedrick, tossing him like rag doll against the wall. A German self-propelled gun idling in the courtyard blasted at the Americans. Though he was badly wounded, Hedrick held

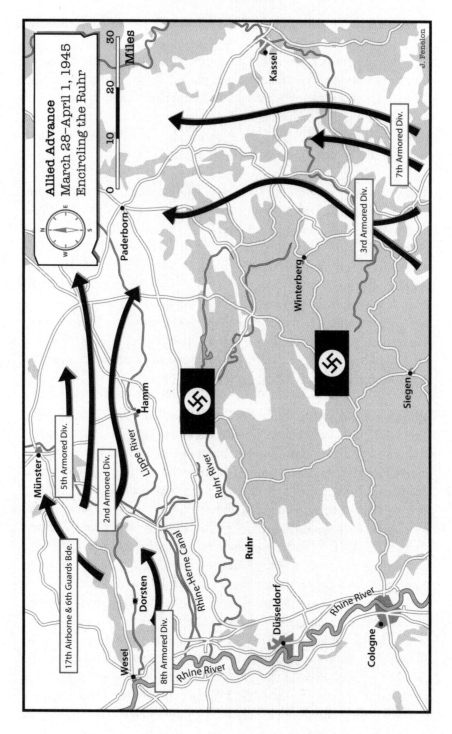

Allied Advance
March 28–April 1, 1945
Encircling the Ruhr

his ground in the sally port, belting out suppressing fire and urging his men to withdraw.

When the glider riders rallied to counterattack back across the moat, they discovered that Hedrick had succumbed to his wounds. Hedrick's father was later presented his son's posthumous Medal of Honor. For those at the tip of the spear, the end of the war was still a hazy concept. In the month of April 1945 the Americans suffered 10,677 killed in action—almost the same butcher's bill as June 1944.

Miley's division was reunited two days later to seize Münster. On the outskirts of town, a *Panzerfaust* streaked out of the dark, detonating into the tank on which Texan Lendy McDonald was riding. He was blasted off the tank and collapsed into a heap. His body lay in the mud until several of his comrades dragged it clear of oncoming tanks. The men left the body there, figuring a Graves Registration team would be along to collect it later. Fortunately, the assessment of McDonald's demise proved premature. He awoke some sixteen hours later in a hospital, unable to speak and with his two legs and right arm paralyzed. That was the end of the war for McDonald. He'd spend the next eight months in Army hospitals before making his recovery.

Münster was taken on the third of April. Thad Blanchard, leading his squad across a bridge into the city, was almost killed by a thirteen-year-old Hitler Youth member sniping from a church steeple. The Ruffians' commander, Edson Raff, had his own close call when a dud artillery shell landed just a few feet from where he stood. Raff and his bodyguard had hightailed it by the time the following three rounds hit.

As Miley's combat teams rambled up the left flank of the encirclement to take the industrial cities of Mülheim, Duisburg, and Werden, Ridgway's XVIII Airborne Corps were going the opposite direction; they'd been relieved on the morning of March 30. With the reassignment of the two airborne divisions, Ridgway's HQ staff began their trek back to Épernay. The 300-mile journey took over twelve hours by jeep due to congestion and poor road conditions.

Tagging along were the OSS agents of Team Algonquin. The rapid advance made further infiltration attempts impractical; they simply couldn't get out in front fast enough to be of use. Team Alsace had been found refusing to leave the DZ, and Team Poissy had returned on the afternoon of March 27, after attempting their second infiltration through Wesel. After several close calls, culminating in artillery shrapnel mangling their radio, they returned to friendly lines. Helmut Steltermann had been evacuated to a hospital in Paris due to his infected wounds. There, wrapped in bandages and in between surgeries, he dictated a letter to his fiancée: "Here I am—happy and well, waiting to be sewn up. I'm walking now. I think a few pieces of shrapnel must still be taken out and then I'm all set. The Doc said I'll be out in 2 weeks so I'm keeping my fingers crossed. . . . The rest I'll tell you personally. That is if you still think the same of me now that I'm air-conditioned . . ."

The speed at which the Allies were slicing across Germany also put the First Allied Airborne Army out of business. The momentum was such that ground commanders were unwilling to wait days for Brereton to marshal his air armada. But Ridgway and his XVIII Airborne Corps were back in the war soon enough. The five divisions under Ridgway's charge became part of the effort to destroy the German forces occupying what was now called the Ruhr Pocket—the 4,000 square miles of surrounded industrial cities. The Allies had closed the noose on April 12. Ridgway's corps attacked north into the Pocket while other corps crashed in from the flanks. Ridgway later described the next eight days of combat as a "meat-grinder."

Certainly, the fight was stiffer than anyone had anticipated. Intelligence officers estimated the Pocket contained 150,000 enemy troops—far fewer than was the actual case. When it was over, Ridgway's corps alone had bagged 160,892 prisoners, with the total number at more than 300,000. More poignant was the liberation of over 200,000 slave laborers and 5,639 Allied POWs.

At the end of April, despite rumors of a jump into Berlin, the troopers of the 17th were relieved from the front and sent to occupy the area surrounding Duisburg, a mere fifteen miles upstream from Wesel, where their journey into the Reich had begun. There they finished out the war as occupation troops, policing and providing local governance functions.

In several of the villages, Miley's paratroopers found local dentists willing to put their skills to work in exchange for liberated *Reichsmarks*. The troopers waited patiently while the dentists drilled small holes in their jump wings, allowing them to attach the much-revered bronze star signifying a combat jump. The troopers of the 17th Airborne were now counted as part of a unique, elite fraternity.

•　•　•

Downstream, the VARSITY battlefields were still littered with crashed gliders, downed aircraft, charred panzers, destroyed anti-aircraft guns, scorched homes, rotting livestock, and dead bodies.

Glider recovery had started almost immediately. GIs sent to prevent further vandalism discovered most of the instruments had already been stripped. The recovery rate was worse than "even the most conservative estimates." Of the 889 American CG-4A gliders that had made it over the Rhine River, only 148 were structurally sound enough for recovery; of the 416 British gliders, 24 could be salvaged. Quartermaster units scoured fields and wrecks for whatever could be reclaimed, filling 47 cargo trucks and 30 trailers with instruments, tires, wheel assemblies, wireless sets, and towropes.

Civilians had been scrounging too. Most of the parachutes had disappeared before they could be recovered; meanwhile, farmers used glider wheels on their carts and mended fences with plywood glider spars.

Families returned to find their homes at best pockmarked by bullets, or at worst burned to the ground. One farmer found a grisly scene in his basement: several dead *Wehrmacht* soldiers, including a gruesome corpse with his jaw torn off by shrapnel and his ring finger cut off by a souvenir hunter.

The Allies had started collecting and evacuating their dead three days after the drop across the Rhine. Over the next several days they recovered hundreds of American, British, and German dead. But many *Wehrmacht* and civilian bodies were left for the local authorities to deal with. The dead had been buried where they lay until they could be formally processed for proper identification. Finding wood for crosses was next to impossible due to the demands of postwar reconstruction. Count Bolko Graf von Stolberg-Wernigerode, the owner of Diersfordt Castle, donated land for a cemetery, which is now the final resting place for 532 German soldiers, including 159 known but to God.

Tragedy continued to plague the farmers even after the guns had stopped. One child lost his hand when playing with a discarded detonator. Another was killed digging through a pile of unexploded ordnance. The massive blast disintegrated the youngster instantly and blew out surrounding windows for several hundred yards.

•　•　•

Troopers of the 17th Airborne were relieved from occupational duty in mid-June, more than a month after the war in Europe ended on May 8, 1945. General Bud Miley's division was then converted to a paper organization, a holding unit, for the transfer of airborne troops back to the zone of the interior—the United States.

GIs were sent home based on a point system that tallied time in service, days in combat, and medals earned. With the exception of veterans in the Ruffians' 507th PIR, who'd been overseas since 1943 and had jumped into Normandy, the majority of Miley's men were shy of the requisite points. They were transferred out to other airborne divisions for continued occupational duty, while men with enough points transferred in to sail home.

Miley's troopers were scattered far and wide, and wherever they were sent, many went alone. Lynn Aas, the trooper who'd taught himself to hate by kicking frozen German corpses, was one such lonely case. His platoon of close to fifty men walked out of the Bulge as an understrength squad, five strong. Of those five, John Madoni was killed in VARSITY, William Simington was wounded in his glider by shrapnel, Richard Elzey lost a leg in Germany, and Aas himself was wounded on March 25. The only original member of their platoon to survive the war unscathed was Private William Mincks. Aas described him as "a Missouri hillbilly who could neither read nor write, the world's worst garrison soldier, but the most reliable in the field of combat. I shared my last foxhole with him."

Lieutenant Frank Dillon, along with many others, was transferred to the 82nd Airborne in Berlin. Thad Blanchard was among those sent to the 101st Airborne. Dozens were sent to the 13th Airborne Division for redeployment to the Pacific for the invasion of Japan. On August 15, 1945, these men were sailing to New York when the Japanese announced their surrender. The whoops of relief most certainly could have been heard for miles.

After two and a half years of existence, the 17th Airborne Division was deactivated on September 16, 1945, having been credited with sixty-six days of combat in three campaigns: Ardennes, Rhineland, and Central Europe. Scattered across those battlefields were 1,382 dead comrades, temporarily interred in cemeteries that marked the division's path across

Europe. Another 4,713 men had been wounded, and at war's end a staggering 420 remained classified as missing in action.

The division's sixty-six days in combat were storied in comradeship, loss, tragedy, and valor, with troopers earning 4 Congressional Medals of Honor—all posthumously—3 Distinguished Service Medals, 43 Silver Stars, and more than 6,200 Purple Hearts.

The final resting place for 279 of Miley's troopers is the Margraten Cemetery in the Netherlands. One of several postwar cemeteries established in Europe, the 65.5 acres contain the graves of 8,301 American dead and a memorial for 1,722 missing. Each headstone, each name, represents a uniquely unfulfilled life of hopes and dreams that was cut short in the battle to stop the Third Reich. Among those buried in Europe is Clyde Haney, whose wife, not yet knowing of her husband's death, wrote to him on March 25, 1945:

> *I have heard the reports on the radio with commentators that were right with the Gliders, & gave a complete description of them landing on the east side of the Rhine. Even told how some of the Gliders crashed. You could even hear the motors of the planes. The radio commentators say that the soldiers of the Glider Infantry are "the finest fighting men of the war." I haven't had any mail from you for nearly 2 weeks now, I think they must be holding it up for awhile while this big push across the Rhine is going on. I sort of wonder if this war in Germany won't be over by the 23rd of April! What an anniversary that would be for us, darling.*

She learned of her husband's death on April 6, 1945, via an official government telegram. Her unread letter was returned with "Deceased" scribbled across the envelope.

There would be no fifth wedding anniversary celebration.

EPILOGUE

While America's 17th Airborne Division played a crucial role in VAR-SITY, so too did the British 6th Airborne Division, which seized the village of Hamminkeln and repelled German counterattacks in their sector. Equally critical were the glider and troop carrier pilots of both the US Air Force and the RAF who skillfully delivered their cargo into battle.

The combined effort across multiple branches of two Allied nations made VARSITY the largest single-day airborne mission of World War II. VARSITY's massive display of power reflected the Allies' industrial advantage at the time: their combined resources marshaled an air armada of 1,596 transports, 1,348 gliders, and 240 B-24 bombers to deliver 19,782 armed men, 133 howitzers, and well over 1,800 tons of ammunition, medical supplies, gasoline, and communications equipment.

All arrived roughly on target, within four hours.

The ambition, scope, and execution of Operation VARSITY remains unparalleled in the annals of warfare. The invasion was the culmination of Allied airborne experience earned the hard way over the previous three years. The Supreme Commander, Dwight Eisenhower, later declared VARSITY the "most successful airborne operation carried out to date."

But kicking in the door of Adolf Hitler's Third Reich exacted a steep price. The 17th Airborne Division sustained 1,307 casualties, including 430 killed in action. British airborne troops suffered another 347 dead, 731 wounded, and dozens missing. The glider pilots of both nations were also hard hit: British casualties in this group included 38 killed and 77 wounded while the American losses stood at 35 dead and 106 wounded. The power aircrews—pilots, navigators, crew chiefs, and radio operators—of the parachute transports and glider tugs also paid a price: the US Air Force totaled 41 such personnel killed, 316 wounded, and 163 missing; the RAF added another 23 dead. The B-24 crews of the Eighth Air Force, flying in on the tail end of the armada, were even more badly mauled: 109 bomber personnel were killed and dozens more wounded.

The losses spurred postwar questions regarding the operation's necessity and effectiveness. The controversy appears to have started with the publication of the US Army's official history of the war's final phase, *The Last Offensive*, written by Charles MacDonald. MacDonald debated "whether under the prevailing circumstances an airborne attack [was] necessary or . . . even justified." He based his skepticism on three assertions: (1) that the airborne bridgehead did not add appreciable depth to PLUNDER's perimeter, (2) that ground troops could have taken the same objectives without "undue difficulty and probably with considerably fewer casualties," and (3) that the drop did not expedite engineering efforts to span the Rhine with pontoon bridges.

To take each point in turn: regarding the depth of the airdrop's penetration into Germany—which was 6.5 miles—it's important to remember that depth wasn't one of VARSITY's objectives. Dempsey and Ridgway debated how far inland to drop the troops during their planning, and both agreed that the strength of German defenses closer to the Rhine was the larger concern. VARSITY's primary objective was to block German counterattacks into the bridgehead by specifically seizing crossing points on the Issel River and Canal. The airborne bridgehead therefore was as deep as it needed to be to encompass the most threatening German artillery positions and the vital Issel crossings.

As for MacDonald's second assertion, there's no denying that the airborne objectives could have been taken by ground troops—ground troops have been occupying terrain since the dawn of conquest. The more pertinent question is whether ground troops could have achieved VARSITY's objectives as *rapidly* as airborne troops. Comparing British and American infantry advances on VARSITY's flanks—which ranged from two to four miles on the first day—the answer must be "doubtful." The arrival by air of over 19,000 combatants in four hours is what secured the thirteen crossings over the Issel and prevented German armor from hampering the Allied advance.

VARSITY's lightning bolt strike behind the enemy's main line of defense disrupted the German commanders' abilities to orchestrate an effective defense and netted over 3,000 POWs. When thousands of *Wehrmacht* soldiers found themselves surrounded by Allied airborne troops—essentially cutting off any escape—they had to make choices that a conventional assault wouldn't have forced. Those Germans caught in the VARSITY landings were prevented from fighting a delaying action as they gradually retreated. Had the Germans been able to destroy the Issel bridges, they would have preserved a natural line of defense—one that would have delayed the Allied breakout to the Ruhr.

Regarding MacDonald's claim that the speed of bridge building along the Rhine didn't proceed at a materially faster rate in the vicinity of Wesel than it did elsewhere, that is only partially correct. While upstream bridges were in operation on D-Day, downstream—where the Germans held the high ground—bridges weren't in operation until the day after.

Besides, expediting a faster crossing was not a VARSITY objective per se. The point of occupying the high ground in Diersfordt Forest was to knock out German artillery batteries and deny observers a point of view from which they could interfere with Allied engineering efforts. VARSITY's vertical envelopment of two German divisions and its destruction or capture of ninety enemy howitzers ensured that construction could proceed apace and vindicated Montgomery's belief in the need to secure the far bank as quickly as possible.

VARSITY veterans, unsurprisingly, aren't much interested in armchair debates. They were soldiers, given a task that they executed with the violence expected of them. It was a sound mission, with a good plan that adhered to the tenets of World War II airborne doctrine. Those veterans still alive more than half a century later bristle at philosophical arguments that appear to diminish the sacrifices of their dead comrades.

The survivors' reflections on VARSITY, and the war, vary by individual personality. Some are intensely proud of their contribution; some never want to speak of it. All were changed by their experiences. The pressures of combat forged some men into diamonds; others it crushed into dust. Most were content with merely surviving. Those who did make it home wrestled for the rest of their lives with the dichotomy of their combat experience: mixed in with the terror and suffering was a daily appreciation for life and an intense camaraderie. Of all the things they held sacred, it was that most of all: the pride of standing with, and for, each other.

ACKNOWLEDGMENTS

I first learned of Operation VARSITY in 1988 when I was an eighteen-year-old private going through the US Army's Airborne school at Fort Benning, Georgia. One weekend I went to the Infantry Museum and saw a plaque listing US combat jumps in Europe during World War II. Listed last was the 17th Airborne Division's drop across the Rhine. I was surprised that I'd never heard of it since I foolishly assumed my high school history class had taught me everything about the war. My cursory exploration of the museum proved how wrong I was, but it wasn't until 1999 that I became serious about studying VARSITY and learning more about the troopers of the 17th Airborne Division.

The task was harder than I anticipated. The official Army history devoted barely a dozen pages to VARSITY and the operation received scant attention outside of obscure official after-action reports and commentary buried in larger volumes. While I was able to glean high-level details of the operation from these sources, they didn't provide any insight into the actual experience of jumping into Nazi Germany. I wanted to know more.

Eventually, I attended several veteran reunions where I met glider pilots, troop carrier pilots, glider riders, anti-tank gunners, artillerymen, and paratroopers. A lot of these elderly men were still as rough and gruff as they were in 1945. They were welcoming but also leery of outsiders. At one reunion, I was recruited into some late-night shenanigans by a group of drunken glider pilots who needed help. They were wheeling one of their passed-out comrades down the hallway on a luggage trolley. Their plan was to leave their inebriated cargo in front of his hotel room door, knock, and run away before the man's wife could open the door and catch the bad influences in the act. The hitch was, they were all at least eighty years old and were concerned that they weren't fast enough to make a clean getaway. That's where I came in. After the pilots had hidden themselves around the corner, I pounded on the door

343

and bolted. Following outbursts of laughter and much backslapping, they made it clear I was "in." We retired to the bar where more drinks were poured and the stories flowed. This is what I'd been missing: firsthand accounts of the VARSITY battle. And after I'd regaled my wife with these secondhand stories, she suggested I write the book I'd long been looking for. Thus began my efforts—while working full-time—to interview more veterans, collect more personal accounts, and dig through the archives for more supporting material. Over a decade later, you hold the final results in your hands.

"The narrative historian's true calling," said author Rick Atkinson, "is to bring back the dead." If I've managed to accomplish that via *Four Hours of Fury*, it's due to the support of VARSITY's veterans and their families. Without their willingness to help, I wouldn't have been able to obtain the level of detail that the story has always deserved. I'm thankful to all the veterans who contributed material, all of whom are acknowledged in the book's endnotes, but there are a few who deserve special mention. Frank Dillon and his family welcomed me into their home and were a constant fan base over the many years it took me to complete this project. Frank's friendship was an unexpected gift and I regret I couldn't write faster so that he could have read a completed draft before he made his final jump. He is missed. John Chester's candid storytelling helped form much of the narrative's backbone. He was a paratrooper to the end. Glider pilot Don Pinzel's warmth and friendship was a steady companion during the early stages of the project and his many introductions to fellow pilots were extremely valuable. Gene Herrmann's wealth of archival documents, personal correspondence, and eternal patience with my dozens of questions are beyond appreciated. His documentation and recall are so accurate that I was literally able to locate one of his mortar team's old foxholes in Belgium, dug by them decades ago as they slogged through the Battle of the Bulge. I couldn't have told the story of Team Algonquin, the OSS team of agents infiltrating enemy lines in German uniforms, without the trust and support of Anneliese Steltermann and her daughter Linda. Their willingness to share family letters and personal anecdotes made the story that much richer.

One of the thrills of researching VARSITY was the privilege of handling original documentation and artifacts from the battle, an effort that was facilitated by many archivists, historians, and librarians in four countries. In the course of my research I enjoyed meeting many of them who shared an interest and passion for history. In North America I am thankful for the helpful staff at the US National Archives and Records Administration (at College Park, Maryland), the US Army Military History Institute (at Carlisle, Pennsylvania), the US Army Center for Military History (at Fort McNair, Washington, DC), the Silent Wings Museum (the Glider Pilot museum in Lubbock, Texas), the Air Force Historical Research Agency (at Maxwell Air Force Base, Alabama), and the Library and Archives Canada (at Ottawa). In the United Kingdom, the staff at the Imperial War Museums' Research Room was very helpful. I would also like to extend much appreciation to the staff at the National Archives (at Kew, London): they're an efficient and well-organized machine, making any visit there incredibly productive. In Germany, Johann Nitrowski, a longtime resident of Hamminkeln and expert on the battles fought throughout the surrounding area, offered his help and friendship, for which I'm grateful. Together Johann and I walked the ground where the characters in this book landed on March 24, 1945. I relied heavily on his book, *Die Luftlandung*, to gain an understanding of VARSITY's impact on German civilians.

I'm indebted to a cadre of advance readers who gave me their feedback and advice to help ensure that the narrative of this book flowed well. I'm thankful for the time and effort they invested. Among them are: Robert Lindsey, who read virtually every draft and never let his enthusiasm wane or his pencil dull; Steve Jensen, whose attention to detail was invaluable and unwavering; my longtime friend and fellow writer Mark Bristol, who pushed me to improve the prose with each draft; and Chris Schorre and Julie Pesche, both of whom provided valuable notes peppered with insightful thoughts and deep questions. My mom, Michael Southard, diligently reviewed the final manuscript multiple times and launched a one-woman campaign to drive pre-sales. Many thanks also go to Shannon Hollis, Sandy McClarty, Paul Madden, Andrei Faji, Wayne Carelock, and Robi Polgar for their insight, support, and valuable feedback. The list of family and friends who offered encouragement during the project is too long to mention, and I'm thankful for their support.

A special thanks to my wife, Melanie, who not only provided priceless assistance of every kind—from soundboarding ideas to transcribing veteran interviews to endless edits of every draft—but also tolerated years of my early hours and late nights as I sequestered myself to complete the project. This book wouldn't have been possible without her help.

My agent, Jim Hornfischer, was an unceasing advocate and a skilled mentor who helped me navigate the adventure of publishing my first book. I'm grateful for his support. Rick Horgan, my editor at Scribner, provided steady guidance throughout the process and his many pages of feedback not only improved my writing craft but also the strength of the book's narrative. Rick's team at Scribner is top-notch and a joy to work with. I'm appreciative of the efforts and help of Emily Greenwald, Dani Spencer, Jason Chappell, Rick Willett, Joshua Cohen, and Erich Hobbing.

While I've endeavored to write an unvarnished account of VARSITY's tragedy and heroism, I'm sure that my love and admiration for the American airborne trooper has shown through. In that regard, I'm biased, having had the honor to have served briefly with a gang of devils who did their best to carry on the traditions and standards set by their WWII predecessors: Sergeant Payne, Brian, Billy, Jay, Mark, Nando, Nick D, Uncle Pester, Bubba, Chet, Yawn, Goblin, Mr. Rey, Marty, Mikey, Clayton, Tom, Jackson, George, and the Cobra Commander. Thanks, brothers, I learned more from you than you'll ever know. This book is dedicated to those men and women who served and those who continue to stand ready to jump into the fray when our country needs them.

Note on Sources

Four Hours of Fury's narrative core is based on primary, contemporaneous sources, including diaries, letters, after-action reports, communications logs, and combat interviews. The locations of specific events were plotted on period maps using coordinates documented by the troopers themselves, either in communications logs or after-action reports. The timing of events is based on those recorded in unit logs. All quotes expressed as dialogue or thoughts in italics are taken verbatim from a memoir, letter, communications log, diary, or interview.

Several sources were of particular value while conducting research. Clay Blair's biography of Matthew B. Ridgway, *Ridgway's Paratroopers*, provided insight into the stoic character of one of our nation's greatest leaders. For the section on the B-24 resupply mission I relied heavily on material generously provided by Dave Shafer, son of B-24 pilot Tom

Shafer, as well as Peter Loncke's self-published report, *The Liberators Who Never Returned*. Peter was retired from the Belgian Air Force and an expert on WWII aviation and the Eighth Air Force's VARSITY mission. Richard Chancellor, in the UK, kindly supplied me with copious amounts of research and period documentation covering VARSITY's US Troop Carrier missions.

The German perspective is based on multiple sources including period Allied intelligence assessments, intercepted German communications (via ULTRA), POW interrogation reports, and postwar interviews/monographs. Anyone seeking to better understand the Germans' willingness to stand and fight against such overwhelming Allied firepower should read *The Wehrmacht's Last Stand* by Robert Citino.

Given all of the above, I must express, however, that I accept full responsibility for any errors of fact or judgment that might be found within this book.

ABBREVIATIONS

The following abbreviations appear
in the notes and selected sources:

17ABN	17th Airborne Division
17ADA	17th Airborne Division Association
21AG	21 Army Group
AEB	Airborne Engineer Battalion
AMC	Airborne Medical Company
AOMC	Airborne Ordnance Maintenance Company
AQ	*Airborne Quarterly*
AQQC	Airborne Ordnance Quartermaster Company
CJB	Clay and Joan Blair Collection
CMH	Army Center of Military History, Carlisle, Pennsylvania
CNA	Canadian National Archives
FAAA	First Allied Airborne Army
FLP	Floyd Lavinius Parks Papers
FMS	Foreign Military Studies Series
GFAB	Glider Field Artillery Battalion
GIR	Glider Infantry Regiment
GPM	Silent Wings Glider Pilot Museum, Lubbock, Texas
LAC	Library and Archives Canada
MBR	Matthew B. Ridgway Papers
NARA	National Archives and Records Administration, College Park, Maryland
NPRC	National Personnel Records Center, St. Louis, Missouri
OSS	Office of Strategic Services
PFAB	Parachute Field Artillery Battalion
PIR	Parachute Infantry Regiment
S&S	*Stars and Stripes*
SHAEF	Supreme Headquarters Allied Expeditionary Force
TBD	Tank Destroyer Battalion
TCC	Troop Carrier Command
TCG	Troop Carrier Group
TCW	Troop Carrier Wing

TFH	*Thunder from Heaven*, News Bulletin of the 17th Airborne Division Association
UKNA	United Kingdom National Archive, Kew, UK
WBB	Papers of William B. Breuer

NOTES

Prologue

xv *55,000 dug-in* Wehrmacht *troops*: Estimated enemy strength as noted in FAAA, "HQ Operations Reports, 1944–1945," March 21, 1945. **xvi** *"I am writing from a plane"*: John Chester, letter to the author, September 1, 2007. **xviii** Looks like we are going to be real shorthanded: Ibid., November 15, 2007. Boatner survived as related by Chester: "Try as we may, no one in our outfit was able to learn anything about Boatner for about five months. . . . The war had ended. . . . I was with a group to be flown to the town of Nice on the French Riviera. Would you believe our pilot was the same one who had flown us on Boatner's fateful trip? . . . The pilot had visited Boatner three times in the hospital. He said the doctors had indicated that if they were able to save the leg, Boatner would have little or no use of it."

PART I DECEMBER 1944–MARCH 1945

Chapter 1 "Where in the hell is everybody at?"

3 *digging foxholes in the Meuse-Argonne Cemetery*: King Harris, *Adventures of Ace Miller*, 57. For their first action, the 17th Airborne Division was attached to the US VIII Corps, under the command of General Troy Middleton; elements of the 513th PIR's 2nd Battalion dug positions in the cemetery. **3** This is war: Lynn Aas, "Remembering the Price of Freedom," 6. **5** *His units were still assembling at their line of departure*: William M. Miley, unpublished manuscript, 29, and David P. Schorr, letter to Gene Herrmann, September 26, 1990. **5** *Just as the forward elements began their advance*, Oberst *Otto-Ernst Remer's*: Antony Beevor, *Ardennes 1944*, 336. **5** *Confronted by the heavily armed and battle-hardened*: Ibid., 336. **6** *Izzy's actions disrupted the enemy attack*: Isadore S. Jachman Medal of Honor Citation. **7** *a German counterattack led by fifteen Mark IV and Mark V Panzers*: Talon, 6, and 17ABN, *Summary of Operations*, 3. **7** *Patton, learning of the attack's ferocity*: Lewis Brereton, *The Brereton Diaries*, 394. **7** *"The 17th saved the day"*: Ibid., 394. **7** *"The 17th has suffered a bloody nose"*: Antony Beevor, *Ardennes 1944*, 337, quoting Major Chester B., Omar Bradley's aide. **7** *"God, how green we are"*: Charles MacDonald, *The Last Offensive*, 38, quoting James R. Pierce, commander of the division's 194th Glider Infantry Regiment (GIR). **7** *519 men killed in action and almost 3,500 wounded*: William C. Mitchell, *17th Airborne Casualties*, 1. **7** *"long nightmare"*: William M. Miley, unpublished manuscript, 29. **7** *Quartermaster troops piled the dead*: John Chester, letter to the author, November 15, 2007. **8** *to those of wildflowers*: Oscar B. Franklin, WWII Veteran Survey, CMH. **8** *long-abandoned trenches from World War I could still be seen*: Richard H. Haney, *When Is Daddy Coming Home?*, 75. **8** *on what they christened the* Diarrhea Express: Ben Scherer, *Soldiers and Brothers Under the Canopy*, 41. **9** *a company commander joked*: Ibid., 42, quoting Captain John Spears. **9** *camps set up three or four miles out in the surrounding countryside*: The Talon Crosses the Rhine, 1. **10** *varied civilian occupations*: John Chester, "They Called It Varsity," 54. **10** *Private George Holdren and his squad*: George Holdren, *WWII Memoir*, 37. Holdren was a member of the 155th Airborne Anti-Tank Battalion. **10** *Its units could bathe, examine, and clothe 2,500 men in ten hours*: FM 10-10, *Quartermaster Service*, 47, and 17ABN, "Operational Diary," 19. **11** *entered the shower six at a time*: Bud Dudenhoeffer, *JUMP!*, 87. **11** *each man underwent a quick medical examination*: FM 10-10, 47. **11** *Chester jolted awake*: John Chester, letter to the author, November 15, 2007. **11** *They pitched additional tents and improved paths and roads*: 17ABN, *Historical Report of Operation Varsity*, i. **11** *"We got more rest at the front"*: History 139th Airborne Engineers, 19. **11** *Laid out according to Army regulations*: FM 10-10, 322. **12** *"I see you are from Iowa"*: George Holdren, *WWII Memoir*, 37. **12** *local Frenchmen hired to assist the cooks*: 17ABN, "Operational Diary," 19. **12** *Censors blotted out sensitive details with India ink*: Richard H. Haney, *When Is Daddy Coming Home?*, 41. **12** *Private Joseph Clyde Haney, known as Clyde . . . "Charles Holmen and Larry Owens"*: Ibid., 6–9, 18, 41. Haney was originally assigned to Baker Company of the 193rd GIR. **13** *First Allied Airborne Army . . . designated the 17th a priority recipient of men and materiel*: 17ABN, *Historical Report of Operation Varsity*, 12. And XVIII Corps (ABN), *War Diary*, February 17, 1945. For simplicity's sake in the narrative, I have shortened the reference of First Allied Airborne Army down to Airborne Army. **13** *Five hundred planeloads of supplies*: 17ABN, *Historical Report of Operation Varsity*, i. **13** *needed 4,000 to return to full strength*: Ibid., i. **13** *One of the division's parachute infantry regiments had been reduced*: Kirk B. Ross, *The Sky Men*, 236. The 513th PIR had been reduced to 46 percent of its total manpower with 70 percent of the losses suffered by its front-line rifle companies. **14** *calling for 5,000 replacements in February and another 3,200 in March*: FAAA, "History of Headquarters," 39. **14** *"Where in the hell is everybody at?"*: Kirk B. Ross, *The Sky Men*, 261. **14** *"to be in shock after the violent combat"*: Bart Hagerman, *War Stories*, 188. Tom Funk was assigned as a rifleman to the 513th PIR. **14** *by officially changing their designation to "reinforcements"*: Charles MacDonald, *The Last Offensive*, 334. **14** *Rumors suggesting jailed inmates*: Bud Dudenhoeffer, *JUMP!*, 88. **15** *"two weeks of torturous physical training"*: Bart Hagerman, *War Stories*, 222. **15** *"The first person that we met as we disembarked was"*: Bob Fox, *Memories—The Way I Saw It*, 14. Robert Fox was a new arrival in Easy Company of the 513th PIR. **16** *a running joke among veterans was*: Antony Beevor, *Ardennes 1944*, 53. **16** *With a maximum range of a mere five miles*: John Weeks, *Airborne Equipment*, 86. **17** *Chester worked them through drills*: John Chester, letter to the author, May 17, 2007. **17** *Chester's crew destroyed the German target*: John Chester, letter to the author, September 1, 2007. **17** *HQ posted requirements for issuing passes*: 17ABN, "Operational Diary," 19. **18** *Chester requested only $10.00 per pay period*: John Chester, letter to the author, November 15, 2007. Accounting for inflation of $13.85, total equaled approx. $2,127.36 a month (or approx. $25,528.32 a year). **18** *glass of watery French beer*: The Talon Crosses the Rhine, 1. **18** *children soon learned they could trade bottles of wine for a few cigarettes*: John Yanok, History 155th Airborne Anti-Tank, Anti-Aircraft Battalion, 43. **18** *prohibiting the purchase of local foodstuffs*: 17ABN, "Operational Diary," 21. **18** *formalizing the explicit number* *of passengers allowed per vehicle type*: Ibid., 20. **19** *apprehend offenders with a cordon of surprise checkpoints*: Ibid., 22. **19** *To soldiers returning from the front*: Jack Belden, *Still Time to Die*, 26. **19** *"take advantage of the things that interest you"*: "Paris, Guide for Leave Troops." **20** *George Holdren, with his recently cleaned teeth, won a pass to Paris*: George Holdren, *WWII Memoir*, 37. **21** *Chester dumped the plate*: John Chester, letter to the author, November 15, 2007. **21** *Sally got Baines' full attention*: Bart Hagerman, *War Stories*, 217.

Chapter 2 The Spartan

22 *Roman senator*: "World Battlefronts," *TIME*, 31. **22** *uncanny ability to recall names*: Clay Blair, *Ridgway's Paratroopers*, 6. **22** *"Old Iron Tits"*: Ibid., 225. The Iron Tits nickname was a bit of a misnomer; Ridgway actually wore a grenade taped to his right chest harness and a first-aid kit on his left, which was often mistaken for a second grenade. **22** *"like jumping off the top of a freight car"*: Matthew B. Ridgway, *Soldier*, 35. **25** *"indispensable prerequisite for the final drive into Germany"*: Forrest C. Pogue, *The Supreme Command*, 294. **26** *500 paratroopers rushed*: Martin Middlebrook, *Arnhem 1944*, 143. **26** *1,485 men killed in action and an additional 6,525 missing*: Ibid., 439. **26** *the 101st Airborne Division suffered 2,110 casualties and the 82nd lost 1,432 men*: John C. Warren, "U.S. Airborne Operations in World War II, European Theater," 146. **26** *"ninety percent success"*: Ibid., 146. **26** *"vigorous command supervision"*: Matthew B. Ridgway, *Soldier*, 111. **29** *Simpson's army, consisting of ten divisions of over 300,000 soldiers and 1,394 tanks*: Charles MacDonald, *The Last Offensive*, 137. **29** *which necessitated a naval admiral to oversee the flotillas of landing craft*: Ibid., 301. **29** *VARSITY, like all other Allied operations*: Bill Hines, *Operation CODE-NAME*, 42. **31** *personal aircraft decorated with the moniker* Debonair Duke: Lewis Brereton, *The Brereton Diaries*, 300. **31** *"marginally competent"*: Bradley, quoted in Carlo D'Este *Eisenhower: A Soldier's Life*, 610. **31** *"resisted any effort to work together"*: Bradley interview quote, no date, CBJ, CMH, Box 57. **31** *Brereton himself took a dim view of his airborne assignment*: Lewis Brereton, *The Brereton Diaries*, 308. **32** *Supporting Gale were the twelve men of the Airborne Army's Plans Section*: FAAA, "History of Headquarters," 11. **32** *Airborne Army's Parisian headquarters in the Hôtel Royal*: Ibid., 360, 395. **33** *He'd endured gas attacks*: "Major-General Richard Nelson Gale MC." **33** *Their poor performance had contributed*: Forrest C. Pogue, *The Supreme Command*, 286. **33** *He planned to use Ridgway's corps for the other pending operations*: Clay Blair, *Ridgway's Paratroopers*, 433. **34** *other planned airdrops to cross the Rhine*: FAAA, "Airborne Army Operational Reports, 44–45," report dated February 1, 1945. The other planned drops across the Rhine were Operations CHOKER II and NAPLES II. **34** *Eisenhower reiterated that Montgomery's plan would stand*: Floyd Lavinius Parks Diary, February 8, 1945. **34** *Both he and Bradley were certain*: Clay Blair, *Ridgway's Paratroopers*, 429. **34** *Bradley wanted to keep Ridgway in the fight*: Ibid., 433. **34** *"one that no professional soldier could turn down"*: Matthew B. Ridgway, *Soldier*, 18. **35** *the four principles behind Montgomery's airborne plan*: FAAA, "Airborne Army Operational Reports, 1944–1945 Varsity to Wildgirl," report dated February 9, 1945. **35** *In addition to the two pilots*: AAF Manual No. 50-17, *Pilot Training Manual for the CG-4A Glider*, 50. **35** *At a later phase the 13th Airborne would drop ninety miles*: FAAA, "Airborne Army Operational Reports, 1944–1945, Varsity to Wildgirl," report dated February 9,

1945. **36** *Ridgway sat ramrod straight in his chair*: Clay Blair, *Ridgway's Paratroopers*, 4. **36** *"Absolutely out of the question"*: Floyd Lavinius Parks Diary, February 9, 1945. **36** *the earliest possible date for the operation would have to be April 1*: FAAA, "Airborne Army Operational Reports, 1944–1945, Varsity to Wildgirl," report dated February 9, 1945. **36** *should expect higher casualties*: Ibid., report dated February 9, 1945. **36** *Ridgway dispatched Gale and a small team of British airborne officers to coordinate*: Ibid., report dated February 9, 1945. **36** *the men agreed, Gale's corps would transition to managing the preparation of 6th Airborne*: Floyd Lavinius Parks Diary, February 9, 1945. **37** *Ridgway discussed the matter with Belchem*: XVIII Corps (ABN), "War Diary," February 9, 1945, CMH, MBR, Box 59. **37** *Ridgway left to complete his transfer and relocate his headquarters to Épernay*: Clay Blair, *Ridgway's Paratroopers*, 436. **37** *would withdraw the 6th Airborne to their bases in England no later than February 15*: Floyd Lavinius Parks Diary, February 9, 1945. **37** *The conditions of the twelve French airfields*: Ibid. **37** *The abandoned Luftwaffe airstrips had been bombed*: John C. Warren, "U.S. Airborne Operations in World War II, European Theater," 158. **38** *They had to erect crew barracks and storage facilities*: FAAA, *Operation Varsity*, 19. Additionally, the task consumed "13,719 tons of pierced steel planking, 7,050 tons of tarmac surfacing materiel, 2,500 tons of rock, 100 tons of stone chip screenings, 18,000 gallons of bitumen seal coat, 5,310 rolls of square mesh track, 51,070 rolls of Hessian mat, 53,300 cubic yards of hardcore, 55,686 bales of straw, [and] 300 barrels of tar."

Chapter 3 Thunder from Heaven

39 *To address the shortfalls*: FAAA, "History of Headquarters," 39. **40** *After graduating in 1918*: Jack Miley, "Remarks at Memorial Service," 7. And biographical information provided by 17ADA. **40** *"Hell, there's nothing to it"*: Harris T. Mitchell, *The Story of the First Airborne Battalion*, 9. **40** *Miley organized a prototyping regimen for each platoon*: Ibid., 29. **40** *Rubber soles prevented slipping*: Christophe Deschodt, *D-Day Paratroopers*, 48. **40** *His principles landed him in the hospital*: "Parachute Infantry Fighting Men Are Proud of Their Commander." **41** *"He was always in superb physical condition"*: William P. Yarborough, "Gen. Yarborough's Speech at Pinehurst Memorial Banquet," 53. **41** *"The percentage of failures, which were colorfully described as"*: Maurice Newnham, *Prelude to Glory*, 254. **41** *Miley, after rejecting several disappointing designs*: Harris T. Mitchell, *The Story of the First Airborne Battalion*, 34. **41** *The Army Uniform Board approved the modification*: Gerard M. Devlin, "When was it that U.S. Army paratroopers started the time honored tradition of wearing jump boots with Class A dress uniforms . . . ," 45. **42** *"The dolls don't exactly put on a chill"*: "Parachutist," War Department training film. **42** *Calling the troops together for a "fight talk"*: William M. Miley, unpublished manuscript, 23. **42** *One of Miley's lieutenants created a ceremonial mug*: History of the Prop Blast, 130. The lieutenant was Second Lieutenant Carl Buechner. **43** *"Thunder from Heaven" was inspired by a biblical quote*: Mel Therrien, "Where Did the Words Thunder from Heaven come from?," 7. **43** *This structure, known as the triangular division*: James M. Gavin, *Airborne Warfare*, 164. **43** *"calling in a very large man and saying"*: Matthew B. Ridgway, *Soldier*, 125. **44** *"The only thing to do was to ignore these limitations"*: Ibid., 106. **44** *The reorganization shifted Miley's triangular formation*: Steven J. Zaloga, *US Airborne Divisions in the ETO 1944–45*, 16. And see also James P. Lyke, "The Operations of the 17th Airborne Division in the Crossing of the Rhine River," 24 March 1945. **44** *After completing jump school*: Frank Dillon, *letter to the author*, April 7, 2012. **45** *to storm the heights of "Dead Man's Ridge"*: Ted Velikoff, "Velikoff Diary," 53. And Bart Hagerman, *17th Airborne Division History*, 8. **45** *Denied the extra hazard pay enjoyed by paratroopers*: Gerard M. Devlin, *Silent Wings*, 126. **45** *"Join the glider troops! No flight pay. No jump pay"*: Ibid., 126. **45** *Oh! Once I was happy, but now I'm Airborne*: Thirteenth Airborne Division, 24. **46** *mailing copies of "The Gliderman's Lament" to congressmen*: "FDR Okeh's Glider Pay Bill July 3rd," 68. **46** *same hazardous duty pay as paratroopers*: Gerard M. Devlin, *Silent Wings*, 126. **46** *cutting their trousers off at the knees*: Bart Hagerman, *Granddaddy Was Airborne!*, 109. **46** *when the men were called to formation on a rainy morning in Châlons*: Eugene Herrmann, letter to the author, December 12, 2015. **47** *regimental strength from 1,678 men to 3,114*: FAAA, "History of Headquarters," 38. **47** *allocation of 81mm mortars soared*: Steven J. Zaloga, *US Airborne Divisions in the ETO 1944–45*, 35, and James P. Lyke, "The Operations of the 17th Airborne Division in the Crossing of the Rhine River, 24 March 1945." **48** *yelling, "Pow! Pow! Pow!"*: Frank Dillon, letter to the author, August 18, 2012, and February 7, 2012. **48** *The safest place during a German mortar or artillery barrage*: Antony Beevor, *Ardennes 1944*, 53. **48** *glider fuselages recovered from the Dutch landing zones*: James P. Lyke, "The Operations of the 17th Airborne Division in the Crossing of the Rhine River, 24 March 1945," 16. **48** *due to serving as scouts in the division's reconnaissance platoon*: 466 PFAB, "History of the 466th Parachute Field Artillery Battalion," 1. **49** *"You're doing a fine job and that's why"*: Letter from John Chester to Charles Duree's daughter, July 28, 2004. **50** *outside Châlons where the Air Force provided aircraft*: For simplicity's sake I have shortened the reference of Army Air Force down to Air Force. **51** *wanted one of Ridgway's divisions to seize the town of Wesel*: Floyd Lavinius Parks Diary, February 15, 1945. **51** *"imaginative and bold in their thinking"*: Matthew B. Ridgway, *Soldier*, 93. **51** *"adequate for a maximum of one division"*: XVIII Corps (ABN), "War Diary," February 14, 1945, CMH, MBR, Box 59. **52** *Dempsey's current plans for VARSITY*: Floyd Lavinius Parks Diary, February 15, 1945. The Dempsey-Ridgway disagreements over VARSITY are based on comments made in Parks' Diary and XVIII Corps (ABN), "War Diary." See especially Parks Diary 2/9/45, 2/10/45, 2/15/45, 2/19/45; XVIII Corps (ABN) "War Diary" 2/14/45, 2/19/45, 2/20/45, 2/23/45. **52** *"useless slaughter"*: George C. Mitchell, *Matthew B. Ridgway*, 21, and Matthew B. Ridgway, *Soldier*, 106. **52** *"the hard decisions are not"*: Matthew B. Ridgway, *Soldier*, 82. **52** *Brereton in particular, considered Dempsey*: Lewis Brereton, *The Brereton Diaries*, 342. **52** *"putting the cart before the horse"*: Floyd Lavinius Parks Diary, February 19, 1945. **52** *"insignificant and but a fraction"*: Ibid. **53** *"The ideal airborne landing is to"* James M. Gavin, *Airborne Warfare*, 81. **53** *the Airborne Army's Ground Information Team*: FAAA, "History of Headquarters," 5. **53** *Poorly chosen landing zones in Burma*: Gerard M. Devlin, *Silent Wings*, 153. **53** *over 700 planes short*: FAAA, "Airborne Army Operational Reports, 1944–1945, Varsity to Wildgirl," report dated February 9, 1945. **54** *noticed fresh paint concealing the unit identification*: Frank Dillon, letter to the author, June 30, 2008.

Chapter 4 Deliberate and Disciplined

55 *"a bitter slugging match"*: Eisenhower quoted in Toby Thacker, *The End of the Third Reich*, 92. **56** *undermanned and poorly equipped divisions*: George MacDonald,

The Last Offensive, 5. **56** *every yard of ground*: Ibid., 7. **56** *by more than 40,000 forced laborers*: Steven J. Zaloga, *Defense of the Rhine 1944–45*, 6. **56** *He was convinced that with enough time*: Charles MacDonald, *The Last Offensive*, 8. **57** *take advantage of the river*: Ibid., 294. **57** *"My generals only look behind them"*: Robert M. Citino, *The Wehrmacht's Last Stand*, 23. **58** *inflicting over 20,000 Allied casualties*: Charles MacDonald, *The Last Offensive*, 183. **58** *from Xanten in the north*: Ibid., 179. **58** *One observer offered "anthropoidal"*: "Special Interrogation Report of General Alfred Schlemm," 1. **58** *Now as commander of the I* Fallschirmjäger-Armee: Ibid., 5. **59** *organizing his four parachute divisions*: Charles MacDonald, *The Last Offensive*, 180. **59** *an anxious preoccupation*: "Special Interrogation Report of General Alfred Schlemm," 12. **59** *"[I was] personally responsible"*: Alfred Schlemm. *First Paratroop Army (20 Nov 44 — 21 Mar 45)*, 11. **59** *violated Hitler's order to hold the fortress*: Franz Kurowski, *Hitler's Last Bastion*, 99. **59** *Without seeking permission*: "Special Interrogation Report of General Alfred Schlemm," 10. **60** *"The disadvantage for the enemy was"*: Alfred Schlemm, *First Paratroop Army*, 18. **60** *could have overrun his defenses*: "Special Interrogation Report of General Alfred Schlemm," 11. **60** *the corpses of 276 comrades*: Franz Kurowski, *Jump into Hell*, 327. **61** *"Not in the course of the entire war"*: Franz Kurowski, *Hitler's Last Bastion*, 93. **62** *his life was saved by Schlemm's intervention*: Franz Kurowski, *Jump into Hell*, 330. **62** *the abandoned equipment was pushed off roads and concealed*: "Special Interrogation Report of General Alfred Schlemm," 13. **62** *each unit commander had to testify by signature*: Ibid., 13. **63** *a determined defense took out thirty-nine*: Charles MacDonald, *The Last Offensive*, 183. **63** *From altitudes of over 16,000 feet*: 514 Squadron, RAF War Diary for March 6, 1945. **64** *"The bullets didn't worry us"*: Ed Cunningham, *The Ludendorf Bridge*, 3. **64** *shuttled every howitzer he had across the Rhine*: "Special Interrogation Report of General Alfred Schlemm," 14. **64** *On the morning of March 9*: Ibid., 14. **65** *the Oberstleutnant concurred*: Ibid., 14. **65** *they wouldn't sell so cheaply*: Ibid., 14. **65** *He delayed the destruction by two hours*: Alfred Schlemm, *First Paratroop Army*, 12. **66** *shot at their own engineers*: Franz Kurowski, *Hitler's Last Bastion*, 102. **66** *"in order to use the better defensive lines"*: Franz Kurowski, *Jump into Hell*, 331. **66** *caught the Allies by surprise*: Charles MacDonald, *The Last Offensive*, 183. **66** *executed according to Montgomery's strategy*: Ibid., 178. **67** *The 3,000 German soldiers left*: Franz Kurowski, *Jump into Hell*, 331. **67** *had escaped with only thirty-five tanks*: Justin L. C. Eldridge, *Defense on the Rhine*. **67** *"From the enemy's POV"*: FAAA, "HQ Operations Reports 1944–1945," report dated March 21, 1945. **67** *managed to save almost all of I* Fallschirmjäger-Armee's *remaining artillery*: Alfred Schlemm, *First Paratroop Army*, 21.

Chapter 5 "Fifty percent of two is one"

68 *returned from a week in the hospital*: Thad Blanchard, letter to the author, February 12, 2007. **68** *he joined the regiment in July 1944*: Ibid., March 12, 2007. **69** *considered Raff a "miserable monster"*: C. B. McCoid, letter to Clay Blair, January 16, 1984, CJB, CMH. **69** *Raff as a loudmouth publicity seeker*: Clay Blair, letter to Matthew Ridgway, August 14, 1984, CJB, CMH. **69** *"The squad and platoon must be perfectly trained"*: Edson D. Raff, *We Jumped to Fight*, 202. **70** *Raff let his authority and rank*: "Good God. Gaston." **70** *"clapped up"*: Thad Blanchard, letter to the author, April 3, 2007. **70** *abstained from drinking, gambling, and smoking*: "Good God. Gaston." **70** *including two of Raff's three battalion commanders*: Clay Blair, *Ridgway's Paratroopers*, 425. **71** *inquiries by the House Appropriations Committee*: Guy Richards, *World War II Troop Type Parachutes*, 56 and 72. **71** *the men's main chutes had failed to open*: 224 AMC, "224th Airborne Medical Co., Accumulated Notes," 4. **71** *"Them bazookas were like swatting"*: Kirk B. Ross, *The Sky Men*, 220. **71** *Its rifled barrel, with twenty-four right-handed lands and grooves*: FM 23-80, 3. **72** *German engineers at Krupp*: John Weeks, *Airborne Equipment*, 79. **72** *Supreme Headquarters had requested 200 M18s*: FAAA, Subject File, 411–45, February 20, 1945. **72** *designating the 17th as the priority recipient*: FAAA, Subject File, 411–45, March 5, 1945. **73** *Two men were Normandy veterans*: 507 PIR, "The Operations of Company H," 8. Both men were transferred to another unit and both were decorated in subsequent actions in the Ruhr pocket. **73** *Instead Dempsey selected Ridgway's third option*: XVIII Corps (ABN), "War Diary," February 18, 1945. **73** *"with practically no heavy weapon support"*: Ibid., February, 18, 1945. **74** *Initial plans called for the amphibious assault*: John C. Warren, "U.S. Airborne Operations in World War II, European Theater," 161. **74** Luftwaffe *night fighters posed a legitimate threat*: Ibid., 161. **75** *Ridgway liked Dempsey's plan*: FAAA, "Airborne Army Operational Reports, 1944–1945, Varsity to Wildgirl," report dated February 9, 1945. **75** *It allowed more time for artillery and fighter-bombers*: John C. Warren, "U.S. Airborne Operations in World War II, European Theater," 161. **75** *Miley too conceded that the advantages*: William B. Breuer, *Storming Hitler's Rhine*, 295. **75** *"disrupt the hostile defense of the Rhine"*: XVIII Corps (ABN), "Operation Varsity, 23 March 1945 to 30 March 1945, 1."* **76** *By Dempsey's calculations*: Floyd Lavinius Parks Diary, February 20, 1945. **76** *"how it is intended to employ this additional division"*: 21AG message to SHAEF, dated February 6, 1945, found in 21AG, "Operation Plunder, Airborne Operations, conference notes." **76** *wired Eisenhower requesting permission to reassign*: Floyd Lavinius Parks Diary, March 6, 1945. **77** *"held at all costs"*: XVIII Corps (ABN), "Operation Varsity, 23 March 1945 to 30 March 1945," 5. **77** *division staffs commenced their detailed planning*: FAAA, "History of Headquarters," 80. **77** *enough aircraft to drop about 17,000 troops in a single lift*: Clay Blair, *Ridgway's Paratroopers*, 440. **77** *the Air Force told Miley they could give him 400 parachute aircraft and 588 glider tugs*: John C. Warren, "U.S. Airborne Operations in World War II, European Theater," 158. **77** *held together by over 500,000 rivets*: http://www.dc3history.org/ didyouknow.html, accessed on May 6, 2017. **78** *agreed that the C-46 units would be made available*: John C. Warren, "U.S. Airborne Operations in World War II, European Theater," 169. The 313th Troop Carrier Group flew the C-46s. **78** *providing a total of 610 tugs*: Ibid., 158. **78** *pulling two gliders stretched the fuselage by several inches*: Paul C. Fritz, "From the Glider Tower's Point of View," 30. **78** *designed to expand by 40 percent before snapping*: George A. Larson, "Alliance Army Air Force Base and the Training of Airborne Crews," 21. **79** *the Troop Carrier Commander . . . rebuffed the idea*: Floyd Lavinius Parks Diary, February 16, 1945. **79** *Ridgway favored double tow . . . Brereton was confident*: Ibid., February 16, 1945. **79** *"utilize double tow to the fullest possible extent"*: Ibid., March 1, 1945. **79** *The 610 C-47s would now be pulling 906 gliders*: John C. Warren, "U.S. Airborne Operations in World War II, European Theater," 158. **79** *Stirling and Halifax bombers to install the correct towing equipment*: Ibid., 158. **79** *The shortage reduced his lift capacity by 576 men*: Ibid., 158. **79** *two divisions would be simultaneously*: Ibid., 157. **79** *"Intelligence reports that it has captured a document"*: Lewis Brereton, *The Brereton Diaries*, 367. **80** *"stop this violation of security"*: Floyd Lavinius Parks Diary, March 15, 1945. **80** *"enclosed in a* *folder which gave no indication*": Ibid., March 10, 1945. **80** *At least thirty-two copies of the report*: HQ FAAA memo to HQ 21 Army Group dated March 8, 1945, found in 21AG, "G (Plans), Operation Varsity (Nov 44–May 45)." **80** *assembled a formidable band led by Private Bill Keller*: Verne Galbraith, *A Little Music*, 30. **81** *tentmates pooled various ingredients from belated Christmas packages*: Richard H. Haney, *When Is Daddy Coming Home?*, 77. **81** *"nicest looking medal the Army has"*: Ibid., 75. **81** *was convinced they were off the hook*: Ibid., 77. **81** *dropping into the "Limey's sector"*: Ted Velikoff, "Velikoff Diary," 53. **81** *troops would be jumping in front of Patton's advancing legions*: John Chester, letter to the author, June 6, 2008. **82** *"We are preparing for something big. . . . I can see it in the air"*: Frank Macchiaverna Diary. **82** *Miley's three regimental commanders arrived*: James P. Lyke, "The Operations of the 17th Airborne Division in the Crossing of the Rhine River, 24 March 1945," 26. **82** *briefings were conducted down to the level of company commanders*: Ibid., 26. **83** *visiting senior Air Force pilots were noticed*: David P. Schorr, "Operation Varsity," 13. **83** *"Never yet has [there] been an airborne operation in which"*: James M. Gavin, *Airborne Warfare*, 90. **83** *"each marched half way around the tent"*: Paul Reed, "Operation Varsity—As I Remember It," 30. Reed never learned if the other trooper survived the war. **83** *That same morning Eric Bols, the British general in command*: Napier Crookenden, *Airborne at War*, 90. **84** *his red beret confiscated and the airborne patches roughly cut off his uniform*: Ibid., 92. **84** *"clerks, orderlies and staff officers"*: Ibid., 92. **84** *"unruffled professionalism"*: C. B. McCoid, letter to Clay Blair, January 16, 1984, CJB, CMH. **84** *"The 507th are flying in west to east and jumping here"*: Napier Crookenden, *Airborne at War*, 92, and William B. Breuer, *Storming Hitler's Rhine*, 209. **85** *He'd known Raff since early 1942*: Clay Blair, *Ridgway's Paratroopers*, 66. **85** *Miley shook the hand of each man and presented him a bottle of liberated* Luftwaffe *brandy*: Napier Crookenden, *Airborne at War*, 94.

Chapter 6 Every Hour a Gift

86 The description of Schloss Ziegenberg and *Adlerhorst* have been pieced together from multiple sources, including http://www.militaryhistoryonline.com/wwii/articles/ adlerhorst.aspx/, accessed on August 20, 2017; http://markfelton.co.uk/publishedbooks/ adlerhorst-hitlers-forgotten-headquarters/, accessed on July 2, 2017; https://en.wikipe dia.org/wiki/Adlerhorst, accessed on May 16, 2017; and Winston G. Ramsey (ed.), "FHQu 'Alderhorst.' " **86** *Hitler now placed his confidence in Kesselring*: Franz Kurowski, *Hitler's Last Bastion*, 85. **86** *"I am the new V3!"*: Richard J. Giziowski, *The Enigma of General Blaskowitz*, 385. **87** *far grimmer than the Führer had led him to believe*: Brian Jewell, *Over the Rhine*, 12. **87** *Hitler believed the more immediate threat lay to the east*: Clay Blair, *Ridgway's Paratroopers*, 444. **87** *down to 7,000 men each*: Brian Jewell, *Over the Rhine*, 12. **88** *four American divisions had managed to push across*: Brian Jewell, *Over the Rhine*, 7. **88** *produced 65 percent of its crude steel and 56 percent of its coal*: Charles MacDonald, *The Last Offensive*, 294. **88** *After the Soviets seized Silesia*: Ibid., 294. **88** *manufacturing output that peaked in late 1944*: Pierre Clostermann, *The Big Show*, 149. **88** *25 new U-Boats. Almost 1,600 tanks and self-propelled guns*: Charles MacDonald, *The Last Offensive*, 7. **89** *Schlemm focused on reinforcing his defensive positions*: Rolf Geyer, *Army Group H*, 2. **89** *almost all of his artillery batteries intact*: Alfred Schlemm, *First Paratroop Army*, 14. **89** *his casualties* *were lighter*: FAAA, "HQ Operations Reports 1944–1945," March 21, 1945, and IX TCC, "Field Order No. 5 for Operation Varsity," Amendment No. 2, dated March 22, 1945. **89** *ordered the construction of defensive positions along the east bank of the Rhine*: Richard J. Giziowski, *The Enigma of General Blaskowitz*, 384. **91** 7-Fallschirmjäger-Division . . . *severe losses*: XVIII Corps (ABN), "Periodic Reports," Annex No. 1a to G-2 Periodic Report No. 1. **91** I *Fallschirmjäger-Armee's Order of Battle is based on a com-bination of details from* "Revised Outline Plan for Operation Varsity," March 17, 1945, found in FAAA, "HQ Operations Reports 1944–1945"; Kurt Mehner, *Die Geheimen Tagesberichte Der Deutschen Wehrmachtführung imZweiten Weltkrieg 1939–1945*; and an Allied report dated March 19, 1945, found in FAAA, "Airborne Army Operational Reports, 1944–1945, Varsity to Wildgirl." **91** *with barely 3,000 soldiers each*: Minutes for March 19, 1945, planning conference, found in FAAA, "Airborne Army Operational Reports, 1944–1945, Varsity to Wildgirl." **91** *three parachute infantry divisions on his right flank totaled just 11,000 men*: Justin L. C. Eldridge, *Defense on the Rhine*. **91** *eight new full-strength divisions had been drafted*: Charles MacDonald, *The Last Offensive*, 8. **91** *Among the replacements were thousands of* Kriegsmarine *and* Luftwaffe *person-nel*: Steven J. Zaloga, *Defense of the Rhine 1944–45*, 13. **91** *replacements received only rudimentary infantry training*: Steven J. Zaloga, *Defense of the Rhine 1944–45*, 13, and "Special Interrogation Report of General Alfred Schlemm," 15. **91** *Schlemm inte-grated them into his existing divisions*: "Special Interrogation Report of General Alfred Schlemm," 15. **91** *SS troops were setting up blocking positions*: XVIII Corp (ABN), "Order of Battle Summary for Wesel Bridgehead," 1. **92** *Allied air attacks . . . increas-ing in both intensity and tempo*: Alfred Schlemm, *First Paratroop Army*, 17. **92** *destroy-ing over 100 locomotives and 3,000 railcars*: FAAA, "Operation Varsity," 13. **92** *Over a hundred of the devastatingly lethal 88mm guns*: NARA, "Field Order No. 1, 194 Glider Infantry," enclosure no. 3C. **92** *years of experience combating enemy aircraft in the Ruhr Valley*: Kurt Gabel, *Making of a Paratrooper*, 263. **92** *at the rate of over 3,000 men a week*: Numbers based on intelligence estimates found in FAAA, "HQ Operations Reports 1944–1945," March 21, 1945. The FAAA's intelligence officers estimated the rate of replacements for Schlemm's I *Fallschirmjäger-Armee* at an additional 3,100 troops the week of March 10, 3,600 the week of March 15, 3,600 the week of March 25, and 3,400 the week of March 30. The two reserve units, 116 *Panzer-Division* and 15 *Panzer-Grenadier-Division*, were estimated to receive another 1,000 a week (500 each). **92** *received training units, either in their entirety or cannibalized*: IX TCC, "Field Order No. 5 for Operation Varsity," Annex 1, 9. **93** *dikes that were thirteen feet high and sixty feet wide*: Justin L. C. Eldridge, *Defense on the Rhine*. **93** *fighting posi-tions every twenty to thirty yards*: XVIII Corps (ABN), "Periodic Reports," annex no. 1a to G-2 Report. **93** *some homes concealed as many as four or five machine gun emplace-ments*: Ibid. **93** *many families evacuated, departing in military convoys or*: Johann J. Nitrowski, *Die Luftlandung*, 282. **93** *The* Wehrmacht *had posted hand-painted signs*: Ibid., 274. **94** *"It was extremely dangerous to be in the open fields during the day"*: Ibid., 254. **94** *"faint of heart"*: Ibid., 283. **94** *The Tinnefeld farm had half of their dairy cows confiscated*: Ibid., 279. **94** *was said to have issued execution orders*: "Adolf Doesn't Like Nazis Robbing Nazis," *Stars and Stripes*, 8. **94** *several returned having identified likely crossing points*: Rudolf Langhaeuser, *6 Paratroop Division*, 3. **95** *"Reports from our sys-tematic reconnaissance and careful observation"*: Ibid., 3. **95** *"The results from recon and observation led to the conclusion"*: Ibid., 3. **95** *Schlemm's attention to a thirty-mile stretch*: Charles MacDonald, *The Last Offensive*, 301. **95** *Spies had also parachuted* *into France via captured American bombers*: OSS, "Cover Report 1-15 FEB 45," 4. **95** *some agents resorted to carrier pigeons*: OSS, "Covering Report for OSS/ETO 16–31 March 45." The document noted, "The interception of German agents in France continues and it is obvious to Allied counter-intelligence officers that the enemy still has a thriving intelligence operation at work in France." **95** *refugees were given safe passage into France in exchange for reporting*: Ibid. **95** *agents were aided and sheltered by former members of the* Parti Populaire Français: OSS, "Cover Report 1–15 FEB 45." **95** A *copy of the document made its way to Schlemm*: Justin L. C. Eldridge, *Defense on the Rhine*. **95** *the jets' equally high-speed cameras photographed Allied airfields*: Ibid. See also, IX TCC, "Field Order No. 5 for Operation Varsity": "This aircraft gives the GAF the capabilities of Photo Reconnaissance of our departure airfields as well as a daily effort over the DZ—LZ areas." **96** *The collection of reports, photographs, and sightings provided*: Charles MacDonald, *The Last Offensive*, 301. **96** *the enemy's most likely courses of action*: Rolf Geyer, *Army Group H*, 3. **96** *Kesselring and Blaskowitz both considered the second scenario the more probable*: Rolf Geyer, *Army Group H*, 3. **96** *"Nevertheless,"* wrote Geyer, *"in absence of clear indications to the contrary"*: Rolf Geyer, *Army Group H*, 4. **97** *But only after Blaskowitz had identified the British main point of attack*: Justin L. C. Eldridge, *Defense on the Rhine*. **97** *The sledgehammer consisted of two veteran divisions*: XVIII Corps (ABN), "Periodic Reports," G-2 Periodic Report dated March 24, 1945. The two divisions were the 116 *Panzer* and 15 *Panzer-Grenadier*. **97** *The two divisions contained over 4,000 men each*: FAAA, "Operations Reports 1944–1945," March 21 1945. **97** *During a conference at I* Fallschirmjäger-Armee's *headquarters on Wednesday, March 14*: Charles MacDonald, *The Last Offensive*, 302. **97** *Kesselring was doing what he could to get more men*: Rolf Geyer, *Army Group H*, 9. **98** *"like a concert pianist who is asked to play a Beethoven sonata"*: Charles Whiting, *Bounce the Rhine*, 90. **98** *Motivated by a complicated combination of loyalty*: See Robert Citino's excellent *The Wehrmacht's Last Stand* for insight into the *Wehrmacht* psyche. **98** *to launch coordinated battalion-sized infantry and armor attacks*: Based on intelligence estimates in NARA, "Field Order No. 1, 194 Glider Infantry," enclosure no. 3C. **98** *Schlemm believed the main attack would occur near Wesel*: Justin L. C. Eldridge, *Defense on the Rhine*. **98** *led him to believe the Allies would drop close to the Rhine*: "Special Interrogation Report of General Alfred Schlemm," 15, and Justin L. C. Eldridge, *Defense on the Rhine*. **98** *Blaskowitz suspected they'd land farther north*: Charles MacDonald, *The Last Offensive*, 301. **99** *his staff had been surrounded and taken out of the fight*: Rolf Geyer, *Army Group H*, 9. **99** *used every available asset*: Brian Jewell, *Over the Rhine*, 15. **99** *by March 10, Schlemm's I* Fallschirmjäger-Armee *had already received 18,500 troops*: FAAA, "HQ Operations Reports," March 17, 1945. **99** *"[Allied] preparations of forces on the mainland for an airborne landing"*: "ULTRA Interceptions," March 18, 1945.

Chapter 7 *Sequitis Bastatii*

100 *The reduction of passes was a ploy*: James P. Lyke, "The Operations of the 17th Airborne Division in the Crossing of the Rhine River, 24 March 1945," 62. **100** *officers combed the wards seeking discharges*: Harold Bell, *Meet a Fellow Trooper*, 44. **101** *"became more afraid of the unfavorable opinion"*: William M. Miley, unpublished manuscript, 4. **101** *sentenced the guilty to a week's confinement in camp*: George

L. Streukens, "Personal Manuscript, 194 GIR," 6. **102** *would lack the smoothness of deliberate planning"*: Floyd Lavinius Parks Diary, February 27, 1945, and March 2, 1945. **102** *Sixty thousand tons of artillery shells*: Brian Jewell, *Over the Rhine*, 15. **102** *over 500 tons of provisions per day, per division*: Charles MacDonald, *The Last Offensive*, 295. **102** *advance D-Day by one week*: FAAA. "Airborne Army Operational Reports, 1944–1945, Varsity to Wildgirl," March 5, 1945. **102** *Miley informed his regimental commanders*: David P. Schorr, "Operation Varsity," 14. **102** *the 105mm and 75mm howitzers, were towed away*: Melvin Manley, "A Short History of Battery B of the 680th Glider Field Artillery Battalion," 17. **102** *officers conducted another series of weapon inspections*: 507 PIR, "The Operations of Company H," 9. **103** *"a bunch of very jealous and curious troopers"*: John Chester, letter to the author, July 16, 2009. **103** *"Am in really beautiful ozone training now easy"*: Richard H. Haney, *When Is Daddy Coming Home?*, 119. **104** *pack all of their nonessential articles*: Frank Dillon, letter to the author, March 24, 2008. **104** *keep their mess tins*: 507 PIR, "Field Order No. 1, Inclosure No. 3A." **104** *another thirty-two replacements arrived*: NARA, Morning Reports, March 19, 1945. **104** *remove their golden talon shoulder patches and all other airborne insignia*: NARA, "Field Order No. 1, 194 Glider Infantry," Enclosure No. 3C. **104** *boarded the familiar forty-and-eight boxcars*: Frank Dillon, letter to the author, March 24, 2008. **104** *platoon sergeant, Mardell Kreuzer, asked for a volunteer*: Eugene Herrmann, letter to the author, August 28, 2017. **105** *staging out of twelve camps constructed at the departing airfields*: James P. Lyke, "The Operations of the 17th Airborne Division in the Crossing of the Rhine River, 24 March 1945," 27. **105** *a standard-issue cot and three wool blankets awaiting him*: 507 PIR, "Field Order No. 1, Inclosure No. 3A." **106** *recently emplaced anti-aircraft guns*: Bart Hagerman, *War Stories*, 201. **106** *On display throughout the compounds and inside briefing tents*: DZ Europe, 97. **106** *Communication between the camps would be strictly limited*: James P. Lyke, "The Operations of the 17th Airborne Division in the Crossing of the Rhine River, 24 March 1945," 28. **106** *A segregation system had been established*: FAAA, "Airborne Army Operational Reports, 1944–1945, Varsity to Wildgirl," March 11, 1945. **106** *Separate dining facilities and latrines*: 507 PIR, "The Operations of Company H," 10. **106** *briefed personnel had the code word "UNDERDONE"*: FAAA. "Airborne Army Operational Reports, 1944–1945, Varsity to Wildgirl," undated security procedures memo, 5. **106** *all outgoing mail would be bagged and sent to the censors*: FAAA, "Operation Varsity," 29. **106** *Sporting equipment was made available*: James P. Lyke, "The Operations of the 17th Airborne Division in the Crossing of the Rhine River, 24 March 1945," 28. **106** *Red Cross volunteers were on hand*: The Talon Crosses the Rhine, 1. **106** *Issues of* Stars and Stripes, *the armed forces newspaper*: 17ABN, "Historical Report of Operation Varsity," 31. **106** *Men flipping through the pages read about*: Examples of articles collected from issues of Stars and Stripes dated March 20–March 23, 1945. **107** *Miley's two parachute regiments would be used to attack*: Gerard M. Devlin, *Paratrooper!*, 613. **107** *Hazy intelligence suggested one potential problem*: 194 GIR, "Division Operation Order." **108** *"The reserve activity in this area against airborne operations cannot really be evaluated"*: IX TCC, "Field Order No. 5 for Operation Varsity," Amendment No. 2, dated March 22, 1945. **109** *delaying the drop until after commencing the river assault*: Ibid. **109** *It would be a concentrated drop with the two airborne divisions*: John C. Warren, "U.S. Airborne Operations in World War II, European Theater," 162. **109** *Counterintelligence agents roamed the camp*: 52 TCW, HQ, Operation Varsity. After Action Report, 8. **110** *Here the mess tents had wood flooring* *and electric lighting*: 507 PIR, "The Operations of Company H," 10. **110** *smuggling in bottles of champagne*: Ibid., 10. **110** *Outdoor speakers blared songs . . . The occasional news broadcast*: 17ABN, "Historical Report of Operation Varsity," 31. **110** *"Days before the operation we went to the marshaling area"*: Bart Hagerman, *War Stories*, 269. **110** *"liquidate the enemy" occupying the Diersfordt Forest*: 507 PIR, officer interviews, 4. **111** *He decided they needed to storm Diersfordt Castle*: Ibid., 4, and 507 PIR, "The Operations of Company H," 10. **111** *roads each had twenty-five- to thirty-foot telephone*: IX TCC, "Field Order No. 5 for Operation Varsity, Annex 1," 5. **111** *enemy trenches dug along the road*: Ibid. **111** *road could facilitate the rapid movement of German troops and tanks*: 507 PIR, "The Operations of Company H," 12. **111** *the 464th Parachute Field Artillery Battalion or "Branigan's Bastards"*: 17ABN Biographies, "George Hawley." **111** *"coolly distant, and never really made us feel accepted"*: Edward S. Branigan, "The 464th PFAB in 'Operation Varsity,'" 1. **112** *as a private in 1933*: Ibid. Branigan first served in the 258th FA Regiment, "the Washington Greys." **112** *the paratroopers of the 513th Parachute Infantry Regiment took seventeen hours*: 513 PIR, "After Action Report, 24 to 31 March." **112** *the station's signs had been covered up . . . they were in the sleepy village of Bapaume*: Rex H. Shama, *Pulse and Repulse*, 325. **112** *the regiment's two marshaling camps were located next to each other*: James P. Lyke, "The Operations of the 17th Airborne Division in the Crossing of the Rhine River, 24 March 1945," 27. **112** *"We were called the 'Thirteeners'"*: Ben Scherer, *Soldiers and Brothers Under the Canopy*, 88. **113** *"Matching the thirteen in 513"*: Ibid., 148. **113** *"Little Joi's"* history can be found in 513 PIR, "History of the Regimental Insignia." **113** *"I ranked 20th in my class . . . 20th from the bottom"*: Untitled article featuring an interview with James Coutts, CMH, J. W. Coutts Papers, and letter to Bill Breuer from Colonel J. W. Coutts, dated February 16, 1984, CMH, WBB. **113** *second in his class for horsemanship and excelled at boxing*: Untitled article featuring an interview with James Coutts, CMH, J. W. Coutts Papers. **113** *"Issue the tissue, you're wasting the tax payers' money!"*: Ed Tommasino, *Thanks from a Grateful Nephew*, 10. **113** *"Why ain't you in the Army?"*: "Curtis Gadd," 17ABN Biographies. **114** *private, private first class, technical sergeant* 5: Curtis A. Gadd, letter to the author, February 10, 2006. **114** *attaching the new rank to his fatigues with laundry pins*: Ibid. **114** *his commanding officer "volunteered" Gadd*: "Curtis Gadd," 17ABN Biographies. **114** *In the briefing tent Tommasino*: Dean M. Bressler, "Airborne '44: Allied Forces Breach the Rhine," 23. **114** Description of DZ X is based on IX TCC, "Field Order No. 5 for Operation Varsity, Annex 1," 6. **114** *Gadd's Dog Company and the rest of the 2nd Battalion would seize the high ground*: 513 PIR, "Field Order No. 16, Inclosure No. 3B," and James P. Lyke, "The Operations of the 17th Airborne Division in the Crossing of the Rhine River, 24 March 1945," 24. **114** *each battalion commander to bring mattress covers and safety pins*: 513th PIR, "Field Order No. 16, Inclosure No. 3B." **114** *"had absolutely no apprehension about the jump"*: Curtis A. Gadd, letter to the author, February 10, 2006. **115** *"I am not afraid of anything, and I do not worry about myself"*: Bart Hagerman (ed.), *Seventeenth Airborne Division*, 37. **116** *"There were only about 1,500 of us"*: Ben Scherer, *Soldiers and Brothers Under the Canopy*, 43. **116** *Daily reconnaissance flights provided a mountain of material*: John C. Warren, "U.S. Airborne Operations in World War II, European Theater," 167. **116** *"Sequitis bastatii". . . "It doesn't mean to follow your leader"*: Kurt Gabel, *Making of a Paratrooper*, 107. **116** *they shared the latest scuttlebutt*: John Magill, *We Led from the Sky*, 68. **116** *Some thought Hitler might finally resort to poison gas*: William B. Breuer, *Storming Hitler's Rhine*,

211. **117** *"the possibility that the Germans will employ gas as an extreme measure"*: Floyd Lavinius Parks Diary, March 13, 1945. **117** *"We had direct orders"*: Kirk B. Ross, *The Sky Men*, 282. **117** *"A prisoner is a liability"*: Ibid., 143. **117** *"The Baggy Pocket Butchers"*: Ibid., 143, 248. Kirk covers the debate of taking prisoners very well in several sections of his book. **117** *Their battalion would take off in a serial of forty-five C-47s*: 466 PFAB, "466th PFA Battalion Supporting Data," 1. Serial A-7 consisted of forty-five C-47s, forty-two of which carried the 466 PFAB and three that carried members of the 17th Airborne Division's artillery HQ unit. **118** *Since June 1944, five airborne chaplains had been killed in action*: Lewis Brereton, *The Brereton Diaries*, 399. Led by Captain John F. Taus (the acting division chaplain), eight chaplains and their assistants, were assigned across the combat teams, with five jumping in and the rest going in by glider. **118** *"We had practiced for this event"*: John Chester, letter to the author, May 17, 2007. **118** *one of fifty-one being brought in by the division on D-Day*: John C. Warren, "U.S. Airborne Operations in World War II, European Theater,"168. **118** *they'd be jumping with a carbine*: John Chester, letter to the author, September 1, 2007. **118** *"Capa was notorious for his daring"*: Ernie Pyle, *Brave Men*, 399. **119** *he planned to jump into Germany*: Kirk B. Ross, *The Sky Men*, 286. **119** *Born as Endre Friedmann to Jewish parents in Budapest*: Capa biography and his learning of VARSITY from Elmer Lower is based on Capa's autobiography, *Slightly Out of Focus*. **119** *"none of them well"*: Ernie Pyle, *Brave Men*, 408. **119** *one of his staff officers develop a comprehensive public relations plan*: Floyd Lavinius Parks Diary, March 13, 1945. **119** *All told, there were close to thirty correspondents assigned to cover the operation*: FAAA, *Operation Varsity*, 44, and IX TCC, "Activities Final Phase," 83. **119** *"we had a short time left for the usual preinvasion cleaning of rifles and consciences"*: Robert Capa, *Slightly Out of Focus*, 213. **120** *After a few hours of sleep*: Frank Dillon, letter to the author, March 24, 2008. **120** *They'd arrived at Melun's train station at 02:00*: Ibid. **120** Description and details of Melun: https://en.wikipedia.org/wiki/Melun, accessed on September 23, 2017. **120** *"We saw the situation from the standpoint of armies on large maps"*: Frank Dillon, letter to the author, August 18, 2017, and March 24, 2008. **120** *"I definitely recall there was a general feeling of enthusiasm"*: Ibid. **120** *After the briefing, he took time to review his orders*: Ibid., June 30, 2008. **121** *thirty-six minutes after Raff's Ruffians jumped, the 194th's gliders would be released*: James P. Lyke, "The Operations of the 17th Airborne Division in the Crossing of the Rhine River, 24 March 1945," 24. **121** *a goose egg–shaped area, covering almost four square miles*: 194 GIR, officer interviews, 3. **121** *There they were to await orders as Miley's divisional reserve*: David P. Schorr, "Operation Varsity," 9. **121** *The last four serials into LZ S would be the artillerymen*: Ibid., 10. **121** *Until those heavier guns arrived, the two parachute regiments*: James P. Lyke, "The Operations of the 17th Airborne Division in the Crossing of the Rhine River, 24 March 1945," 25. **121** *there were some misgivings about the bigger plan*: Joseph W. Moscar, "Parts of My Missions." **122** *Both the river and the canal were approximately thirty-five feet across*: David P. Schorr, "Operation Varsity," 6. **122** *"We saw aerial maps and photos taken by reconnaissance planes"*: Frank Dillon, letter to the author, August 18, 2017, and March 24, 2008. **122** *"The briefing was thorough and included photos so detailed"*: Frank J. O'Rourke, "Eyewitness: A Gliderman Across the Rhine." **122** *"The radio news commentator, Kaltenborn, said on the radio tonight"*: Richard H. Haney, *When Is Daddy Coming Home?*, 119.

Chapter 8 Secret Destinations

123 Details of Steltermann's OSS service are based on letters, orders, and period identification documents kindly provided by the Steltermann family, hereafter referred to as: Steltermann Collection. **124** *"a secret operational mission to a secret destination"*: Steltermann Collection (OSS orders dated January 21, 1945). **125** *Rumor had it that in 1940 he carried his ailing Jewish father over the Pyrenees Mountains*: Joe LaGattuta, interview with the author, January 5, 2004, and Robert Staub, OSS Personnel File. **125** *Steltermann was also provided with a* Wehrmacht *driver's license*: OSS, "Cover Report 1–15 MAR 45," and Steltermann Collection. **125** *On March 11, he and Staub reported to the OSS office in Paris*: OSS, "Covering Report 1–15 April 45." **125** *Private First Class David Doyle, assigned to the team in a support function . . . its surrounding grounds as "palatial"*: David W. Doyle, *True Men and Traitors*, 59. **125** *In addition to Steltermann and Staub, the eight other agents*: OSS, "Covering Report 1–15 April 45." **125** *Specialist X First Class Leo Jungen assigned as a wireless operator*: Ibid. **125** *Captain Stephen Vinciguerra commanded the sixteen-man detachment*: Ibid. **125** He'd *served as an instructor for teams parachuting into occupied France*: OSS, Stephen Vinciguerra, "Field Report from ETO." Vinciguerra was awarded the Bronze Star for his service in Holland. **126** He'd *spent the interim working with Ridgway's corps*: Ibid. **126** *Vinciguerra had divided Algonquin's agents into four teams of two*: OSS, "Covering Report 1–15 April 45." **126** *This allowed for quicker processing of agent reports*: OSS, "Strategic Services Detachments with the Army in the Field." **126** *Outfitted with standard US Army radios*: OSS, "Covering Report 1–15 April 45." **126** *They'd then mingle with the inevitable flow of retreating civilians*: David W. Doyle, *True Men and Traitors*, 59. **127** *Team Student, the two French-speaking Belgians*: OSS, "Covering Report 1–15 April 45." **127** *what the OSS called "tourists" drops*: OSS, "HQ Seventh Army G-2, Strategic Services Section." **127** *The OSS had given up on infiltrating agents overland*: Ibid. **127** *Issued what captured German rations were available*: OSS, "OSS Report for OSS/ETO, Continental Operations 10–31 MAR 45." **128** *conceal their German uniforms under olive-drab American mechanic coveralls*: OSS, "Covering Report 1–15 April 45." **128** *pretending to be frantically escaping the Allied landings*: David W. Doyle, *True Men and Traitors*, 60. **128** *"My present schedule may prevent seeing you before you leave"*: Letter from Ridgway to Miley, dated March 20, 1945, CMH, Miley Papers. **128** *Eisenhower had released the 13th Airborne from VARSITY*: Floyd Lavinius Parks Diary, March 10, 1945. **128** *fog "so thick you could tack pin-up pictures to it"*: Duxford Diary, *1942–1945*, 23. **129** *Ridgway opposed this option vehemently and recommended VARSITY be canceled*: Floyd Lavinius Parks Diary, March 14, 1945. **129** *Brereton overruled him*: Ibid. **129** *"forgets that he is dealing with men's lives"*: Matthew B. Ridgway, *Soldier*, 28. **129** *Ideal weather conditions for the drop*: John C. Warren, "U.S. Airborne Operations in World War II, European Theater," 160. **129** *"is not a pleasant month"*: Ibid., 160. **129** *Montgomery believed VARSITY critical enough*: Ibid., 160. **129** *Montgomery now wanted the two divisions to drop twelve miles farther east*: Ibid., 160. **130** *Brereton would rush an alternate plan, but only if*: Floyd Lavinius Parks Diary, March 20, 1945. **130** *The drop area near Erle was barely large enough to accommodate two divisions*: FAAA, "Airborne Army Operational Reports, 1944–1945," report dated March 14, 1945. **130** *flak batteries was described as "a formidable issue"*: Ibid. **130** *distributed to Miley's intelligence officers . . . who tucked them away*: Kirk B. Ross, *The Sky Men*, 280. **130** *"The pain was excruciating"*: Matthew B. Ridgway, *Soldier*, 26. **130** He *spent*

the next several nights trying to sleep on the board: Ibid., 25. **131** *"a glider pilot in Texas once asked me to fly with him"*: Bob Hope, *I Never Left Home*. **131** *the constant exposure of the gliders' wood and fabric to rain*: George A. Larson, "European Theater of Operations Post War Review of Airborne Operations," 27. **131** *low wing load, which gave them a higher glide ratio*: Air Forces Manual No. 3, Glider Tactics and Technique, 3. **131** *"It's all right to fly a box car, but why fly it sideways?"*: James E. Mrazek, *Fighting Gliders of World War II*, 103. **132** *the cargo area had a heavy-duty, honeycombed plywood floor*: Gerard M. Devlin, *Silent Wings*, 62. **132** *gliders "ended up against fences, stone walls, or trees"*: "Development of the Glider," 43. **132** *pilots called for the installation of escape panels*: 441 TCG, "Interrogation Check Sheets, Glider Pilots of the 441st TCG, 99th TCS." **132** *Operation MARKET GARDEN had required using 90 percent*: John C. Warren, "U.S. Airborne Operations in World War II, European Theater," 73. **132** *Normandy, where 97 percent of the gliders*: Ibid., 98. **132** *In many cases, fabric had been ripped off the fuselage in great chunks*: Milton Dank, *The Glider Gang*, 163. **133** *only 281 of the 2,000 gliders*: Gerard M. Devlin, *Silent Wings*, 281. **133** *"present production of gliders is insufficient"*: FAAA, "Outgoing Messages, 1 FEB — 13 MAR 45." **133** *At this stage the gliders battled for priority*: George A. Larson, "European Theater of Operations Post War Review of Airborne Operations," 27. **133** *took a well-trained team almost 250 man hours to reassemble a single CG-4A*: Martin Wolfe, *Green Light!*, 179. **133** *Brereton ordered troop carrier units to curtail training flights*: Floyd Lavinius Parks Diary, February 9, 1945. **133** *Troop Carrier Command confirmed in mid-March that their inventory*: John C. Warren, "U.S. Airborne Operations in World War II, European Theater," 158. **134** *"only in emergencies will there be but one rated pilot in the glider"*: 51 TCW "Standard Operating Procedure for Gliders." **134** *"Each co-pilot's seat was occupied by an airborne trooper"*: James M. Gavin, *Airborne Warfare*, 38. **134** *The Air Force had enough pilots to put two in each cockpit*: John C. Warren, "U.S. Airborne Operations in World War II, European Theater," 152, and Gerard M. Devlin, *Silent Wings*, 246. **135** *"called us out, and when we were all lined up"*: Zane Winters, "The Last Glider Mission, Part 1," 9. **135** *During MARKET GARDEN, hundreds of disorderly pilots*: David P. Schorr, "Operation Varsity," 25. **135** *"They got into Brussels, most of them, and that was it"*: Donald Pinzel, interview with the author, September 20, 2003. **135** *"liability" . . . "not believe there is anyone in the combat area more eager"*: Gerard M. Devlin, *Silent Wings*, 279. **135** *The pre-mission briefings, deemed as "unsuitable"*: John C. Warren, "U.S. Airborne Operations in World War II, European Theater," 153. **136** *"amorphous mass, almost without organization"*: Ibid., 153. **136** *"all glider pilots should be given intensive combat training"*: Air Forces Manual No. 3, Glider Tactics and Technique, 4. **136** *"short and relatively sketchy"*: John C. Warren, "U.S. Airborne Operations in World War II, European Theater," 73. **136** *caused by constantly transferring glider pilots from squadrons*: Ibid., 196. **136** *"a coherent and continuous training program of their own"*: Ibid., 196. **136** *"We were bitter about the up-rootings"*: W. D. Knickerbocker, *Those Damn Glider Pilots*, 4. **137** *The curriculum included 75 hours of weapons training*: IX TCC, "Ground Training for Glider Pilots." **137** *squadron commanders and key personnel had already been briefed*: John C. Warren, "U.S. Airborne Operations in World War II, European Theater," 171. **137** *an Army ordnance depot outside of Paris to scavenge armor plating*: William B. Breuer, *Storming Hitler's Rhine*, 229. **138** Notes on using P-51 external tanks' nose cones for C-46 para-packs: IX TCC, "Activities Final Phase," 11. **138** *the majority of gliders would be equipped with the chutes*: Ibid., 15. **138** Griswold nose notes: Ibid., 15. **138** Corey Skid notes: John C. Warren, "U.S.

Airborne Operations in World War II, European Theater," 72, and Gerard M. Devlin, *Silent Wings*, 125. **138** *Personal survival equipment continued to flow in daily from supply depots*: IX TCC, "Activities Final Phase," 48. **139** *The division's parachute maintenance personnel*: 507 PIR, "Field Order No. 1, Inclosure No. 3A." **139** *"It was psychologically comforting to feel it"*: John Magill, *We Led from the Sky*, 68. **140** *Magill noticed that the veterans preferred to pack extra ammunition*: Ibid., 68. **141** *officers ordered the troopers to tie the packets to the front of their helmets*: David P. Schorr, "Operation Varsity," 15. **141** *bright yellow silk triangular signal panels*: James P. Lyke, "The Operations of the 17th Airborne Division in the Crossing of the Rhine River, 24 March 1945," 28. **141** *the panels could be worn as a scarf, tied over a helmet, across the back*: W. D. Knickerbocker, *Those Damn Glider Pilots*, 215. **141** *instructed to wear theirs looped over one shoulder*: 194 GIR, "Field Order No. 1, 194 Glider Infantry," Enclosure No. 3C. **141** *he cut the last one down the middle and shared it with his platoon sergeant*: Frank Dillon, letter to the author, March 24, 2008. **141** *"Hither-Thither"*: Greg Forster, "Biggest Wartime Drop," 44. **141** Tongue-twisting passwords are discussed by Sergeant Jake McNiece on page 79 of his autobiography, *The Filthy Thirteen* (Casemate, 2003). **142** *confined conditions of the former German airfields hindered ground crews*: IX TCC, "Activities Final Phase," 24. **142** *Anti-aircraft guns ringed each airfield*: Ibid., 25. **142** *"A few spurts of gunfire were heard"*: Michael N. Ingrisano, *Valor Without Arms*, 118. **142** *On the night of March 21, and again at dawn*: Ibid., 123. **142** *Montgomery grew increasingly nervous*: Pierre Clostermann, *The Big Show*, 155. **143** *nose-mounted oblique cameras*: William Green, *Famous Fighters of the Second World War*, 117. **143** *Allied radar stations couldn't fix its echo accurately*: Pierre Clostermann, *The Big Show*, 181. **143** *Tempest, with a max speed of 435 mph*: William Green, *Famous Fighters of the Second World War*, 105. **143** Details of the "rat code" missions can be found in Pierre Clostermann, *The Big Show*, 181. **144** *"DUST MEANS DEATH"*: Brian Jewell, *Over the Rhine*, 14. **144** *German gunners turned Xanten's church tower*: Ibid., 14. **144** *"dummy supply points, parks of inflated rubber vehicles"*: James P. Lyke, "The Operations of the 17th Airborne Division in the Crossing of the Rhine River, 24 March 1945," 15. **145** *Brereton and his Airborne Army staff "definitely disapproved" of the tactic*: Floyd Lavinus Parks Diary, February 27, 1945. **145** *smoke generators, built by the Standard Oil Company*: "Invisible Oil Afforded Screen," *Stars and Stripes*. **145** *billow continuously from sunrise on March 21*: Brian Jewell, *Over the Rhine*, 15. **145** *they taped routes for mustering infantry*: Ibid., 15. **145** *"a mixed blessing"*: Ibid., 15.

Chapter 9 "Satanic plan of annihilation"

146 *The troops closest to the riverbanks donned gas masks*: "Interrogation Report from Gen Meindl and Major General Fiebig," 1. **146** *Apart from causing discomfort and frustration, the smoke didn't particularly alarm*: Ibid., 2. **147** *"purely a case in which the territory most suitable for AFVs"*: Ibid., 2. **147** *Germany could achieve a stalemate*: James Lucas, *Kommando*, 203. **147** *drafted over 500,000 new recruits for national service*: Toby Thacker, *Joseph Goebbels: Life and Death*, 282, and Peter Longerich, *Goebbels: A Biography*, 643. **147** *"Roosevelt and Churchill Agree to Jewish Murder Plan!"*: Michael R. Beschloss, *The Conquerors*, 144. **147** *"The German people must realize that we are engaged in a life and death struggle"*: Forrest C. Pogue, *The Supreme Com-*

mand, 342. **148** *"satanic plan of annihilation"* and *"aim of these conditions, inspired by the Jews"*: Ibid., 342. **148** *"giant potato patch"*: Michael R. Beschloss, *The Conquerors*, 144. **148** *"The conviction that Germany had nothing to expect from defeat but oppression and exploitation"*: Ibid., 171, and excerpt from "New Journal of Zürich," unknown date from December 1944, found on https://en.wikipedia.org/wiki/Morgen thau_Plan. **148** *"worth thirty divisions to the Germans"*: Michael R. Beschloss, *The Conquerors*, 172. **148** *"The struggle for the very existence of our people forces us to seize any means"*: Robert M. Edsel, *The Monuments Men*, 250. **148** *"all types of bridges, tracks, roundhouses, all technical installations"*: Ibid., 273. **149** *Organized into company-sized units of sixty to seventy-five men* (and following description of *Volkssturm* troops and their armament, etc.): XVIII Corps (ABN), "Periodic Reports," interrogation report of captured *Volkssturm* troops, dated March 27, 1945 (Annex No. 2 to G-2 Periodic Report No. 4). **149** *Goebbels claimed his home district alone*: Toby Thacker, *Joseph Goebbels: Life and Death*, 284. **149** *The cloth bands, worn around the left bicep, bore the words* "Deutscher Volkssturm": IX TCC, "Field Order No. 5 for Operation Varsity, Annex 1," 10. **150** *reported to* Wehrmacht *quartermasters who supplied them, as stocks allowed*: Heinrich von Luettwitz, *XLVII Panzer Corps*, 34. **150** *their equipment and training were inadequate to operate independently*: IX TCC, "Field Order No. 5 for Operation Varsity, Annex 1," 11. **150** *"The* Volkssturm *battalion of the 18th Regiment consisted of five companies"*: Rudolf Langhaeuser, *6 Paratroop Division*, 1. **150** *"useless old dodderers"*. . . *Wesel's district commander ordered a squad of eight* Volkssturm *to guard his personal car*: XVIII Corps (ABN), "Periodic Reports," interrogation report of captured *Volkssturm* troops, dated March 27, 1945 (Annex No. 2 to G-2 Periodic Report No. 4). **151** *he cautioned them to the possibility of airborne troops landing among their positions*: "Alertness Against Airborne Landings," translated enemy document dated March 4, 1945, captured by the 17th Airborne, found in XVIII Corps (ABN), "Periodic Reports." **151** *"According to the English system of security"*: Heinz Fiebig, "The 84th Infantry Division During the Fight from Reichwald to Wesel," 16. **151** *He did, however, ensure that combat engineers constructed both actual and dummy minefields . . . Artillery survey teams also preregistered*: TM-E 30-451, *Handbook on German Military Forces*, 53, and James Gavin, *Airborne Warfare*, 66. **151** *Observation posts, often manned by* Volkssturm *troops, were set up to provide*: TM-E 30-451, *Handbook on German Military Forces*, 53. **151** *alternate signals such as the use of red and white flares or sirens were instituted*: Intelligence Bulletin, Vol. II, No. 3, Section III (November 1943), War Department, Military Intelligence Division, 20, and "Defense Against Airborne Landings," dated February 17, 1945, translated document captured by the 17th Airborne, found in XVIII Corps (ABN), "Periodic Reports." **152** *"The commanding general has ordered our highest degree of alertness"*: "Alertness Against Airborne Landings," translated enemy document, dated March 4, 1945, captured by the 17th Airborne, found in XVIII Corps (ABN), "Periodic Reports." **152** *"The gun position was worked on, ammunition storage was made"*: Peter Lonke, *The Liberators Who Never Returned*, 66. **152** *To supplement the fixed anti-aircraft positions*: Charles MacDonald, *The Last Offensive*, 302. **152** *400 guns of various calibers*: Ibid., 302. **152** *Crews positioned their guns*: Richard J. Giziowski, *The Enigma of General Blaskowitz*, 386. **152** *"I stripped the entire Ruhr District of its defensive weapons"*: Gene Sprenger, *Who Was Who—German General Officers, 1946*, 30. **152** *He was not "particularly impressed" by what he saw . . . "left relatively undisturbed"*: Interrogation Report on Major General Fiebig, 6th Airborne Division, "Report on Operation Varsity," Appendix D. **153** *"with suffi-*

cient vigor or determination": Ibid. **153** *"Through very active fighter bomber activity the enemy tried"*: Heinz Fiebig, *The 84th Infantry Division During the Fight from Reichwald to Wesel*, 17. **153** *"targeting of German anti-aircraft weapons made the use of airborne soldiers obvious"*: Justin L. C. Eldridge, *Defense on the Rhine*. **153** *"Many dogs are the rabbit's death"*: Peter Lonke, *The Liberators Who Never Returned*, 66. **153** *an anti*-airborne Kampfgruppe—*battle group—positioned adjacent to the expected landing areas*: "ULTRA Interceptions," February 26, 1945. *Kampfgruppe Karst* only reached a maximum head count of 4,000. **153** *Each combat team contained its own artillery*: POW interrogation report dated March 26, 1945, found in 194 GIR, "Misc. Varsity Documents." **153** *every man would participate in the maximum effort*: "Defense Against Airborne Landings," dated February 17, 1945, translated document captured by the 17th Airborne, found in XVIII Corps (ABN), "Periodic Reports." **154** *Some platoons were issued bicycles to reduce their reaction time*: POW interrogation report dated March 26, 1945, found in 194 GIR, "Misc. Varsity Documents." **154** *Hitting the parachutists before they could consolidate*: TM-E 30-451, *Handbook on German Military Forces*, 53. **154** *"[Allied] preparations of forces on the mainland"*: "ULTRA Interceptions," March 18, 1945. **154** *Kesselring advised Blaskowitz to place his units in a state of alert*: "ULTRA Interceptions," March 18, 1945. **154** *"I tried to sleep at our gun position"*: Peter Lonke, *The Liberators Who Never Returned*, 66. **154** *"in feverish haste"*: Heinz Fiebig, *The 84th Infantry Division During the Fight from Reichwald to Wesel*, 16. **155** *"Officers and men did not fight out of slavish obedience"*: Alfred Schlemm, *First Paratroop Army*, 20. **155** *Increased Allied reconnaissance flights*: Rolf Geyer, *Army Group H*, 9. **155** *March 16 with an air attack on the VI Flakkorps' command post*: Ibid., 9. **155** *Two days later another raid was directed at Blaskowitz's* Heeresgruppe H *headquarters*: Richard J. Giziowski, *The Enigma of General Blaskowitz*, 386. **155** *Blaskowitz managed to escape without injury, but his dentures did not*: Ibid., 424. **156** The attack on Kesselring is based on http://www.militaryhistoryonline.com/wwii/articles/adlerhorst.aspx and http://markfelton.co.uk/publishedbooks/adlerhorst-hitlers-forgotten-headquarters/, both accessed on August 25, 2017. **156** *resulted in Blaskowitz ordering all of his troops into an even higher state of alert*: Rudolf Langhaeuser, *6 Paratroop Division*, 4. **156** The attack on Schlemm is based on Justin L. C. Eldridge, *Defense on the Rhine*, and "Special Interrogation Report of General Alfred Schlemm." **156** *"Allied airborne landings on a large scale to establish bridgeheads"*: Lewis Brereton, *The Brereton Diaries*, 403. **156** *"the pattern of our air attacks and various other factors"*: Ibid., 403. **156** *"Come on Seventeenth, we're waiting for you."*: Paul Reed, *OPERATION VARSITY—As I Remember It*, 30. Many 17th Airborne Division veterans claim to have heard the Axis Sally broadcast, but the exact verbiage varies. **157** *"But we enjoyed the music"*: Thad Blanchard, letter to the author, February 12, 2007.

Chapter 10 "Two if by sea"

158 *"It looked like a reinforced egg crate and I admit I had my doubts"*: Bart Hagerman, *War Stories*, 281. **159** *load-bearing capacity of over 4,000 pounds*: James E. Mrazek, *Fighting Gliders of World War II*, 111. **159** *the glider pilots were ultimately responsible for conducting the final inspection*: David P. Schorr, "Operation Varsity," 16. **159** For correspondent Hamilton Whitman's account, see Hamilton Whitman, "Airborne Operation: Mission Completed," 3. **160** *glider pilot Bob Casey waited to be told what was* *happening*: Robert Casey, personal diary. **160** *liked to wear his flight hat at a rakish angle*: from Casey photo in *World War II Glider Pilots*, 81. **160** *"God to give those going on the mission the strength, the skill and the courage"*: Milton Dank, *The Glider Gang*, 230. This briefing vignette is based on multiple accounts, but most notably Milton Dank's. **160** *visibility was expected to be over four miles with no low cloud cover*: FAAA, "Outgoing Messages, 13–31 MAR 45," March 23, 1945. **160** *They accounted for the varying airspeeds of C-46s, C-47s*: IX TCC, "Activities Final Phase," 67. **161** *The armada of over 1,500 powered aircraft and 1,300 gliders*: John C. Warren, "U.S. Airborne Operations in World War II, European Theater," 163. For aircraft numbers here and elsewhere, I have relied on John Warren's numbers. **161** *At MARFAK the armada would form three lanes*: Ibid., 162. **162** *radio beacons and visual markers would be set up at key checkpoints*: Ibid., 163. **162** *Pilots were to maintain radio silence during the flight in*: IX TCC, "Field Order No. 5 for Operation Varsity," 6. **162** *"Now this is a small town called 'Wesel,'"*: W. D. Knickerbocker, *Those Damn Glider Pilots*, 282. **162** *The daisy-chain effect of lead serials reducing*: IX TCC, "Activities Final Phase," 44. **162** *it should take two hours and thirty-seven minutes*: John C. Warren, "U.S. Airborne Operations in World War II, European Theater," 163. **162** *"have a definite part of the area assigned to him in which to spot [land] his glider"*: Air Forces Manual No. 3, Glider Tactics and Technique, 17. **162** *"You could give odds that a large number of gliders would head for the obvious fields"*: W. D. Knickerbocker, *Those Damn Glider Pilots*, 165. **163** *intelligence estimated the* Luftwaffe *had nearly 900 available offensive aircraft*: IX TCC, "Field Order No. 5 for Operation Varsity, Annex 1," 7. **163** *downing seven B-17 bombers in just eight minutes*: Donald Miller, *Masters of the Air*, 448. **163** *the Air Force had spent the last three days bombing every enemy airfield*: XVIII Corps (ABN), "Operation Varsity, 23 March 1945 to 30 March 1945." **163** *Air Force planners hoped that between the damaged airfields*: IX TCC, "Field Order No. 5 for Operation Varsity, Annex 1," 8. **163** *Escorting the American column would be over 300 Air Force P-47 Thunderbolt*: John C. Warren, "U.S. Airborne Operations in World War II, European Theater," 172. **163** *"Those orange pins represent flak positions"*: DZ Europe, 97. **163** *They knew that for every AA gun spotted in an aerial photograph*: Milton Dank, *The Glider Gang*, 231. **163** *"antiaircraft fire might inflict losses such as the command had never before encountered" . . . "chief anxiety"*: John C. Warren, "U.S. Airborne Operations in World War II, European Theater," 167. **163** *Germany had committed one-third of its industrial artillery production*: Donald Miller, *Masters of the Air*, 481. **163** *putting the number of 37mm and 20mm AA guns around Wesel anywhere between 300 and 400*: FAAA, "Operation Varsity," 7, and FAAA, "Airborne Army Operational Reports, 1944–1945, Varsity to Wildgirl," report dated March 10, 1945. **164** *In MARKET GARDEN anti-flak attacks nearly decimated two fighter groups*: George A. Larson, "European Theater of Operations Post War Review of Airborne Operations," 32. **164** *Attacks on identified batteries were being held off until the next morning*: John C. Warren, "U.S. Airborne Operations in World War II, European Theater," 167. **164** *Artillery and aircraft would have to cease their attacks*: FAAA, "Operation Varsity," 27. **164** *"Don't forget to wear GI shoes"*: DZ Europe, 97. **164** *He warned the pilots not to expect help from the locals*: Milton Dank, *The Glider Gang*, 226. **164** *they should surrender to uniformed military personnel*: 52 TCW, HQ, "Operation Varsity. After Action Report," 7. **164** *Miley had designated his 3rd Battalion as divisional reserve—the 875 glider pilots*: David P. Schorr, "Operation Varsity," 27. **164** *two of the companies . . . would plug gaps in the perimeter; a third would*: Ibid., 27. **165** *"responsi-*

ble for reporting promptly to their Group assembly area: IX TCC, "Field Order No. 5 for Operation Varsity, Amendment No. 2," 1. **165** *"Well here we go again! May your dog tags never part!"*: DZ Europe, 98. **165** *Aerial photographs, taken that morning, revealed . . . Do they know we're coming?*: Frank Dillon, letter to the author, March 24, 2008. **165** *"Most of the men were on edge and that news didn't help any"*: "Diary of B Co. — 194th Glider Infantry," 46. **165** *Word was passed around that, after chow, movies would be shown*: Frank Dillon, letter to the author, March 24, 2008. **165** *"spent the last few hours before going to bed"*: Ibid., 59. **165** *Clyde Haney, also at A-55, attended a Catholic service to take Communion*: Richard H. Haney, *When Is Daddy Coming Home?*, 79. **165** *"It was mighty solemn. . . . During that Mass they knelt and bowed their heads"*: Martin Wolfe, *Green Light!*, 383. **165** *"exciting and thrilling and yet the undercurrent of danger was there"*: Melvin Manley, A Short History of Battery B of the 680th Glider Field Artillery Battalion," 17. **166** *One of Manley's comrades, Private Rocco, shot himself with his carbine*: 680 GFAB, "Historical Record of the 680th Glider Field Artillery Battalion," 26. **166** *The division's medical unit would be using 53 of the division's*: James P. Lyke, "The Operations of the 17th Airborne Division in the Crossing of the Rhine River, 24 March 1945," 55. **166** *into twenty-five of the gliders . . . There were enough supplies*: Details of the division's medical units/plans: 224 AMC, "224th Airborne Medical Company, Inclosure 24." **166** *The Graves Registration Collecting Point*: James P. Lyke, "The Operations of the 17th Airborne Division in the Crossing of the Rhine River, 24 March 1945," 55. **167** *The SOP required red and yellow be used for ammunition and explosives*: Brian N. Siddall, *507th in Germany*, and Steven J. Zaloga, *US Airborne Divisions in the ETO 1944–45*, 46. **167** *Airborne Army had managed to procure thirty of them*: James P. Lyke, "The Operations of the 17th Airborne Division in the Crossing of the Rhine River, 24 March 1945," 18. **167** *"Respect property rights, vandalism is inexcusable"*: *Pocket Guide to Germany*. **168** *Wouldn't it be a thrill*: Bart Hagerman, *War Stories*, 193. **168** *six bundles had the added complexity of being daisy-chained together*: TM 9-319, *75mm Pack Howitzer M1A1 and Carriage M8*, 46. **168** *"broom handles"*: John Chester, letter to the author, February 17, 2008. **168** There is a job to be done and I am going to do it!: Ibid., November 15, 2007. **169** *"They may have been a lot of things"*: Ibid. **169** *"belle indifférence"*: Roy R. Grinker and John Spiegel, *Men Under Stress*, 104. **169** *"Before their battles"*: Robert Capa, *Slightly Out of Focus*, 215. **169** *spent the evening with their comrades talking and playing cards*: Ben Scherer, *Soldiers and Brothers Under the Canopy*, 148. **170** *"You had to look pretty hard to be sure it was a mock dance"*: Bud Hutton, "Airborne Armies Join Invasion of Nazi Heartland," 1. **170** *"he was going all out"*: Homer K. Kessler, *My Front Line Experience*, 3. **170** *Team Algonquin had split up that morning*: OSS, "Covering Report 1-15 April 45." **171** *Novocain*: Clay Blair, *Ridgway's Paratroopers*, 449. **171** *"sour faced bugger"*: Charles Whiting, *Bounce the Rhine*, 60. **171** *"Without benefit of aerial bombardment"*: Ibid., 85. **171** *"Brad, all the world must know"*: Franz Kurowski, *Hitler's Last Bastion*, 124. **171** *"Had Monty crashed the river on the run"*: Richard H. Haney, *When Is Daddy Coming Home?*, 86. **172** *The Supreme Commander of the Allied forces*: Lewis Brereton, *The Brereton Diaries*, March 23, 1945. **173** *The terror raids have destroyed our cities*: James Lucas, *Kommando*, 213. **173** *"drown the enemy in a sea of blood"*: This quote and additional *Werwolf* information based on James Lucas, *Kommando*, 212. Even though almost all *Werwolf* incidents were later attributed to regular forces, there still existed at the time a concern based on propaganda and rumors. **174** *barrage fired from over 3,400 howitzers*: James P. Lyke, "The Operations of the 17th Airborne

Division in the Crossing of the Rhine River, 24 March 1945," 29. **174** *"breathtakingly fearful but"*: Brian Jewell, *Over the Rhine*, 18. **174** *"Two if by sea"*: Charles Whiting, *Bounce the Rhine*, 97. **174** *Brereton had given formal approval for VARSITY*: John C. Warren, "U.S. Airborne Operations in World War II, European Theater," 173. **174** *Over 200 bombers roared over Wesel*: FAAA, "Operation Varsity," 15, and XVIII Corps (ABN), "Operation Varsity, 23 March 1945 to 30 March 1945." **174** *"It was the single most terrifying spectacle I have ever seen"*: Howard K. Smith quoted in Paul Hollister and Robert Strunsky (eds.), *D-Day Through Victory in Europe*, 142. **175** *"Are you awake?"*: Thad Blanchard, letter to the author, February 12, 2007.

PART II MARCH 24, 1945

Chapter 11 "Good hunting"

179 *"Okay, off and on. Chow in ten minutes. Fallout, column of twos"*: Frank J. O'Rourke, "Eyewitness: A Gliderman Across the Rhine." O'Rourke was at camp A-58 with C Co. **179** *"I couldn't eat much of my eggs"*: Ted Velikoff, "Velikoff Diary," 54. **179** *"The best part of it was we could take all"*: Joseph W. Moscar, "Parts of My Missions." **181** *The pilots received a last-minute briefing at the control tower*: Robert Casey Diary. **181** *"Purple Shaft No. 2, Is this trip necessary?"* etc.: Glider names collected from several sources listed in bibliography. **181** *By the time they'd emerged from the previous night's briefing*: David P. Schorr, "Operation Varsity," 17. **181** *"There was little margin for error"*: Milton Dank, *The Glider Gang*, 232. **182** *The pilots ensured that the nose locks*: Elbert Jella, documents and notebook. **182** *"looked like a typical glider pilot". . . Herman Clausen, to land their crate*: Frank J. O'Rourke, "Eyewitness: A Gliderman Across the Rhine." **182** *"There was no outside sign of fear. It was strange to think of fear"*: Frank Dillon, letters to the author, August 18, 2017, and March 24, 2008. **182** *"piece of cake"*: George Buckley, "Mission Impossible — Operation Varsity," 76. **182** *Zane Winters also readied his glider at A-55*: Zane Winters, "The Last Glider Mission, Parts 1 and 2." **183** *"Having crossed the Rhine"*: Don Campbell, "Glider Yanks Sprawl, Yawn, Then Go Over," 13. **183** *one flight officer passed around a flask of Cognac*: Edmund Wienczak, personal diary. **183** *Each trooper positioned his folded blanket*: Frank Dillon, letter to the author, March 24, 2008. **183** *the pilots had steel plates under their seats*: Ibid., April 19, 2008. **183** *The ground crew had staged the gliders*: John Schumacher, "Two Years in the Life of John J. Schumacher: 1944–1946." **184** *Inspectors ensured towropes were properly S-rolled*: Air Forces Manual No. 3, Glider Tactics and Technique, 6. **184** *double-tow combo every sixty seconds*: Ibid., 12. **184** *the signalman flashed his panel*: 51 TCW. "Standard Operating Procedure for Airborne Operations." **184** *Dillon looked to his right*: Frank Dillon, letter to the author, March 24, 2008. **184** *Lumbering down the runway*: Franklin Dentz, "Operation Varsity Glider Ride to Wesel." **185** *single 350-foot towrope was equivalent to*: William H. Nicholas, "Gliders — Silent Weapons of the Sky," 154. **185** *Knickerbocker contemplated the same number of women*: W. D. Knickerbocker, *Those Damn Glider Pilots*, 212. **185** *Each aircraft had a designated jumpmaster*: FM 31-30, *Tactics and Technique of Air-borne Troops*, 63. **185** *The last point of the inspection verified that the static line*: Ibid., 65. **186** *Raff had made Blanchard and several other squad leaders*: Thad Blanchard, letter to the author, April 3, 2007. **186** *Lieutenant Langland Van Cleef, who'd skipped* *his breakfast*: Frederick Graham, "1,500 Planes Fly in Biggest Airborne Push," 4. **186** *traded insults and cursed their equipment*: Ibid., 4. **186** *"Give the goddamned bastards hell, men!"*: William B. Breuer, *Storming Hitler's Rhine*, 231. **186** *"Forget good sportsmanship on the battlefield"*: Edson D. Raff, *We Jumped to Fight*, 202. **187** *Chalk 1, piloted by Colonel Joel Couch*: John C. Warren, "U.S. Airborne Operations in World War II, European Theater," 177. And for wager see IX TCC, "Activities Final Phase," 77. **187** *Underneath Raff's aircraft, the stick had strapped*: Brian N. Siddall, *507th in Germany*, and Steven J. Zaloga, *US Airborne Divisions in the ETO 1944–45*, 46. **187** *"We had no time for [that] at the moment"*: Harold E. Barkely, letter from Barkely to Breuer, January 13, 1984, CMH, WBB. **187** *By 07:00 the troopers had pulled themselves up*: Ibid., and 507 PIR, "Historical Report on Operation Varsity," 1. **187** *Blanchard was unimpressed with his pilot*: Thad Blanchard, letter to the author, February 12, 2007. **187** *Raff's aircraft rolled down the runway at 07:25*: John C. Warren, "U.S. Airborne Operations in World War II, European Theater," 177. **187** *Bill Consolvo noted that his fellow troopers were quiet*: Bart Hagerman, *War Stories*, 194. **188** *The Bastards were already one man down*: 464 PFAB, "After Action Report," 1, and William L. Pandak, undated letter to Bill Breuer, CMH, WBB. **188** *One of the division's most notorious*: "17th Airborne. The Bulge to The Rhine." **188** *Miley had decided to establish his command post*: James P. Lyke, "The Operations of the 17th Airborne Division in the Crossing of the Rhine River, 24 March 1945," 24. **188** *the division's chain of command was split up*: Ibid., 25. **189** *The remaining twenty-three able-bodied troopers*: 513 PIR, officer interviews, 13, and Kirk B. Ross, *The Sky Men*, 288. **189** *"We're on our way"*: Eric Friedheim, "Rhineland Rendezvous." Friedheim was in the first plane of the second serial. **190** *"No one needs a reserve chute at 500–700 feet"*: Dean M. Bressler, "Airborne '44—Allied Forces Breach the Rhine," 25. **190** *"fucked up door"*: 513 PIR. I Co., "World War II: Battle of the Bulge and Rhine Jump," E3. **190** *"a killer and an instructor of killers"*: Kurt Gabel, *Making of a Paratrooper*, 106. **190** *serial of forty-five C-47s departing from A-80*: 466 PFAB, "466th PFA Battalion Supporting Data," 1. **190** *"wearing a bull's-eye"*: John Chester, letter to the author, June 6, 2008. **191** *"Your Colonel wants us to drop you"*: Bill Smith, *Heroes*, 96. **191** *RAF fighters arrived above enemy airfields at dawn*: FAAA, "HQ Operations Reports," March 21, 1945. **191** *1,430 four-engined bombers*: Supreme Headquarters Allied Expeditionary Force, "A-3 Div. Report of Allied Air Operations in Preparation for Operations Plunder & Varsity." **191** *The Air Force lost eight bombers on the raids*: John C. Warren, "U.S. Airborne Operations in World War II, European Theater," 172. Various sources claim differing numbers of airfields attacked. I have used numbers as found in Ibid. **191** *Another wave of almost 3,500 bombers*: John C. Warren, "U.S. Airborne Operations in World War II, European Theater," 167. **191** *Another sortie of 2,090 bombers dropped 6,600 tons of bombs*: Ibid., 172. **191** *Targets within VARSITY's actual assault zones*: Ibid., 168. **191** *a stream of US B-24 bombers flying from their Italian bases*: SHAEF, "A-3 Div. Report of Allied Air Operations in Preparation for Operations Plunder & Varsity." **191** *The RAF also made diversionary attacks*: Ibid. **192** *Two hours into their flight*: John C. Warren, "U.S. Airborne Operations in World War II, European Theater," 177. **192** *departed from eleven airfields in England at 07:09*: Ibid., 174. **192** *Their route took them over Waterloo*: Brian Jewell, *Over the Rhine*, 30. **192** *one of the massive Hamilcar gliders folded in on itself*: Ibid., 30. **192** *Close to 500 British and American fighters*: John C. Warren, "U.S. Airborne Operations in World War II, European Theater," 172. **192** *the populace gazed skyward*: Charles Whiting, *Bounce* *the Rhine,* 113. **192** *over three hours for the armada to pass:* Milton Dank, *The Glider Gang,* 240. **192** *trailing by approximately 160 feet and offset:* IX TCC, "Activities Final Phase," 141. **193** *"The troop carriers looked sleek and well fed":* Richard C. Hottelet, *Big Jump into Germany,* 13. **193** *Carrying the gliders into LZ S:* John C. Warren, "U.S. Airborne Operations in World War II, European Theater," 163. **193** *single-tow gliders going into LZ N were last:* IX TCC, "Field Order No. 5 for Operation Varsity." **193** *The seven single-tow serials of forty to forty-eight aircraft:* John C. Warren, "U.S. Airborne Operations in World War II, European Theater," 163. **193** *a secure and interference-free method:* Air Forces Manual No. 3, Glider Tactics and Technique, 8. **193** *"To us they were a joke":* W. D. Knickerbocker, *Those Damn Glider Pilots,* 162. **193** *tug's aircrew would stand in the astrodome and flash colored lights:* 51 TCW, "Standard Operating Procedure for Gliders." **194** *"Son of a bitch!":* Seymour H. Tuttle, "Over the Rhine at Wesel, March 24, 1945," CMH, WBB. Tuttle was in B Battery of the 680th GFAB. **194** *"We ought to paint 'V-3' on the side":* Howard Cowan, "Glider Men Get Revenge for Set-Back," 13. **194** *causing him to worry about a midair collision:* Lewis Brereton, *The Brereton Diaries,* 409. **194** *"Hell yes, I'm tired":* Milton Dank, *The Glider Gang,* 242. **195** *only one of Dillon's men barfed:* Frank Dillon, letter to the author, March 24, 2008. **195** *"That glider was one big stinking mess":* Bart Hagerman, *War Stories,* 222. **195** *"This is it!":* Gerald Bonnesen, "Operation Varsity—The Rhine Crossing: The Beginning of the End for Germany," 1. **196** *Liberator could carry 2.5 tons of supplies:* FAAA, "Operation Varsity," Appendix 9, Annex A. **196** *To facilitate even more cargo the ball turret was removed:* John C. Warren, "U.S. Airborne Operations in World War II, European Theater," 188. **196** *all twenty-one bundles could be out in six seconds:* IX TCC, "Activities Final Phase," 56. **196** *shifted from colorful villages and idyllic farms* 507 PIR, "Historical Report on Operation Varsity," 1.

Chapter 12 "Let's go!"

197 *German* Fallschirmjäger *used interlocking fields of machine gun fire:* John C. Warren, "U.S. Airborne Operations in World War II, European Theater," 173. **197** *"It says a lot for the morale":* Lieutenant General Sir Brian Horrocks, the XXX Corps commander, quoted in Brian Jewell, *Over the Rhine,* 19. **197** *Progress was being made, however, in the center sector:* John C. Warren, "U.S. Airborne Operations in World War II, European Theater," 174. **198** *Gathered on a small balcony overlooking the Rhine:* Charles Whiting, *Bounce the Rhine,* 114. See also Eisenhower's *Crusade in Europe* and period film footage. **198** *But the fighter pilots, circling overhead:* 406th Fighter Group, 513th Fighter Squadron. "Downed Aircraft Report for P-47, Louise, 42-28672." **198** *Flying in groups of twelve:* Peter Lonke, *The Liberators Who Never Returned,* 202. **198** *"When you're flying 20 feet off the ground":* Tom Glenn quoted in Linda Shiner "Republic P-47 Thunderbolt." **198** *Pilot Charles Bennett's aircraft:* XXIX TAC, 366th Fighter Group, 390th Fighter Squadron, "Downed aircraft report for P-47, 42-29245." The British RAF also lost at least seventeen aircraft in anti-flak attacks, see John C. Warren "U.S. Airborne Operations in World War II, European Theater," 173. **199** *"They're coming! . . . They're coming!":* Charles Whiting, *Bounce the Rhine,* 114. **199** *"There seemed no end to the lines of planes":* Eric Sevareid quoted in Paul Hollister and Robert Strunsky (eds.), *D-Day Through Victory in Europe,* 145. **199** *Raff's Ruffians had arrived eight minutes early:* John C. Warren, "U.S. Airborne Operations in

World War II, European Theater," 174. The barrage was cut short at 09:30. **199** The jump command sequence is based on author's experience and Kurt Gabel, *Making of a Paratrooper*, 87. Little has changed in the US Army's jump procedures since World War II. **200** not as bad as we expected: 507 PIR, officer interviews, 12, and Frederick Graham, "1,500 Planes Fly in Biggest Airborne Push," 4. **200** *Yellow smoke drifted up from a clearing*: James M. Gavin, *Airborne Warfare*, 134. **200** *Colonel Joel Couch crossed the Rhine at a sharp bend near Xanten*: John C. Warren, "U.S. Airborne Operations in World War II, European Theater," 174. **200** *his main checkpoint: a narrow lake*: Ibid., 177. **201** *smoke screen had been turned off the day before*: Brian Jewell, *Over the Rhine*, 18. It had been turned off at 17:30 on March 23, 1945. **201** *They could smell the smoke*: Frederick Graham, "1,500 Planes Fly in Biggest Airborne Push," 4. **201** *Sergeant Harold Barkley followed Raff out the door*: Letter from Harold E. Barkely to Breuer, January 13, 1984, CMH, WBB. **201** *Blanchard's assistant squad leader yelled . . . "I'll see you on the ground!"*: Thad Blanchard, letters to the author, February 12, 2007, and April 23, 2007. James Simon was Blanchard's assistant squad leader. **202** *"It was obvious we could do no more"*: Peter Lonke, *The Liberators Who Never Returned*, 202. **202** *Realizing he was drifting over the trees*: Thad Blanchard, *A Trooper Remembers*, 57. **202** *"Get me down!"*: Thad Blanchard, letter to the author, February 12, 2007. **203** Sergeant Robert Vannatter's story is based on Lew Good, "Dedication of the 17th Airborne Plaque," 60. **203** *the nearly 500 Ruffians of the first serial*: 507 PIR, officer interviews, 2. And see also John C. Warren, "U.S. Airborne Operations in World War II, European Theater." **203** *The murky haze reduced visibility*: 507 PIR, officer interviews, 13. **203** *Incoming fire, from the same high ground*: Ibid., 3. **205** *known to GIs as "Hitler's buzz saw"*: Robert Bruce, *German Automatic Weapons of World War II*, 69. **205** *They suffered some casualties*: 507 PIR, "Historical Report on Operation Varsity." Unfortunately the report does not list those killed or give specific numbers for this engagement. **205** *could hear a battery of German heavy artillery*: 507 PIR, "Varsity Narrative." **205** *Map study and information from a POW confirmed*: James P. Lyke, "The Operations of the 17th Airborne Division in the Crossing of the Rhine River, 24 March 1945," 33. **205** *under the command of Major Paul Smith*: 507 PIR, officer interviews, 14. **205** *Smith soon came to the same conclusion*: Ibid., 14. **205** *They assaulted forward*: 507 PIR, "Historical Report on Operation Varsity," 3, and 507 PIR, "Varsity Narrative." **206** *Harvey . . . organized several parties to fan out and spike the guns*: 507 PIR, officer interviews, 16. **206** *Among the sixty POWs*: Ibid., 16., and 507 PIR, "Historical Report on Operation Varsity," 3. **207** *Ruffians estimated they'd killed fifty-five*: 507 PIR, "Varsity Narrative." **207** *As the troopers floated down, tracer rounds arched past*: 507 PIR, officer interviews, 25. **207** *Four aircraft were hit by antiaircraft fire*: 52 TCW, HQ, *Operation Varsity, After Action Report*, 5. **207** *The jumpmaster escaped*: 507 PIR, officer interviews, 25. The crash also killed all four of the farm's dairy cows: Johann J. Nitrowski, *Die Luftlandung*, 279. **207** *The woods to the north and west*: John C. Warren, "U.S. Airborne Operations in World War II, European Theater," 178. **207** *They ran past the twisted dead bodies*: 507 PIR, "Varsity Narrative." **207** *Richard Boe found a lone German*: Richard Boe, *Unpublished Memoir*. **208** *The dead crew's range card confirmed suspicions*: 507 PIR, "Varsity Narrative." **208** *The lead pilot gave the jump signal five seconds late*: 507 PIR, officer interviews, 29. **208** *Westcott had jumped with his Thompson at the ready*: 507 PIR, "Historical Report on Operation Varsity," 11. **208** *Private Bob Baldwin was rocked by the sudden explosion*: Dominique François, *The 507th Parachute Infantry Regiment*, 77. **208** *the plight of Technician*

Fourth Grade Charles Rushing: 507 PIR, "Historical Report on Operation Varsity," 10. **209** George Peters' account and eyewitness accounts can be found in "Airborne Infantryman Awarded Medal of Honor Posthumously" and Manuel Gorriaran, Jr., "Honors for George Peters," 55. **210** *One aircraft, with an engine shot out*: 52 TCW, HQ, *Operation Varsity, After Action Report*, 5. **210** *"Meet me over at that bundle!"*: Gerard M. Devlin, *Paratrooper!*, 619. **210** *"We sure as hell"*: William B. Breuer, *Storming Hitler's Rhine*, 240. **210** *security detail establishing a perimeter . . . two of Miley's intelligence officers*: James P. Lyke, "The Operations of the 17th Airborne Division in the Crossing of the Rhine River, 24 March 1945," 49. **211** *Lieutenant George Hawley, was so focused*: George Hawley, "A Trooper With No Strings Attached," 68, and "George Hawley," 17ABN Biographies. **211** *Lieutenant Colonel Branigan landed*: William B. Breuer, *Storming Hitler's Rhine*, 241. **211** *Branigan rounded up five troopers*: Ibid., 242. **211** *One of the troopers rushed up to the second floor*: 464 PFAB, "After Action Report," 7. This was Private Robert Grubb. **211** *Branigan realized that the house*: 464 PFAB, "After Action Report," 2. **211** *the Bastards soon had two more of their heavy .50-caliber machine guns*: William B. Breuer, *Storming Hitler's Rhine*, 241. **211** *provided essential cover for the crews*: 464 PFAB, "After Action Report," 2. **212** *Crews leveled their 75mm howitzers in direct fire*: Ibid., 2. **212** *fought to establish a perimeter on the northeast*: Ibid., 2. **212** Pandak's story is based on William L. Pandak, undated letter to Bill Breuer, CMH, WBB. **212** *The biggest prize, however, was a captured 81mm mortar*: 507 PIR, officer interviews, 17. **212** *the defenders in the castle, who barraged the tree line*: 507 PIR, "Historical Report on Operation Varsity," 3. **213** *Blanchard spotted a group of Germans sprinting to their Mark IV*: Thad Blanchard, letter to the author, February 12, 2007. **213** *the Ruffians' 3rd Battalion departed*: 507 PIR, "The Operations of Company H," 11. **213** *a dug-in tank fired into their right flank*: Ibid., 16. **214** *Able Company to hold their position*: 507 PIR, officer interviews, 17. **216** *Around noon, two companies of the Ruffians' 3rd Battalion*: James P. Lyke, "The Operations of the 17th Airborne Division in the Crossing of the Rhine River, 24 March 1945," 35. **216** *Able Company used their captured 81mm mortar*: 507 PIR, officer interviews, 17. **216** *But the white phosphorus shells fell short*: 507 PIR, "The Operations of Company H," 17. **216** *Ruffian Ivey Hutchinson leapt up*: Ibid., 17. **217** *They opted to run back toward*: Ibid., 17. **217** *the Ruffians along the embankment launched their attack*: 507 PIR, "Varsity Narrative." **217** *at 13:00 every trooper along the perimeter would unleash*: 507 PIR. "The Operations of Company H," 18.

Chapter 13 "The Yanks are coming!"

218 *Their mission was to seize*: James P. Lyke, "The Operations of the 17th Airborne Division in the Crossing of the Rhine River, 24 March 1945," 37. **218** *"We could see planes coming out"*: Rex H. Shama, *Pulse and Repulse*, 340. **218** *their primary checkpoint—a double-track rail line*: John C. Warren, "U.S. Airborne Operations in World War II, European Theater," 178. **218** *fired small arms and light flak up at the C-46s*: Ibid., 180. **218** *In Private Tom Funk's aircraft*: Bart Hagerman, *War Stories*, 188. **219** *The lead pilot chopped his power back*: Rex H. Shama, *Pulse and Repulse*, 340. **219** *The sudden deceleration had a domino effect*: John C. Warren, "U.S. Airborne Operations in World War II, European Theater," 179. **219** *It was close to stalling speed . . . dove into the ground, killing everyone*: Ibid., 180, and Rex H. Shama, *Pulse and*

Repulse, 358. **219** *20mm anti-aircraft guns opened up*: John C. Warren, "U.S. Airborne Operations in World War II, European Theater," 180. **219** *At 10:09 the pilot in the lead aircraft*: 513th PIR, "After Action Report, 24 to 31 March," 7. **219** *Just after Chalk 1's troopers cleared the cargo doors*: 313 TCG, 49 TCS, "Missing Aircrew Report for Aircraft: 44-77472," and Rex H. Shama, *Pulse and Repulse*, 340. **219** *killing Sergeant Tom Harvey*: Kirk B. Ross, *The Sky Men*, 296. Harvey's body was later recovered. **220** *"I'll admit that when we stood up in the plane"*: Lew Good, "Dedication of the 17th Airborne Plaque," 60. **220** *"I was scared shitless"*: Kirk B. Ross, *The Sky Men*, 289. **220** *Mac McKirgan was the last man*: Ben Scherer, *Soldiers and Brothers Under the Canopy*, 44. **220** *"He was just a sheet of flames"*: Patrick K. O'Donnell, *Beyond Valor*, 316. **220** *"I started to think over my whole life"*: Robert Capa, *Slightly Out of Focus*, 216. **220** *Coutts spotted blood*: Letter to Bill Breuer from Colonel J. W. Coutts, dated February 16, 1984, CMH, WBB. **221** *Texan Lendy McDonald, hooked-up and waiting*: Ben Scherer, *Soldiers and Brothers Under the Canopy*, 62, and McDonald interview with the author. **221** *"Jump the other door!"*: Ben Scherer, *Soldiers and Brothers Under the Canopy*, 62. **221** *"Our right wing tank was opened up"*: Rex H. Shama, *Pulse and Repulse*, 342. **221** *Bad luck continued to plague Chalk 13*: 513 PIR, officer interviews, 13, and John C. Warren, "U.S. Airborne Operations in World War II, European Theater," 177. **221** *In Noah Jones' plane*: Ben Scherer, *Soldiers and Brothers Under the Canopy*, 133. By my count thirty-three Thirteeners did not jump, most due to blocked doors or wounds. See also 52 TCW, HQ, *Operation Varsity, After Action Report*, 37. **223** *nine minutes to drop the Thirteeners* 52 TCW, *Operation Varsity*, 32 and 34. **223** *fourteen of the seventy-two C-46s*: John C. Warren, "U.S. Airborne Operations in World War II, European Theater," 180. The C-46 losses were attributed to "the arrangement of the wing tanks which, when they were hit, caused gasoline to travel along the inside of the wing toward the fuselage." As they were not equipped with self-sealing gas tanks, they were particularly vulnerable. **223** *"We lay flat on the earth"*: Robert Capa, *Slightly Out of Focus*, 216. A photograph taken about this time by Capa, while lying on the drop zone, is included in this book's collection of photos. **223** *"Stop those Jewish prayers"*: Ibid., 219. **223** The B-17 account is based on Richard Hottelet, *Big Jump into Germany*, 13, and Paul Hollister and Robert Strunsky (eds.), *D-Day Through Victory in Europe*, 146. Baldwin had wanted to jump too, but his ripcord was accidently pulled. He rushed back to the cockpit and regained control of the B-17 in time to crash land. **224** *"just before the plane disappeared"*: Robert Capa, *Slightly Out of Focus*, 219. **224** *rifles, machine guns, 20mm cannons*: 513 PIR, officer interviews, 2. **224** *"two bullets hit the dirt"*: Rex H. Shama, *Pulse and Repulse*, 342. **224** *"Soldat? Soldat?"*: Johann J. Nitrowski, *Die Luftlandung*, 249. The medics were unable to reattach Hani's finger and it later had to be amputated. **225** *a paratrooper gunned him down*: Ibid., 250. **225** John Magill's account of being on the DZ is based on John Magill, *We Led from the Sky*, 72–74. **226** *The forty-five C-47s of serial A-7*: 466 PFAB, "466th PFA Battalion Supporting Data," 1. **226** *sixteen had been damaged, with just one shot down*: 52 TCW, HQ, *Operation Varsity, After Action Report*, 5. **226** *crashed into a heap fifty yards from his howitzer*: John Chester, letters to the author, May 7, 2007, and September 1, 2007. **226** *"had friends and plenty of ammunition"*: John Chester, letter to the author, February 1, 2007. **227** *"I'd better get on with the fight"*: Ibid. **227** *Captain Charles Duree, had taken a bullet*: 466 PFAB, "466th PFA Battalion Supporting Data," 4, and John Chester, letter to the author, September 1, 2007. "I was told that Duree took bullet in the stomach." **227** *Duree's second in command was* *killed*: 466 PFAB, 466th PFA Battalion Supporting Data," 3. **227** *And inexplicably, one entire planeload was missing*: One aircraft dropped its stick and their howitzer west of the Rhine River, ten minutes prior to reaching the DZ. Accounts vary as to how this happened, with the troopers claiming the crew chief gave them the jump signal too soon. Once on the ground, the troopers collected themselves, commandeered two cargo trucks, and made their way over the Rhine to the 466th's position. Their howitzer was in place and ready to fire by 08:30 on March 25. **227** *Lieutenant Colonel Kenneth Booth, landed just twenty yards from*: 466 PFAB, "466th PFA Battalion Supporting Data," 1. **227** *Two troopers crashed through the roof*: Ibid., 4. The two troopers were First Sergeant John Bennick and Private Dan Morgan, both of B Battery. **227** *"I got hung up in this goddamn tree"*: William B. Breuer, *Storming Hitler's Rhine*, 254. **227** *"8-ball, who spent half his time"*: John Chester, *Collection of Personal Memoirs*, "This 8 Ball Was Also a First Class Hero." **228** *Before Buswell could fire again*: Ibid. **228** *Trooper Anthony Moon*: John Chester, letter to the author, September 1, 2007. **228** *There were at least eight 20mm guns*: Samuel C. Myer, "Varsity's Organic Artillery," 674. **229** *The Germans shifted fire*: Greg Forster, "Biggest Wartime Drop," 43. **229** *Rifle grenades eliminated one 20mm position*: 466 PFAB, "466th PFA Battalion Supporting Data," 4. **229** *A captured gun was pressed into action*: Ibid., 2. Sergeant Joseph Flanagan manned the gun. **229** *one of their own howitzers on the far side of the DZ*: Ibid., 4. Chester's A Battery had two guns assembled by 11:00. **229** *A crew led by Sergeant James Guy*: Ibid., 5. **229** *One of the first to realize he'd been dropped in the wrong place*: King Harris, *Adventures of Ace Miller*, 2. **229** *Miller rushed in from the flank*: Ibid., 6. **230** *He spotted the double-track railroad*: 513 PIR, officer interviews, 14. **230** *reportedly even firing his pistol*: Jim Conboy, "My Part in Operation Varsity," 63. **230** *Those two troopers—along with Miller's two runners*: 513 PIR, officer interviews, 14. **230** *"erratic at best"*: Kirk B. Ross, *The Sky Men*, 237. **230** *"Boots and Helmet" . . . "one tended not to see"*: King Harris, *Adventures of Ace Miller*, 6, and Curtis A. Gadd, letter to the author, April 9, 2007. **230** *took turns saluting*: Kirk B. Ross, *The Sky Men*, 271. **230** *let the colonel lie on top of him*: Ibid., 246. **230** *a 1936 graduate of West Point*: King Harris, *Adventures of Ace Miller*, 7. **231** *"He would do some horribly irrational acts"*: Kirk B. Ross, *The Sky Men*, 247. **231** *ran into multiple enemy strongpoints*: James P. Lyke, "The Operations of the 17th Airborne Division in the Crossing of the Rhine River, 24 March 1945," 38. **231** *"Get that damn machine gun"*: Kirk B. Ross, *The Sky Men*, 309. **231** *"I can't, I can't"*: Dean M. Bressler, "Airborne '44—Allied Forces Breach the Rhine," 25. **232** *"Over here! D Company"*: Ibid., 26. **232** *Ed Tommasino, had been gunned down*: Ibid., 26. **232** *Gadd had crashed to earth under fire*: Curtis A. Gadd, letter to the author, February 10, 2006. **232** *aimed between his feet*: Curt Gadd, *To Set the Record Straight*, 29. **232** *"Look out! Gliders"*: Dean M. Bressler, "Airborne '44—Allied Forces Breach the Rhine," 26. **232** *Trooper Ken Eyers watched another glider crash*: Bart Hagerman, *War Stories*, 230. **232** The British area should be well north: Dean M. Bressler, "Airborne '44—Allied Forces Breach the Rhine," 26. **232** *For Jim Coutts, the Thirteeners' commander*: James M. Gavin, *Airborne Warfare*, 135–137, and letter to Bill Breuer from Colonel J. W. Coutts, dated February 16, 1984, CMH, WBB. **233** *the Thirteeners' concentrated landing*: WSEG, "A Historical Study of Some World War II Airborne Operations," 61. **233** *"Try 250 yards!"*: Letter to Bill Breuer from Colonel J. W. Coutts, dated February 16, 1984, CMH, WBB. **233** *German Mark IV rolled out*: 513 PIR, officer interviews, 15. **234** *The M22's 25mm armor*: John Weeks, *Airborne Equipment*, 151. **234** *When the crew piled out*: 513 PIR, officer interviews, 15. **234** Mac McKirgan's account is based on Ben Scherer, *Soldiers and Brothers Under the Canopy*, 44–45. McKirgan was a member of A Company, 513th PIR. **235** *"And much as I hate to"*: Robert Capa, "This Invasion Was Different, 28. **236** *Jim Conboy, a nineteen-year-old private*: Jim Conboy, "My Part in Operation Varsity," 63. **236** *left him for dead*: Ibid., 63. Conboy woke up in the field later that night. He was held prisoner for several hours before the group of Germans holding him surrendered. He was taken to an aid station and later had his right foot amputated. **236** *the artillerymen on DZ X had seven howitzers*: 466 PFAB, "466th PFA Battalion Supporting Data," 2. **236** *they'd captured ten 76mm gun positions*: John C. Warren, "U.S. Airborne Operations in World War II, European Theater," 181. **237** *the artillery would be firing toward them*: James P. Lyke, "The Operations of the 17th Airborne Division in the Crossing of the Rhine River, 24 March 1945," 40. **237** *John Chester moved confidently*: John Chester, *Collection of Personal Memoirs*, "What About Capital Punishment?" **237** *"I've not got time to fool around"*: John Chester, letter to the author, May 7, 2007. **237** *"No, better not do that"*: John Chester, letter to the author, February 1, 2007. **237** *Chester had spoken to him yesterday*: Ibid., September 1, 2007.

Chapter 14 "Now is when you pray"

238 *pilots strained to keep them steady*: David P. Schorr, "Operation Varsity," 18. **238** *pilots and copilots swapping turns at the controls*: John C. Warren, "U.S. Airborne Operations in World War II, European Theater," 182. **238** *Staff Sergeant Jimmie Taylor screamed over the racket*: James E. Taylor, manuscript from presentation at Kate Duncan Smith Dar School. **238** *The rudimentary instrument panel consisted of*: Pilot's Flight Operating Instructions for Army Model CG-4A Glider, 2. **239** *an obsessive tic of tapping the instruments' glass*: James E. Mrazek, *Fighting Gliders of World War II*, 111. **239** *He was shaken by the sight*: George Buckley, "Mission Impossible— Operation Varsity," 76. **239** *twenty-one gliders were lost on the way . . . "structural weaknesses"*: John C. Warren, "U.S. Airborne Operations in World War II, European Theater," 182. **239** *The accidents reduced the glider riders' strength*: Ibid., 183. **239** *Major Carl Peterson caught a glimpse of the war correspondents' damaged B-17*: 194 GIR, officer interviews, 2. Peterson was the regiment's operations officer (S-3). **239** *"Kansas City Kitty-Mary Lou"*: Milton Dank, *The Glider Gang*, 248. **239** *"I figured the dice were cast"*: John Yanok, History 155th Airborne Anti-Tank, Anti-Aircraft Battalion, 34. **240** *creating two distinct landing patterns*: John C. Warren, "U.S. Airborne Operations in World War II, European Theater," 183. **240** *VARSITY planners had assigned pilots specific sectors*: Ibid., 182. **240** *The gliders in the lead serial were to land in the*: James P. Lyke, "The Operations of the 17th Airborne Division in the Crossing of the Rhine River, 24 March 1945," 43. **240** *Pandemonium struck when the aircraft of the middle serial*: Rex H. Shama, *Pulse and Repulse*, 363. This was serial A-10 of the 436th TC Group; the third serial into LZ S. **240** *The stack-up caused the following serial*: Ibid., 364. **240** *Red lights flashed from the navigator's glass astrodome*: Air Forces Manual No. 3, Glider Tactics and Technique, 16. **240** *"rotten egg stench"*: David E. Mondt, untitled VARSITY article, 20. **240** *whose weapons were designed to engage*: "FLAK," War Department training film, TF I-3389. **241** *The two lead aircraft were shot down*: 52 TCW, HQ, *Operation Varsity, After Action Report*, 7, and John C. Warren, "U.S. Airborne Operations in World War II, European Theater," 183. **241** *Ideally* *they'd approach into the wind*: Air Forces Manual No. 3, Glider Tactics and Technique, 16. **241** *Reducing speed before touching down was critical . . . Arresting chutes helped*: Ibid., 34. **241** *Protocol called for the short tow pilot*: Elbert Jella, documents and notebook, and George A. Larson, "Alliance Army Air Force Base and the Training of Airborne Crews," 20. **241** *In the space of the next hour*: John C. Warren, "U.S. Airborne Operations in World War II, European Theater," 183. **241** *"Going down!"*: Lewis Brereton, *The Brereton Diaries*, 409. **243** *unaware that a fouled towrope had damaged*: Charles O. Gordon, "Burp Gun Corner," 24. The two pilots were Flight Officers Heelas and Hyman of the 78th TCS, 435th TCG. Glider pilots released the towrope first, which would later be jettisoned by the cargo pilots as they were back over friendly lines and passing over the designated rope drop-point. They tried to recycle as many of the nylon ropes as possible. **243** Peter Emmerich's account based on Peter Lonke, *The Liberators Who Never Returned*, 67. The 883rd Light Flak Battalion was part of the 64th Flak Regiment under the 4th Flak Division. Source: usacac.army.mil/CAC2/CGSC/CARL/nafziger/939GXLE.PDF, accessed on July 6, 2014. **244** *In the opinion of nineteen-year-old pilot George Buckley . . . "A C-47 in front of us with one engine out"*: George Buckley, "Mission Impossible—Operation Varsity," 76. **245** *Copilot Lieutenant Harry Dunhoft took over*: 435 TCG, "Interrogation Check Sheets. Glider Pilots." **245** *The glider riders had been briefed about them*: Ted Velikoff, "Velikoff Diary," 53. **245** *They were hit again fifty feet off the ground*: OSS, Covering Report 1–15 April 45," and Steltermann Collection (letter to his fiancée, May 5, 1945). **245** *Jungen covered their escape*: Based on Jungen's Recommendation for Silver Star as written by Steltermann, December 6, 1945. **246** *He'd been hit multiple times*: Steltermann Collection (Bronze Star citation, extract from radiologic report, Medical Department, April 8, 1945). **246** *Steltermann watched dozens of gliders*: Steltermann Collection. **246** *"Four birds at three o'clock!"*: Zane Winters, *The Last Glider Mission*, Part 2, 10. **246** *the position of the glider's pitot tube*: AAF Manual No. 50-17, *Pilot Training Manual for the CG-4A Glider*, 10. **246** *The pilot in front of them wasn't as fast*: Zane Winters, *The Last Glider Mission*, Part 2, 10. The destroyed glider was flown by Fred Daughtery and Walter Chandler. **246** *Winters kicked his way out of the cockpit*: Ibid. Winters later tried to kick his way out of a grounded glider to emulate his VARSITY escape—no matter how hard he kicked he could never muster the strength he did that morning on the LZ. The window would not budge. **246** *To Major Carl Peterson*: 194 GIR, officer interviews, 14. **247** *fired his tommy gun through the nose of his glider*: Don R. Pay, *Thunder from Heaven*, 39. **247** *platoons of the first serial were assembled*: John C. Warren, "U.S. Airborne Operations in World War II, European Theater," 185. **247** *Trooper Harry Ellis, first out of his glider*: Harry Ellis, "Airborne Landing Across the Rhine," 24. Ellis later received the Bronze Star for his actions. **248** *Bud Dudenhoeffer and his squad*: Bud Dudenhoeffer, JUMP!, 93. **248** *Another twenty-one gliders were raked by small arms fire*: 52 TCW, HQ, *Operation Varsity, After Action Report*, 7. **248** *"To Hitler from the 194"*: Talon, 17th Airborne Division newsmagazine, June 15, 1945, 5. **248** *Dillon and his men could now*: Dillon's account based on Frank Dillon, multiple letters to the author. **249** *By 11:10, 75 percent*: James P. Lyke, "The Operations of the 17th Airborne Division in the Crossing of the Rhine River, 24 March 1945," 44. **249** *Clyde Haney felt his pilot bank right*: The account of Haney's death is based on Richard H. Haney, *When Is Daddy Coming Home?*, 84. **250** *George Buckley's load of troopers jumped out*: George Buckley, "Mission Impossible—Operation Varsity," 76. **250** *Artillerymen of the 680th unloaded*: Jack P. Ancker, email to the author, July 8, 2009. **251** *two battery com-*

manders were killed: 680 GFAB, "680th Journal," 13, and 17ABN, After Action Report Narrative, 24–31 March 1945, 2. **251** *Jim Lauria's 75mm howitzer*: Jim Lauria, interview with the author, March 25, 2007. **251** *11:55*: The time is based on John C. Warren, "U.S. Airborne Operations in World War II, European Theater," 186. **251** *The armada's last seven serials*: James P. Lyke, "The Operations of the 17th Airborne Division in the Crossing of the Rhine River, 24 March 1945," 47. **251** *the final serials would deliver 1,321 more troops*: John C. Warren, "U.S. Airborne Operations in World War II, European Theater," 186. **251** *By the time the single-tow glider serials passed over*: Ibid., 186. **252** *One of the first gliders released*: History 139th Airborne Engineers, 22. **252** *The Air Force lost another three transports*: John C. Warren, "U.S. Airborne Operations in World War II, European Theater," 186. **252** *Over 50 percent of the gliders came in too fast*: Ibid., 187. **252** *Flight Officer Wes Hare's glider smacked in hard*: Hare's account is based on Johann J. Nitrowski, *Die Luftlandung*, 316, and Milton Dank, *The Glider Gang*, 251. **252** *George Holdren . . . couldn't see much*: George Holdren, WWII Memoir, 42. **252** *The fluctuating airspeeds had disrupted*: John C. Warren, "U.S. Airborne Operations in World War II, European Theater," 186. **252** *"like a string of firecrackers going off"*: Holdren's account based on George Holdren, WWII Memoir, 42. **253** *"every man for himself"*: John C. Warren, "U.S. Airborne Operations in World War II, European Theater," 187. **253** LZ conditions based on 441 TCG, 99TCS, "Interrogation Check Sheets. Glider Pilots," and 314 TCG, 62 TCS, "Interrogation Check Sheets." **253** *Several of the gliders landed on the southern perimeter*: John Chester, letter to the author, February 1, 2007. **254** *Joseph Shropshire and his load of two troopers*: David E. Mondt, untitled VARSITY article, 15. **254** *By Shropshire's estimate*: 314 TCG, 62 TCS, "Interrogation Check Sheets. Glider Pilots." **254** *certain he would be killed*: David E. Mondt, untitled VARSITY article, 15. **254** *he was killed the next day*: http://history.union.lib.nc.us/GoldStarMothers/helmst.htm, accessed on May 25, 2018. **254** *In the same LZ, Bill Knickerbocker and his copilot ran*: W. D. Knickerbocker, *Those Damn Glider Pilots*, 296. **255** *Fifty-three gliders*: 224 AMC, "224th Airborne Medical Company, Inclosure 24." **255** *As the casualties arrived, medics divided them*: Edmund A. Wienczak, personal diary. **255** *"four medics in my glider were shot thru the head"*: 441 TCG, "Interrogation Check Sheets. Glider Pilots of the 441st TCG, 99th TCS." **255** *"His lower extremities were missing"*: Edmund A. Wienczak, personal diary. **255** *Sergeant Paul Totten dashed out*: History 139th Airborne Engineers, 25. Totten was a medic with the 139th. **256** *One ingenious medic had had enough*: Johann J. Nitrowski, *Die Luftlandung*, 346. **256** *Sixteen medics were killed*: 224 AMC, "224th Airborne Medical Company, Inclosure 24." **256** *German POWs were put to work*: Ibid. **256** *Members of George Company*: 194 GIR, officer interviews, 5. **256** *Squads of well-armed Germans had barricaded*: Ibid., 5. **256** *Private Robert Geist let the first tank . . . Private William Paliwoda took out the second*: Napier Crookenden, *Airborne at War*, 134. **257** *The company already had two coups to their credit*: 194 GIR, officer interviews, 6. The regimental CP was that of the German 1052 Infantry Regiment. See also 194 GIR, "2nd Battalion Activities," 2. **257** *In a similar attack*: 194 GIR, officer interviews, 6. **257** *including maps marked with gun positions*: Michael Seaman, "18th Corps Handled Wesel Airborne Job While 17th Division's 194th Inf. Carried Ball," 5. **257** *"consequent disorganization"*: 194 GIR, officer interviews, 7. **257** *Private Robert Weber unlimbered his bazooka*: 194 GIR, "2nd Battalion Activities," 3. **257** *"all but disintegrated"*: Don R. Pay, *Thunder from Heaven*, 40. **257** *After knocking out several German outposts*: 194 GIR, officer interview, 8. **258** *George Company lay in wait*: 194

GIR, "2nd Battalion Activities," 2. **258** *After chasing them out a few times*: Ted Velikoff, "Velikoff Diary," 54. **258** *Herrmann and Snow sprinted across*: Eugene Herrmann, letter to the author, July 1, 2016. **259** *The medics told him his injury*: Ibid., September 16, 2015. **259** *Baker Company went into reserve*: 194 GIR, "Misc. Varsity Documents." **259** *The troopers tasked with seizing Bridges 7 through 10*: 194 GIR, officer interviews, 4.

Chapter 15 "I shall fear no evil"

260 *The formations of supply-carrying B-24s, aligning for the target*: John C. Warren, "U.S. Airborne Operations in World War II, European Theater," 188. **260** *visibility was reduced to a mere half mile*: Ibid., 189. **260** *Shafer . . . going under the power lines*: Tom Shafer, interview with author and *My Heroes*. **260** *The lead formations veered south*: John C. Warren, "U.S. Airborne Operations in World War II, European Theater," 189. **261** *"We saw the US Army in action"*: Dave Shafer, "Combat Log," 60. **261** *The Ruffians were supposed to have*: John C. Warren, "U.S. Airborne Operations in World War II, European Theater," 165, 188. **261** *Fortunately the navigator in the lead aircraft*: Peter Lonke, *The Liberators Who Never Returned*, 226. **261** *Shafer raised Ole King Cole's nose*: Tom Shafer, interview with author, August 18, 2013. **262** *"The air was filled"*: Peter Lonke, *The Liberators Who Never Returned*, 226. **262** *Shafer brought Ole King Cole back down to fifty feet*: Dave Shafer, *Combat Log*. **262** *The explosion's huge ball of flame*: Dick Howell quoted in *My Heroes*. **262** *"four engines rolling across the field"*: Ibid., 64, and Peter Lonke, *The Liberators Who Never Returned*, 230. **262** *"Because of ground fire"*: Tom Shafer, interview with the author, August 18, 2013. **262** *"everybody was scared"*: *My Heroes*. **262** *"It is almost certain"*: Dave Shafer, *Combat Log*, 64. **263** *Instead of jettisoning the supplies*: Donald Frank, "Running the Gauntlet from Hell to Main Street." **263** *"Tracers flashed up from 20mm cannons"*: Jack Young's account based on "Jack's Story," http://www.aeroc.dbnetinc.com/artist.html. **264** *"The wing dropped and the pilot lost about 25 feet"*: Peter Lonke, *The Liberators Who Never Returned*, 208. **264** *"Gun ready!"*: Emmerich's account is based on Peter Lonke, *The Liberators Who Never Returned*, 70. After dark Emmerich's AA Battery moved to new positions to avoid being overrun by American troops. Emmerich took advantage of the move to desert, hiding at a nearby farm. The farmer, who had lost sons in the war, kept Peter hidden until late April, when Emmerich made his way back home to Duisburg. On March 25, twenty-one members of Emmerich's battery were killed and nine captured. **265** *Flying* E-for-Easy, *Second Lieutenant Jack Hummel*: Ibid., 21. **265** *In the bomb bay Corporal James Deaton*: "Target: DZ-Wesel, 392nd Bomb Group, Mission #268, 24 March 1945." **265** *The nose gunner and the navigator jumped*: Peter Lonke, *The Liberators Who Never Returned*, 30, and ibid.; Morse made it, but Knudson's chute failed to open. **265** *"Lord, it is all up to you now"*: The E-for-Easy crew account is pieced together from several crew accounts found in Peter Lonke, *The Liberators Who Never Returned*.

Chapter 16 "Are they going to shoot us now?"

268 *A few plucky sharpshooters clanged the bell*: James P. Lyke, "The Operations of the 17th Airborne Division in the Crossing of the Rhine River, 24 March 1945," 35. **268** *Frightened civilians*: Johann J. Nitrowski, *Die Luftlandung*, 282. **269** *After two hours of mopping up*: James P. Lyke, "The Operations of the 17th Airborne Division in the Crossing of the Rhine River, 24 March 1945," 35. **269** *The castle's owner, Count Bolko Graf von Stolberg-Wernigerode*: Johann J. Nitrowski, *Die Luftlandung*, 283; account of Brigitte Müller, daughter of the parish priest in Diersfordt, Superintendent D. Heinrich Müller. **269** *He'd watched the airdrop from the Allied side*: Ridgway's crossing is based on Matthew B. Ridgway, *Soldier*, 133, and Clay Blair, *Ridgway's Paratroopers*, 467. Brigadier General John Whitelaw, the 17th Airborne's assistant division commander, also crossed with Ridgway. **270** *Ridgway arrived at the Ruffians' command post*: 507 PIR, "Varsity Narrative." The 507th PIR's S-3 journal states Ridgway arrived at 15:26. **270** *losses at ninety-nine casualties*: James P. Lyke, "The Operations of the 17th Airborne Division in the Crossing of the Rhine River, 24 March 1945," 36. **270** *A patrol sent toward the Rhine had made contact*: Ibid., 32. The Ruffians made multiple contacts with the Scottish division between 13:02 and 14:34. **270** *Several of the troopers who'd scampered out*: 507 PIR, "The Operations of Company H," 18. **271** *Raff felt that if the criteria for Ridgway's award*: Edson Raff, unpublished manuscript, 18 and 25. **271** *Equally egregious, Ridgway had elected to cross the Rhine*: Ibid., 29. **271** *Miley also had radio contact with his chief of staff*: This was Colonel Willard Liebel, who arrived by glider in serial A-18. **272** *One of Branigan's crew muscled a howitzer*: 464 PFAB, "After Action Report," 2. This crew was led by a Lieutenant Richardson. I have been unable to confirm his first name. **272** *As the enemy armor loitered*: 17ABN, "After Action Report Narrative, 24–31 March 1945," 2. **272** *Raff's 1st Battalion, standing by*: 507 PIR, "The Operations of Company H," 15. B Company was sent to furnish close-in protection for the 464th, and according to 507 PIR, officer interviews, "17th Airborne Division, Crossing Rhine, Operation Varsity, 24–31 March 1945," Able Company was sent to clear the woods northwest of the artillery positions. **272** *They now packed up*: 507 PIR, officer interviews, 18. **273** *"Everywhere was a grey uniform"*: Thad Blanchard, letter to the author, February 12, 2007. **274** *From the way some of the bodies were positioned*: Johann J. Nitrowski, *Die Luftlandung*, 280. As told by Berhardine and Maria Hegmann, who witnessed the bodies as they came out of their cellar. **274** *As the Ruffians flushed the trenches*: 507 PIR, officer interviews, 18. **274** *Tragically, only two of the group*: Johann J. Nitrowski, *Die Luftlandung*, 281. **274** *With Ridgway tagging along*: James P. Lyke, "The Operations of the 17th Airborne Division in the Crossing of the Rhine River, 24 March 1945," 48. **274** *Twenty-one-year-old Private Robert Watson*: Bart Hagerman, *War Stories*, 193. **274** *The diehards filed out*: Ibid. **274** *Staff Sergeant Bill Consolvo was hailed*: Consolvo's account is based on ibid. Consolvo later recalled: "When I go to the reunions, however, and see that old Nazi flag laying there on the table, I can't help but think of that day and how excited I was when I hauled it down. And, then I think about how many good men fell that day just so we could accomplish our mission." **274** *One bumped into a squad*: 507 PIR, "Varsity Narrative." **275** *Downstairs they found his sister*: The account of Vicar Heinrich Müller is based on Johann J. Nitrowski, *Die Luftlandung*, 282. **275** *Americans shooting through the window*: Ibid., 316. **275** *The troopers segregated the civilians*: John C. Warren, "U.S. Airborne Operations in World War II, European Theater," 193. **275** *The local English teacher, Frau*

Bruns: Johann J. Nitrowski, *Die Luftlandung,* 283. **276** The murder of Major Gordon Fowler is based on Fowler's 406th Fighter Group downed aircraft report and Peter Lonke, *The Liberators Who Never Returned,* 202. **276** *Two tommy gun–toting MPs:* James P. Lyke, "The Operations of the 17th Airborne Division in the Crossing of the Rhine River, 24 March 1945," 51.

Chapter 17 "A very dirty business"

277 *By 11:30 the medics, led by Captain Loran Morgan:* 466 PFAB, "466th PFA Battalion Supporting Data," 6. **277** *Medic Steve Miladinovich moved between rooms:* 466 PFAB, "History of the 466th Parachute Field Artillery Battalion," 12. **277** *To deliver his cargo Lefler had landed:* Ibid., 12. Lefler was promoted to corporal for his efforts. **278** *they had nearly fifty dead:* Ibid., 11. **278** *In exchange for those losses:* James P. Lyke, "The Operations of the 17th Airborne Division in the Crossing of the Rhine River, 24 March 1945," 42, and 466 PFAB, "466th PFA Battalion Supporting Data," 7. **278** *"had a highly desirable trait":* John Chester, letter to the author, September 1, 2007. **278** *A Battery, in addition to losing their officers:* 466 PFAB, "466th PFA Battalion Supporting Data," 3. **278** *Their drop had started badly:* 466 PFAB, "History of the 466th Parachute Field Artillery Battalion," 13. **278** *"Before the jump, I'd removed my plate":* Greg Forster, "Biggest Wartime Drop," 44. **278** *"In the Horsa!":* John Chester, letter to the author, February 1, 2007. **279** *"The inhabitants of a territory":* FM 27-10, *Rules of Land Warfare,* 4. **279** *"war can be somewhat beyond":* John Chester, letter to the author, February 1, 2007. **279** *B Battery, already in position:* 466 PFAB, "466th PFA Battalion Supporting Data," 4. **279** *The first groups filtered in:* John C. Warren, "U.S. Airborne Operations in World War II, European Theater," 181. **280** *Lieutenant Peter Scotese from Philadelphia:* Don R. Pay, *Thunder from Heaven,* 37. Private First Class John Dobridge of Jersey City and Private First Class Kenneth A. Braun of Brooklyn were the other two privateers. **280** *A proactive lieutenant:* 513th PIR, "Narrative of Action. 1st Battalion," 8, and 513 PIR, officer interviews, 2. The lieutenant was Richard E. Cosner of HQ Co. **280** *The latest intelligence indicated:* 513 PIR, officer interviews, 4. **280** *They were responsible for occupying a mile-long gap:* Ibid., 26. **280** *A group of fifty troopers led by Lieutenant Eugene Crowley:* 513 PIR. I Co., "World War II: Battle of the Bulge and Rhine Jump," E4, and 513 PIR, "Narrative of Action," 10. **280** *Next to arrive was a group of 150 troopers:* Ibid., E6, and Ibid., 4. **281** *Kent's group, while en route to the DZ:* 513 PIR, officer interviews, 27. **281** *"The Krauts had some stuff":* Bud Hutton, "Airborne Yanks, British Swarmed Into Nazi Ambush in Rhine Jump," 3. **281** *"Are you friendly":* 513 PIR. I Co., "World War II: Battle of the Bulge and Rhine Jump," E26 and E54. **282** *"What in God's name are you lugging":* Letter to Bill Breuer from Colonel J. W. Coutts, dated February 16, 1984, CMH, WBB. **282** *Miley and Ridgway's jeep convoy:* J. W. Coutts, February 8, 1984, questionnaire. **282** *Ridgway jestingly rebuked him:* Ibid. **282** *By the time Miley and Ridgway arrived:* 513 PIR. I Co., "World War II: Battle of the Bulge and Rhine Jump," E7. **282** *Having carefully studied maps:* Ibid., E7. **282** *But they'd recovered only fourteen* 513 PIR, officer interviews, 26. **282** *Attempts to recover equipment bundles:* Ibid., 3. **282** *Resourceful troopers forced some of their prisoners:* Robert F. Gill, "Things and Events as I Remember Them 50 Years Later," 21, and James P. Lyke, "The Operations of the 17th Airborne Division in the Crossing of the Rhine River, 24 March 1945," 56. **282** *Several patrols had* *been dispatched across*: 513 PIR. I Co., "World War II: Battle of the Bulge and Rhine Jump," E7. **282** *As far as Coutts could tell, his 3rd Battalion*: Ibid., E8. **283** *He and his executive had been captured*: 513 PIR, "Narrative of Action," 2. They both returned to their unit around 16:30. **283** *With the 1st Battalion in position*: 513th PIR, "Narrative of Action. 1st Battalion," 8. **283** *No contact had yet been made*: 513 PIR, officer interviews, 16. **283** *Perhaps the delay was due to*: Ibid., 16. **283** *By late afternoon he'd collected*: Ibid. **283** *They radioed back to Miller for artillery support*: Ibid. **283** *Miller ordered Bressler*: 513 PIR, officer interviews, 16. **283** *Finally at 19:00 . . . Coutts . . . ordered Miller to seize his objective*: 513th PIR, "Narrative of Action. 2nd Battalion," 4. **283** *Miller's men, moving in a skirmish formation*: 513 PIR, officer interviews, 16. **283** *The fire was coming from a cluster of brick buildings*: Ibid., 16. **284** *Among the paratroopers*: War Department, "Oregon Airborne Infantryman Awarded Medal of Honor Posthumously." **284** *Still suffering from the lingering symptoms*: This according to trooper Buck McKendrick, found on 17ABN Biographies. **284** *They made it about fifty yards*: War Department, "Oregon Airborne Infantryman Awarded Medal of Honor Posthumously." **284** *About twenty-five yards from the German's perimeter*: Ibid. **284** *For his critical role in spearheading the assault*: Ibid. **284** *They dropped several shells*: This according to trooper Bob Patterson, found on 17ABN Biographies. **285** *An Unterwachtmeister (artillery sergeant)*: Johann J. Nitrowski, *Die Luftlandung*, 316. **285** *Paratrooper Robert Gill*: Robert F. Gill, "Things and Events as I Remember Them 50 Years Later," 21. **285** *Entering the château, they fired up*: This according to trooper Buck McKendrick, found on 17ABN Biographies. **285** *Hollis Powell watched*: Peter Lonke, *The Liberators Who Never Returned*, 29. **285** *A gaggle of over 200 enemy prisoners*: This according to trooper Buck McKendrick, found on 17ABN Biographies. **285** *A shot rang out*: Peter Lonke, *The Liberators Who Never Returned*, 31. **286** *"I got him!"*: Ibid., 29. **286** *16 B-24s had been shot down*: James P. Lyke, "The Operations of the 17th Airborne Division in the Crossing of the Rhine River, 24 March 1945," 56. **286** *It was a tactical mistake*: For criticism, see ibid., 65. **286** *Unfortunately, its radio was beyond repair*: OSS, "Covering Report 1–15 April 45." **286** *They found an aid station bustling with activity*: Steltermann Collection (letter written to his fiancée, May 5, 1945). **286** *Team Alsace, the other uniformed agents*: OSS, Stephen P. Vinciguerra, "Field Report from ETO." **287** *Vinciguerra and Steltermann dismounted*: OSS, "Covering Report 1–15 April 45." **287** *While Steltermann and Staub interrogated*: Ibid. **287** *They'd taken all of their objectives*: 194 GIR, "2nd Battalion Activities," 3. **287** *Elements of Kampfgruppe Karst*: 194 GIR, "Misc. Varsity Documents." Balish took command after the CO, Colonel W. S. Stewart, had been wounded; Major Pleasant Martin had been in command temporarily before Balish took over. **287** *Troopers repelled the attack*: 194 GIR, "Regimental Journal," 2. This attack tool place at 15:40. **288** *At 16:00 Kampfgruppe Karst launched*: 194 GIR, "2nd Battalion Activities," 3. **288** *Forward observer Lieutenant Herman Lemberger*: Don R. Pay, *Thunder from Heaven*, 42. **288** *Again British artillery from the far bank*: 194 GIR, "2nd Battalion Activities," 3. **288** *After the dust settled, both George and Fox Companies*: 194 GIR, "Regimental Journal," 2. These radio calls were received at 16:20. **288** *twenty-five cows were milked*: "681st GFAB, 681st Glider Field Artillery Battalion," 10. **288** *From crashed gliders and supply bundles*: Don R. Pay, *Thunder from Heaven*, 4. **288** *But stout, well-armed German defenders stopped them*: 194 GIR, "2nd Battalion Activities," 4. **289** *As the sun dipped below the horizon*: Ibid., 3. **289** *Lieutenant John Robinson eyed the graying sky*: Ibid., 3. **289** *With the Commandos' location uncertain*: 194 GIR, officer interviews, 6. Eventually almost 275 POWs were taken out of the area, "after the most generous use of Corps artillery and WP." **289** *"be careful"*: J. W. Coutts, February 8, 1984, questionnaire. **290** *Thus far the division had collected prisoners*: 194 GIR, "Regimental Journal," 4, and Ozzie Gorbitz, *Blood on the Talon*, 185. **290** *The kitchen had been well stocked*: John Chester, "They Called It Varsity," 54. **290** *Before sending their prisoners to the holding area*: Ibid., 54. **290** *Commo wire had been laid*: John Chester, letter to the author, September 1, 2007.

Chapter 18 "We had luck with us"

291 *"We didn't know where"*: Matthew B. Ridgway, *Soldier*, 134. **291** *Sporadic gunfire and the* crumping *of grenades*: Ibid., 134. **291** *The Americans finally arrived at 22:45*: Ibid., 134, and 6th Airborne Division, "Report on Operation Varsity and the Advance from the Rhine to the Baltic," 20. **291** *The command post—established in the single-story brick farmhouse*: BAOR, "Report on Operation Varsity," 56. **291** *A group of civilians huddled together*: Johann J. Nitrowski, *Die Luftlandung*, 234. **291** *In the pig barn was a dead American parachutist*: Ibid., 236. **292** *The kitchen had been converted*: Ibid., 235. **292** *A British officer, attempting to get a few minutes of sleep*: BAOR, "Report on Operation Varsity," 56. **292** *British General Eric Bols greeted Ridgway*: Johann J. Nitrowski, *Die Luftlandung*, 237. **292** *Since Ridgway was the first emissary*: BAOR, "Report on Operation Varsity," 56. **292** *"fighting like stink for the first day"*: Napier Crookenden, *Airborne at War*, 125. **292** *Within four hours of their landing*: George Chatterson, *The Wings of Pegasus*, 8, and John C. Warren, "U.S. Airborne Operations in World War II, European Theater," 177. **292** *Bols' men had repelled multiple*: Brian Jewell, *Over the Rhine*, 40. Later that night, during a German counterattack, the British troopers blew the bridge west of Ringenberg to prevent German tanks from crossing. **292** *The British fighters would be credited with*: John C. Warren, "U.S. Airborne Operations in World War II, European Theater," 191. The Forward Visual Control Party assigned to the 17th Airborne landed in the British sector and were unable to make it to Miley's HQ until D+1. **292** *Reports were incomplete, but*: Napier Crookenden, *Airborne at War*, 143, and John C. Warren, "U.S. Airborne Operations in World War II, European Theater," 177. The 6th Airborne suffered 347 KIA and another 731 WIA. **292** *The three generals crowded*: Matthew B. Ridgway, *Soldier*, 134. **293** *Bols would hold his current positions*: 6th Airborne Division, "Report on Operation Varsity and the Advance from the Rhine to the Baltic," 20. **293** *There was still heavy German resistance*: Brian Jewell, *Over the Rhine*, 39. **293** *In turn, German engineers*: XVIII Corps (ABN), "War Diary," March 25, 1945. **293** *Allied engineers strung chains*: Charles Whiting, *Bounce the Rhine*, 129. **293** *His vision had returned*: Justin L. C. Eldridge, *Defense on the Rhine*, and "Special Interrogation Report of General Alfred Schlemm," 15. **293** *Montgomery's staggered attacks*: "Special Interrogation Report of General Alfred Schlemm," 16. The attack schedule: 21:00 British XXX Corps attacked, 22:00 Commandos crossed into Wesel, 02:00 British XII Corps attacked, and two hours later, at 04:00, just before dawn on March 24, the US Ninth Army attacked, followed by VARSITY at 10:00. Timing based on Montgomery's 21AG Diary, 305. **293** *While Schlemm had been unconscious*: Justin L. C. Eldridge, *Defense on the Rhine*. **293** *Allied fighters strafed his staff car*: "Special Interrogation Report of General Alfred Schlemm," 16. **293** *Indeed, the Allies' patrolling of the road networks*: William B. Breuer, *Storming*

Hitler's Rhine, 216. **294** *He spent the next two days*: Justin L. C. Eldridge, *Defense on the Rhine*. On March 28 command of I *Fallschirmjäger-Armee* was transitioned to General Gunther Blumenritt. Schlemm spent rest of war in a hospital, until his capture. **294** *The column of jeeps nudged their way*: Miley's and Ridgway's return journey is based on Matthew B. Ridgway, *Soldier*, 134, and James P. Lyke, "The Operations of the 17th Airborne Division in the Crossing of the Rhine River, 24 March 1945," 51. **294** *"Aaah, go sit in your hat"*: Matthew B. Ridgway, *Soldier*, 135. Ridgway quotes the paratrooper as saying "go sit in your hat"—personally I think he opted to edit out the "h." **295** *The four platoons of the 435th Troop Carrier Group*: Johann J. Nitrowski, "Varsity Folder," letter from William Horn, September 9, 1990. **295** *The 78th was located to the rear*: Hans den Brok, *Battle of Burp Gun Corner*, 49. **295** *The four corners of the intersection*: Johann J. Nitrowski, "Varsity Folder," letter from William Horn to Parks, August 31, 1989. **295** *Several of the "volunteer" power pilots grumbled*: 435 TCG, "Interrogation Check Sheets. Glider Pilots," Floyd Hand. **295** *The pilots quickly realized*: Charles O. Gordon, *Burp Gun Corner*, 18. **295** *"The rank didn't necessarily denote leaders"*: 435 TCG, "Interrogation Check Sheets. Glider Pilots," Richard Barthelemy. **296** *Civilians were ushered out*: Charles O. Gordon, *Burp Gun Corner*, 9. **296** *In one house a squad of pilots rescued*: Ibid., 13. Lieutenant Donald Patterson led this squad. **296** *He ushered the Germans*: 435 TCG, "Interrogation Check Sheets. Glider Pilots." I have opted to leave out this pilot's name, but the curious can find his full account in the above source. **296** *The Luftwaffe pilot was dazed*: Charles O. Gordon, *Burp Gun Corner*, 9. **296** *In a gesture of unnecessary chivalry*: Doug Wilmer, "The Battle of Burp Gun Corner." **296** *Whoever was coming toward them*: Johann J. Nitrowski, "Varsity Folder," letter from William Horn, April 11, 1988. **296** *It wasn't until the advancing unit*: 435 TCG, "Interrogation Check Sheets. Glider Pilots," Frederick Mitchell. **296** *The pilots snapped off shots*: Doug Wilmer, "The Battle of Burp Gun Corner," and 435 TCG, "Interrogation Check Sheets. Glider Pilots," Jacob Zichterman. Accounts vary as to whether the armored vehicle was a self-propelled assault gun (Stug) or an actual tank. Glider pilot Robert Campbell, one of the more experienced pilots, identified it as a Mark IV tank. I have used the generic term "tank" in my account to cover either scenario. **297** *He heaved them*: 435 TCG, "Interrogation Check Sheets. Glider Pilots," Raye Niblo. **297** *From his foxhole, Valton Bray*: Ibid., Valton Bray. **297** *The gun was destroyed*: Ibid., Emmett Huff. **297** *"We were afraid to open fire"*: Ibid., Albert Hurley. **297** *As they advanced behind the tank*: Ibid., Frederick Mitchell. **297** *"There must have been about a hundred"*: Elbert Jella, documents and notebook. **297** *The explosion was tremendous*: 435 TCG, "Interrogation Check Sheets. Glider Pilots," Garnett Holland. **298** *They squeezed off short bursts*: 435 TCG, "Interrogation Check Sheets. Glider Pilots," Chester DeShurley. **298** *The shell cracked two feet over*: Ibid. **298** *The interior of the two-story brick structure*: Hans den Brok, *Battle of Burp Gun Corner*, 58. **298** *They rescued an elderly couple*: Johann J. Nitrowski, "Varsity Folder," letters from William Horn, September 27, 1987, and April 11, 1988, and Horn to Parks, August 31, 1989. **298** *Their machine gunners on their flanks*: 435 TCG, "Interrogation Check Sheets. Glider Pilots," Richard Barthelemy. **298** *"Things were plenty SNAFU"*: 435 TCG, "Interrogation Check Sheets. Glider Pilots," Albert Hurley. **298** *Most of the 77th Platoon*: See multiple accounts in 435 TCG, "Interrogation Check Sheets. Glider Pilots." **298** *Claims would later be made*: Charles O. Gordon, *Burp Gun Corner*, 14. Despite postwar claims by those manning the Glider Pilot CP that word was sent out to the platoons, the pilot statements made within days of the action make it clear no one on the line knew what was happening. **299** *"During the attack five of our squadron deserted"*: 435 TCG, "Interrogation Check Sheets. Glider Pilots," William Bruner. **299** *Just two superficial head wounds*: Johann J. Nitrowski, "Varsity Folder," letter from William Horn, April 11, 1988. **299** *The "Battle for Burp Gun Corner"*: Elbert Jella, documents and notebook. The skirmish got its name from a *Stars and Stripes* article (April 1, 1945) that covered the event. **299** *A jumpy pilot shot*: Charles O. Gordon, *Burp Gun Corner*, 9. **299** *A burst from the .30-caliber*: 435 TCG, "Interrogation Check Sheets. Glider Pilots." Again I have opted to leave out this pilot's name, but the curious can find his full account in the above source. **299** *The only sign of Wittig's patrol*: 194 GIR, "2nd Battalion Activities," 3. **299** *Robinson's platoon hunkered down*: Ibid., 3. **300** *Colonel Harry Balish dispatched another platoon*: Ibid., 3. **300** *After a few miserable minutes*: Ibid., 4. **300** *But the field telephone lines*: Ibid. **300** *A burst of fire spit out*: Ibid. Technical Sergeant Lyman Wisler was killed in action here. **300** *"Firing 310 degrees . . ."*: 194 GIR, "Regimental Journal," 6. **301** *Repeated attempts to*: 194 GIR, "2nd Battalion Activities," 4. **301** *Creeping up on the bridges*: Ibid., 4. Robert Sheehy and John Kovacs were the two scouts. **301** *Anderson's troopers loaded up*: Ibid., 4. **301** *Sheehy led them to Bridge 2*: Ibid. **301** *The platoon watched in silence*: Ibid. **301** *They could find no trace of GIs*: 194 GIR, officer interviews, 8. **302** *No one had been able to*: 194 GIR, "2nd Battalion Activities," 5. **302** *The low-level gun run was ineffective*: Ibid., 5. **303** *Fox Company's machine gunners*: Ibid., 5. **303** *At 22:00 the Germans broke through at Bridge 7*: 194 GIR, "Misc. Varsity Documents." **303** *women were pretending*: 194 GIR, "Regimental Journal," 5. **303** *It worked once*: Michael Seaman, "18th Corps Handled Wesel Airborne Job While 17th Division's 194th Inf. Carried Ball," 5. **303** *A reliable source indicated*: 194 GIR, "Regimental Journal," 7. **303** *The attack was brushed off*: 194 GIR, "Misc. Varsity Documents." **303** *In one such engagement, Sergeant William Wolf*: *The Talon Crosses the Rhine*, 8, and Don R. Pay, *Thunder from Heaven*, 42. **304** *Private Levert Smith, Jr., apparently fumbled his*: 17ABN Biographies, "Levert Lindell Smith, Jr." **304** *"We heard the shells coming"*: Frank J. O'Rourke, "Eyewitness: A Gliderman Across the Rhine." **304** *Lieutenant Joseph Kormylo*: The Kormylo patrol is based on 507 PIR, "Varsity Narrative," and Richard A. Boe, unpublished memoir. **305** *They should expect*: 194 GIR, "Regimental Journal," 8.

Chapter 19 "Organized resistance has now ceased"

306 *Scattered around the glider riders' positions*: 194 GIR, "2nd Battalion Activities," 5. **306** *Efforts to reach them had failed*: Ibid., 5. Part of the confusion was due to the canal being below street level in this part of Wesel. **306** *Thirty minutes later*: Ibid., 6, and 194 GIR, officer interviews, 14. As one can imagine, prisoner counts vary by source. The officer interviews document states that on the morning of D+1, "the regiment had by actual count, captured 1,153 POWs." While the 2nd Battalion Activities report states "That night Lt Cunningham, S-2, revealed that his count showed 1,157 prisoners for the two days [D+2]." **307** *Wittig's men had wiggled their way*: 194 GIR, "2nd Battalion Activities," 6. **307** *Despite the successful counterattack*: Ibid., 6. **307** *It wouldn't be until mid-afternoon*: 194 GIR, "Regimental Journal," 10. **307** *"I don't know who killed him"*: Ben Roberson, WWII Veteran Biographical Sketch, CMH. **307** *Daylight also revealed the toll on the bridges*: The state of the bridges are based on numerous reports from surveys conducted by the 139th AEB, specifically: "Daily Engineer Situation

Report No. 2" and "Daily Engineer Situation Report No. 3." A Lieutenant Evans, whose first name I have been unable to determine, defused the demolition charges. **307** *Gene Herrman's crew was instructed*: Eugene Herrmann, letters to the author, September 16, 2015, and August 29, 2017. **309** *Medic Joseph Moscar witnessed the drama*: Joseph W. Moscar, "Parts of My Missions." **310** *Half a mile northwest of Bridge 2*: The number of German casualties at Burp Gun Corner varies. I have based the count on the April 1, 1945, *Stars and Stripes* article, which states, "They counted 13 dead Germans at or near the corner; 45 wounded POWs. . . . Unwounded POWs were well over 80." **310** *"I still remember today very vividly"*: Johann J. Nitrowski, "Varsity Folder," letter from William Horn, September 27, 1987. **310** *The pilots weren't sure*: Ibid., letter from William Horn, April 11, 1988, and 435 TCG, "Interrogation Check Sheets. Glider Pilots," Garnett Holland. **310** *Since the pilots realized the Germans hadn't retreated*: Charles O. Gordon, *Burp Gun Corner*, 9. **310** *A four-pilot patrol party left*: Ibid., 10. **310** *At 14:00 word came down*: Ibid., 10. **310** *"I only used fifteen rounds"*: Zane Winters, "The Last Glider Mission, Part 2," 10. **311** *In the vanguard of the supply columns*: 717 AOMC, "After Action Report," 1. **311** *From a reception station*: IX TCC, "Activities Final Phase," 51. **311** *Cots and rations were provided*: Ibid., 51. **312** *"These missions are no longer any fun"*: Howard G. Schultz, "Account of Glider Pilot in Varsity," 2. **312** *"Any Glider Pilots picked up"*: Harry W. Andrews, untitled personal account, 5. **312** *Despite transportation delays*: IX TCC, Control Team No.2, "Activities of Control Team No. 2 on Varsity Mission." **312** *And within six days*: John C. Warren, "U.S. Airborne Operations in World War II, European Theater," 191. **312** *Bill Knickerbocker returned to his unit*: W. D. Knickerbocker, *Those Damn Glider Pilots*, 315. **312** *Combat engineers tinkered*: 139 AFB, "Monthly After Operations Report," 2. **312** *The Thirteeners' 2nd Battalion*: 513 PIR, "Narrative of Action," 2. Fox Company was in the lead, with Dog Company in trail. See also 513 PIR, "After Action Report, 24 to 31 March," 3. **313** *Two platoons of* Grenadiers: The German troops occupying the Diersfordt Forest were primarily from the *84 Infanterie-Division*, whose three line regiments were the 1051, the 1052, and the 1062 Grenadier Regiments. **313** *Thirteeners' final D-Day objective fell at 07:30*: 513 PIR, "Narrative of Action," 5. **313** *While Miller awaited the Tommies*: Ibid., 4, and Napier Crookenden, *Airborne at War*, 111. **313** *The clearing operation netted*: 513 PIR, "After Action Report, 24 to 31 March," 2. **313** *Bicycles and horses became popular*: Kirk B. Ross, *The Sky Men*, 427. **313** *"I didn't want to go"*: Bart Hagerman, *War Stories*, 188. **314** *Their company had captured*: 513 PIR, I Co., "World War II: Battle of the Bulge and Rhine Jump," E26. **314** *"I think I see a jeep"*: Ibid. **314** *Parachute infantry regiments had only 15*: Steven J. Zaloga, *US Airborne Divisions in the ETO 1944–45*, 26. **314** *"Like hell you will"*: 513 PIR, I Co., "World War II: Battle of the Bulge and Rhine Jump," E27. **315** *A spatter of carbine fire*: 466 PFAB, "History of the 466th Parachute Field Artillery Battalion," 2. **315** *Unless the situation was dire*: Ibid., 3. **315** *By one o'clock that afternoon*: Ibid. "By 13:00, the last howitzer of Battery A, which was dropped west of the Rhine River arrived with the complete gun crew. The battalion has all 15 howitzers in action." **315** *Incoming artillery rounds silenced*: 513 PIR, officer interviews, 27. **316** *Two hundred–odd rounds crashed in*: 513 PIR., I Co., "World War II: Battle of the Bulge and Rhine Jump," E9. Casualties were twenty-six wounded and six killed. **316** *"No snow, no ice, no howling wind"*: Ben Scherer, *Soldiers and Brothers Under the Canopy*, 64. **316** *They were to occupy LONDON*: 513 PIR, officer interviews, 4. **316** *Large explosions from a dreaded 88*: Ben Scherer, *Soldiers and Brothers Under the Canopy*, 170, and 513 PIR, "Narrative of Action," 8. **316** *Not* *far from McDonald, Ben Scherer's squad*: Scherer's account is based on Ben Scherer, *Soldiers and Brothers Under the Canopy*, 170. Scherer was later evacuated to a hospital near Liege, Belgium, where he met up with a paratrooper from the 13th Airborne who got them several bottles of American whiskey. "We drank Early Times and Seagram's Seven without chasers and loved every drop of it." **316** *It took several lucky artillery rounds*: Ben Scherer, *Soldiers and Brothers Under the Canopy*, 170. **317** *"A squad leader who makes"*: Kurt Gabel, *Making of a Paratrooper*, 75. **317** *"it was too dark"*: Ben Scherer, *Soldiers and Brothers Under the Canopy*, 64. **317** *"You tell General Miley"*: Ibid. **317** *"as welcome as Betty Grable"*: Hamilton Whitman, "Airborne Operation: Mission Completed," 3. **317** *The gun teams of the 605th . . . The other twenty-four guns*: 605 TBD, "After Action Report," 1. **318** *The patrol radioed back at 12:50*: 507 PIR, "Varsity Narrative." **318** *After getting the report, Raff*: Ibid. **318** *With one battalion on their left*: 507 PIR, "The Operations of Company H," 19. **318** *The approaches to Wesel were cluttered*: 507 PIR, "Varsity Narrative." **318** *The crews shuttled the howitzers forward*: 464 PFAB, "After Action Report," 2. **319** *It took the combined firepower*: 507 PIR, "Varsity Narrative." **319** *"The city had been pulverized"*: 507 PIR, officer interviews, 19. **319** *They held Bridge 3*: 194 GIR, "2nd Battalion Activities," 6. **319** *They'd have a few hours*: 507 PIR. "Varsity Narrative." **319** *"Organized resistance has now ceased"*: 194 GIR, "Regimental Journal," 12. **320** *At Bridge 6, the German attack*: Ted Velikoff, "Velikoff Diary," 54. **320** *By the next morning*: 194 GIR, "Misc. Varsity Documents, (Narrative of facts: 1st Battalion)," 11.

Chapter 20 "This is a pursuit"

321 Description and history of the 771st is based on Edwin Castagna, *History of the 771st Tank Battalion*. **322** *Cochrane's tankers found the Thirteeners at 03:30*: 513 PIR, "After Action Report, 24 to 31 March." **322** *Coutts explained that the assault companies*: 513 PIR, I Co., "World War II: Battle of the Bulge and Rhine Jump," E10. **322** *The Nazis ground attack commenced*: 17ABN, "Operational Diary," 25. **322** *A mortar shell killed Able's radio operator*: Ben Scherer, *Soldiers and Brothers Under the Canopy*, 86. **322** *Eyes wide, MacFarlane nodded and scrambled*: Ibid. The machine gun position was manned by Privates Ken Eyres, Joe Timinski, and John Peagler. **322** *Private Noah Jones found himself*: Ibid., 134. **323** *Cochrane's Shermans plastered them*: Edwin Castagna, *History of the 771st Tank Battalion*, 61. **323** *As the three-man mortar squad*: Ben Scherer, *Soldiers and Brothers Under the Canopy*, 134. **323** *Daylight confirmed what they'd suspected*: Ibid., 65, and 17ABN, "Operational Diary," 24. **324** *The tanks ceased fire at 08:00*: 513 PIR, I Co., "World War II: Battle of the Bulge and Rhine Jump," E30. **324** *Fifteen troopers were cut down*: Ibid. **324** *Lieutenant Dean Swem's platoon advanced*: Ibid. **325** *"maniacal frenzy"*: Ibid. **325** *The Thirteeners pressed their attack*: Ibid., E31. **325** *The last remaining obstacle*: Ibid. **325** *To crack it the Thirteeners called*: 466 PFAB, "History of the 466th Parachute Field Artillery Battalion," 3. **325** *George Holdren, who'd been advancing*: George Holdren, WWII Memoir, 47. **325** *they were Volkssturm troops*: Ibid., 47. **325** *At the cost of three wounded troopers*: 513 PIR, I Co., "World War II: Battle of the Bulge and Rhine Jump," E31. **326** *"there were only about fourteen"*: George Holdren, WWII Memoir, 47. **326** *Coutts had suffered thirteen KIA*: 17ABN, "17th Airborne Casualty Rate, Daily By Unit." **326** *Was she a frightened German*: George Holdren, WWII Memoir, 48. **326** *He craned skyward as* Messerschmitts *and Spitfires*: Ibid., 46. **326** *"the necessity of that sort of thing"*: Ibid., 47. The burning of houses is also discussed in Ted Velikoff, "Velikoff Diary," 54. **326** A *search of the house*: George Holdren, *WWII Memoir*, 48. **327** *"There is evidence of considerable looting"*: 17ABN, "Looting Memorandums." **327** *"personnel of this command are ransacking"*: 17ABN, "After Action Report for HQ, Apr. 2, 1945," Inspector General's Section. **327** *"I have personally seen and stopped"*: 17ABN, "Looting Memorandums." **327** *"This part of Germany wasn't hurt much"*: John Yanok, History 155th Airborne Anti-Tank, Anti-Aircraft Battalion, 35. This was Lieutenant Colonel Bill Paddock, CO of the 155th. **327** *Using tanks and artillery*: "Diary of B Co. — 194th Glider Infantry," March 26, 1945. **327** *All told they bagged 250 prisoners*: 194 GIR, "Misc. Varsity Documents," 8, and 17ABN, "17th Airborne Casualty Rate, Daily By Unit." **327** *Captain George Streukens and his men captured a creamery*: George L. Streukens, "Personal Manuscript, 194 GIR," 8. **327** *The Ruffians, despite constant shelling*: 507 PIR, "Varsity Narrative." **327** *On Montgomery's right flank, the US 30th*: Ibid. **328** *"assigned objectives for operation"*: Ibid. **328** *Captain Ernest Carpenter needed a drink*: Accounts of Carpenter and Wienczak based on Edmund A. Wienczak, personal diary. **328** *One of the patients was a Ruffian*: Ibid. The Ruffian was Joesph Kowalski. **328** *The medics had been ferrying*: 224 AMC, "224th Airborne Medical Company, Inclosure 24." **328** *Braving stray artillery rounds*: Ibid. **328** *As such the wounded were lifted*: Ibid. **328** *They arrived at the 17th Airborne Division's aid station*: William B. Breuer, *Storming Hitler's Rhine*, 276. **329** *The clearing medics loaded up*: 224 AMC, "224th Airborne Medical Company, Inclosure 24." **329** *When the Rhine bridges opened up*: Ibid. **329** *The patients' first stop*: Everett C. Johnston, CMH, "WWII Veteran Survey." **329** *Care stations had been organized*: Bill Tom, untitled article, 8. **329** *"There was no discrimination"*: Quinn A. Whiting, "Memories of World War II," 9. **329** *A grievously wounded paratrooper*: Ibid., 9. **330** *The announcer declared*: XVIII Corps (ABN), "Periodic Reports," a review of German broadcasts. **330** *The two airborne divisions' three-day*: 17ABN, "Operational Diary," 25, and XVIII Corps (ABN), "Operation Varsity," 6. **330** *"there is nothing left"*: Lewis Brereton, *The Brereton Diaries*, 407. **330** *Brereton . . . uncharacteristic visit*: Ibid., 408. **330** *Ridgway had the operation well in hand*: FAAA press release dated March 26, 1945, FLP, CMH. **330** *"Have not received any copy"*: FAAA, "Outgoing Messages, 13–31MAR45," March 24, 1945. **330** *"Okay, fellows, unload your rifles"*: Lewis Brereton, *The Brereton Diaries*, 408. **331** *"disregard . . . to obtain maximum exploitation"*: Matthew B. Ridgway, "An Airborne Corps Operations," 7. **331** *"Advance to Dorsten. This is a pursuit"*: John C. Warren, "U.S. Airborne Operations in World War II, European Theater," 190. **331** *"Their columns sometimes resembled"*: Edwin Castagna, *History of the 771st Tank Battalion*, 63. **331** *To take advantage of*: Brian Jewell, *Over the Rhine*, 45. **331** *The Thirteeners served as*: Ibid., 45. The Thirteeners served as infantry support for the British 6th Guards Armored Brigade, the Ruffians went to XIX Corps (Guards Armored Brigade), and the glider riders were farmed out to the 95th Infantry Division. **331** *Simultaneously, American units having*: Matthew B. Ridgway, *Soldier*, 138. **331** *"sporadic and rang[ing] from"*: Kurt Gabel, *Making of a Paratrooper*, 266. **331** *"They [the Germans] were in the woods"*: Ben Scherer, *Soldiers and Brothers Under the Canopy*, 134. **332** *"a long, unwieldy, weapon"*: Richard W. Homan, "Donations Needed for Memorial to Pendleton County WWII Hero." **332** *VARSITY was his second*: War Department, untitled press release. **332** *Hedrick's squad, according to*: Ibid. **332** *"It makes no difference"*: Ibid. **334** *When the glider riders rallied*: Richard W. Homan, "Donations Needed for Memorial to Pendleton County WWII Hero." **334** *Hed-*

rick's father was later: War Department, untitled press release. **334** *In the month of April*: Rick Atkinson, *The Guns at Last Light* (Henry Holt and Company, LLC, 2013), 596. **334** *On the outskirts of town*: Ben Scherer, *Soldiers and Brothers Under the Canopy*, 6. **334** *Münster was taken on*: FAAA, "History of Headquarters," 88. **334** *Thad Blanchard, leading his squad*: Thad Blanchard, letter to the author, February 12, 2007. **334** *The Ruffians' commander, Edson Raff*: Dominique François, *The 507th Parachute Infantry Regiment*, 80. **334** *With the reassignment of*: FAAA, "History of Headquarters," 88. The 17th Airborne was assigned to the XIII Corps, while the 6th Airborne went to VII Corps. **334** *The 300-mile journey*: OSS, "Covering Report 1–15 April 45." **334** *Team Alsace had been found*: Ibid. **335** *Helmut Steltermann had been evacuated*: OSS, Stephen P. Vinciguerra, "Field Report from ETO." **335** *"Here I am—happy and well"*: Steltermann Collection. **335** *The speed at which the Allies*: Lewis Brereton, *The Brereton Diaries*, 416. **335** *The Allies had closed the noose*: Bart Hagerman, "17th Airborne Division History," 9. **335** *Ridgway's corps attacked north*: Matthew B. Ridgway, *Soldier*, 139. The divisions attached to Ridgway's corps included four infantry divisions (the 9th, 78th, 86th, and the 97th) and an armored division, the 13th. **335** *"meatgrinder"*: Ibid. **335** *160,892 prisoners*: Lewis Brereton, *The Brereton Diaries*, 421. **335** *More poignant was the*: Matthew B. Ridgway, *Soldier*, 140. **335** *There they finished out*: FAAA. "History of Headquarters," 89. **335** *In several of the villages*: 513 PIR, I Co., *World War II: Battle of the Bulge and Rhine Jump*, E58. **336** *GIs sent to prevent*: IX TCC, "Activities Final Phase," 85. **336** *"even the most conservative"*: FAAA, *Operation Varsity*, 48. **336** *Of the 889 American*: Ibid. **336** *Quartermaster units scoured fields*: Ibid. **336** *Most of the parachutes*: Boyd Daniels, *The Riggers Cross the Rhine*, 43, and Johann J. Nitrowski, "Varsity Folder." **336** *One farmer found a*: Johann J. Nitrowski, *Die Luftlandung*, 310. **336** *Over the next several days*, 411 AQQC, "After Action Report," 1. **336** *Count Bolko Graf von Stolberg-Wernigerode*: Johann J. Nitrowski, *Die Luftlandung*, 286. **336** *One child lost his hand*: Ibid., 239. **336** *Another was killed digging*: Ibid., 238. **337** *Troopers of the 17th Airborne*: Bart Hagerman, "17th Airborne Division History," 10. **337** *They were transferred out*: Kurt Gabel, *Making of a Paratrooper*, 271. **337** *"a Missouri hillbilly who"*: Lynn W. Aas, "Remembering the Price of Freedom," 8. **337** *Dozens were sent to the*: Bart Hagerman, "17th Airborne Division History," 10. **337** *After two and a half years*: Ibid. **337** *Scattered across those battlefields*: Compiled from *Army Battle Casualties and Non-Battle Deaths in World War II: Final Report* (Washington, DC: Statistical and Accounting Branch, Office of the Adjutant General, 1953), 80. **338** *The division's sixty-six days*: John Kormann, *Little Known Sacrifices*, 11. **338** *The final resting place*: 17ABN Biographies, "Stephen Milewski." **338** *I have heard the reports*: Richard H. Haney, *When Is Daddy Coming Home?*, 84.

Epilogue

339 *made VARSITY the largest single-day airborne mission of World War II*: While MARKET GARDEN dropped three divisions, it used less aircraft and delivered troops over a period of five days, making VARSITY the largest single-day drop of the war. **339** *their combined resources marshaled an air armada of 1,596 transports*: Aircraft numbers are based on John C. Warren, "U.S. Airborne Operations in World War II, European Theater," 228. **339** *deliver 19,782 armed men*: Troop numbers are again based on Warren, which consists of 8,834 American, Canadian and British paratroopers (there was

SELECTED SOURCES

Books

Beevor, Antony. *Ardennes 1944: The Battle of the Bulge*. New York: Penguin Random House LLC, 2015.

Belden, Jack. *Still Time to Die*. Philadelphia: The Blakiston Company, 1944.

Beschloss, Michael R. *The Conquerors: Roosevelt, Truman and the Destruction of Hitler's Germany, 1941–1945*. New York: Simon and Schuster, 2002.

Blair, Clay. *Ridgway's Paratroopers: The American Airborne in World War II*. Garden City, NY: The Dial Press, 1985.

Brereton, Lewis H. *The Brereton Diaries*. New York: William Morrow and Company, 1946.

Breuer, William B. *Storming Hitler's Rhine: The Allied Assault: February–March 1945*. New York: St. Martin's Press, 1985.

Bruce, Robert. *German Automatic Weapons of World War II*. Wiltshite, UK: The Crowood Press Ltd., 2000.

Capa, Robert. *Slightly Out of Focus*. New York: The Modern Library, 1999.

Castagna, Edwin. *History of the 771st Tank Battalion*. Berkeley: Lederer, Street & Zeus Co., Inc., 1946.

Chatterson, George. *The Wings of Pegasus: The Story of the Glider Pilot Regiment*. Nashville, TN: The Battery Press, Inc., 1982.

Citino, Robert M. *The Wehrmacht's Last Stand: The German Campaigns of 1944–1945*. Lawrence, KS: University Press of Kansas, 2017.

Clostermann, Pierre. *The Big Show: Some Experiences of a French Fighter Pilot in the RAF*. New York: Random House, 1951.

Crookenden, Napier. *Airborne at War*. New York: Charles Scribner's Sons, 1978.

Dank, Milton. *The Glider Gang: An Eyewitness History of World War II Glider Combat*. New York: J. B. Lippincott Co., 1977.

den Brok, Hans. *Battle of Burp Gun Corner: 435th Troop Carrier Group, Operation Varsity, 24–25th March 1945*. New Orleans: Walka Books, 2014.

Deschodt, Christophe, with Laurent Rouger. *D-Day Paratroopers: The Americans*. Paris: Histoire & Collections, 2004.

D'Este, Carlo. *Eisenhower: A Soldier's Life*. New York: Henry Holt and Company, 2002.

Devlin, Gerard M. *Paratrooper! The Saga of the U.S. Army and Marine Parachute and Glider Combat Troops During World War II*. New York: St. Martin's Press, 1979.

——. *Silent Wings: The Saga of the U.S. Army and Marine Combat Glider Pilots During World War II*. New York: St. Martin's Press, 1985.

Doyle, David W. *True Men and Traitors: From the OSS to the CIA, My Life in the Shadows*. New York: John Wiley & Sons, Inc., 2001.

Dudenhoeffer, Bud. *JUMP! A Paratrooper's Life Before, During and After World War II*. Jefferson City, MO: Aardvark Global Publishing, 2009.

Duxford Diary, 1942–1945. Cambridge, UK: East Anglian Aviation Society, 1975.

DZ Europe: The Story of the 440th Troop Carrier Group. United States Army Air Forces, 440th Troop Carrier Group. Place and date of publication not identified, ~1945.

Edsel, Robert M. *The Monuments Men: Allied Heroes, Nazi Thieves, and the Greatest Treasure Hunt in History*. New York: Center Street, 2009.

Enjames, Henri-Paul. *Government Issue Collector's Guide, Volume I*. Paris: Histoire & Collections, 2009.

Esvelin, Philippe. *D-Day Gliders*. Bayeux, France: Heimdal, 2001.

François, Dominique. *The 507th Parachute Infantry Regiment*. Bayeux, France: Heimdal, 2000.

Gabel, Kurt. *Making of a Paratrooper: Airborne Training and Combat in World War II*. Lawrence: University Press of Kansas, 1990.

Gavin, James M. *Airborne Warfare*. Washington, DC: Infantry Journal Press, 1947.

Giziowski, Richard J. *The Enigma of General Blaskowitz*. New York: Hippocrene Books, Inc., 1997.

Goldman, Curtis. *Silent Warrior: A Photo Journal Account of a WWII Combat Glider Pilot*. Springfield, MO: 21st Century Press, 2008.

Gorbitz, Ozzie. *Blood on the Talon: 139th Airborne Engineer Battalion 1943–1945, Volume 1: Unit History*. Roswell, NM: Castraponere Publishing, 2013.

Green, William. *Famous Fighters of the Second World War*. New York: Hanover House, 1957.

Grinker, Roy R., and John Spiegel. *Men Under Stress*. Philadelphia: Blakiston, 1945.

Hagerman, Bart. *Granddaddy Was Airborne!* Paducah, KY: Turner Publishing Company, 1997.

———. (ed.). *Seventeenth Airborne Division*. Paducah, KY: Turner Publishing Company, 1999.

———. (ed.). *War Stories, The Men of the Airborne*. Paducah, KY: Turner Publishing Company, 1993.

Haney, Richard H. *When Is Daddy Coming Home?* Madison: Wisconsin Historical Society Press, 2005.

Hollister, Paul, and Robert Strunsky (eds.). *From D-Day Through Victory in Europe*. New York: Columbia Broadcasting System, 1945.

Hope, Bob. *I Never Left Home*. New York: Simon & Schuster, Inc., 1944.

Ingrisano, Michael N. *Valor Without Arms. A History of the 316th Troop Carrier Group, 1942–1945*. Bennington, VT: Merriam Press, 2001.

Jewell, Brian. *Over the Rhine: The Last Days of War in Europe*. New York: Hippocrene Books, Inc., 1985.

Knickerbocker, W. D. *Those Damn Glider Pilots*. College Park, GA: Static Line Books, 1993.

Kurowski, Franz. *Hitler's Last Bastion: The Final Battles for the Reich, 1944–1945*. Atglen, PA: Schiffer Military History, 1998.

———. *Jump into Hell: German Paratroopers in World War II*. Mechanicsburg, PA: Stackpole Books, 2010.

Longerich, Peter. *Goebbels: A Biography*. New York: Random House, 2015.

Lucas, James. *Kommando: German Special Forces of World War Two*. Edison, NJ: Castle Books, 2003.

MacDonald, Charles B. *The Last Offensive: U.S. Army in World War II*. Washington, DC: Center of Military History, United States Army, 1990.

Mehner, Kurt. *Die Geheimen Tagesberichte Der Deutschen Wehrmachtführung im Zweiten Weltkrieg 1939–1945*. Osnabrück, Germany: Biblio-Verlag, 1993.

Middlebrook, Martin. *Arnhem 1944: The Airborne Battle*. Boulder, CO: Westview Press, 1994.

Miller, Donald. *Masters of the Air: America's Bomber Boys Who Fought the Air War Against Nazi Germany*. New York: Simon and Schuster, 2006.

Mitchell, George C. *Matthew B. Ridgway: Soldier, Statesman, Scholar, Citizen*. Mechanicsburg, PA: Stackpole Books, 2002.

Mitchell, Harris T. *The Story of the First Airborne Battalion*. Rockville, MD: Twinbrook Communications, 1996.

Mrazek, James E. *Fighting Gliders of World War II*. New York: St. Martin's Press, Inc., 1977.

Newnham, Maurice. *Prelude to Glory: The Story of the Creation of Britain's Parachute Army*. London: Sampson Low, Marston & Co., Ltd., 1947.

Nitrowski, Johann J. *Die Luftlandung und das Kriegsende im Gebiet der Städte Hamminkeln und Wesel*. Hamminkeln, Germany: self-published, 1997.

O'Donnell, Patrick K. *Beyond Valor: World War II's Ranger and Airborne Veterans Reveal the Heart of Combat*. New York: The Free Press, 2001.

Pay, Don R. *Thunder from Heaven. Story of the 17th Airborne Division, 1943–1945*. Birmingham, MS: BOOTS, *Airborne Quarterly*, 1947.

Pogue, Forrest C. *The Supreme Command: U.S. Army in World War II*. Washington, DC: Center of Military History, United States Army, 1989.

Pyle, Ernie. *Brave Men*. Mattituck, NY: Aeonian Press, 1978.

Raff, Edson D. *We Jumped to Fight*. New York: Eagle Books, 1944.

Richards, Guy. *World War II Troop Type Parachutes. Allies: U.S., Britain, Russia*. Atglen, PA: Schiffer Military History, 2003.

Ridgway, Matthew B. *Soldier: The Memoirs of Matthew B. Ridgway*. New York: Harper & Brothers, 1956.

Ross, Kirk B. *The Sky Men: A Parachute Rifle Company's Story of the Battle of the Bulge and the Jump Across the Rhine*. Atglen, PA: Schiffer Publishing Ltd., 2000.

Scherer, Ben F. (ed.). *Soldiers and Brothers Under the Canopy*. St. Petersburg, FL: Southern Heritage Press, no date of publication given.

Shama, Rex H. *Pulse and Repulse: Trooper Carrier Airborne Teams in Europe During World War II*. Austin, TX: Eakin Press, 1995.

Siddall, Brian N. *507th in Germany. Complete Jump Rosters & Aircrews for Operation Varsity*. Ithaca, NY: EQS Press, 2006.

Thacker, Toby. *The End of the Third Reich*. Stroud, UK: Tempus Publishing, Ltd., 2006.

——. *Joseph Goebbels: Life and Death*. New York: Palgrave Macmillan, 2010.

Weeks, John. *Airborne Equipment: A History of Its Development*. New York: Hippocrene Books, Inc., 1976.

Whiting, Charles. *Bounce the Rhine*. Briarcliff Manor, NY: Stein and Day, Inc., 1986.

Wolfe, Martin. *Green Light! Men of the 81st Troop Carrier Squadron Tell Their Story*. Philadelphia: University of Pennsylvania Press, 1989.

World War II Glider Pilots: National World War II Glider Pilots Association. Paducah, KY: Turner Publishing Company, 1991.

Zaloga, Steven J. *Defense of the Rhine 1944–45.* Long Island City, NY: Osprey Publishing, 2011.

——. *US Airborne Divisions in the ETO 1944–45.* New York: Osprey Publishing, 2007.

Periodicals and Newspapers

Aas, Lynn W. "Remembering the Price of Freedom." *University of North Dakota Alumni Review* (September/October 2001): 6+.

"Adolf Doesn't Like Nazis Robbing Nazis." *S&S* (Nancy Edition, March 31, 1945): 8.

"Airborne Troop Carrier of World War II." *TFH* (October/November 1996): 74.

Andrews, Harry W. Untitled personal account. *The Yacht Club Association of the 62nd Troop Carrier Squadron* (October 1998): 4+.

Bell, Harold. "Meet a Fellow Trooper—Harold Bell." *TFH* (July/August 1997): 44.

Blanchard, Thad. "A Trooper Remembers." *TFH* (December 2006): 57.

Bonnesen, Gerald. "Operation Varsity—The Rhine Crossing: The Beginning of the End for Germany." *389th Bomb Group and Attached Units Newsletter* (Spring 2007): 1.

Bressler, Dean M. "Airborne '44—Allied Forces Breach the Rhine." *Assembly, West Point Alumni Magazine* (March 1995): 22+.

Buckley, George. "Mission Impossible—Operation Varsity." *TFH* (Summer 1993): 76+.

Campbell, Don. "Glider Yanks Sprawl, Yawn, Then Go Over." *TFH* (Winter 1997): 13+.

Capa, Robert. "This Invasion Was Different." *TIME*, April 2, 1945, 28.

Conboy, Jim. "My Part in Operation Varsity." *TFH* (December 2003): 63.

Cowan, Howard. "Glider Men Get Revenge for Set-Back." *TFH* (Winter 1997): 13+.

Chester, John. "They Called It Varsity." *TFH* (August 2006): 54+.

Cunningham, Ed. "The Ludendorf Bridge." *Yank, The Army Weekly*, Continental Edition, April 1, 1945, 3+.

Daniels, Boyd. "The Riggers Cross the Rhine." *TFH* (August 2006): 43.

Davis, Luther. "G Stands for Guts!" *Air Force, The Official Journal of the USAAF* (March 1945): 10+.

Dentz, Franklin. "Operation Varsity Glider Ride to Wesel." *TFH* (November 1999): 55+.

"Development of the Glider." *TFH* (Fall 1995): 43+.

Devlin, Gerard M. "When was it that U.S. Army paratroopers started the time honored tradition of wearing jump boots with Class A dress uniforms . . ." *TFH* (August 2006): 45+.

"Diary of B Co. 194th Glider Infantry—1st Platoon, 1st Squad." *TFH* (Fall 1993): 46+.

Eldridge, Justin L.C. "Defense on the Rhine." *Military Intelligence Bulletin* (January–March 1995): printout, no page numbers.

Ellis, Harry. "Airborne Landing Across the Rhine." *TFH* (October 2001): 24.

"FDR Okeh's Glider Pay Bill July 3rd." *TFH* (Summer 1993): 68.

Forster, Greg. "Biggest Wartime Drop." *Military History Magazine* (April 1994): 38+.

Fox, Bob. "Memories—The Way I Saw It." *TFH* (July/August 1996): 14+.

Frank, Donald. "Running the Gauntlet from Hell to Main Street." *389th Bomb Group and Attached Units Newsletter* (Spring 2007): 17.

Friedheim, Eric. "Rhineland Rendezvous." *Air Force, The Official Journal of the USAAF* (May 1945): 4+.

Fritz, Paul C. "From the Glider Tower's Point of View." *TFH* (Fall 1995): 30+.

Gadd, Curt. "To Set the Record Straight." *TFH* (Spring 1995): 29.

Galbraith, Verne. "A Little Music." *TFH* (June 1999): 30.

Gill, Robert F. "Things and Events as I Remember Them 50 Years Later." *TFH* (March/April 1998): 21.

Good, Lew. "Dedication of the 17th Airborne Plaque in Arlington National Cemetery on 05 JUN 93." *TFH* (Summer 1993): 60.

"Good God. Gaston." *TIME*, October 12, 1942, Time.com, no page number.

Gorriaran, Manuel, Jr. "Honors for George Peters." *TFH* (Fall 1994): 55.

Graham, Frederick. "1,500 Planes Fly in Biggest Airborne Push." *New York Times*, March 25, 1945, 1+.

Hagerman, Bart. "17th Airborne Division History." *AQ* (Summer 2007): 8+.

Harris, King. "Adventures of Ace Miller." *Alta Vista Magazine*, January 27, 1991, 6+.

Hashway, Thomas. "Post Traumatic Stress Disorder." *TFH* (November 1999): 82+.

Hawley, George. "A Trooper with No Strings Attached." *TFH* (Winter 1997): 68.

Hines, Bill. "Operation CODENAME." *Infantry Journal* (March 1947): 42+.

"History of the Prop Blast (One Version Anyhow)." *AQ* (Fall 1999): 130+.

Homan, Richard W. "Donations Needed for Memorial to Pendleton County WWII Hero." *Pendleton Times*, May 24, 1990, no page number.

Hottelet, Richard C. "Big Jump Into Germany." *Colliers* (May 1945): 13+.

Hutton, Bud. "Airborne Armies Join Invasion of Nazi Heartland." *S&S*, Nancy Edition, March 25, 1945, 1.

———. "Airborne Yanks, British Swarmed into Nazi Ambush in Rhine Jump." *S&S*, Nancy Edition, March 29, 1945, 3.

"Invisible Oil Afforded Screen." *S&S*, Nancy Edition, March 29, 1945, 2.

Kormann, John. "Little Known Sacrifices." *TFH* (March/April 1998): 11.

Kormas, Ancel. "Rations for Airborne and Other Mobile Troops." *TFH* (Summer 2003): 92.

Larson, George A. "Alliance Army Air Force Base and the Training of Airborne Crews." *AQ* (Fall 1998): 20+.

———. "European Theater of Operations Post War Review of Airborne Operations." *AQ* (Fall 2009): 27+.

Miley, Jack. "Remarks at Memorial Service—Mt. Airy Resort—September 16, 1998." *TFH* (November 1998): 7+.

Mondt, David E. Untitled VARSITY article. *The Yacht Club Association of the 62nd Troop Carrier Squadron* (March 1991): 1+.

Myer, Samuel C. "Varsity's Organic Artillery." *Field Artillery Journal* (November 1945): 673+.

Nicholas, William H. "Gliders—Silent Weapons of the Sky." *National Geographic* (August 1944): 150+.

O'Rourke, Frank J. "Eyewitness: A Gliderman Across the Rhine." *World War II*, April 2004, 42.

"Parachute Infantry Fighting Men Are Proud of Their Commander." *Charlotte Observer*, May 5, 1942, clipping from CMH, CJB, Box 60.

Ramsey, Winston G. (ed.). "FHQu 'Alderhorst.'" *After the Battle* 19 (1977): 51.

Reed, Paul. "Operation Varsity—As I Remember It." *TFH* (July 2000): 30+.

Ridgway, Matthew B. "An Airborne Corps Operations." *Military Review* (November 1945): 14.

Seaman, Michael. "18th Corps Handled Wesel Airborne Job While 17th Division's 194th Inf. Carried Ball." *S&S*, Nancy Edition, April 8, 1945, 5.

Shiner, Linda. "Republic P-47 Thunderbolt." *World War II in the Air (Collector's Edition) Air & Space* (Summer 2018): 80.

Smith, Bill. "Heroes." *TFH* (Summer 2003): 96.

Sprenger, Gene. "Who Was Who—German General Officers, 1946." *TFH* (Summer 1993): 30.

Therrien, Mel. "Where Did the Words Thunder from Heaven Come From?" *TFH* (Spring 1994): 7.

Tom, Bill. Untitled article. *Thunder Mail Call, 17th Airborne Division's Post-Dissolution Newsletter* (Greenwald Edition, June 2008): 8.

Tommasino, Ed. "Thanks from a Grateful Nephew." *TFH* (July/August 1996): 10.

Velikoff, Ted. "Velikoff Diary" *TFH* (Spring 1994): 53+.

Whitman, Hamilton. "Airborne Operation: Mission Completed." *S&S*, Nancy Edition, April 1, 1945, 3.

Wilmer, Doug. "The Battle of Burp Gun Corner." *Static Line* (April 2003): 10.

Winters, Zane. "The Last Glider Mission, Part 1." *Silent Wings Newsletter* (Fall 2003): 9.

——. "The Last Glider Mission, Part 2." *Silent Wings Newsletter* (Winter 2003): 10.

"World Battlefronts." *TIME*, April 2, 1945, 27+.

Yarborough, William P. "Gen. Yarborough's Speech at Pinehurst Memorial Banquet." *TFH* (Fall 1994): 53+.

Field Manuals

AAF Manual No. 50-17. *Pilot Training Manual for the CG-4A Glider*. Headquarters AAF, Office of Flying Safety, March 1945.

Air Forces Manual No. 3, Glider Tactics and Technique. January 24, 1944.

FM 10-10. *Quartermaster Service in Theater of Operations*. War Department, March 2, 1942.

FM 23-80. *57-MM Rifle M18*. Department of the Army Field Manual, June 1948.

FM 27-10. *Rules of Land Warfare*. War Department Field Manual, October 1940.

FM 31-30. *Tactics and Technique of Air-borne Troops*. Department of the Army Field Manual, May 20, 1942.

FM 101-10. *Staff Officer's Field Manual: Organizational, Technical and Logistical Data*. War Department, June 15, 1941.

Intelligence Bulletin, Vol. II, No. 3, Section III (November 1943). War Department, Military Intelligence Division.

Pilot's Flight Operating Instructions for Army Model CG-4A Glider. Technical Order (TO) No. 09-40CA-1. June 15, 1944.

Pocket Guide to Germany. Army Information Branch, United States Army, 1944.

TM 9-319. *75mm Pack Howitzer M1A1 and Carriage M8*. Department of the Army, November 1948.

TM-E 30-451. *Handbook on German Military Forces*. War Department Technical Manual, March 15, 1945.

Reports and Manuscripts

IX TCC, US Army Air Forces, HQ. "Activities Final Phase—European War" (June 1945). GPM.
——. Control Team No. 2. "Activities of Control Team No. 2 on Varsity Mission" (March 30, 1945). GPM.
——. "Field Order No. 5 for Operation Varsity" (March 16, 1945). GPM.
——. "Ground Training for Glider Pilots" (December 15, 1944). GPM.
——. "SOP for Troop Carrier-Airborne Operations" (May 2, 1944). NARA.
XVIII Corps (ABN). "Operation Varsity, 23 March 1945 to 30 March 1945" (April 25, 1945). 17ADA.
——. "Order of Battle Summary for Wesel Bridgehead" (March 7, 1945). Courtesy of Steltermann family.
——. "Periodic Reports." NARA.
——. "War Diary." CMH, MBR.
XXIX TAC, 366th Fighter Group, 390th Fighter Squadron. "Downed Aircraft Report for P-47, 42-29245" (flown by Charles E. Bennett) (March 27, 1945).
FAAA. "Airborne Army Operational Reports, 1944–1945, Varsity to Wildgirl." NARA.
——. "History of Headquarters, First Allied Airborne Army. August 2, 1944–May 20, 1945." Compiled by Historical Division, 9th Information and Historical Service.
——. "HQ Operations Reports, 1944–1945." NARA.
——. "Operation Varsity." NARA.
——. "Outgoing Messages, 1 FEB–13MAR45." NARA.
——. "Outgoing Messages, 13–31 MAR45." NARA.
——. "Subject File, 411–45, Personnel and Training—US ABN Action Files." NARA.
6th Airborne Division. "Report on Operation Varsity and the Advance from the Rhine to the Baltic, March 24th–May 2nd, 1945." UKNA.
17ABN. "After Action Report Narrative, 24–31 March 1945" (April 10, 1945). NARA.
——. 17th Airborne Casualty Rate, Daily by Unit.
——. "Division Chaplain's Report, After Action Report for HQ, 17th ABN" (April 2, 1945). NARA.
——. "Historical Report of Operation Varsity." 17ADA.
——. "Inspector General's Section," After Action Report for HQ, 17th ABN (April 2, 1945). NARA.
——. Looting Memorandums (March 25, 1945, and March 28, 1945). NARA.
——. "Operational Diary, Covering January 1, 1945 to April 10, 1945." 17ADA.
——. "Summary of Operations: 3 Jan. 45 to 31 Jan. 45." 17ADA
21AG. "Correspondence and Signals (Between C-in-C and CofS)." UKNA.
——. "G (Plans), Operation Varsity (Nov. 44–May 45)." UKNA.
——. "Operation Plunder, Airborne Operations, conference notes." UKNA.
——. "Orders for the Battle of the Rhine, M559" (March 9, 1945). UKNA.
51 TCW, HQ. "Standard Operating Procedure for Airborne Operations" (August 2, 1944).
——. "Standard Operating Procedure for Gliders" (August 17, 1943). GPM.
52 TCW, HQ. "Operation Varsity. After Action Report" (April 20, 1945). GPM.

139 AEB. "139th Airborne Engineer Battalion Monthly After Operations Report" (April 18, 1945). NARA.

———. "Daily Engineer Situation Report No. 2" (March 25, 1945).

———. "Daily Engineer Situation Report No. 3" (March 26, 1945).

194 GIR. "Division Operation Order (19 March 1945)."

———. "2nd Battalion Activities (March 24, 25, 26)." NARA.

———. "Field Order No. 1, 194 Glider Infantry" (March 19, 1945). NARA.

———. "Misc. Varsity Documents." NARA.

———. Morning Reports. NPRC.

———. Officer interview, Major Carl A. Peterson, Regt. S-3. GPM.

———. "Regimental Journal 2 (4 March 45–26 March 45)." NARA.

224 AMC. "224th Airborne Medical Co., Accumulated Notes." 17ADA.

———. "224th Airborne Medical Company, Inclosure 24." NARA.

313 TCG, 49 TCS. "Interrogation Check Sheets. Glider Pilots of the 314th TCG, 62nd TCS." GPM.

———. "Missing Aircrew Report for Aircraft: 44-77472" (April 18, 1945).

406th Fighter Group, 513th Fighter Squadron. "Downed Aircraft Report for P-47 Serial Number: 44-33308" (Major Fowler, Gordon W.) (March 26, 1945).

———. "Downed Aircraft Report for P-47, Louise, 42-28672. (Altnoff, Erwin. MIA) (March 26, 1945).

411 AQQC. "After Action Report, Inclosure (Apr. 3, 1945)." NARA.

435 TCG. "Interrogation Check Sheets. Glider Pilots of the 435th TCG, 77th TCS." GPM.

441 TCG. "Interrogation Check Sheets. Glider Pilots of the 441st TCG, 99th TCS." GPM.

464 PFAB. "After Action Report" (April 1, 1945). NARA.

466 PFAB. "466th PFA Battalion Supporting Data." Courtesy of John Chester.

———. "History of the 466th Parachute Field Artillery Battalion." NARA.

507 PIR. "Field Order No. 1, Inclosure No. 3A" (March 20, 1945). NARA.

———. "Historical Report on Operation Varsity." Courtesy 17ADA.

———. Officer interviews, "17th Airborne Division, Crossing Rhine, Operation Varsity, 24–31 March 1945." GPM.

———. "Varsity Narrative." NARA.

513 PIR. "After Action Report, 24 to 31 March." NARA.

———. "Field Order No. 16, Inclosure No. 3B" (March 17, 1945). NARA.

———. "History of the 513th Parachute Infantry." War Department, the Adjutant General's Office. NARA.

———. "History of the Regimental Insignia." NARA.

———. "Narrative of Action." NARA.

———. "Narrative of Action. 1st Battalion, 513th Parachute Infantry Regiment." NARA.

———. Officer interviews, "17th Airborne Division, Crossing Rhine, Operation Varsity, 24–31 March 1945." GPM.

605 TDB. "After Action Report." (May 4, 1945).

680 GFAB. "Historical Record of the 680th Glider Field Artillery Battalion." NARA.

———. "680th Journal. 0645 20 March–2400 31 March 1945." NARA.

681 GFAB. "681st Glider Field Artillery Battalion." NARA.

717 AOMC. "After Action Report. Inclosure 20." NARA.

British Army on the Rhine. "Report on Operation Varsity." 17ADA.

Fiebig, Heinz. "The 84th Infantry Division During the Fight from Reichwald to Wesel." Manuscript B-843, FMS, CMH.

Geyer, Rolf. "Army Group H (10 Mar–9 May 45)." Manuscript B-414, FMS, CMH.

"Interrogation Report from Gen Meindl and Major General Fiebig" (August 6, 1945). CNA.

Langhaeuser, Rudolf. "6 Paratroop Division (11 Mar–1 Apr 45)." Manuscript B-453, FMS, CMH.

Lyke, James P. "The Operations of the 17th Airborne Division in the Crossing of the Rhine River, 24 March 1945 (Personal Experience of the Aide-de-Camp to the Commanding General)." Advanced Infantry Officers Course, Class No. 2, 1948–1949. Courtesy Frank Dillon.

OSS. "Cover Report 1–15 FEB 45" (February 19, 1945). NARA.

——. "Cover Report 1–15 MAR 45" (March 19, 1945). NARA.

——. "Covering Report for OSS/ETO 16–31 March 45" (April 4, 1945). NARA.

——. "Covering Report 1–15 April 45" (April 18, 1945). NARA.

——. "HQ Seventh Army G-2, Strategic Services Section" (April 10, 1945). NARA.

——. "OSS Report for OSS/ETO, Continental Operations 10–31 MAR 45" (April 5, 1945). NARA.

——. Staub, Robert, OSS Personnel File. NARA.

——. Steltermann, Helmet, OSS File. NARA.

——. "Strategic Services Detachments with the Army in the Field." NARA.

——. Vinciguerra, Stephen P. "Field Report from ETO." NARA.

Schlemm, Alfred. "First Paratroop Army (20 Nov 44–21 Mar 45)." Manuscript B-084, FMS, CMH.

Schorr, David P., Lieutenant Colonel. "Operation Varsity. Airborne Assault Crossing of Rhine River, Vicinity Wesel Germany, 24 March 1945." School of Combined Arms Regular Course, 1946–1947, Command and Staff College, Fort Leavenworth, Kansas.

"Special Interrogation Report of General Alfred Schlemm, Commander First Parachute Army." LAC.

Supreme Headquarters Allied Expeditionary Force. "A-3 Div. Report of Allied Air Operations in Preparation for Operations Plunder & Varsity. ETO, 1945." CMH.

"ULTRA Interceptions" (February 27, 1945; March 19, 1945). UKNA.

von Luettwitz, Heinrich. "XLVII Panzer Corps (08 Mar–16 Apr 45)." Manuscript B-198, FMS, CMH.

Warren, John C. "U.S. Airborne Operations in World War II, European Theater. U.S.A.F. Historical Studies: No. 97." Maxwell Air Force Base, Alabama: Air University U.S.A.F. Historical Division Study, 1956.

Weapons System Evaluation Group (WSEG). "A Historical Study of Some World War II Airborne Operations" (Staff Study No. 3).

Papers, Letters, Collections, Personal Narratives, and Diaries

CMH Papers and collections: Clay and Joan Blair Collection, William B. Breuer Papers, J. W. Coutts Papers, William M. Miley Papers, Floyd Lavinius Parks Papers and Diary, Matthew B. Ridgway Papers.

Letters to the author: Ancker, Jack P. (680 GFAB); Blanchard, Thad (507 PIR); Chester, John (466 PFAB); Dillon, Frank (194 GIR); Gadd, Curtis A. (513 PIR); Herrmann, Eugene (194 GIR).

513th PIR, I Co. "World War II: Battle of the Bulge and Rhine Jump." Collected, unpublished memories and official documents. Courtesy of John Vafides (513 PIR).

Boe, Richard A. "Unpublished Memoir." Courtesy of Richard A. Boe.

Branigan, Edward S. "The 464th PFAB in 'Operation Varsity'" (January 11, 1984). CMH, WBB.

Casey, Robert. Personal diary. GPM.

Chester, John. *Collection of Personal Memoirs.* Courtesy of John Chester.

Holdren, George. *WWII Memoir.* Courtesy of George Holdren.

Jella, Elbert. Documents and notebook. GPM.

Kessler, Homer K. "My Front Line Experience." Courtesy of Homer K. Kessler.

Macchiaverna, Frank. Personal diary. Author's collection.

Magill, John. "We Led from the Sky: A Combat Paratroopers Story." CMH.

Moscar, Joseph W. "Parts of My Missions." CMH, WWII Veteran Surveys.

Nitrowski, Johann J. "Varsity Folder," pertaining to Battle of Burp Gun Corner. GPM.

Schorr, David P. Letter to Herrmann, September 26, 1990. Courtesy of Eugene Herrmann.

Schultz, Howard G. "Account of Glider Pilot in Varsity." GPM.

Schumacher, John. "Two Years in the Lift of John J. Schumacher: 1944–1946." Courtesy of John Schumacher.

Steltermann, Helmut. Collection of wartime documentation. Courtesy of the Steltermann family.

Stephens, Howard. "The Operations of Company H, 507th PIR. 24 March 1945 to 5 May 1945. Personal Experience of a Company Commander" (May 13, 1945). Courtesy of the Infantry School, Ft. Benning, GA.

Streukens, George L. "Personal Manuscript, 194th GIR." George L. Streukens Papers, CMH.

Whiting, Quinn A. "Memories of World War II." 17ADA.

Wienczak, Edmund A. Personal diary. Found in "224th Airborne Medical Company, Accumulated Notes." 17ADA.

Interviews

Aas, Lynn (194 GIR); Brooks, Arly (507 PIR); Davis, Al (517 Sig.); Doyle, David (OSS); Gadd, Curt (513 PIR); Kormann, John (17 ABN); LaGattuta, Joe (OSS); Lambrecht, Jack (glider pilot); Lauria, Jim (681 GFAB); McDonald, Lendy (513 PIR); Miley, John (son of William Miley); Muncy, Herbert (glider pilot); Pierce, Ed (513 PIR); Piergiovanni, Peter (155 Anti-Tank Co.); Pinzel, Donald (glider pilot); Powers, Chuck (C-47 pilot); Shafer, Tom (B-24 pilot); Schumacher, John J. (194 GIR); Theis, George (glider pilot); Von der Brugge, John (513 PIR).

Miscellany

17ABN Biographies. Collection of documents on CD-ROM provided by the 17ADA.

"17th Airborne. The Bulge to the Rhine. 681st Glider Field Artillery Battalion—Battery B." VHS, 1990 Kenwood Productions, Inc.

514 Squadron, RAF War Diary for March 6, 1945. http://www.514squadron.co.uk/, accessed on January 1, 2017.

"Airborne Infantryman Awarded Medal of Honor Posthumously." War Department press release (February 11, 1946). Contains eyewitness accounts of George Peters' actions.

Biographical Sketch of Major General (Ret.) William Maynadier Miley, Father of the American Paratrooper. 17ADA.

Felton, Mark. "Adlerhorst—The Führer's Secret Castle." http://markfelton.co.uk/pub-lishedbooks/adlerhorst-hitlers-forgotten-headquarters/, accessed on August 25, 2017.

Franklin, Oscar B. CMH, WWII Veteran Survey.

"FLAK." War Department training film, TF I-3389. Army Signal Corps, 1944.

Gordon, Charles O. "Burp Gun Corner, 24 March 1945." Courtesy of Charles Gordon.

History 139th Airborne Engineers. Printed by Alfred Sleb, Muelheim (Ruhr). No date.

"Jack's Story." http://www.aeroc.dbnetinc.com/artist.html, accessed on July 3, 2009.

Johnston, Everett C. CMH, WWII Veteran Survey.

Kappes, Irwin J. "Hitler's Ultra-Secret *Adlerhorst*." http://www.militaryhistoryonline.com/wwii/articles/adlerhorst.aspx, accessed on August 25, 2017.

Lonke, Peter. *The Liberators Who Never Returned.* Self-published study of Operation Varsity's downed B-24 bombers. Courtesy of Peter Lonke.

"Major-General Richard Nelson Gale MC." http://www.pegasusarchive.org/normandy/richard_gale.htm, accessed on August 4, 2015.

Manley, Melvin (ed.). "A Short History of Battery B of the 680th Glider Field Artillery Battalion, 17th Airborne Division." Courtesy of John D. Kaminski, 17ADA.

Miley, William M. Unpublished manuscript, no date. 17ADA.

Mitchell, William C. "17th Airborne Casualties. Some Figures and Comments." No date. 17ADA.

"Morgenthau Plan." https://en.wikipedia.org/wiki/Morgenthau_Plan, accessed on October 12, 2017.

My Heroes. Documentary on Shafer's B-24 Crew. Directed and edited by Dave Shafer, 2005. Courtesy of Dave Shafer.

"Oregon Airborne Infantryman Awarded Medal of Honor Posthumously." War Department, Bureau of Public Relations, Press Branch, December 19, 1945.

"Parachutist." War Department training film, Misc. 924. Produced by the Signal Corps.

"Paris, Guide for Leave Troops." United States Army, WWII era, no date. Author's collection.

Raff, Edson. Unpublished Manuscript. CMH, CJB.

Roberson, Ben. WWII Veteran Biographical Sketch. CMH.

Shafer, Dave. "Combat Log. B-24 Liberator Crew." Self-published compilation of crew interviews, diaries, and documentation of Tom Shafer's B-24 crew. Courtesy of Dave Shafer.

Talon, 17th Airborne Division newsmagazine, June 15, 1945. CMH.

The Talon Crosses the Rhine: A Pictorial History of the 17th Airborne Division's Airborne Mission Across the Rhine. Paris: 17th Airborne Division, 1945.

The Talon, with the 17th in Ardennes. Paris: 17th Airborne Division, 1945.

"Target: DZ-Wesel, 392nd Bomb Group, Mission #268, 24 March 1945." http://www .b24.net/missions/MM032445.htm, accessed on March 15, 2009.

Taylor, James E. Manuscript from presentation at Kate Duncan Smith Dar School in Grant, Alabama, November 10, 2004. Courtesy of James Taylor.

Thirteenth Airborne Division. Atlanta, GA: Albert Love Enterprises, 1944.

War Department press release, October 26, 1945. NARA, Records of the Army Staff, Public Information Division, News Branch, Medal of Honor, US Army 1946–48. Press release containing eyewitness accounts of Clinton M. Hedrick's actions.

Wiegand, Brandon T. (ed.). *Index to the General Orders: 17th Airborne Division.* Creighton, PA: D-Day Militaria, 2004.

———. *Index to the General Orders: 513th Parachute Infantry Regiment.* Creighton, PA: D-Day Militaria, 2004.

Yanok, John (ed.). History 155th Airborne Anti-Tank, Anti-Aircraft Battalion, 17th Airborne Division, 1995. Courtesy of John Yanok.

INDEX

*Numbers in **bold** font refer to pages with images.*